The Peoples of the British Isles

Also available from Lyceum Books, Inc.

The Peoples of the British Isles: A New History from Prehistoric Times to 1688, 3E by Stanford E. Lehmberg and Samantha A. Meigs

The Peoples of the British Isles: A New History from 1688 to 1870, 3E by Thomas William Heyck

The Peoples of the British Isles: A New History from 1870 to the Present, 3E by Thomas William Heyck

The New Nature of History by Arthur Marwick

The Middle Classes in Europe 1789–1914 France, Germany, Italy, and Russia by Pamela M. Pilbeam

The Transformation of Intellectual Life in Victorian England by Thomas William Heyck

The Peoples of the British Isles
A New History

From 1870 to the Present

Third Edition

Volume Three

Thomas William Heyck
Northwestern University

LYCEUM
BOOKS, INC.

5758 S. Blackstone Ave.
Chicago, Illinois 60637

© Lyceum Books, Inc., 2008
Published by

LYCEUM BOOKS, INC.
5758 S. Blackstone Ave.
Chicago, Illinois 60637
773+643-1903 (Fax)
773+643-1902 (Phone)
lyceum@lyceumbooks.com
http://www.lyceumbooks.com

12 11 10 09   2 3 4 5

ISBN: 978-1-933478-24-1

Library of Congress Cataloging-in-Publication Data

Lehmberg, Stanford E.
    Peoples of the British Isles : a new history / Stanford E. Lehmberg, Samantha A. Meigs. — 3rd ed.
        p. cm.
    Vols. 2–3 by Thomas William Heyck.
    Includes bibliographical references and index.
    ISBN 978-1-933478-01-2 (v. 1 : alk. paper) — ISBN 978-1-933478-23-4 (v. 2 : alk. paper) — ISBN 978-1-933478-24-1 (v. 3 : alk. paper)
    1. Great Britain—History. 2. Ethnology—Great Britain. 3. Ireland—History. 4. Ethnology—Ireland. I. Meigs, Samantha A., 1958– II. Heyck, Thomas William, 1938– III. Title.
DA30.L44 2008
941—dc22   2007047345

For Hunter and Shannon, literally

Contents

List of Illustrations

List of Maps

Preface

The purpose of this book is to tell the story (or rather, stories) of the peoples of the British Isles in the most recent period. It is a great story, full of drama and relevance to the history of the United States. The book is meant to be different from the conventional English history textbooks in two ways. First, it covers *British* and not just English history. Second, it takes as its central focus the lives of all the peoples of the British Isles, not just those of the political elite. Because England has long been the largest and most powerful country in the British Isles, English history will receive the most coverage. Indeed, one of the main themes of British history in the modern period—that is, since the end of the seventeenth century—has been the expansion of English power and influence within the British Isles. But Wales, Scotland, and Ireland have in the last forty years or so become the subjects of vital, growing, and fascinating historiographies that demand the attention of students of British history. The histories of the peoples of what came to be called "the Celtic fringe" often had much in common with the history of the English, but at times they diverged sharply. To study comparatively the development of the different societies in the British Isles often throws new light on seemingly well-known events. Moreover, the Welsh, Scots, and Irish were often "problems" for the English, but the English were problems for them as well. To treat the Celtic peoples as mere intrusions into the English story yields not only a deformed historical account of Wales, Scotland, and Ireland but also an incomplete history of the British Isles as a whole.

Economic, social, and cultural history form the backbone of this account. The book thus follows the most exciting trends in recent historiography. When dealing with national politics, the book offers analysis of the structure, functions, and impact of the political system as it evolved rather than a detailed narrative. It places "high politics" in the context of the whole way of life of the peoples of the British Isles. The focus, then, throughout is on the lives of "real" people—how they made a living, how they organized their society and institutions, how they related to each other individually and in groups, and how they understood themselves and their world. What was it like to be a member of the urban working class in the 1890s? How did the long period of unemployment in the 1920s and 1930s affect popular culture? What was the impact of total war in the twentieth century on coal miners or women munitions workers? What were the consequences of postwar affluence and the welfare state? This book will attend to these kinds of questions.

Each of the historical eras spanned by the centuries since 1870 has its own character, its own special mix of economic arrangements, social structure, political style, and cultural expressions. The three parts of the book are meant to mark out for analysis these historical eras—the decline of Victorian society; the age of total war; and postwar Britain. The flow of historical events is continuous, and certain themes tie the historical eras of the modern period since 1688 together. One is the expansion of English influence within the British Isles and the formation under English leadership of the multinational British state. Related to that is the development of separate national identities in the Celtic countries. A second theme is the rise of Great Britain to great power status and then its decline to the rank of an ordinary European power. A third is the remarkable economic expansion of the late eighteenth and nineteenth centuries, which made Britain the first industrial nation in the world and which has been followed by a long and painful relative economic contraction. Fourth, there is the theme of changing social structure and social relations—the origins and development of class society from the social hierarchy of preindustrial Britain. Finally, there is the theme of the evolving structure of the state and the political system, which involves not only the expansion of the role of the state in the British economy and society but also the development of democratic institutions.

If this book succeeds, it will be by helping students understand the peoples of the British Isles in the in the early twenty-first century—why they are the way they are. It should also help American students understand themselves and their own society a little better, for the British are enough like the Americans to make comparisons numerous and enough different to make contrasts revealing.

A NOTE ON TERMINOLOGY

Because Britain is a multinational state that does not now include all of the peoples of the British Isles, it is important to be very careful about using labels like "English" and "British." But this is an area in which it is difficult to be perfectly consistent and to avoid irritating nationalist sensibilities. Geographically speaking, "Britain" correctly denotes the whole island composed of England, Wales, and Scotland, but not Ireland. But "Britain" has also been used by people around the world to refer to the United Kingdom, which came to existence only in 1707, which included Ireland from 1801 to 1921 but which today includes only Northern Ireland as well as England, Wales, and Scotland. For much of the nineteenth century, "Britain" meant not only the United Kingdom but also the British Empire. At the same time, many people both within the British Isles and around the world said "England" when they meant "Britain," and by force of habit many people still do. Today, "Britain" technically means "the United Kingdom of Great Britain and Northern Ireland," but it would make no sense to apply that usage to any historical period before 1921.

I have done my best to refer to the English, Welsh, Scots, and Irish as the circumstances require, to be careful when speaking of "Britain," and to be accurate in distinguishing the political entity of England from that of Great Britain.

ACKNOWLEDGMENTS

I would like to thank a number of people for the help they have provided in the writing of this book. First and foremost are all the scholars of modern British and Irish history on whose work this volume depends. They are too numerous to name here, and even the Suggested Readings after each chapter give only a partial indication of my debt to them; but I hope that all will understand how much I appreciate their contributions even where I have given them my own twist. I have learned a great deal over the years from Larry McCaffrey of Loyola University, Emmet Larkin of the University of Chicago, and from my colleagues and friends at Northwestern, Lacey Baldwin Smith, Tim Breen, and Harold Perkin. My undergraduate students at Northwestern have played a larger role in this book than they know and I am grateful to them and to my energetic and resourceful research assistants, Kevin Mahler, Jill Marquis, Helen Harnett, and Suzette Lemrow. Thanks go to the scholars who have read and commented on all or parts of the book: Stewart J. Brown, James Cronin, Stanford Lehmberg and Standish Meacham. Thanks also go to the reviewers: Nancy Fix Anderson, Loyola University, New Orleans; George L. Bernstein, Tulane University, New Orleans; Anna Clark, University of North Carolina, Charlotte; Kimberly K. Estep, Auburn Univesity; Walter R. Johnson, Northwestern Oklahoma State University, Alva; Neil Rabitoy, California State University, Los Angeles; Karl Von den Steinen, California State University, Sacramento; and Meredith Veldman, Louisiana State Univesity, Baton Rouge, for their helpful comments. Ron Warncke was supportive in earlier stages of the work, and David Follmer has given much support and assistance for more than a decade. Greatest thanks of all go to my wife, Denis Heyck, who willingly helped in countless ways since the inception of this project.

Part **I**

The Decline of
Victorian Britain

1870–1914

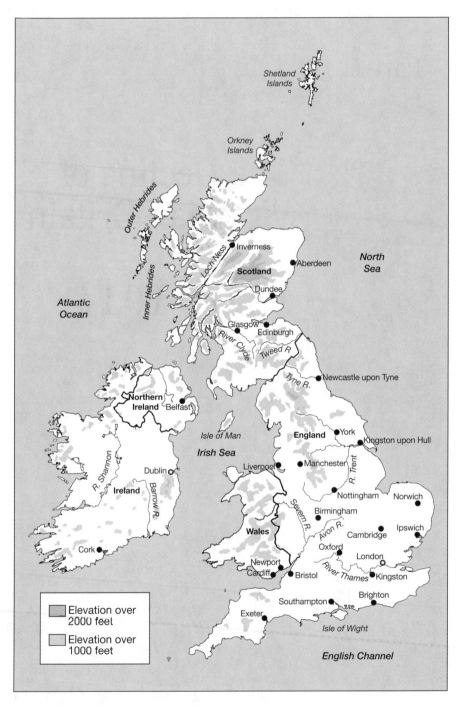

Topography of the British Isles

Chapter 1

Troubles in Economy and Society, 1870–1914

The "long century" from about 1870 to the present forms a unified chapter in the history of the peoples of the British Isles. In the eighteenth and nineteenth centuries, Britain had become the first industrial nation and the strongest power on earth. British industry, based on a technology of steam power and iron machines, dominated global trade even as it helped generate the world's first class-based society—the three-level pyramid of the landed class, middle class, and working class. The British state, centered on England itself, encompassed all of the British Isles. In the first seventy years of the nineteenth century, a remarkable culture known as Victorianism had been built on the foundations of prosperity and progress; it symbolized the expansive achievement of the British peoples between 1688 and 1870. During the course of the next century and a quarter, all of the prominent features of this society and culture were subjected to change, sometimes because of forces imposed on Britain from the outside but sometimes because of the dynamics generated from within.

In the years between 1870 and 1914, the foundations of Victorian culture were seriously eroded, so that the whole structure was toppled by the First World War. Some historians make a sharp distinction between the "late-Victorian" period (1870–1901), which ended with the death of Queen Victoria, and the "Edwardian" period (1901–1914), which took its name from Victoria's eldest son and successor, Edward VII. Indeed, there were certain differences of mood and fashion—late-Victorian angst (anxiety) and Edwardian gaiety—but these were less important than the long-run trends that tied the whole together. These were the years when Britain's economy began to descend from the heights of world preeminence; when social change again intensified class antagonism; when Victorian confidence turned to uncertainty and anxiety; and when intellectual rebellion began to create modernism from the scattered pieces of the Victorian mind. One well-informed journalist observed in 1913:

> We have a society in which political power rests with the mass of its poorer members; in which education, carried up to a certain level, is general; in which an unprecedented mental restlessness has been stimulated by the diffusion of reading matter, and the facilities of rapid communication; in

which class barriers are still rigid, though the physical, temperamental, and personal differences, which formerly divided classes from one another, have been attenuated; in which moral sanctions and conventions, handed down by tradition, and based ultimately on Christian theology have lost much of their force. . . .*

All of these observations were true, and they marked dramatic changes from the mid-Victorian decades. No one factor caused the changes in late Victorian and Edwardian Britain; indeed, the fascination of the period arises from the interplay of political, economic, social, and cultural themes. But just as industrial and agricultural change altered the face of Britain in the years from 1780 to 1840, so economic and social difficulties in the period from 1870 to 1914 provided a framework in which the other factors operated.

Between 1870 and 1914, British economic growth began to falter, and foreign rivals started to catch up. The mood of expansive confidence characteristic of the upper classes in the mid-Victorian period slowly evaporated and was replaced by one of anxiety and concern. The relative social peace of that seemingly golden age of the 1850s and 1860s consequently degenerated into class conflict. To be sure, there was no outright collapse of trade and industry, and Britain remained a great economic power in 1914. Many a British businessman could sit down every morning to his breakfast and newspaper with pride in his company's profits and his country's successes. Many another, however, could hardly bring himself to read the morning's paper, for fear of finding news of declining profits, or of yet another demonstration by militant feminists, or of a strike in a vital industry, or of a heated political stalemate, or worse yet of another trade in which Germany had pulled ahead.

THE LATE-VICTORIAN ECONOMY, 1870–1900

The economy of late-Victorian Britain had a very mixed record. Many businessmen thought that the economy had taken a radical turn for the worse, and their concern inspired the government to appoint a Royal Commission on "The Great Depression in Trade and Industry," which reported in 1886. There was, in fact, no depression of the sort that was to come in 1929: no reversal of growth, no mass unemployment, no collapse of the industrial sector. The British economy continued to grow throughout the last quarter of the nineteenth century, and it continued to produce significant advances in the material standard of living. Yet there were serious economic difficulties, especially compared to the mid-Victorian years: the economy as a whole grew more slowly, the agricultural sector was badly shaken, and newly industrializing nations began to overtake the British headstart. Two simple facts are very revealing: first, overall economic growth from 1870 to 1900 averaged about 2 percent a year, as opposed to almost 3 percent a year for the first three quarters of the century; second, in 1900, both the United States and Germany produced more iron and steel than Britain did.

---

*Sidney Low, The Governance of England (New York, G. P. Putnam's, 1913), p. xxxvii.

Throughout the period, certain parts of the economy performed very well, whereas others lagged behind. To take agriculture first: there was a sharp decline of cereal (mainly wheat) farming in the Midlands and South of England—long the grain belt of the nation and the seat of the landed elite's political and social prestige. The causes of this decline were (1) a series of exceptionally cold and wet winters in the latter 1870s and (2) the collapse of grain prices in Britain. The former cause was short term and its impact eventually disappeared, but the price collapse had effects that lasted through the 1930s.

What happened was that cheap foreign wheat flooded the British market from the 1870s on. Imports of wheat doubled between 1870 and 1890, and the prices that British cereal farmers earned for their crops fell drastically. The farmers had no control over this calamity. Vast plains were brought under the plow in the United States, Canada, Argentina, and Australia after the 1860s. Railways and steamships made exportation of wheat from these newly productive areas very cheap. By the 1880s, in economic terms Chicago was as close to London as a Midlands estate. Since the Com Laws had been repealed in 1846, there was nothing to discourage the importation of wheat. By 1900, the price of wheat in Britain had fallen 50 percent. Livestock farmers fared better, but from the 1880s, refrigerated ships made it possible to export to Britain beef from Argentina and lamb from New Zealand. By 1900, more than one-third of the meat consumed in Britain came from abroad.

One result of the collapse of wheat prices was the restructuring of English farming. Because cattle grazers (at first) and dairy and vegetable farmers did better than grain growers, there was a shift away from cereal to mixed farming. Acreage devoted to fruit and market gardening increased. The most dramatic shift was from wheat cultivation to pasturage. Acreage in wheat was halved between 1871 and 1900, whereas land devoted to pasturage increased by 4 million acres. These tendencies continued in the early twentieth century. By 1913, more than three times as much land in England was in pasturage as in grains of all kinds.

As prices for cereals fell, the traditional landowners and tenant farmers of the Midlands and southern counties were hard pressed. Some farmers diversified, others scrimped on maintenance of fields and farm buildings, and some received rent abatements from their landlords. Many tenants, however, could not survive the crisis. By 1900, many tenancies stood vacant. Moreover, 340,000 agricultural laborers left rural life for urban occupations or overseas.

The landlords themselves, who had been under pressure from middle-class rivalry for most of the century, now found it hard to sustain their luxurious style of life. Many discovered that their incomes were cut in half as rent-rolls declined but that their cost of living remained high. Late-Victorian landlords typically sought outside income by investing in business and industry; by 1890 any self-respecting bank or railway could boast of several titled nobles on its board of directors. At the same time, many landlords retrenched by cutting back on household staff, by closing a house in town or in the country, or by entertaining less lavishly. In 1870, for example, the earl of Verulam's family drank 590 bottles of sherry and 250 of brandy, but in 1880, they consumed a mere 298 of sherry and 75 of brandy!

The industrial sector continued to grow as a portion of the British economy, but here too there were signs of trouble. Industrial output continued to expand, and by 1900 trade and industry accounted for 64 percent of the total national income and agriculture only 6 percent. British exports (almost all of which were manufactured goods) went up by 50 percent between 1870 and 1900. The two key problems were (1) that industrial production grew less rapidly than before—from over 3 percent per year before 1870 to 2 percent between 1870 and 1914 and (2) that British industrial production now grew more slowly than that of two giant foreign rivals—Germany and the United States. Thus Britain's share of world manufacturing output gradually shrank:

Table 1.1: Relative Shares of World Manufacturing Output

	1860	1880	1900
Britain	19.9	22.9	18.5
Germany	4.9	8.5	13.2
United States	7.2	14.7	23.6

Source: Paul Kennedy, *The Rise and Fall of the Great Powers* (New York: Random House, 1987), p. 149

For the first time since industrialization began, Britain now had economic rivals. All around the world, British businessmen met competition in the sale of manufactured goods. They did not find it pleasant or think it fair. Both Germany and the United States protected their industries by tariffs, but British industry labored under free trade. By the 1880s, some British businessmen had come to think that Britain ought to adopt protective tariffs in order to create conditions of "fair trade," but the mystique of free trade remained influential, and most commercial men realized that Britain needed free trade in order to have the widest markets possible. In any case, resentment toward Germany grew. In 1896, for instance, E. E. Williams published a book entitled *Made in Germany* in which he claimed that competition from the Germans in Britain and abroad had become "a deliberate and deadly rivalry."

In addition, many British manufacturers found the prices of their products falling and their profit margins squeezed. Prices for manufactured goods fell by about 25 percent in the late-Victorian years, which was a great boon for consumers but a source of concern for industrialists. Profits are very difficult to measure, but all contemporary observers testified that profits were depressed. The lower level of profits denied British industry part of its traditional source of investments—plowed back from the industry itself.

The industries that had the most serious difficulties in the late-Victorian period were the old staples of the Industrial Revolution—cotton textiles, iron, and, to a lesser extent, coal. The problems in all three areas resulted from competition from newly industrializing countries, all of which adopted the most up-to-date technologies, while the British lagged behind in technical innovation. The British were slow to adopt the faster ring-spinning and automatic looms in the cotton textile industry; they were slow to shift from Bessemer converters to the more efficient Siemens-Martin furnaces in making steel, and slow to adopt the Gilchrist-Thomas process for making iron and steel from low-grade ore; and they did not adopt mechanical coal cutting in the coal industry, even though the increasing depth and expense of mining required it. Of the older industries, only in shipbuilding did the British increase their lead.

At the same time, the British failed to keep pace in several new heavy industries based on advanced technologies. Of these, the electrical and chemical were the most important. The industrial use of steam and gas was deeply entrenched in Britain; thus the new electric power industries that grew rapidly in Germany and the United States met strong resistance in Britain. In industrial chemicals as in electricity, British scientists made many of the fundamental discoveries, while industrialists of other nations made the practical applications. German industry, for instance, made great advances in the production of aniline dyestuffs, which were first discovered in Britain. In the production of alkali, British manufacturers stuck to the old Leblanc process, while the Germans and Americans adopted the newer and cheaper Solway process.

Where the British excelled in the late-Victorian years was in light industries and domestic retailing. New light industries such as sewing machines, armaments, and above all, bicycles were founded on the solid base of mechanical craft skills of the Midlands. The bicycle industry of Coventry was, moreover, the first British industry to adopt American mass production methods. In retail sales, new entrepreneurs brought about major changes by establishing retail chains that sold standardized items in the high streets of every village and town: Boots the Chemists (drug stores), Sainsbury (groceries), and Thomas Lipton (groceries). W. H. Smith established book stalls in every railway station, selling cheap reading matter to travelers and commuters, and commercially oriented publishers established mass circulation newspapers in the cities.

How can the relatively poor performance of British industry in the late nineteenth century be explained? The big issue to be understood is how the most prosperous and industrially advanced economy began to falter and fall behind. Part of the explanation must simply be that as other nations began to industrialize, they would by definition break Britain's monopoly in industrial production and inevitably take some share of the world's markets. Furthermore, other nations could (and did) industrialize with the latest technology and business methods and thus to an extent were able to leap frog over the British, who had a huge investment in somewhat older plants and technology. To a degree, inertia was bound to be a bigger problem in Britain than in countries with new industries.

Comparison of the British performance after 1870 with those of Germany and the United States thus suggests that British industry was handicapped by its great headstart. To be sure, British industry by the 1870s and 1880s produced huge income for the nation as a whole, and this could have been transformed into capital investment that would have kept British industry ahead. But as the economy matured, British society unconsciously opted more for consumer pleasures than for capital investment—as seems the fate of most industrial societies—and the British also habitually invested huge sums of money abroad. The British exported capital throughout the nineteenth century and at a greater rate after 1870 than before: British assets abroad exceeded £1 billion in 1875 and £2 billion in 1900. They did so because the rate of return on foreign investments—mainly railways in the United States and elsewhere—was higher than at home. The maturing domestic economy, with its relatively older technology and expanding service sector, did not produce returns on investment to match those in newly industrializing areas. Given the British commitment to laissez-faire policies, the government would not consider policies that might have kept that capital at home.

The British headstart in industrialization also created psychological and structural disadvantages. While foreign entrepreneurs aggressively pursued innovations in order to catch up, British industrialists found it hard to break with old habits in management, sales, and industrial relations. They tended to look to the past as the model for success. Similarly, British capitalists were reluctant to discard the factories and machines that they and their workers knew well; hence they tended to squeeze profits from existing technology by incremental changes rather than undertake wholesale recapitalization. British entrepreneurs were slow to adopt new forms of industrial organization emerging in Germany and the United States—cartels and trusts. Although British business did gradually shift from individually owned firms and partnerships to public and private companies, the ordinary firm was much smaller than in Germany or America. British firms did grow in size, and this slowly brought about a split between ownership and management. But British commerce and industry remained comparatively splintered. In the British coal industry, for instance, there were nearly 1,600 coal companies in 1913.

The traditionalism of British industry and the burden of past habits affected the late-Victorian economy in another way: they retarded the deliberate application of science to industry, which was the wave of the future. Theoretical or "pure" science in Britain was second to none: in addition to Darwin and the evolutionists in geology and biology, the British could boast of John Dalton and Lyon Playfair in chemistry and Michael Faraday and James Clerk Maxwell in physics. But the British lagged behind Germany and the United States both in the industrial application of science and in the scientific training of the work force at every level. German and American factories regularly had research laboratories by the late nineteenth century, but hardly any British industry did. The British preferred design by "rule of thumb" that had served so well in the past. Britain had no state school system until 1870 and relatively few secondary schools until after the Great War. British higher education remained open only to the few and concentrated on the liberal arts and sciences, while despising technology and engineering. In 1913, Britain had only 9,000 university students, whereas Germany had nearly 60,000, and Britain graduated only 350 students in all fields of science and mathematics, whereas Germany graduated 3,000 in engineering alone.

The attitudes that limited the educational system in Britain arose in part from a commitment to laissez-faire but mainly from certain cultural assumptions inherited from the past. The landed gentleman remained the ideal for most British businessmen. British capitalists yearned to emulate the landed orders—to make a fortune, buy an estate, and retire to a gracious life untainted by trade. Self-interest and profit, like industry and cities, were regarded as distinctly inferior to selfless public service and country life. The public schools (that is, exclusive private boarding schools), in which an increasing proportion of middle-class boys were educated, inculcated these values of the leisured landowner and the amateur public servant. British literary culture from the romantic period on taught the superiority of the preindustrial world and the life of the mind. By the late-Victorian period, the hard edge of many industrial families had been worn down, and what the British middle class gained in culture, it lost in drive and entrepreneurship.

EDWARDIAN FALSE DAWN, 1900–1914

In the years between 1900 and 1914, the British economy in certain ways seemed to recover. Large numbers of businessmen enjoyed sharply improved standards of living and indulged in bouts of consumer spending that approached the spectacular. The upper classes still found it possible to find cheap domestic help, and they built handsome homes in the country or suburbs that would make later middle-class housing seem cramped. The well to-do could afford the latest item of consumer pleasure—the automobile, noisy and dusty as it was. These features of Edwardian life were later (after the First World War) to glow in the memories of the rich as the "good old days." Such memories selectively forgot the less pleasant features of the Edwardian economy: the enormous gap between rich and poor, the obtrusive evidence of poverty, and the growing conflict in industrial relations. In E. M. Forster's marvelously perceptive novel, *Howards End* (1910), the well-to-do businessmen and reformist intellectuals could enjoy their lives only because they felt that the working people were "in the abyss," beyond help. In fact the main economic themes that had emerged in the late-Victorian years remained in place. What later was remembered as a golden age was in fact a false dawn.

The principal factor in the apparent prosperity before 1914 was a recovery of prices. The twin causes of this price rise were the continuing increase in the size of the population, which reached more than forty-five million in 1914, and the general long-term improvement in incomes and standards of living: more people had more money to spend. Overall, the prices of food and manufactured goods went up between 20 and 25 percent from 1900 to 1914. As usual, this increase cut different ways in different social classes: manufacturers, financiers, commercial men, and their families enjoyed higher profits again, whereas the working class, whose wages did not go up as fast, found their consuming power stagnant. This they found a bitter pill after the improvement in real wages of the 1880s and 1890s.

Meanwhile, many long-term trends remained unfavorable for the economy. Economic growth slowed between 1900 and 1914 and by some calculations stopped altogether. Productivity (production per capita) slowed, and Britain's share of the world's manufacturing output fell to slightly less than Germany's and less than half of America's. Capital was formed at a lower rate than at any time in the nineteenth century and at a rate much lower than in Germany or the United States. The British in the Edwardian period had a more favorable balance of payments than in the late-Victorian years, but that positive balance was much more dependent on "invisible income" and the sale abroad of capital goods—that is, on shipping, the sale of financial services, and earnings from investment, and on the sale of coal, steam engines, and industrial machinery. By 1914, the British economy had become more vulnerable to both disturbances in the pattern and volume of world trade and industrialization of previously underdeveloped regions in the British spheres of influence.

However, it is important to keep these gradual changes in perspective. Britain in 1914 was still one of the three great economic powers in the world. Britain was the third largest industrial producer on earth, and the British enjoyed the second highest (behind the United States) per capita income. Britain remained the greatest trading and financial nation in the world, the leading power in shipping, international banking and finance, and overseas trading services.

SOCIAL CHANGE, 1870–1914

Though not as well known to students of history as the "heroic" age of class formation and industrialization, social change in the late nineteenth and early twentieth centuries was as profound as in any period of similar length in the British past. Social change occurred in four main patterns between 1870 and 1914: (1) an alteration of the social structure, in which the landed class and the upper middle class merged to form a "plutocracy"; (2) the deliberate limitation by married couples of the number of children, resulting in much smaller families; (3) the beginnings of a widespread women's movement; and (4) the solidification of working-class culture in the context of heightened class tensions.

The first of these changes—the formation of a plutocracy, or class that ruled by means of its wealth—basically was the result of economic troubles among the aristocracy and gentry. As men in the landed orders sought to bolster their incomes by investing in business and industry and by lending their names to commercial enterprises, they blurred the line that had long divided the landed class from the middle class. They came to understand better the point of view of the wealthy bourgeoisie. As we have seen, the businessmen met them halfway, by buying estates and country villas as soon as their fortunes permitted and by sending their sons to the elite public schools, which inculcated many of the values and life-styles of the traditional governing class. By 1914, the upper class was no longer *landed* but simply *propertied*.

The rapid expansion of the professions accentuated this structural change. The British professions stood between the landed and middle classes, often drawing their recruits from the middle class but functioning in close relationship to the gentry. The professionals thereby mediated between the landed and the middle

81 Banbury Road, Oxford. A typical home of the substantial middle class in late-Victorian Britain. Note the Ruskinian (or Gothic) influence.

classes, transmitting both values and personnel from one to the other. The professions had grown throughout the nineteenth century, but now their numbers expanded at an accelerated pace. A reasonable estimate is that the number of professionals rose from about 2.5 percent of the work force in 1861 to 4 percent in 1901, and given their wealth and status, they exercised power and influence all out of proportion to their numbers. By 1914, the professional ranks included not only military officers, clergymen, doctors, and lawyers but also teachers, artists, architects, surveyors, engineers, and accountants.

Another development that contributed to the formation of a single, propertied upper class was suburbanization. Social class was (and is) as much a state of mind as an expression of occupation and wealth. Ownership of a piece of land, no matter how small, tended to make a late-Victorian businessman think like a property owner. It was, in fact, the closest that most of them could come to having a country house. Suburbs were not new in Britain in 1870, but their expansion accelerated in the half-century between 1870 and 1914. Thus, whereas the first half of the nineteenth century was characterized by the concentration of masses of people in urban centers, the second half was marked by an "exhaling" of large numbers into concentric rings around the great cities. Railroads made this process easier but did not cause it. Middle-class people moved to the suburbs because they feared the crime, filth, and disease of the cities and because they found it possible in the suburbs to satisfy their needs for privacy and domesticity.

The second major category of social change—family limitation—was tied directly to the economic pressures on the professional and middle-class people of the late-Victorian period. In Britain, the practice of birth control began among these middle and upper-class families; its main impact on working-class families did not come until after 1900. Birth control was not the result of the invention or discovery of contraceptive devices but rather of the adoption of existing techniques in order to maintain high standards of living. During the mid-Victorian decades, middle-class couples had on average about six children during the span of marriage. They apparently thought that they could keep up their high level of consumption, employ the proper number of servants, and provide for their children (including the appropriate education) even with such large families. Indeed, bourgeois couples of the expansive mid-Victorian decades came to expect ever-increasing standards of living and therefore to become accustomed to increasing their outlay on homes, food, domestic servants, and all the other paraphernalia of respectability—holidays, fine clothes, carriages, and the like.

Once the economic difficulties of the late-Victorian years began to beset middle-class families, however, couples began to recognize the expense of children, especially because the increasing complexity of society required more years of education and professional training. The average age at marriage already was high—not far below thirty years of age for men; thus there was little opportunity to delay it further. Birth control proved to be the answer. The techniques and devices—the "safe" period, coitus interruptus, condoms, and diaphragms—had long been known. They received much attention in the 1860s, and even more during the trial (for obscenity) of two birth-control advocates, Charles Bradlaugh and Annie Besant, in 1877. Working-class couples, however, remained suspicious of bourgeois ways, and illiteracy kept many of them socially conservative until the years between 1900 and 1914, when they, too, began limiting the size of their families.

The demographic results of the spread of birth control are clear. The average number of children in each family in Britain (not counting Ireland) fell from about six in 1870 to a little over three in the early twentieth century. By the 1920s, it had fallen to just over two per marriage. The population growth that had exploded upward in the eighteenth century began to slow down, *even though the mortality rate was falling*. The declining birth rate, then, slowed the population increase: the growth of the population, which had reached 17 percent per decade in the 1810s and held at 11 percent per decade in the 1850s and 1860s, declined to about 10 percent per decade in the early 1900s. All mature industrial nations have seemed to experience such a "demographic transition"; Britain's came earlier than most, in the period between 1870 and 1914. By the 1920s, the British population was barely growing at all.

The social consequences of this revolution in family size were perhaps most important for women. Because the reduction of family size was brought about by

New kinds of women's work: typists. With the increasing growth of the service sector of the British economy and the invention of the typewriter came the expansion of clerical jobs for women.

the middle class first, the effect was felt initially by middle-class wives and mothers, and only later by working-class women. For wives in middle-class and professional families, the reduction of the number of children served as a liberation from some of the burdens of childbearing and child care and therefore as a release for activities outside the home. One result was an increase in the number of women involved in philanthropy and other "good causes" such as temperance reform and social work in the slums. Well-to-do women still found paid employment scarce and socially unacceptable. Voluntary social work gave them an alternative outlet for their energy and talent; it was an extension outside the home of the traditional female role of moral care. By such philanthropic activity, thousands of upper-class women gained valuable experience and expertise in public life.

At the same time, as middle-class males put off marriage or emigrated, the number of unmarried women grew. The goal for respectable women was still marriage, but the number of unmarried women had risen markedly between 1851 and 1871: in the 1870s almost one out of every three British women between twenty-four and thirty-five was unmarried. As a result, the number of middle-class women who went to work outside the home increased sharply. Not only were more middle-class women (almost all of them single) seeking work, but also the economy was producing more jobs suitable for respectable women. No longer was the middle-class girl in need of income restricted to becoming a governess; the more service-oriented economy opened positions for nurses, teachers, clerks, shop assistants, and secretaries.

All of these changes made powerful contributions to a women's movement and to feminism, which together formed one of the most widely discussed phenomena of the late nineteenth century and which formed a powerful political force in the years just before the First World War. The liberated "intellectual woman" showed up in British fiction as a new character type—from Sue Bridehead in Thomas Hardy's *Jude the Obscure* to Margaret and Helen Schlegel in E. M. Forster's *Howards End*. The early women's movement was not by any means a single, well-organized force in the late Victorian period. The women who composed it had different values and different targets. Some, like Sophia Jex-Blake and Elizabeth Garrett Anderson, worked to break the male monopoly over the professions. They succeeded: Jex-Blake opened even the medical schools to women in the 1880s, despite Queen Victoria's vehement disapproval. Others, such as Emily Davies, sought to establish women's colleges even within the staunch male preserves, Oxford and Cambridge. They succeeded to the extent of founding colleges for women in both of the ancient universities, despite the fears on the part of some males that academic standards would be lowered and male undergraduates would be distracted from their work. (Women were not allowed to take degrees from Oxford until 1921 and from Cambridge until 1948.) Josephine Butler and others attacked the notorious Victorian double standard in sexual morality by campaigning to have the Contagious Diseases Act abolished. This act, passed in the 1860s, enabled police in army and navy towns to force prostitutes to submit to medical inspection for venereal disease. After a long campaign, in which Butler called on men to practice the same chastity they preached to women, Parliament repealed the act in 1886.

Some late-Victorian feminists felt that marriage was so unequal as to further the traditional weakness and subservience of women; hence another element in the women's movement worked to reform the legal position of women in marriage. Frances Power Cobbe agitated successfully in the 1860s and 1870s to enable magistrates to impose more severe sentences on wife beaters. Women gradually won some custody rights over their children in divorce cases. By a series of laws culminating in 1882, married women were allowed to retain their property. Divorce, however, was not granted to women on the same grounds as men until 1923; until then, they still had to prove something in addition to adultery to win a divorce.

Finally, there was a campaign to win votes for women. Given the importance of Parliament in British life, the women's movement, which never included a majority of women, inevitably focused most of its energy on gaining the right to vote. Beginning with J. S. Mill's famous essay, *The Subjection of Women* (1869), a slowly growing number of men and women argued that women were as capable of that reasoned behavior required by the suffrage as were men. In the late-Victorian years, various women's suffrage societies (combined into one society in 1897), led by Lydia Becker and Millicent Fawcett, campaigned for women's votes ("on the same terms as men") by means of persuasion: reasoned appeals, lobbying, petitions, and political pressure. This essentially middle-class movement met staunch resistance from people—female as well as male—who believed that the vote would spoil the innocent purity of women, or that it would ruin marital harmony, or that the justifiable claims of women were being met without it. A few Liberal members of Parliament (including Mill in his one term) were for women's suffrage, but the leadership remained solidly opposed; a few Conservative leaders might have accepted it, but the rank and file resisted. Most women, like most men, continued to think that the proper sphere for women was the home and that the proper woman's role should be, as one wife wrote, that of "a quite unillustrious, more or less hampered dependent wife and mother." But by the early twentieth century, feminists routinely criticized marriage as corrupt in that it subjected women to "sexual slavery," and they rejected the Victorian doctrine of the separate spheres for men and women.

In the early twentieth century the relatively sedate tactics of the suffragists were upstaged by the militant tactics of the suffragettes, a highly visible minority in the feminist movement. The central figures in this new phase of the feminist movement were Mrs. Emmeline Pankhurst and her two daughters, Christabel and Sylvia. Mrs. Pankhurst, wife of a radical Manchester lawyer, founded the Women's Social and Political Union in 1903. From its beginning the WSPU showed interest in both votes for working-class women and the social condition of working-class women. Within two years of its founding the WSPU had turned toward militant action: disruption of political meetings, demonstrations, political marches, and, from 1912, window smashing, arson, and even physical assault. In 1913, a suffragette threw herself under the hooves of the king's horse on Derby Day and was killed. Others who were imprisoned went on hunger strikes and were subjected to ghastly force-feedings. Whether such tactics did the cause of women's suffrage more good than harm remains a heated question to this day. Certainly, the Liberal prime minister, H. H. Asquith (1906–1916), was very hostile to the women's behavior, and the turn of the Pankhurst daughters against men and marriage split the movement. In any case, women did not get the vote until after the Great War, by which time the militant agitation had been set aside.

WORKING-CLASS CULTURE, 1870–1914

Meanwhile, in the years between 1870 and 1914 British working people, whose experiences were now predominantly industrial and urban, settled into a distinct pattern of life—to use one historian's phrase, "a life apart."* The comfortable lives, the conspicuous consumption, and the aspirations for progress of the upper classes all depended on the drudgery and low wages of the working people, but these

---

*Standish Meacham, *A Life Apart: The English Working Class, 1890–1914* (Cambridge, Mass., Harvard University Press, 1977).

segments of the population occupied different worlds. The working class of the late nineteenth and early twentieth centuries made up 75 percent of the British population (as opposed to 5 percent for the plutocracy and 20 percent for the middle class). By the early 1900s, the great majority of workers were employed in trade and industry; less than 10 percent were now working in agriculture. A majority of the employed working class were males, but nearly 10 percent of working-class women also held jobs outside their homes, the largest number of them as domestic servants. Except for the domestics, few of these people had much to do with the upper classes; the face-to-face contacts of the preindustrial world were almost entirely gone, and suburbanization had completed the geographical segregation of the classes.

Despite a century of industrial expansion, the standard of living for the urban working class remained low. During the late-Victorian years, the decline of prices brought substantial improvement in real wages for *employed* working men and women—perhaps as much as a 40 percent improvement—but price increases rolled back some of this gain after 1900. The average wage for a working man was no more than £60 or £70 a year, as opposed to £200 a year for the middle class and £1,000 a year for the upper class. The long-standing wage differential between the skilled workers and the less-skilled tended to diminish, as the progress of both management techniques and technological development in mass industry worked towards de-skilling of the artisanal elite. Moreover, both *unemployment* and under-employment posed serious problems for the working class—so serious that the word unemployment was invented in the 1880s. In the worst years for unemployment, 1886-1887, thousands of angry working people repeatedly demonstrated and rioted in London. On "Bloody Sunday," in November 1887, squadrons of red-coated Life Guards cleared a massive gathering of workers from Trafalgar Square in the most dangerous expression of class conflict since the 1840s.

The severe poverty suffered by many working-class people was amply demonstrated by sociological research. In the mid-1880s, Charles Booth, a wealthy manufacturer, began a massive survey published in 1889–1902 as the *Life and Labour of the People in London*. Booth intended to disprove socialist claims about the dire poverty among working people, but he found the opposite of what he expected. Defining the poverty line stringently—as the amount above which a family was barely able to maintain "decent independent life"—Booth discovered that about 30 percent of London's population lived at or below the line. In 1901, another social investigator, Seebohm Rowntree, and others realized what working people knew firsthand: that all of the working class, except for the skilled artisans (who were about 10 percent of the total) lived on the edge of the abyss of poverty and would fall into it if they lost employment or fell ill.

The grinding poverty of many in the working class had dire effects on their health and way of life. Most men and women worked fifty-four hours a week or more, when they could get work. For this labor, they lived on forty-five shillings a week per family, spending over half on an unvarying diet—bread (thirty-three pounds a week per family), potatoes (in the North, porridge), butter, sugar, a dozen eggs, and some meat. As the chief wage earners, men were given the choicest food;

Late-Victorian urban poverty: Saltney Street, Liverpool. This photo shows the common pump and open drain in a cramped street in working-class Liverpool.

children got what was left. Boys and girls regularly went to work at eight or nine years of age even after compulsory education brought them into school for part of the day. A large percentage of children suffered from rickets, open sores, and other diseases related to malnutrition. When the Boer War (1899–1902) brought thousands of volunteers to the army, two of every three from the working class were rejected as physically unfit. Working-class youths at age thirteen were 2 or 3 inches shorter and 15 pounds lighter than the average public school children of the same age.

Survival was the main objective of most working-class families. Ties of kinship enabled families to come to each other's rescue in a crisis, and working-class families tended to be very close. Likewise, neighbors, who lived cheek-by-jowl in the densely crowded cities, felt obliged to help out. Thus neighborhoods, or inner-city "villages," were the principal means by which working people shaped their lives and provided mutual support. Neighbors saw each other regularly in the neighborhood institutions—pubs, groceries, shops, and pawnbrokers. Any urban neighborhood contained its own social hierarchy: an elite (the skilled workers), unskilled workers, and the down-and-out of the streets. Social status and public behavior were carefully observed and policed by a matriarchy, composed of the married women of the neighborhood. No one escaped their oversight. The wives and mothers also served as the treasurers of their families' meager resources—planning, scrimping, saving, shopping, and pawning household items at the beginning of the week. A family's status was known by the items it pawned: pawning good shoes and clothes denoted high status and respectability, as opposed to rugs, pots and pans, and bed clothes, which revealed low wages or imprudent living. Showing respectability was crucial. The better-off families showed it by dressing in their Sunday best (reclaimed from the pawn broker each Saturday) and attending chapel; families that could not afford to own (or reclaim) Sunday-best clothing stayed home so as not to display their hardship.

Women typically had to hold their families together. Women were clearly subordinate to their husbands, who usually asserted their independence and manliness by dominating their wives in a world that otherwise kept them powerless. Men ate first and best, and men kept their special preserves—the pubs—off limits to women. About a fifth of all employed women were married, though many worked at home to make ends meet. Rarely did any working woman make wages equal to those of men, nor did women in many industries participate in trade unions. Yet, as one observer wrote, "When the mother dies the family goes to pieces." One of Charles Booth's investigators reported:

> If she be a tidy woman, decently versed in the rare arts of cooking and sewing, the family life is independent, even comfortable, and the children may follow in the father's footsteps or rise to better things. If she be a gossip and a bungler—worse still, a drunkard—the family sink to the lowest level of the East London street; and the children are probably added to the number of those who gain their livelihood by irregular work and by irregular means.

One of the most important changes in the history of the working class between 1870 and 1914 was the introduction of a state school system in 1870. The need for a comprehensive elementary educational system had long been recognized in Britain, but education was a divisive issue, one that polarized Anglicans from nonconformists and advocates of local control from centralizers. But after the second great measure of political reform was passed in 1867 (see Chapter 4), members of the governing elite thought that the need to educate the new voters was urgent. Moreover, the strength of foreign economic competition persuaded them that action could not wait. The Liberal government was finally able to find a compromise of the religious differences in 1870: the existing system of "voluntary" schools (most of which were Anglican) was retained and supplemented by the building of locally controlled "Board" schools where the existing schools were nonexistent or inadequate. In 1880, schooling was made compulsory for children under eleven years old, and in 1902, another major act doubled the number of secondary schools. All of these acts, as we will see, were intensely controversial, but the effects of the new school system were clear: before 1870, the rate of illiteracy among men was 33 percent and among women 50 percent; by 1900, illiteracy had been abolished.

The abolition of illiteracy was eventually to have a powerful impact on working-class culture. It would radically increase the ability of working men and women to develop their own systematic analyses of the political and economic systems—and to construct their own ideology and policies appropriate to a working-class point of view. But the results of universal literacy did not come suddenly, and by 1914 they had only begun to work. The elementary schools for the poor that were set up in the late nineteenth century often were badly overcrowded and poorly taught. Their lessons were not meant to help boys and girls to improve their social status but to prepare them for the station into which they were born. Patriotism, imperialism, and respect for their social superiors were the main themes. Many working-class families were suspicious of the new schools—as they were of most governmental intervention in their lives—and besides, they needed their children to work. Working-class families generally took their children out of school as soon as possible. In 1906–1907, for example, only 35 percent of fourteen year olds were still in school, and only 18 percent of sixteen year olds. Consequently, the level of literacy that the schools inculcated was low, and before 1914, a majority of the working class still could not comprehend a text containing any but simple ideas and one-syllable words. The entrepreneurs of journalism recognized this fact and simplified and trivialized their mass-circulation papers.

The urgency of the problems of survival for many working-class families and the low level of reading ability retarded the spread of trade unions and working-class radicalism. Nevertheless, the state of the economy led many working-class leaders into more aggressive and extreme ideas and action between 1870 and 1914. The waning of the expansive and (relatively) generous attitude of commercial and industrial men, their attempts to cut wages and increase factory efficiency so as to shore up profits, and the rise of unemployment all contributed to the spread of socialism in the working-class leadership on the one hand and a much more inclusive and aggressive trade unionism on the other.

In Britain, as we will see in Chapter 2, socialism was largely a movement of middle-class intellectuals. But its influence began to penetrate small circles in the working class in the 1880s. By 1900, there were perhaps thirty thousand socialists in Britain. Some of these late-Victorian socialists were Marxists, some were Fabians (that is, social science experts and gradualists), and some were Christian socialists. After 1900, syndicalism (a French term for the ideas that unions should control their industries and that militant industrial action would be more effective than political reform) won a foothold in some of the biggest unions, most notably the coal miners. Most working-class socialists, however, were not doctrinaire but idealistic, deriving their ideals of equality and community from the prophecies of Carlyle and Ruskin. They wanted an end to the worship of money, a reinvigoration of craftsmanship, and the restoration of independence and dignity to workers. Such views were expressed by the socialist most widely read by British working people, Robert Blatchford, whose paper, the *Clarion*, sold forty thousand copies a week in 1894.

Socialism was one factor contributing to the new-style unionism of the 1880s and after; economic conditions were the other. The "new unionism" involved both the organization of semiskilled and unskilled workers in industries not organized before and the adoption of much more aggressive tactics by all unions, old and new. A socialist, Annie Besant, helped the London match girls win a dramatic strike in 1888. Working-class socialists such as Tom Mann, John Burns, and Will Thorne organized the gas workers in 1889. Later that year Mann and others helped the dockers, who had always been casual (that is, hourly) laborers, organize and strike for higher wages and more regular work. After a bitter and well-publicized struggle with their employees, the dockers won. Union membership more than doubled, reaching two million in 1901—about 20 percent of male manual workers.

During the 1890s employers counterattacked against the unions, slowing their growth and weakening their legal position. The big blow came in 1901: after a strike on the Taff Vale railway in South Wales, the company sued the union, and the House of Lords ruled in favor of the company that unions were liable for damages in a strike. This decision would have made strikes impossible, and it tended to make workers more militant than ever. Parliament reversed the Taff Vale decision in 1906, but with the spread of syndicalism and the downturn in real wages, industrial relations remained very tense anyway. Serious strikes occurred in the coal and railway industries and on the docks as trade unions tried to secure the eight-hour day and a living wage. In 1912, British industry lost six times as many working days to strikes as the annual average in the previous twenty years. Some union organizers tried to revive the old "one big union" idea in preparation for a general strike; although that effort failed, the miners, railwaymen, and transport workers did create a "Triple Alliance" in 1913. Many employers by then believed that the trade unionists were seeking a general confrontation between capital and labor.

The spread of socialism and the growth of trade unions both expressed and contributed to an intensified class consciousness. By 1914, as Professor Meacham has put it, there was in Britain "a sense of impending crisis." As we will see in subsequent chapters, the women's movement, Irish nationalism, and foreign affairs also contributed to the crisis atmosphere. However, it is important to remember that only a minority of working people participated in either socialism or the trade unions. As Robert Roberts recalled from his boyhood in Salford, near Manchester: "Before 1914 the great majority of the working class were ignorant of Socialist doctrine in any form, whether 'Christian' or Marxist." Even the union movement, which was much bigger than socialism, included only four million people in 1914, about 45 percent of all manual workers, or 10 percent of the total population.

The broadest, most inclusive trend between 1870 and 1914 was not socialism or the new unionism, but the extension and solidification of urban working-class culture. Work, which began at 6:00 A.M. and lasted until 5:30 P.M., dominated the lives of working-class people, even though the industrial worker rarely regarded it as fulfilling. British workers kept work sharply separate from leisure time. They spent their weekday evenings after work in the pub, and they spent Saturday afternoons (which an increasing number had free) in relaxing over tea and newspapers like *Tit-Bits*, the *Daily Mail*, and *Answers*. Sundays they rarely dedicated to church or chapel, but to "sleeping in" and visiting with friends. Few had paid holidays; thus most working men and women spent their holidays at home or on day excursions to the country or the seashore.

Besides work, the neighborhood, the pub, and the pawnshop, three other institutions became crucial to urban working-class culture after 1870: the music hall, professional football (soccer), and fish and chips. Music halls, which were lowbrow variety theaters for the masses, offered bright lights, music, comedy, and drink. Their songs and jokes were drawn directly from working-class experience—"pop" music and entertainment by the pop stars of the day, themselves working-class people. Football, a medieval village sport, was revived in the 1860s by upper-class men who wished to involve working men in a vigorous and "wholesome" recreation. But in the 1880s, working men began to form their own football clubs, which quickly became professional as competition among them intensified. These clubs—Manchester United, Shefffield United, West Ham, and so on—provided focal points for local pride, rituals of communality, and diversions from dismal living conditions. As for fish and chips (a great British contribution to human civilization): British workers had consumed little seafood until the late nineteenth century, when rapid transportation and refrigeration made fresh fish available in all the big cities. By 1914, fish and chips had become a key element in the working-class diet.

In creating these institutions, as well as in participating in socialism and trade unionism, the British working class was developing its own life apart from that of the plutocracy and middle class. The boundary between working-class and middle-class status, never easily penetrated, became more impermeable than ever before, especially for working-class males. Working people in growing numbers during the late-Victorian and Edwardian years rejected the moralistic preachings of their "social superiors," preferring to go their own way. Church and chapel played a role in the lives of a diminishing number of working people—and the farther down the social ladder, the smaller the role. It remained the case that many members of the working class retained an informal, diffuse, non-churchgoing form of Christian beliefs, which held that God exists but does not actively intervene in worldly affairs, that good behavior would be rewarded in the afterlife, and that it was not necessary to go to church to be a good person. Few working men or women held an elaborate political or economic ideology, for experience taught them that tomorrow would be much like today. As one working man wrote, "One can dream and hope, and if by chance God gives such a one imagination, it is more of a curse than a blessing." Yet the late Victorian and Edwardian working people did have a strong class consciousness, expressed in terms of "them" and "us." The ups and downs of life lived on the brink of destitution typically made working people "cheeky" and wise in their own way—inclined to let things roll off their backs, not to take themselves too seriously, and above all not to accept that "them" were better than "us."

Suggested Reading

Alford, B. W. E., *Britain in the World Economy since 1880* (New York: Longman, 1996).

Banks, J. A., and Olive Banks, *Feminism and Family Planning* (New York: Schocken, 1964).

Booth, Alan, *The British Economy in the Twentieth Century* (New York: Palgrave, 2001).

——— , *Prosperity and Parenthood* (London: Routledge & Kegan Paul, 1969).

Caine, Barbara, *English Feminism, 1780–1980* (New York: Oxford University Press, 1997).

Cannadine, David, *The Decline and Fall of the British Aristocracy* (New Haven: Yale University Press, 1990).

Floud, Roderick, and Donald McCloskey, eds., *The Economic History of Britain Since 1700: Volume 2: 1860 to the 1970's* (New York: Cambridge University Press, 1981).

Gourvish, T. R., and Alan O'Day, eds., *Later Victorian Britain, 1867–1900* (New York: St. Martin's, 1988).

Harris, José, *Private Lives, Public Spirit: A Social History of Britain, 1870–1914* (New York: Oxford University Press, 1993).

———, *Unemployment and Politics* (Oxford: Clarendon Press, 1972).

Jones, Gareth Stedman, *Outcast London* (Oxford: Clarendon Press, 1971).

Kirk, Neville, *Change, Continuity and Class: Labour in British Society, 1850–1920* (Manchester: Manchester University Press, 1998).

Landes, David, *The Unbound Prometheus* (Cambridge: Cambridge University Press, 1969).

Levine, Phillippa, *Victorian Feminism, 1850–1900* (Tallahassee: Florida State University Press, 1989).

McKibbin, Ross, *The Ideologies of Class: Social Relations in Britain, 1880–1950* (New York: Oxford University Press, 1990).

Meacham, Standish, *A Life Apart: The English Working Class, 1890–1914* (Cambridge, Mass.: Harvard University Press, 1977).

Pollard, Sidney, *Britain's Prime and Britain's Decline: The British Economy, 1870–1914* (London: Edward Arnold, 1989).

Prochaska, F. K., *Women and Philanthropy in Nineteenth Century England* (New York: Oxford University Press, 1980).

Read, Donald, *England, 1868–1914* (New York: Longman, 1979).

Roberts, Elizabeth, *A Woman's Place: An Oral History of Working-class Women, 1890–1940* (Oxford: Basil Blackwell, 1984).

Roberts, Robert, *The Classic Slum* (Manchester: Manchester University Press, 1972).

Rubenstein, W. D., *Capitalism, Culture, and Decline in Britain, 1750–1990* (New York: Routledge, Chapman & Hall, 1993).

Saul, S. B., *The Myth of the Great Depression, 1873–96* (London: Macmillan, 1976).

Thompson, F. M. L., *English Landed Society in the Nineteenth Century* (London: Routledge and Kegan Paul, 1963).

———, *Gentrification and English Culture, 1780–1980* (New York: Oxford University Press, 2001).

Thompson, Paul, *The Edwardians* (London: Weidenfeld & Nicolson, 1975).

Vicinus, Martha, ed., *A Widening Sphere: Changing Roles of Victorian Women* (Bloomington: Indiana University Press, 1977).

Walkowitz, Judith, *Prostitution and Victorian Society* (New York: Cambridge University Press, 1980).

Chapter 2

Crisis of Confidence, 1870–1914

The economic and social changes of the late-Victorian and Edwardian years contributed to a crisis of confidence. Orthodox Christianity had been shaken by Darwinism, and now the difficulties of the economy, the revelation of enduring poverty, and the alteration of the social structure threw many Victorian ideas into doubt. To many men and women in the educated classes—especially younger people—Victorian ideas and values no longer seemed satisfying. Consequently, in cultural life, the years between 1870 and 1914 in Britain were filled with exploration and speculation as people searched for new ordering principles. Fundamental assumptions and doctrines about the economic and social systems came under attack and new ones emerged. For a time, even the traditional British philosophical style, empiricism, was overturned, and the Benthamite and Coleridgean strands of thought, which had seemed mutually supportive in the mid-Victorian years, sharply diverged. There was an explosion of "isms": in addition to feminism there were scientific naturalism, New Liberalism, socialism, imperialism, and aestheticism. Thus, although this was a troubled period in British cultural history, it was also one of the most exciting.

SCIENTIFIC NATURALISM

One of the most influential intellectual efforts to find a new ordering principle for both an understanding of the natural world and a guide for behavior was scientific naturalism. This was the British variety of a cult of science that emerged in most of the Western world in the late nineteenth and early twentieth centuries. As the influence of Christianity declined, science, which was as yet seen as incapable of doing any harm, seemed to be the best alternative. As one English writer said in 1878, "In the struggle of life with the facts of existence, Science is the bringer of aid; in the struggle of the soul with the mystery of existence, Science is the bringer of light." Many scientists in the late-Victorian period, including Herbert Spencer, T H. Huxley, John Tyndall, and Francis Galton, aggressively asserted the claims of science as a new religion and of scientists as a new priesthood.

The British scientific naturalists intended to create nothing less than a science-based culture. Their doctrine was composed of six basic points. First, they held that the universe, or nature, is a mechanism, and therefore all events have material causes, in the sense of being mechanically determined like the movement of cogs in a machine. Second, they believed that evolution describes the working of this machine. Third, they claimed that thought and ideas cannot cause the natural world to move and interact; all causes are material. Fourth, as Huxley said, there is "but one kind of knowledge and but one method of acquiring it": empirical science, which should be extended to all realms of thought, including ethics and social behavior. Fifth, they contended that because it is not possible to have any knowledge of the supernatural, the correct outlook is agnosticism: not the claim that God and the supernatural do not exist but simply that one cannot have any valid knowledge about them at all. Sixth and finally, they insisted that ethics and morals must be derived from the facts of the natural world, not from the "unknowable."

Perhaps the greatest—certainly the most prolific and famous—scientific naturalist was Herbert Spencer (1820–1902). It is hard to overestimate the influence of Spencer in late-Victorian Britain (and America, where he was even more influential). In the 1890s, a letter was delivered to him addressed: "Herbt. Spencer, England, and if the postman doesn't know where he lives, why, he ought to." Widely regarded as a prodigious genius, Spencer tried to create a comprehensive philosophy by universalizing science. He was trained as a civil engineer, and his philosophy always reflected that no-nonsense background. Impenetrably self-confident, Spencer acquired his fundamental ideas early and never swerved from them: (1) that evolution, operating through "survival of the fittest" (a phrase he invented), is the explanation of change in nature, human life, and society; (2) that evolution moves from "simple homogeneity" to "complex heterogeneity"—that is, there is in society as in nature a continuous specialization of function; and (3) that every event is caused, but "every cause produces more than one effect."

Spencer drew from these evolutionary views a strong defense of laissez-faire economics and an anti-interventionist attitude toward government policy. He believed that because it is impossible to predict the effects of economic or social legislation, governments should try to do as little as possible. Furthermore, Spencer believed that social welfare policies only prevent people from adapting to their environment, which they must do to survive. He thought that social progress is inevitable if people are left alone, since the natural evolution of society is toward more complex specialization and interdependence. Such views became the stock-in-trade of defenders of capitalism and opponents of governmental social reform after 1870. Spencer's ideas seem to resemble those of Adam Smith, for both thinkers believed that progress would occur only if people are left alone, but whereas Smith thought that this progress would be the result of each individual's efforts to maximize his or her production, Spencer saw society in biological terms: "I have contended that policies, legislative and other, while hindering the survival of the fittest, further the propagation of the unfit [and] work grave mischiefs."

Spencer's application of evolutionary theory to social policy places him among the most prominent type of scientific naturalists of the late-Victorian and Edwardian years, the Social Darwinists. In fact, however, Spencer's view of evolution was not exactly that of Darwin, for Spencer believed in the inheritance of acquired char-

Herbert Spencer. The most famous evolutionary philosopher in late-Victorian Britain and one of the most influential thinkers in the Western world at the time.

acteristics, and Darwin did not. The Social Darwinists applied Darwinian theory to society as a whole, sometimes (as we will see below) in support of imperialism abroad and sometimes in support of capitalism and laissez-faire policies at home. The Social Darwinists who, like Benjamin Kidd and Karl Pearson, applied evolution to whole nations could advocate domestic social reform to make the society more "efficient." But Social Darwinists who applied evolution to the internal condition of British society almost invariably opposed measures of social reform on the same grounds as did Spencer.

This "internalist" variety of Social Darwinism could be extraordinarily harsh in its attitude toward social life. As Spencer wrote, they thought it wrong to interfere with the "progressive" forces of nature: "There is no greater curse to posterity than that of bequeathing to them an increasing population of imbeciles and idlers and criminals." These conservative Social Darwinists believed that private charity was adequate for all reasonable relief of poverty and that state intervention would block the natural struggle of life and prevent the beneficial weeding out of the weak. To interfere with this process would be harmful to the "British race" and to the world. Alfred Marshall, the leading economist of the late 1800s, wrote:

> . . . if the lower classes of Englishmen multiply more rapidly than those which are morally and physically superior, not only will the population of England deteriorate, but also that part of the population of America and Australia which descends from Englishmen will be less intelligent than it otherwise would be.

Such views obviously were racist—a common failing of Social Darwinism— and also led logically to eugenics, the idea of deliberately improving the genetic pool of the population. The leading British eugenicist was Francis Galton (1822–1911),

Social Darwinist, social scientist, and statistician. Galton argued that accepting evolution as the key to progress meant that natural selection should be assisted in doing its work. "Eugenics," he said, "cooperates with the workings of Nature by securing that humanity shall be represented by the fittest races. What Nature does blindly, slowly, and ruthlessly, man may do so providently, quickly, and kindly." Society, consequently, should not attempt to cut the high mortality rate of the poor by social legislation, but it should promote the marriage and fertility of "the fit" by measures such as creating a register, for interbreeding purposes, of the best families. Other eugenicists later advocated policies to discourage marriage and reproduction among the criminal, disabled, or chronically ill segments of the population.

Social Darwinism enjoyed its heyday in the 1880s and 1890s in Britain, and it retained a wide popularity in more or less diluted form among the middle class through the twentieth century. The well-to-do found Social Darwinism a satisfying explanation of why they were at the top of the heap and the poor were at the bottom. But in the years between 1900 and 1914, it received an abrupt rejection from certain academic philosophers who took the whole theory of scientific naturalism in a new direction. The rejection of Social Darwinism as a basis for ethics was first articulated by two young philosophers at Cambridge University, G. E. Moore (1873–1958) and Bertrand Russell (1872–1970). By means of highly technical logical analysis, Moore and Russell showed that the logical base of Social Darwinism—indeed, of utilitarianism and all other previous ethical systems—was vague and indefensible.

Yet Moore and Russell themselves clearly stood in the broad tradition of British empiricism and the scientific approach to knowledge. Moore, an analytical philosopher of ethics, set as his goal the foundation of "any ethics that can claim to be scientific." Russell, a mathematical logician of scintillating genius and acerbic wit, wanted to make philosophy consistent with modern science and indeed to reshape philosophy according to the latest scientific and mathematical discoveries. In a large number of popular lectures and books, most notably *Why I Am Not a Christian*, Russell carried on the tradition of Huxley and Tyndall in attacking what he regarded as the hypocrisy, cruelty, and irrationalism of Christianity. Throughout the twentieth century in Britain, this has been the position of a broad stream of progressive (often left-wing), scientifically oriented intellectuals, the heirs of David Hume and the Enlightenment.

THE NEW LIBERALISM

The search for a new ordering principle for society also produced a new direction for liberalism—the "New Liberal" movement. Between 1870 and 1914, the New Liberals, a group of intellectuals, most of whom were professional writers and journalists rather than businessmen, broke with Victorian liberalism in certain ways by calling for greater concern with society as a whole and for a more positive role for the state. Often referred to as "collectivists" in their own day, the New Liberals never captured the rank and file of the Liberal party; nevertheless, they were extremely influential in creating both the philosophy and the reality of the British welfare state.

Like their Victorian Liberal predecessors, the New Liberals were individualists, but they had very different ideas concerning how the good of the individual was to be promoted. Earlier British Liberals, as we saw in Volume II, Chapter 13, believed in the rationality and perfectibility of individuals, in constitutional liberty and representative government, and in the self-regulation of the free-market economy. They thought that the natural action of economic and social forces, if unimpeded by either privilege or the state, would maximize freedom and prosperity. But the "discovery" of chronic poverty by social investigators like Booth and Rowntree and by social activists like the Reverend Andrew Mearns (author of a best-selling pamphlet in 1883, *The Bitter Cry of Outcast London*) proved that the economic and social systems had not, in fact, worked for all. Moreover, as we will learn in Chapter 4, working men received the vote in two stages, 1867 and 1884, and this new body of voters demanded the attention and concern of Liberals as well as Conservatives. By the 1880s, a full-scale reconsideration of political philosophy was underway. The New Liberals led the reconsideration within the liberal movement; they insisted that the state would have to intervene in society to correct the shortcomings of capitalism.

Over the course of years from 1880 to 1914, the New Liberals generated a substantial body of reform proposals, including old age pensions, unemployment insurance, health insurance, and a minimum wage. As we will see, much of this program was eventually enacted, but for now we will focus on their philosophy of "positive freedom," which underlay the legislative proposals. This philosophy held that the historic role of liberalism—the abolition of obstacles to individual liberty of action—was over, and that the time had come for constructive action by the state to create an environment in which all individuals had freedom *to* act, not just freedom *from* arbitrary authority. Thus the New Liberals shifted the focus of liberalism from the autonomous person to the person as part of a whole society, and they conceived of the state as society's agency for producing democracy and equality. As one New Liberal wrote: " 'New Liberalism' differed from the old in that it envisaged more clearly the need for important economic reform, aiming to give a positive significance to the 'equality' which figured in the democratic triad of liberty, equality, and fraternity."

There were three intellectual sources for the New Liberal philosophy. One was the thought of John Stuart Mill, the great mid-Victorian liberal. During his lifetime Mill had shifted the emphasis of liberalism from material to moral self-development of the individual. From the 1860s on, British liberal thinkers concerned themselves with establishing the conditions in which individuals had maximum opportunity for moral improvement. Furthermore, Mill had altered utilitarian theory by arguing that altruism, not self-interest, brings the highest pleasure. Mill himself had concluded by the end of his life that the values, if not the system, of socialism were preferable to capitalism. It was a short step for his successors to conclude that the state should actively create conditions in which people—even the working class—could exercise genuine freedom of moral choice: conditions that would be free of poverty, misery, disease, ignorance, and economic servitude.

The second intellectual source of New Liberalism was evolutionary thought. Whereas evolution taught some thinkers like Spencer that survival of the fittest required laissez-faire policies, it taught others that society is an organism, with the well-being of any individual depending on the well-being of the others. By this view, the direction of social evolution is toward cooperation, not competition, and cooperation can be assisted by the rational use of state power.

The third source of New Liberal thought was philosophical idealism, particularly the ideas of T. H. Green (1836–1882). Green was an Oxford philosopher and a teacher who possessed great personal magnetism. Like many of the other idealist philosophers of his generation, Green was the son of an Evangelical clergyman, and, like the other idealists, he found that modern science and scholarship made adherence to orthodox Christianity impossible. For Green an idealist philosophy drawing on the German thinkers Kant and Hegel provided a rational substitute for religion. As he put it, his interest in philosophy was wholly religious, in the sense that it is "the reasoned intellectual expression of the effort to get to God." Green's philosophy, like that of all the British idealists, was highly technical and ridden with Germanic jargon, yet it became the dominant style of philosophy in the British universities in the late-Victorian years.

The idealists sought to see all things—nature, the universe, experience—as a whole and to show how the mind itself plays a role in constituting what we perceive as reality. In this regard, it was antiscientific, for scientists liked to investigate nature one piece at a time and to regard each bit as existing independently of the human mind. Moore and Russell after 1900 led a terrific attack on idealism on behalf of the scientific outlook, but in the meantime, idealism had become the influential mode of philosophy. To Green, God was the infinite and eternal unifying feature of the world, expressed in people as generous and altruistic morality. People express their "best selves" and find unity with God by high-minded, socially oriented behavior. In other words, people reach their highest ethical potential only in society and only in sacrifice of their own interests for others. Thus for Green, and for his many disciples among the New Liberals, individualism was related not to the pursuit of self-interest but to self-sacrifice.

Green inspired a generation of Oxford students and gave them a motive for social action. Many of the New Liberals themselves had lost their religion and were seeking a substitute. Many of them as members of the elite felt a sense of guilt in the wake of revelations of poverty and class divisions. Some, like Arnold Toynbee, devoted themselves to healing the gap between working class and upper class by living in settlement houses, the most important being Toynbee Hall (founded in East London in 1884). Others involved themselves in adult education in the industrial cities. Still others took up the cause of propagandizing for New Liberal ideas and programs.

The two leading New Liberal intellectuals were J. A. Hobson and L. T. Hobhouse, neither of them a thinker on the level of Mill but together an influential duo.

Hobson (1858–1940) was a heretical economist and prolific writer on social subjects. He contended that the economic system did not regulate itself automatically. In fact, the unequal distribution of incomes allowed the rich to save too much and therefore to depress consumption, and underconsumption caused periodic depression and chronic unemployment. These ideas later were to influence the work of the great economist John Maynard Keynes. Meanwhile, in *Imperialism: A Study* (1902), Hobson applied his theory of malfunctioning capitalism to imperialism, to show that the motives for empire were not as noble as they professed to be. Hobhouse (1864–1929) was a philosophical sociologist who gave an evolutionary and empirical basis for New Liberal thought. He often called himself a "collectivist" to distinguish his brand of social evolutionism from Spencer's. In Hobhouse's view, human evolution involved progress toward intellectual and moral improvement; therefore, the state could (and should) intervene rationally in society to create the environment that in turn shapes the development of individuals.

Many of the New Liberals were concerned about the potential danger of class conflict. C. F. G. Masterman, an effective journalist and politician, emphasized the connection between the ostentatious consumerism by the upper class and the poverty of the working class. In *The Condition of England* (1909), Masterman drew on the work of Carlyle and Ruskin to portray English society as poised on the precipice of social disaster, for the pursuit of extravagant wealth by the plutocracy left the working class without genuine opportunity to become fully developed individuals. In the modern urban crowd there is danger and tragedy:

> . . . one feels that the smile may turn suddenly into fierce snarl or savagery, no less than happiness or foolish praise. But more than the menace, the overwhelming impression is one of ineptitude; a kind of life grotesque and meaningless.

SOCIALISM

Among the various efforts to find a new ordering principle, the one that most upset conventional middle-class businessmen was socialism. Socialism had (and has) many different types, but generally it may be defined as any ideology that holds cooperation rather than competition as the organizing principle of society; hence socialism focuses on the social as opposed to the individual aspect of human nature. In the late nineteenth century socialism became widely adopted in Britain for the first time, and though it has never been accepted by a majority of Britons, it has exercised a greater influence in Britain than in the United States. In the late-Victorian and Edwardian years, many people, most of them from the middle class, began to think that socialism offered a better analysis of poverty as well as more idealistic values than capitalism.

Socialism had first appeared in Britain in the early years of the nineteenth century, as some radicals adopted cooperative plans to express their desire for community in the face of industrialization. That early socialism took two different forms: utilitarian and romantic. The most famous utilitarian-style socialist was

Robert Owen (1771–1858), a successful and benevolent cotton manufacturer. He believed that competition destroys natural, communally oriented moral values, and therefore if the social environment were changed, people could learn to live together in rational cooperation. Owen in the 1820s tried to establish utopian socialist villages in Britain and overseas, the most famous attempt being a short-lived utopian community in New Harmony, Indiana.

The romantic variety of early British socialism had both Christian and aesthetic impulses. Mid-nineteenth century Christian Socialists like F. D. Maurice and J. M. Ludlow hoped to reestablish a Christian commonwealth in which God's love, incarnate in Christ, served as the model for social relations. The aesthetic strand derived from the ideas of Thomas Carlyle and John Ruskin. Carlyle's vehement critique of industrial capitalist society, with its "cash nexus" as the main relation among people, emphasized the interdependence of society and the values of work, duty, and obedience. Ruskin learned much from Carlyle and then applied his own view of the visual arts to Britain with devastating effect. Ruskin believed that art and architecture reflect the moral and spiritual health of a society; hence the ugliness that he saw in Victorian painting and buildings reflected the ugliness of social relations. His own proposals for change were less effective than his critique: they added up to an impractical vision of an idealized medieval social order, complete with a coherent social hierarchy, loyal peasants, and craftsmen organized in a guild system.

Karl Marx (1818–1883) offered a very different brand of socialism from either the utilitarian utopianism of Robert Owen or the romantic medievalism of John Ruskin. Marx set out a "scientific" analysis of classical political economy and of British society under capitalism. Marx, of course, was German, but he worked as an exile in London from 1849 until his death. In his mature work, *Das Kapital (Capital)*, first published in German in 1867, Marx combined German philosophy, French socialist theory, and British political economy. He regarded capitalism, of which Britain was the most advanced example, as a system that necessarily exploited its workers. The key, he thought, is that the value of any object is equal to the labor that went into its production; yet a worker in capitalist industry produces objects worth much more than is needed to give him or her subsistence. An oversupply of laborers ("the reserve army of labor") keeps wages at a subsistence level. The difference between the value of what the worker produces and what he or she is paid is profit, and the capitalist takes all of it for his own purposes.

Marx also believed that when capitalism had reached maturity, it would cause its own collapse. As capitalists exploited their workers more and more ruthlessly, the workers would spontaneously rebel and establish a socialist state. The failure of British workers to revolt in the 1850s and 1860s frustrated Marx. He believed that the concern of British artisans and skilled workers to establish trade unions was a result of "false consciousness"—that is, they misunderstood the real structure of capitalism and their own real interests and thus tried by unionizing to secure a place within the system. British trade unionists sent delegates (along with some

Owenites and former Chartists) to the International Workingmen's Association (the "First International") in 1864, and Marx became one of the leaders of this new organization. On the whole, however, British working men and women held back from socialism during the flourishing days of the Victorian economy, not least because they disliked Marx's tendency to look on unions as useful mainly for recruiting socialists.

Marxism had little impact in Britain until the 1880s, when the troubles in the British economy gave it some credibility. Even then, many British socialists rejected Marxism, and where Marxism was accepted it was usually altered by one or the other of the native British traditions. *Capital* was not published in English until 1887; thus British radicals knew of Marx's ideas only through pamphlets or summaries published by people other than Marx himself. Nevertheless, as "collectivists" of all sorts, including socialists, began to multiply and organize clubs and societies in the 1880s, Marxist ideas formed one of the traditions that they made use of.

One of the leading figures in this early socialist revival was H. M. Hyndman, who was also one of the British socialists most heavily influenced by Marx. A businessman and utilitarian, Hyndman read a French translation of *Capital* in 1880. At about the same time he began organizing the Social Democratic Federation, a club that included both middle-class and working-class radicals. In his book, *England for All*, Hyndman borrowed extensively from Marx (and, much to Marx's annoyance, without acknowledgment). But in certain ways Hyndman's views differed from those of Marx. In particular, Hyndman tended to think that significant change could occur through gradual state and local social reforms, whereas Marx preferred not to cooperate with existing institutions.

In any case, Hyndman had a domineering personality, and this caused a break with the most creative and brilliant of British socialists, William Morris (1834–1896). Morris went on to found a new organization, the Socialist League. Morris was a multitalented genius—poet, painter, designer, architect, social critic, and founder of the British arts-and-crafts movement. He followed a path from High Church Anglicanism to socialism because of the influence of Ruskin's aesthetic rejection of British society. Morris wrote:

> Apart from the desire to produce beautiful things, the leading passion of my
> life has been and is hatred of modern civilization. . . . The struggle of
> mankind for many ages had produced nothing but this sordid, aimless, ugly,
> confusion.

Like Ruskin, Morris was a romantic medievalist, an admirer of the Gothic style, the coherent medieval culture, and the craftsmanship of the medieval guilds. He wanted above all to create a society in which the ordinary worker took joy in producing genuinely useful and beautiful objects.

Morris grafted Marxism onto this aesthetic vision. He believed that Marx explained what Ruskin had observed: that modern industry turned the craftsman into a cog in the industrial machine. He thought a profound revolution in both

William Morris's bed in his home at Kelmscott Manor. This splendidly crafted piece of furniture shows how medievalism, socialism, and aestheticism came together in the arts-and-crafts movement inspired by Morris.

social relations and individual values was needed, and to this end he devoted himself, not to politics or trade union organization but to raising the consciousness of both the middle class and the working class by writing and speaking. In *News from Nowhere* (1891) Morris presented an anarchistic utopia: a society in which all political, economic, and social regulations had disappeared and the individual was free to create spontaneously. Such aesthetic views were too impractical to attract more than a small following, but in a more general way they became very influential in a romantic and idealistic stream of British socialism. Morris's ideas have repeatedly emerged in Christian, guild, and anarchist types of socialism in Britain.

The dominant form of British socialism in the years between 1880 and 1914 could not have been more different: Fabianism. Fabian socialism was utilitarian, practical, and gradualist, and it was committed to social efficiency and rule by experts in social science. The leading Fabians of the day were middle-class intellectuals, most of whom had close friends and associates among the New Liberals. Fabianism grew out of an organization characteristic of late-Victorian Britain—the Fellowship of the New Life, a society of young men and women of deep ethical concerns, looking for a new principle to live by. The founders of the Fabian Society in 1884 were the more practical members of this group. Over time, they developed from their ethical interests a distinctive socialist outlook and program.

The leading Fabians were George Bernard Shaw, Graham Wallas, and Sidney and Beatrice Webb. Shaw was a brilliant wit, playwright, and publicist, at heart a radical individualist and anarchist. At first a Marxist, Shaw in the latter 1880s abandoned the labor theory of value but retained the Marxian interpretation of the historical development of production and exploitation. Wallas was the son of a clergy-

Sidney and Beatrice Webb. This photo shows the great Fabian socialist husband-and-wife team outside the Royal Academy of Arts.

man, but he abandoned his parents' religion without giving up his deep ethical commitment. He eventually became a social scientist devoted to creating a just society. Sidney and Beatrice Webb became the most influential of all the Fabians. Husband and wife as well as partners in economic and social research, the Webbs had a high regard for bureaucrats and expertise (Sidney was a civil servant and Beatrice a professional social scientist). As Beatrice was later to say, she and Sidney were "benevolent, bourgeois, and bureaucratic." They were also people of unflagging industry, a formidable if rather strange pair. It was Sidney who, although well informed in Marxian theory, rooted Fabian economics in the British tradition of political economy.

The essence of Fabian doctrine was that social institutions, not the whole culture or human nature itself, needed reform. Parliament and local government provided the means to reform; thus revolution was neither necessary nor desirable. Sidney Webb even accepted the importance of individual self-interest: "It is the business of the community not to lead into temptation this healthy natural feeling but so to develop social institutions that individual egoism is necessarily directed to promote the well-being of all." The key to implementing this idea was to extend the idea of rent, as it had been set out in classical political economy, to other forms of property. Ever since the early 1800s, British political economists like David Ricardo and J. S. Mill had argued that rent in modern society goes up because of

Imperialism: missionaries at a dispensary in East Africa. Late-Victorian Britain was inspired by the humanitarian impulses of imperialism.

the growth of the population and the economic development of the community, not because of the landowner's efforts. The community is justified, therefore, in taxing this "unearned increment" of rent to its full value, and in turning it to the use of the community. The Fabians extended this theory to capital and "special skills," for they believed that these forms of property were also socially created wealth and eligible for state expropriation for the good of all.

The Fabians' admiration of the expert and the state, their practicality, and their interest in social efficiency led them into some unusual alliances in the early twentieth century. In the 1880s and 1890s, the Fabians sought to "permeate" the Liberal party, hoping to accomplish their goals through this well-established reformist party. But the Webbs' concern for national efficiency and their belief in the superiority of progressive nations like Britain made them enthusiasts of empire. Such views linked them to the imperialists in the Conservative party as well as the Liberal party. At the time of the Boer War (1899–1902), the Webbs' imperialism caused a controversy among the Fabian Society's leadership, for many socialists blamed the war on capitalism, but the Webbs kept the Society in line.

This orientation attracted the interest of the young social and utopian novelist H. G. Wells. As an advocate of science and technology, Wells believed in rule by an expert administrative elite, which he sometimes called the "Samurai." This gave him common ground with the Webbs. But Wells was a maverick and was much more devoted to the radical transformation of social institutions than were the Webbs, who intended to reform and build on such institutions. Wells eventually challenged the Webbs for leadership of the Fabians, making the Edwardian years troublesome for the Webbs. However, by 1909, the Webbs had prevailed, and Fabianism remained on its gradualist, administrative, democratic, and reformist path. This would prove to be the mainstream of British socialism for the next seventy years.

IMPERIALISM

The years between 1870 and 1914 are rightly known as the "Age of Imperialism" in British history. The British Empire expanded at a rapid rate as areas that had been part of the "informal empire" came under formal rule and as new areas were annexed (see Chapter 5). In 1871, the Empire included 235 million people and almost 8 million square miles; in 1900, it encompassed 400 million people and 12 million square miles—almost one-fourth of the earth's land surface. Yet just as important as expansion itself in designating these years as the Age of Empire was the elaboration of an ideology of imperialism. Through most of the nineteenth century the British had increased their imperial holdings but had lacked a positive rationale for empire. As one statesman said, the colonies seemed to have been acquired "in a fit of absence of mind." But from the 1870s, new foreign rivalries and economic pressure caused the British not only to expand aggressively but also to justify their actions by an imperial ideology.

British imperialism was a strange compound of confidence and anxiety. The more confident element arose from long-standing pride in British achievements overseas and above all in British governing institutions. People of all parties shared this feeling. As an editorial in *The Times* (1867) put it, "We are all proud of our empire, and we regard our Colonies and dependencies as the various members of such a family as earth never yet saw." This pride was consistent with the view of the so-called Little Englanders that as the colonies of white settlement grew to maturity they would drop like ripe fruit off the imperial tree. Increasingly in the late nineteenth century, however, the Little Englanders' outlook came to be rivaled by the imperialists' notion that the colonies should be bound more closely to Britain. Imperial consolidation came to be associated with the Conservative party, though there were "Liberal imperialists" who believed in it as well. As early as 1872, the Conservative leader, Benjamin Disraeli, in a famous speech at the Crystal Palace, had committed the Conservatives to protection of the nation's institutions and preservation of the Empire.

Pride in the Empire included a sense of trusteeship that all members of the governing elite could share. The British regarded themselves as the new Romans, bringing religion and progress to backward peoples, and as specially talented in the techniques of government. Justifiably proud of their parliamentary system, they believed that they had much to offer the world. Around the Empire, declared the colonial secretary in 1878, "We have races struggling to emerge into civilization, to whom emancipation from servitude is but the foretaste of the far higher law of liberty and progress to which they may yet attain." The British governing class was confident in Britain's ability to carry out this mission of noble trusteeship. Joseph Chamberlain, perhaps the most eminent imperialist politician, put it bluntly in 1895: "I believe that the British race is the greatest of the governing races that the world has ever seen."

The more anxious and defensive side of imperialism arose from the perception that Britain was locked in a global economic and political rivalry with other nations, most notably Germany. In this regard, imperialism was a matter of power: the British simply wanted to continue to count heavily in the councils of the world. *Realpolitik* ("realistic" geopolitics) became the fashion in British governing circles, and imperialism was part of it. According to the *Pall Mall Gazette* in 1885:

> In times past . . . we did what we pleased, where we pleased, and as we pleased. All that has changed. . . . At every turn we are confronted with the gunboats, the sea lairs, or the colonies of jealous and eager rivals.

The imperialists believed that "pegging our claims" around the world would give Britain refuge from the huge economic and military powers that seemed to threaten Britain. The issue, they thought, was whether Britain would rise to the challenge of international struggle and imperial expansion or go the way of Rome. Biological metaphors dominated their minds: "The truth is," one imperialist wrote in 1896, "that what we call national rivalry is to all intents and purposes part of the universal scheme that makes Nature 'red in tooth and claw.' " British national interests demanded self-sufficiency through empire: securing of imperial possessions as markets and investment opportunities for British goods and capital, and cultivation of colonies that would assist Britain in global rivalries, including war.

Social Darwinism contributed to this concept of imperialism. Many Social Darwinists believed that the British had to achieve greater "social efficiency" to survive in international competition. Empire requires an "imperial race"; thus, oddly enough, many imperialists were also social reformers. Social Darwinists thus shared a widespread concern about the "degeneration" of what they called "the British race." Some Social Darwinists like Karl Pearson put their hope in eugenics; others, like Benjamin Kidd, argued for reforms such as improved education and nutrition to make the working class stronger and healthier potential soldiers. Likewise, they hoped to inculcate through sports and paramilitary organizations habits of order and discipline. The cult of school sports, the Boy Scouts (1908), and the numerous cadet brigades were all results of the quest for social efficiency. As the Social Darwinists put it, the struggle was racial:

> The facts are patent. Feeble races are being wiped off the earth, and the few, great incipient species arm themselves against each other. England, as the greatest of these—greatest in race-pride—has avoided for centuries the only dangerous kind of war. Now, with the whole earth occupied and the movements of expansion continuing, she will have to fight to the death against successive rivals.

As this passage shows, the racist quality of imperialist thought was ambiguous: imperialists tended to be both anxious about the quality of "the British race" and confident of Britain's racial superiority. One Fabian socialist said, "If we are breeding the people badly neither the most perfect constitution nor the most skillful diplomacy will save us from shipwreck." On the other hand, imperialists believed that the British or "Anglo-Saxon race" (note the exclusion of the Celtic peoples) was superior to black, brown, and yellow races (not to mention Slavic, Mediterranean, and Celtic peoples), and that this justified rule by the British. Indeed, they thought, the "colored" races were childlike and incapable of ruling themselves, whereas the British stood at the top of the evolutionary mountain. The *Daily Mail* caught this racial pride in exclaiming about the white troops in the Jubilee parade of 1897: ". . . every man such a splendid specimen and testimony to the Greatness of the British race . . . the sun never looked down until yesterday on the embodiment of so much energy and power."

Racial pride and the sense of Britain's unique governing ability enabled British imperialists to think of imperialism as a duty rather than as a naked expression of economic and political power. Psychologically this was very important. All over Britain, upper middle-class and professional families sent their sons out to the Empire in the spirit of sacrificing self-interest to a noble burden. This helps explain why British proconsuls in fact set such a high standard of fairness and incorruptibility, if not cultural sensitivity. The spirit of duty was caught perfectly by Rudyard Kipling in his "White Man's Burden" (1899):

> Take up the White Man's Burden–
>   Send forth the best ye breed–
> Go bind your sons to exile
>   To serve your captives' need.
>
> Take up the White Man's Burden–
>   And reap his old reward:
> The blame of those ye better,
>   The hate of those ye guard.

Racial pride, noble sacrifice, global struggle, heroic adventures, faraway exotic places—all constituted a heady brew that affected popular emotions more than did Liberal collectivism or socialism. The imperialists in the elite had an instinctive sense of public relations. Imperial pride was inculcated in the new state schools; every child learned to recognize the pink or red areas on the map as "theirs." History textbooks glorified the exploits of soldiers, sea captains, and explorers. Mass-circulation newspapers celebrated jingoism, and cheap literature for children linked imperialism with enthusiasm for the monarchy and the army. *The Boys Own Paper* and dozens of other magazines played on related themes of athleticism, militarism, violence, and empire. The most famous writer for the youth market, G. A. Henty, thrilled a generation of boys with his eighty-two novels, many of which purveyed an imperial ideology: the superior vigor, initiative, decency, and pluck of the British race. The monarchy itself became identified with empire: in 1876, Parliament granted Queen Victoria the title "Empress of India," and in 1887 and 1897 the queen's jubilees treated the London masses to spectacular parades of British and imperial troops. Just how far working people accepted the ideas behind imperialism is subject to debate, but it seems clear that imperial patriotism was an important counterbalance to class consciousness.

AESTHETICISM

New Liberalism, socialism, and imperialism were all directed toward political and social action. But the other main "ism" of the years between 1870 and 1914 was a very different kind of movement: aestheticism. There were many varieties of aesthetes in late-Victorian and Edwardian Britain—cultural critics, bohemian poets, urbane dandies, ardent modernists—but all of them rejected conventional Victorian attitudes in favor of art, beauty, and intellect, each to be exercised for its own sake. Out of this anti-utilitarian and antimoralistic revolt was born the dominant theme in twentieth-century British high culture—modernism (a cultural movement devoted to aestheticism, formalism, experimentation, and anti-Victorianism).

In producing an aesthetic movement in art and literature, the British were about a generation behind the French, whose aestheticism blossomed in the works of Gustave Flaubert and Charles Baudelaire. But the British aesthetes were part of a long native tradition of opposition to industrial society and its dominant middle class. From the time of the romantic poets through Carlyle and Dickens, many British writers had tried to speak as prophets or preachers to the general reading public, warning of the disastrous cultural consequences of industrialization, self-interest, and greed. Now, in the 1860s and 1870s, writers sympathetic to this tradition began to turn away from the public, to write for each other, and to preserve a refuge for art. They consequently adopted from Flaubert and Baudelaire the doctrine of "art for art's sake."

How can this turn in the romantic tradition be explained? Partly, it was due to the receding of the tide of religion, which left many British intellectuals stranded on the shoals of doubt and disbelief; for them art became yet another substitute for religion. Partly, this turn was due to the loss of confidence characteristic of so many late-Victorians, an unease that the aesthetes shared. Partly, it was due to the disillusionment they felt on realizing the failure of earlier prophets like Carlyle and Dickens to reverse the values of upper-class British society. And partly, the aesthetic turn of mind was due to the sense among serious writers that they were losing control over their audience. In the earlier Victorian period, writers knew their audience was relatively compact, middle class, and influential, and they instinctively understood this audience. But with the spread of state schools, a new, massive, semiliterate, working-class audience came into existence. Journalists and hack writers given to sensationalism could reach this audience, but serious writers felt bewildered and threatened by it. They lost confidence in themselves as prophets or preachers and increasingly sought to write only for each other.

The seeds of this aesthetic tendency began to germinate in the ideas of John Ruskin and Matthew Arnold in the 1860s. Ruskin's belief that the moral and social conditions of a society inform its art clearly pitted art against life. For him, art is superior to society. Arnold (1822–1888), the greatest literary critic of nineteenth-

Bloomsbury: Bertrand Russell, John Maynard Keynes, and Lytton Strachey in 1915. These three intellectuals were among the members of the Bloomsbury Group, which dominated British high culture in the early years of the twentieth century.

century Britain, was also a profound social observer. He believed that the Victorian age, with its materialism, its devotion to self-interest, its class conflict, its political battles, was a supremely un-poetic age. Modern life seemed to him diseased, "with its sick hurry, its divided aims/Its heads o'ertaxed, its palsied hearts." By the latter 1860s, Arnold believed that class conflict, in which the middle class (or "Philistines," as he labeled them) was dominant, was creating a kind of spiritual anarchy. He believed that because Christianity no longer could supply the necessary coherence, culture must be the antidote to anarchy. He defined *culture* in a highly intellectualized way—the pursuit of perfection by the study of the best that has been thought and said in the world.

Both Ruskin and Arnold still held on to the hope for social revitalization. But many of their disciples in the late-Victorian years found it impossible to sustain that hope. Many of them felt so alienated from the values of bourgeois society that they could not engage in socially constructive writing. In reaction, they idealized a life spent in the rarified atmosphere of art, spirit, and intellect. They aggressively rejected the notion that society had any claims on their art. They insisted that all art—painting, writing, music—ought to be judged by standards peculiar to itself. Art was for art's sake only.

The twin themes of aestheticism—that one's life itself should be a work of art and that art is independent of social usefulness—appeared in much late-Victorian literature, including the novels of Henry James, Samuel Butler, and George Gissing; the poetry of Algernon Swinburne and William Butler Yeats; and the painting of James McNeill Whistler. But they were expressed most clearly in the life and work of Walter Pater, an Oxford tutor, literary critic, and novelist. Pater insisted that art is to be judged by its own standards of perfection and that the goal of life "is not action, but contemplation—being as distinct from doing—a certain disposition of mind." One should seek always to burn with a "hard, gem-like flame" of aesthetic ecstacy. For such aesthetes, art had become the new religion.

In the 1890s, this doctrine spawned a small circle of artists who took it to the extreme—the decadents, as they came to be called. The most famous of these glitterati were the novelist and playwright Oscar Wilde and the artist Aubrey Beardsley. They loved to shock the bourgeoisie of London by their clever and ironic turn of phrase, their praise of exotic (and erotic) beauty, their exploration of the pleasures of evil, and their dandified dress and manners. Wilde confronted Victorian values with decadent epigrams in the Preface to his novel, *The Picture of Dorian Gray*:

> The artist is the creator of beautiful things . . .
> They are the elect to whom beautiful things mean
>   only Beauty.
> There is no such thing as a moral or immoral book.
> Books are well written, or badly written. That
>   is all . . .
> All art is quite useless.

Decadence was a dead end, but aesthetic ideas about life and art helped shape the outlook of the most famous literary and intellectual circle of Edwardian Britain, the Bloomsbury Group (named after the area in London in which many of them lived between 1905 and 1925). Most of the male members of the Bloomsbury Group (Leonard Woolf, Lytton Strachey, E. M. Forster, and J. M. Keynes) were students at Cambridge around the turn of the century, and most had been members of a secret undergraduate society called the Apostles. The dominant figure of the Apostles was the unworldly but personally charismatic young philosopher G. E. Moore. He taught his students and friends to adopt a refreshingly rigorous analytical style of thought and to accept the elitist view that the two highest values were states of mind: the contemplation of beautiful objects and the enjoyment of personal friendships. The Apostles believed that these doctrines liberated them from the restrictions and oppressions of Victorian convention. As they moved to Bloomsbury from Cambridge and rounded out the group with two sisters, Virginia and Vanessa Stephen (who married Leonard Woolf and Clive Bell, respectively), they made Moore's philosophy into a creed: "We repudiated entirely," Keynes wrote, "customary morals, conventions, and traditional wisdom."

The aesthetic theory of the Bloomsbury Group was a foundation stone of modernism in Britain. Because, in their view, contemplation of beautiful objects is a complex and learned activity, in practice it is only suitable for an artistic elite. The "Bloomsberries" were snobs, and by the same token, they thought that art is the only refining activity in life, apart from cultivation of the most exquisite personal relationships. They tended to think that all political and social policy should be directed to the creation and support of art. They thought that ultimately art would recivilize society, but not by direct social action. Works of art, they believed, are not the servants or the mirrors of society; their role is not social instruction or propaganda. A true work of art is autonomous: a painting is not a photograph, a biography is not a slavish chronology, nor is a novel a realistic description or a moral lesson. Art calls for an emotion of its own ("the aesthetic emotion"), which arises from the relations among the formal elements of the work—the lines, volumes, colors, images, and symbols. Bloomsbury theory thus added formalism, an important ingredient of modernism, to aesthetic values.

The aesthetic belief in the special role of the artist or intellectual revived the romantic belief in symbolism. Symbolists believed that by symbols alone can truths about the "unseen" or supernatural world be communicated. The greatest symbolist poet writing in English in this period was the Irishman William Butler Yeats, about whom more will be said in Chapter 3. Here it should be noted that Yeats was one of the founders of modernism. Symbolism was also practiced by two English Edwardian novelists, who were in other ways about as different as two writers can be: E. M. Forster and D. H. Lawrence. Forster (1879–1970) was from the upper middle class; was a Cambridge graduate, a writer of mild temperament, and an unforceful Liberal; and had a refined sensibility. In *Howards End* Forster took a country house as the symbol for England itself; its inheritance, like that of the country itself, is viewed as contested for by the pushy business class and the sensitive intellectuals.

D. H. Lawrence (1885–1930) was the first great English working-class novelist. He was the son of a coal miner and had to battle the industrial and class systems themselves to break through their constrictions on his life. He also had to break away from the oppressive affection of his mother, an emotionally tortuous process that gave him a homegrown Freudian insight into personal relations and individual development. Together, his social and psychological vision gave Lawrence a unique perspective on society, personality, and sexuality and informed a series of novels of astonishing energy and originality, including *Sons and Lovers*, *Women in Love*, and *Lady Chatterly's Lover*. Lawrence was not the greatest modernist novelist (that honor goes to the Irishman James Joyce, who will be discussed in Chapter 3), but his hostility to Victorian moral, social, and literary convention clearly showed that modernism had emerged in full force.

Suggested Reading

Beckson, Karl E., *London in the 1890s: A Cultural History* (New York: W. W. Norton, 1992).

Bowler, Peter J., *Reconciling Science and Religion: The Debate in Early Twentieth-Century Britain* (Chicago: University of Chicago Press, 2001).

Burton, Antoinette, *Burdens of History: British Feminists, Indian Women, and Imperial Culture, 1865–1914* (Chapel Hill: University of North Carolina Press, 1994).

Brown, Judith M., and W. Roger Louis, eds., *The Twentieth Century*, Vol. 4 of *The Oxford History of the British Empire*, ed. W. Roger Louis (Oxford: Oxford University Press, 1999).

Buettner, Elizabeth, *Empire Families: Britons and Late-Imperial India* (Oxford: Oxford University Press, 2004).

Collini, Stefan, *Liberalism and Sociology: T. L. Hobhouse and Political Argument in England, 1880–1914* (Cambridge: Cambridge University Press, 1979).

Colls, Robert, *Identity of England* (Oxford: Oxford University Press, 2002).

Crook, D. P., *Benjamin Kidd: Portrait of a Social Darwinist* (Cambridge: Cambridge University Press, 1984).

Freeden, Michael, *The New Liberalism* (Oxford: Clarendon Press, 1978).

Harrison, Royden J., *The Life and Times of Sidney and Beatrice Webb: The Formative Years* (London: Palgrave Macmillan, 2001).

Heyck, T. W., *The Transformation of Intellectual Life in Victorian England* (New York: St. Martin's, 1982).

Hough, Graham, *The Last Romantics* (London: Duckworth, 1949).

Hynes, Samuel, *The Edwardian Turn of Mind* (Princeton, N.J.: Princeton University Press, 1968).

Koebner, Richard, and H. D. Schmidt, *Imperialism: The Story and Significance of a Political Word* (Cambridge: Cambridge University Press, 1964).

MacDonald, Robert H., *The Language of Empire: Myths and Metaphors of Popular Imperialism, 1880–1918* (Manchester: Manchester University Press, 1994).

Mackenzie, John M., *Propaganda and Empire* (Manchester: Manchester University Press, 1984).

MacKenzie, Norman, and Jeanne MacKenzie, *The Fabians* (New York: Simon & Schuster, 1977).

MacLeod, Diane Satchko, *Art and the Victorian Middle Class: Money and the Making of Cultural Identity* (Cambridge: Cambridge University Press, 1997).

McBriar, A. M., *Fabian Socialism and English Politics, 1884–1918* (Cambridge: Cambridge University Press, 1962).

McLeod, Hugh, *Religion and Society in England, 1850–1914* (New York: St. Martin's Press, 1996).

Owen, Alexandra, *The Place of Enchantment: British Occultism and the Culture of the Modern* (Chicago: University of Chicago Press, 2004).

Peel, J. D. Y., *Herbert Spencer: The Evolution of a Sociologist* (London: Heinemann Educational, 1971).

Pierson, Stanley, *British Socialists: The Journey from Fantasy to Politics* (Cambridge, Mass.: Harvard University Press, 1979).

Porter, Bernard, *The Absent-Minded Imperialists: Empire, Society, and Culture in Britain* (New York: Oxford University Press, 2006).

———, *The Lion's Share* (London: Longman, 2004).

Richter, Melvin, *The Politics of Conscience: T. H. Green and His Age* (Cambridge: Cambridge University Press, 1964).

Searle, G. R., *The Quest for National Efficiency* (Berkeley: University of California Press, 1971).

Soloway, Richard, *Birth Control and the Population Question in England, 1877–1930* (Chapel Hill: University of North Carolina Press, 1982).

Thompson, Andrew, *The Empire Strikes Back? The Impact of Imperialism on Britain from the Mid-Nineteenth Century* (London: Longman, 2005).

Thompson, E. P., *William Morris* (New York: Pantheon Books, 1977).

Thornton, A. P., *The Imperial Idea and Its Enemies* (London: Macmillan; New York: St. Martin's Press, 1959).

Turner, Frank Miller, *Between Science and Religion* (New Haven: Yale University Press, 1974).

Waters, Chris, *British Socialists and the Politics of Popular Culture, 1884–1914* (Stanford: Stanford University Press, 1990).

Chapter 3

Revival on the "Celtic Fringe"

During the nineteenth century, Britain, with England as its core, achieved a fairly high degree of national integration—higher, for instance, than the Austro-Hungarian Empire and stronger in some ways even than Germany. Industrialization, the market economy, the railways, the expansion of printing and literacy in English, the geographic mobility of the ruling and intellectual elites, and the opportunities of the Empire all helped form bonds of unity that—with the important exception of Ireland—withstood even the pressures of total war between 1914 and 1918. But the extent to which this British nation represented a *blending* of the nationalities within the British Isles is problematical. England was by far the biggest and strongest segment of Great Britain, having in 1911 approximately 75 percent of all the people of the British Isles. The English were quick to assume that what was good for England was good for the rest of Britain. They habitually said "England" when they meant "Britain." On the basis of prejudice rather than science, they asserted that the "Anglo-Saxon race," from which English men and women allegedly descended, was far superior to the "Celtic race" of Wales, Scotland, and Ireland.

During the course of the century, therefore, the Welsh, Scots, and Irish were marginalized—treated as of marginal importance to Britain—as well as partially integrated with England. In the late-Victorian years, Wales, Scotland, and Ireland came to be known in England as "the Celtic fringe"—a perfect verbal symbol of their marginal status in the minds of the English. In reaction to being marginalized, political and cultural leaders in each of the three Celtic countries asserted their own national identities and sponsored national cultural revivals. These revivals were largely independent of each other, though they shared certain common qualities; thus each national revival took a different form and achieved a different expression of national identity. There was revival on the Celtic fringe, not revival *of* the Celtic fringe. Viewed together, these revivals composed an important force in British political and cultural history; they helped create the political and cultural contexts in which millions of inhabitants of the British Isles have identified themselves.

WALES: INDUSTRY, NONCONFORMITY, AND NATIONALISM

There were five main themes in Welsh history between 1860 and 1914: (1) poor relations between landlords and tenants in the countryside; (2) rapid growth

South Wales coal miners. The densely populated mining valleys of South Wales in the late nineteenth and early twentieth centuries were a notable feature of the British industrial landscape and home to Welsh nonconformity and radicalism.

of industry, especially in the coalfields of South Wales; (3) the dominance of nonconformist Christianity; (4) attachment of Welsh nonconformists to the British Liberal party; and (5) cultural revival. These five themes were tightly interrelated.

The ownership of land in nineteenth-century Wales was even more concentrated than in England. In the 1870s, about 570 families owned 60 percent of the land; very little tilled land was owned by the people who occupied and farmed it. Until the 1880s, Welsh society and politics were dominated by a few great landed families—the Wynns, the Vaughns, the Butes, and others. Most of these aristocratic and gentry families were highly anglicized in taste and interests, just as they were Anglican in religion. The tenants and farm laborers, however, were solidly nonconformist. Landlord-tenant relations were very poor, especially after the latter 1870s, when agricultural depression worked severe hardship on the tenantry. Welsh landlords used their authority blatantly to intimidate tenants into voting Tory; tenants who did not knuckle under often were evicted. Antilandlord sentiment became an enduring theme in Welsh popular politics.

At the same time, industry became increasingly dominant in the Welsh economy. As we saw in Volume II, Chapter 10, the iron industry attracted dense concentrations of capital and labor to South Wales during the first decades of industrialization. In the second half of the nineteenth century, coal became the great Welsh industry, the famous coal mines of the Rhondda valleys opening in 1851. By 1913, South Wales was producing one-third of the world's coal exports, and more than 250,000 men worked in the Welsh coalfields.

Unlike the ironmasters, the entrepreneurs of the Welsh coal industry were largely Welsh-born and nonconformist in religion. Thus the Welsh middle class of the coal-mining areas shared the language and the religion of their workers, who were mostly Welsh-speaking and almost entirely nonconformist. Until the twentieth century, when class conflict overcame these bonds, the Welsh middle and working classes shared common ground and ranged themselves against the anglicicized and Anglican traditional elite.

The Welsh "industrial enclave," concentrated so densely in South Wales, was therefore thoroughly Welsh in culture to the end of the nineteenth century. But for a number of reasons English influence grew relentlessly. English was the language of the government, the courts, education, the professions, and high-level commerce. There was a heavy inflow of Scottish and English migrants into South Wales. As the coal owners grew richer and more established, they became more English. Finally, Welsh coal miners came to understand that they had the same problems as English workers, and they found their strongest support among English and Scottish trade unionists. Class identity in this sense functioned as a strong pan-British integrative force. By the early 1900s, Welsh miners were holding their meetings in English. Industrialization, which in its early stages had helped preserve the Welsh language and culture, in the long run corroded Welshness.

In the last half of the nineteenth century, however, there was still a high correlation between Welsh-speaking areas and nonconformist areas: to be Welsh was to be nonconformist. As we saw in Volume II, Chapter 12, evangelicalism took Wales by storm; by the 1850s, the Welsh were people of the chapel rather than the church. By the late nineteenth century, almost 90 percent of the Welsh were nonconformists, and many of them belonged to the more puritanical sects—Baptists, Congregationalists, and Calvinistic Methodists. The Church of England (the established church in Wales) had made little attempt to reach out to the people at large: the first Welsh-speaking bishop in more than a century was appointed only in 1870. As one Welsh Anglican said: "Churchmen in Wales were comprised almost exclusively of the richer portions of society . . . so that they had in Wales a church kept up for the rich man at the expense of the poor majority."

Welsh popular culture revolved around nonconformity. Chapel vestries dominated their communities, offering chapel members places to meet, adult education, Sunday schools, and above all choirs to sing in. Nonconformists imposed their Sabbatarianism on Wales, making the Welsh Sunday peculiarly bleak even by Victorian standards. But nonconformist ministers also were the heart and soul of the literary celebrations of Welsh culture, the annual *eisteddfoddau,* both national and local; they were in a sense the new bards, evangelical style.

Nonconformity inevitably became the strongest political force in late-Victorian Wales. In the first half of the century, popular radicalism was even more widespread in Wales than in England. Food riots in the 1810s and 1820s, agitation and violence over parliamentary reform in 1831, anti-Poor Law demonstrations in the 1830s, antiturnpike turbulence (the "Rebecca Riots") from 1838 to 1842, and strikes in the coalfields throughout the period were symptoms of a popular movement with which most middle-class Welsh men and women had little sympathy. But once Chartism (itself quite violent in Wales) had faded, middle- and working-class Welsh nonconformists were able to join in a national nonviolent radical movement. In 1867, the Second Reform Act (see Chapter 4) empowered this Welsh nonconformist movement by granting urban male householders the vote. Beginning with some sensational electoral victories in 1868, Welsh radical nonconformity became a steamroller. Allied with the British Liberal party, Welsh radicals won twenty nine of thirty-two Welsh parliamentary seats in 1880, and at least that many in every election until 1922. As we will see, Welsh nonconformity formed one of the big battalions in the late-Victorian and Edwardian Liberal army.

Participation in the British Liberal party helped keep Welsh nonconformist radicalism from becoming a separatist movement. Nevertheless, political radicalism represented a form of Welsh nationalism. What had mobilized the Welsh nonconformists in the first place was the "Treason of the Blue Books" in 1847, a report by a parliamentary commission on Welsh education that called for education of Welsh children in English only. It treated Wales as a backward and immoral region. Welsh nonconformists felt offended because of both their religion and their Welshness. Similarly, the Welsh nonconformist agenda—abolition of the tithe to the Church of England, winning of nonconformist rights in marriage and burial laws, disestablishment of the Church of England in Wales, and reform of landlord-tenant relations—expressed dissent from the English church and from the power of the anglicized elite. Welsh nonconformists found allies in the Liberal party because the Liberals generally supported the cause of nonconformists against the privileges of the established church and the claims of the middle class against the landlords. The Welsh nonconformists did not want independence for Wales, for they believed that the Welsh economy was far too dependent on England's to survive alone. But in the 1880s and 1890s, some militant young Welsh politicians like Tom Ellis and David Lloyd George earned great influence in the Liberal party and won commitment of the party not only to disestablishment but also to Home Rule (a degree of regional autonomy) for Wales.

At the same time, a cultural nationalist movement took root in Wales. It was not separatist, for even Welsh cultural nationalists were comfortable with two patriotisms—British and Welsh. Almost all of the Welsh nationalists of the years between 1880 and 1914 identified themselves as British as well as Welsh. Their *British* identity pertained to matters external to the British state, whereas their *Welsh* identity concerned things internal to the British Isles. The Welsh nationalists took pride in the British monarchy and Empire, but they also emphasized Welsh distinctiveness, glorified the allegedly virtuous and independent Welsh peasant, and reveled in the Welsh language. Welsh cultural nationalists like John Morris-Jones and Owen Edwards worked to collect and revive Welsh literature, to celebrate the Welsh past, and to save the Welsh language. They urged establishment of a

Welsh national museum, library, and university—all of which had been accomplished by 1914. Briefly, in 1894–1896, a Young Wales (Cymru Fydd) movement attempted to fuse cultural and political nationalism, but interest in Welsh independence was too slight for Cymru Fydd to thrive. What Welsh cultural nationalism did achieve was to spread an enduring sense of the Welsh past and of the differentness of Welsh culture. For the time being, that was enough.

SCOTLAND: INDUSTRY, LIBERALISM, AND IDENTITY

Next to the national revivals in Wales on the one hand and Ireland on the other, the revival in late-Victorian Scotland seems a pale creation. But that is in part because the Scots brought into the period a strong sense of historical identity, one that needed cultivation rather than revival. As a result of centuries of independent existence, followed by the negotiated Union of 1707, the Scots had retained their own established (Presbyterian) church, system of laws and courts, and educational structure. The romantic movement had revived a sense (admittedly somewhat bogus when it came to kilts and tartans) of historic distinctiveness. Even Lowland Scots came to celebrate Scottish heroes like Robert Bruce, William Wallace, Mary Queen of Scots, and Bonnie Prince Charlie. After the Battle of Culloden in 1746, and the subsequent destruction of Highland culture, Scotland settled into a century of acclimatizing to English culture and the British state, but the sense of Scottish distinctiveness remained strong.

For this and other reasons, the main themes in Scottish history between 1860 and 1914 were not quite the same as those in Wales. For example, relations between Scottish landlords and tenants were poor, but this was largely due to the fact that many Scottish landlords did not want any tenants at all. They preferred to turn their estates into pastures for sheep or game preserves for deer and grouse. The Highlands had been depopulated by 1860: whereas the Highlands had once been home for half the Scottish people, by 1900 less than 25 percent of the Scots lived there. The Highlands for the remaining peasantry was a scene of poverty and precarious livelihoods. The luckiest of the poor in rural Scotland lived by raising sheep and eating potatoes. The unlucky, especially in the western Highlands and islands, were under constant threat of eviction, for most landlords sought to clear the land even further of its tenant population. Scottish landlords, Highland as well as Lowland, continued to anglicize themselves: they spoke English and sent their sons to English public schools and, when possible, to Oxford and Cambridge. The peasantry of the western Highlands and islands, known as "crofters" (from their tiny land holdings called "crofts"), often isolated by their Gaelic tongue, scraped out an existence next to vast sheep runs and deer preserves. Their resentment finally boiled over in the 1880s, when they openly and violently resisted eviction. The Liberal party, which gradually came to speak for the crofters, gave them security of tenure in 1886, but poverty remained the central fact of crofters' lives.

The most prosperous—and densely populated—part of Victorian Scotland was the industrial and commercial belt extending across the Lowlands from the Firth of Clyde to the Firth of Forth. In this part of Scotland, per capita productivity and income began to catch up with those of England, though the problems of urban poverty and housing were at least as bad as England's. Of the Scottish industries, shipbuilding and marine engineering fared best in the hard years of the late nineteenth and early twentieth centuries. Industrial relations in the late-Victorian period were full of turmoil, especially in the coal industry, not least because Scottish coal mine owners imported both Catholic and Protestant workers from Ireland in order to dilute and divide the miners. In Glasgow, Catholic-Protestant tension separated even working-class football fans, Catholics supporting Glasgow Celtic and Protestants the Glasgow Rangers. Scottish miners struggled to win recognition of their unions in the 1870s and 1880s, but ran up against an unusually stubborn and autocratic breed of employers. By 1914, though they were divided by religion (Protestant versus Catholic), Scottish workers were breaking out of their traditional passivity, while their employers were digging in their heels.

Scotland in the late 1700s and early 1800s had a tiny electorate (less than five thousand voters) and therefore was ruled from London by patronage distributed by the landlords. The Scottish landlords were in the pocket of the Tory wirepullers. Gradually, however, Whig influence began to grow, spreading outward from the great journal, the *Edinburgh Review*. Then, in 1843, an event occurred that shook up Scottish life and gave a boost to Scottish liberalism: the disruption of the Church of Scotland. For about ten years before 1843, evangelicals within the Scottish church had fought the moderate ruling body over a number of issues, most notably patronage. The evangelical Presbyterians insisted that each congregation could call its own minister, whereas the moderates supported the right of patrons to appoint the ministers. Led by Thomas Chalmers, the evangelicals in 1843 split off to form the Free Church, taking about 40 percent of the clergy with them.

The Free Church spread rapidly, especially in the Highlands. Though Free Churchmen still believed in the principle of an established church, they wished to disestablish the Church of Scotland, on grounds that the Free Church was the true Presbyterian church. Their support for disestablishment aligned them with the bulk of the Scottish middle class, most of whom were drawn to evangelicalism. This ecclesiastical dispute, added to the middle class's predictable opposition to the landlords, gave liberalism and the British Liberal party overwhelming dominance in Scottish politics for most of the rest of the century.

But, as in Wales, Scottish liberalism did not become a separatist movement. Most Scots, after all, were Protestants and felt no ultimate grievance with English culture. The Gaelic language was dying out, and traditional Scottish (that is, Highland) society had been destroyed. Most Scots were content with a dual identity— British and Scottish. There was a Gaelic revival in the 1870s that built on romantic idealization of Highland life, and this largely academic revival combined with radical liberalism over the plight of the crofters. But Gaelic was not taught in the state schools, and cultivation of Gaelic language and literature remained an academic pastime. As one statesman said, "No Scotsman, except a handful of Celtic enthusiasts in the Highlands, wants a separate parliament for Scotland."

Yet there was in Scotland a growing sense that Scottish rights within the United Kingdom needed vindication. Following the Irish example (see below, this chapter), many Scottish Liberals committed themselves to Scottish Home Rule in 1886. In 1900, some militant Liberals founded the Young Scots Society. The feeling in Scotland that Scottish rights would be protected only if Scotland enjoyed greater regional autonomy produced four Scottish Home Rule bills between 1886 and 1914. None was passed, but in 1885 the British government created the position of secretary of state for Scotland, with supervision over a number of Scottish administrative boards, many of them already in existence. The British also granted fairer distribution of governmental expenditures, and a Scottish Grand Committee, made up of the Scottish members of Parliament (M.P.s) only, was given limited control over purely Scottish legislation. Thus a limited degree of "devolution" was established in recognition of the strong Scottish sense of distinctiveness.

IRELAND: FROM THE FAMINE TO THE HOME RULE MOVEMENT

Both political nationalism and "celtic" cultural nationalism blossomed most vigorously in Ireland. These movements grew out of a changing economic and social structure. The Famine of 1845–1850 proved to be the watershed in modern Irish history. For one thing, many of the tiny agricultural holdings of the pre-Famine years disappeared. In 1910, Ireland still had sixty-two thousand holdings of less than 5 acres, but this was only one-third of the pre-Famine number. For another, Irish farmers shifted away from growing wheat toward pasturage, causing a sharp decline in the number of agricultural laborers. Emigration from the Irish countryside continued at a high rate. After 1873, the worldwide decline of agricultural prices brought bad times for the Irish tenants, but in general, the tenants were better off than before 1845 and better able to mobilize to win relief.

In terms of social change, the post-Famine years saw four major trends. One was a tendency among the peasantry toward later marriage and fewer children, which of course contributed to population decline. At the same time, the disastrous custom among the tenants of subdividing their holdings for their children gave way to new desire to keep holdings intact. The Famine had taught a severe lesson, encouraging the tenants to hold down the number of children, and the shift to pasturage encouraged them to expand their holdings whenever possible. Third, the spread of education had a great impact on the illiteracy of the Irish peasants. Although state efforts to expand education in Ireland were hampered by incessant bickering between Catholics and Protestants, by 1910 illiteracy had largely been eliminated. The education offered in Irish state schools was thoroughly English, for its purpose was to make of each student "a happy English child"; nevertheless, neither the political nationalism nor the cultural revival of late-Victorian Ireland would have been possible without the national schools. Fourth, with the growth of industry and commerce in Belfast and Dublin, there was by 1900 in Ireland not only a much larger middle class but also the makings of an urban working class.

Meanwhile, Irish Catholicism underwent a "devotional revolution"—a revitalization and "Romanizing" of Catholic worship. Led by Archbishop Paul Cullen, the Irish Catholic hierarchy built new churches and convents, raised the standards of the parish clergy, and multiplied and regularized religious services. Cullen looked to Rome for guidance and spread practices that were popular in the Vatican—novenas, the rosary, and so on. The Irish Catholic laity became one of the most devout Catholic populations in the world. Ireland produced a surplus of priests and nuns, many of whom carried Irish Catholicism to the English-speaking world. Cullen was strongly conservative and opposed militant Irish nationalism. Nevertheless, his policies in a sense tightened the bond between Irish Catholicism and Irish nationalism: "faith and fatherland" was his ideal—that is, to be a patriot was to be a Catholic.

In the decades after the Famine and the collapse of Young Ireland, Irish nationalism was highly political. It swung between two poles: one was constitutional and devoted to parliamentary action, and the other was unconstitional and inclined toward revolutionary violence. In the 1850s, some Irish M.P.s founded the Independent Irish Party, hoping to defend the rights of Irish Catholics and to win some security for Irish tenants. But, like so many Irish parliamentary factions since the Union of 1801, the Independent Irish Party could claim no more than a small minority in the British Parliament; it became demoralized and soon fell apart. Constitutional Irish politics slipped into the doldrums. Irish landowners dominated many constituencies, and most of them were staunchly pro-British and Tory. Liberalism fell on relatively stony soil in Ireland for several reasons: the Irish middle class was small, nonconformists amounted to less than 10 percent of the population, and Irish Catholicism was generally illiberal. By the end of the 1850s, constitutional politics had reached a dead end.

The nationalist pendulum now swung to a new revolutionary society—the Irish Republican Brotherhood, or Fenians (so called because of the legendary warrior band, the Fianna). The Fenians had no political program except overthrow of British rule by force. Led by two veterans of the Young Ireland fiasco of 1848, James Stephens and John O'Mahoney, the Fenians (or IRB) sought to establish an independent and nonsectarian Irish republic.

They met strong opposition from the Irish Catholic bishops but received much assistance from Irish émigrés in America, who, remembering the Famine, tended to be aggressively anti-British. The Fenians organized themselves in a complicated ladder of "cells," "circles," and one "center," which were supposedly secret but were soon penetrated by British agents. The Civil War in America distracted the Irish-American Fenians and forced the IRB to delay its revolution. In 1865, British authorities shut down the Fenian newspaper and arrested many Fenian leaders. In 1866, about six hundred American Fenians "invaded" Canada but were quickly forced back across the border. Finally, in 1867 the remaining Fenian leaders in Ireland defiantly staged a rebellion before they could be arrested. It was quickly suppressed.

Given the futility of the Fenians' efforts, it is surprising how much influence they exercised. After 1867, Irish nationalism swung back to the constitutional path, but the IRB continued to exist as an underground stream of the most militant nationalists. They claimed not only the mantle of "true" Irish nationalism but also the control of money from Irish-Americans.

Charles Stewart Parnell, the charismatic and tough-minded leader of the Irish Home Rule movement.

The constitutional effort that replaced Fenianism was the Home Rule movement. Its founder was Isaac Butt, a Conservative Irish barrister who was concerned about the potential consequences of class conflict and revolution in Ireland, which would surely occur, he believed, if the legitimate grievances of the Irish people were not settled. Already, the Liberal government led by William E. Gladstone had addressed some of those grievances by disestablishing the Anglican church of Ireland (1869) and by passing an Irish Land Act (1870). Butt favored both policies but feared that radicalism might go on to destroy Irish property and stability. His solution was neither independence nor repeal of the Union, but federalism. By Home Rule, then, Ireland would have its own Parliament for Irish affairs yet would be subordinate to the Parliament at Westminster. Butt imagined that one day Wales, Scotland, and England would also have their own Parliaments, all federated under the British Parliament.

In the general election of 1874, the new Home Rule party, founded only four years before, won 59 of the 105 Irish seats in the House of Commons. Butt did his best to persuade the British Parliament to accept Home Rule, but he did not succeed. To the British, Home Rule, no matter how restricted the powers of an Irish Parliament might have been, was simply a plan to turn over Ireland and its Protestant garrison to papists and to split the Empire at its core. Butt's politics of persuasion soon dissatisfied Irish nationalists who preferred the tactics of confrontation—specifically, to obstruct the proceedings of Parliament. If Britain, they said, would not let Irishmen rule Ireland, then the Irish would not let Parliament rule Britain. Between 1877 and 1880, one of the advocates of the confrontational approach—the more forceful and militant nationalist, Charles Stewart Parnell—supplanted Butt as leader of the Home Rule movement.

Parnell (1846–1891) was, along with Daniel O'Connell, one of the two towering figures in nineteenth-century Irish nationalism. A Protestant landlord and a man of icy demeanor, Parnell achieved an iron discipline over the Home Rule party and an almost magical hold on the imagination of the Irish people. The secrets of his success were his personal charisma, his supreme self-confidence, his passionate dislike of England, and his political ruthlessness. By refusing to bend to English will and yet staying just inside the boundaries of the law, Parnell managed to bind together the constitutional and the revolutionary wings of Irish nationalism. He simultaneously won control over three groups: the Home Rule parliamentary party, the political organization of Irish men and women in Britain, and the organized force of militant tenants in Ireland, the Land League. By his confrontational tactics in the House of Commons, he won the support of the IRB; hence, in the so-called New Departure, Parnell allied himself with the near-revolutionary mass agitation for tenant rights controlled by the most militant and violence-prone nationalists. The Parnellite Home Rule movement had a constitutional (if aggressive) parliamentary force backed up by agrarian agitation and violence at home.

From 1880 to 1882, Parnell managed this unwieldly weapon with great skill. Though he never publicly advised Irish tenants to commit acts of agrarian terrorism, he plainly sympathized with the tenants and sought to assist those who were evicted or needed legal aid. In 1880, he urged tenant farmers to shun the landlords' agents or other tenants who took over farms from evicted families. The application of this treatment to one estate manager, Captain Boycott, gave the name *boycott* to the English language. Ireland seemed to be descending into violence and anarchy—cattle were maimed, property was destroyed, and landlords and their men were attacked. Finally, in 1881, the Liberal government tried to pacify the country by passing a Land Act. It gave Irish tenants the "Three F's": fixity of tenure, fair rents (set by a court), and free sale by the tenants of their improvements. But the Liberals also moved against agrarian terrorism by passing a stringent coercion bill. In 1882, the government imprisoned Parnell for advising the tenants not to accept the Land Act.

Imprisonment made an even greater hero of Parnell in the hearts of his countrymen. But later in 1882, he reached an agreement with Prime Minister Gladstone, according to which Parnell would be released and the Irish tenants would receive additional relief, in return for Parnell's support of the Land Act. This Liberal–Home Rule alliance (the "Kilmainham Treaty") survived even the brutal assassination of the Liberal chief secretary for Ireland by some IRB men. Through 1885, Parnell was able to control the violent elements in his movement while supporting the Liberal government in Parliament.

Parnell, however, had no intention of allowing the quest for Home Rule to die. In 1885, he returned to his confrontational politics in hopes of forcing one British party or the other to grant Home Rule. In the general election of that year, he instructed Irish voters living in Britain to vote Conservative, his aim being to bring about a deadlock in the House of Commons, to which the Home Rule party would

The Liberal leader, William E. Gladstone, being kicked up in the air over Irish Home Rule by an unusual combination of opponents. From left to right: John Bright, Joseph Chamberlain, Randolph Churchill, Lord Salisbury, and Stafford Northcote.

hold the key. As luck would have it, the election results did hand him the balance of power: neither party would be able to form and sustain a government without the support of the eighty-six Home Rulers. Parnell would be able to turn out of office one cabinet after another. Gladstone thought this situation was constitutionally intolerable and grasped the nettle by committing himself to Irish Home Rule.

As we will see in Chapter 4, this commitment to Home Rule was the most dramatic event in late-Victorian politics. It split the Liberal party, but it did not achieve Home Rule. Twice a Liberal government—in 1886 and in 1893—introduced Home Rule bills, at great electoral cost to themselves, and twice they were defeated. By the time the second Home Rule bill was rejected, the Liberal–Home Rule alliance had collapsed and Parnell was dead.

The fall of Parnell became a tragedy of mythic proportions in Irish popular culture. As the so-called Uncrowned King of Ireland, Parnell had become the new Irish national hero. He enjoyed a sensational victory in 1889, when he proved in court that criminal accusations brought against him by the vehemently anti–Home Rule London *Times* were based on forged letters. But later that same year, it was revealed that Parnell had taken as a mistress one Kitty O'Shea, wife of a member of the Home Rule party. Parnell's adultery was intolerable to the British nonconformists who made up the backbone of the Liberal party and, subsequently, the Irish Catholic bishops. The Catholic clergy hounded Parnell, and the Liberals demanded that the Home Rule party depose Parnell. After a bitter fight, the party majority did the Liberals' bidding. Parnell, however, fought back, claiming that the Catholic clergy and the anti-Parnellite Home Rulers had betrayed Irish nationalism. Parnell's health was destroyed in this last desperate campaign. When he died in 1891, he was elevated into national martyrdom alongside Wolfe Tone and Robert Emmet by those who regarded themselves as the true heirs of Irish nationalism.

IRELAND: FROM HOME RULE TO CULTURAL RENAISSANCE

For nine long years after 1891, the Irish Home Rule party was bitterly divided between Parnellites and anti-Parnellites. British politicians were able to put Home Rule on the back burner. But the Home Rule party finally reunited in 1900, and once the Liberals came back into office, the Home Rulers (as we will see) were again able to press their claims effectively. In 1912, the Liberal government (now led by H. H. Asquith) proposed a third Home Rule bill, which was eventually passed into law but never implemented due to the outbreak of world war in 1914. The Home Rule party thus managed to retain its hold on the middle-class voters who dominated conventional parliamentary politics in Ireland right down to 1914. Yet in the years between Parnell's death in 1891 and the passage of the third Home Rule bill, new expressions of Irish nationalism emerged with which Home Rule had little contact, and compared to which the Home Rulers seemed stodgy and obsolete.

One of the reasons that Home Rule was unable to sustain its grass-roots popular fervor was that the Irish land problem was solved. The tenants had received some security of tenure by the Land Act of 1881; in effect, the act made them co-owners of their holdings with the traditional estate owners. Given this situation, many of the Irish aristocracy and gentry found landowning much less attractive than before. Furthermore, the Conservative governments of 1886–1892 and 1895–1905 decided to "kill Home Rule with kindness." The key to their Irish policy was land purchase: by a series of laws culminating in "Wyndham's Act" of 1903, the British government loaned money to Irish tenants on very favorable terms so that the tenants could buy their holdings from the landlords. Wyndham's Act also gave the landlords bonuses to sell out. By 1920, the old problem of landlordism in Ireland had been eliminated.

By the early twentieth century, however, the Irish desire for some kind of national autonomy was so wide and deep that it could not be killed with kindness by the British government. There had taken root in late-Victorian Ireland a *cultural* nationalism that could not be satisfied with material progress. One aspect of this cultural revival was "Celticism," a pro-Celtic reaction against the Anglo-Saxonism prevalent in late-Victorian England. Celtic history, fairy tales, and folklore were told and retold so as to recall the supposed excellence of ancient Celtic society and to celebrate legendary heroes like Cuchulain and Finn MacCuchail. The historian Standish O'Grady's *History of Ireland* (published in 1878–1880) opened up to the Irish imagination the lost realms of Celtic culture and literature. The Irish peasants, allegedly descended from the ancient Milesians, were portrayed as racially pure, morally virtuous, politically democratic, and instinctively heroic—as opposed to the stolid and unimaginative "Sassennachs."

The organization that popularized the values of the Celtic revival was the Gaelic Athletic Association (GAA). Established in 1884 by Michael Cusack, an Irish-speaking teacher of civil service candidates, the GAA aimed at replacing English games like cricket and soccer with Irish games like hurling and Gaelic football. By attracting young men into Irish-style (and often extremely rough) games, the GAA developed a fierce local and national pride and anti-English attitude. Inevitably, these emotions had political consequences: support for the more aggressive varieties of nationalism. In 1891, for instance, two thousand GAA hurlers marched in Parnell's funeral as an expression of approval of Parnell's final defiance of the English.

The intellectual and scholarly aspects of the Irish Celtic revival found expression in a host of antiquarian, literary, and folklore societies. The most important of these was the Gaelic League, established in 1893. Its leading figures were Eoin Mac-Neill (an Ulster Catholic) and Douglas Hyde (a southern Irish Protestant). Their objectives were to preserve the Irish language, to extend its use among the people again, and to cultivate a new literature in Ireland. The phrase "Irish-Ireland" summed up their philosophy. Hyde gave voice to it in a famous lecture called "The Necessity of de-Anglicizing Ireland." He argued that Irish men and women were stuck in a "half-way house" between Irish and English culture: they hated the English but imitated them. Only if the Irish deliberately cultivated Irish literature, customs, games, names, and above all language would they be able to sustain a distinctive Irish national identity.

The Gaelic League and "Irish-Ireland" were eventually to have a profound impact. As we will see, their vision led to a separatist politics that was much more radical than Home Rule. Even by 1910 the Gaelic League had made significant progress on the cultural front: although by then the Irish language was spoken by only about 12 to 13 percent of the Irish people, Irish was being taught for the first time in Ireland's state schools, and Irish was now required for entry into the new Irish National University (established in 1908).

Yet the great literary revival that blossomed in Ireland between 1880 and 1914 was not in Irish but in English. This splendid movement was one of the finest achievements in all the history of high culture in the British Isles; its roll call of participants comprised a close-knit band of literary talents of the first rank: Lady Augusta Gregory, George Russell (known simply as "AE"), John Millington Synge, William Butler Yeats, James Joyce, and Sean O'Casey. All of these except Joyce were descendants of the Anglo-Irish Protestant population, yet all drew on the revived interest in Celtic folklore, mythology, and literature. And all sought in their individual ways to give substance to a nonsectarian sense of the Irish identity.

The causes of any such sudden cultural flowering must remain to a degree mysterious, and this generalization seems especially true of the Irish literary renaissance. One explanation for it may simply be that these writers shared the widespread reaction against "Anglo-Saxonism" and discovered that they could draw creatively on the fresh materials of the Celtic revival. Another explanation may be that because of a series of events (the disestablishment of the Irish church in 1869, the land war of the 1870s and 1880s, and the Home Rule movement), a younger generation of the Anglo-Irish elite was the first to realize that the days of the Protestant ascendancy were numbered. By this second interpretation, the Irish literary renaissance was a product of post-colonialism: a profound attempt by the colonists to come to terms with the culture of the colonized. Whatever the explanation, their conscious objective was to create, as Professor F. S. L. Lyons wrote, "a modern Irish literature in English."

All of the leading figures in the Irish literary revival struggled with either or both of two sets of problems: first, the difficulties arising from a divided cultural identity—Irish and Anglo-Irish; second, the opposing claims of nationalism and artistic creativity. The most brilliant playwright among them, J. M. Synge (1871–1909), sought to render the rhythms and patterns of the Irish language into English, and he succeeded wonderfully. But in his two best plays, *In the Shadow of the Glen* and *The Playboy of the Western World* (1907), Synge also portrayed the Irish peasants as they really were. Advocates of "Irish-Ireland" and Catholic nationalists alike found the reality unacceptable, for they had idealized the peasantry. As one Irish-Irelander declared, "All of us know that Irish women are the most virtuous in the world"; he refused to let Synge, or the newly founded Abbey Theatre, say otherwise.

W. B. Yeats (1865–1939) was by far the greatest poet of the Irish literary revival and arguably the greatest English-language poet of the twentieth century. Yeats was a believer in magic and the occult and in the reality of a supernatural world; thus he was drawn both to the premodern outlook of Irish folklore and to the symbolist style of poetry. An avid collector of Irish folktales, Yeats turned the materials of Celtic legend into beautiful English language modernist poetry. He was a nationalist, with connections to the IRB; his play *Cathleen ni Houlihan* led one playgoer to wonder whether such patriotic plays should be produced "unless one was prepared for people to go out and shoot and be shot." But Irish nationalism, which demanded the artist's total commitment, proved too restrictive on Yeats's creativity. The nationalists' criticism of Synge's plays repelled Yeats, and thereafter Yeats tended to adopt an aristocratic disdain for the common and vulgar features of Irish life.

James Joyce (1882–1941), the most innovative of all writers of English language fiction in the modernist movement, reacted even more strongly against conventional Irish life. He left Ireland in 1904 and spent the rest of his life on the European continent. Yet he was a product, in spite of himself, of Ireland and of the Irish literary renaissance, both of which he rejected. As he showed in *A Portrait of the Artist as a Young Man* (1916), Joyce abandoned Catholicism and took up literature as his vocation in one defiant act. He believed Irish culture—or at least that of Dublin—to be paralyzed and paralyzing: priest-ridden, whiskey-soaked, intellectually degraded, and politically hypocritical. During his life on the Continent, Joyce was aggressively cosmopolitan rather than Irish. Yet he knew Ireland intimately and set all his important work in Ireland, including the highly experimental novel *Ulysses* (1922). In it, as in all his mature work, Joyce managed to combine symbolism with realism, and mimicry with experiment in the use of language. Cosmopolitan and modernist as his novels are, he painted an indelible portrait of the culture of the Irish nation.

IRELAND: CULTURAL RENAISSANCE TO THE BRINK OF CIVIL WAR

The Irish cultural revival proved to be inseparable from politics. The strong sense of Irish nationality led to political ideas of national self reliance, and the ideas led to organization. Beginning in 1898, self-reliance was expressed as an ideology under the banner of "Sinn Fein" (ourselves alone) by the journalist and intellectual Arthur Griffith. Griffith wanted not only to establish an independent Irish literature, history, and language but also to free Ireland from economic and political dependence on England. He proposed policies of economic self-sufficiency and political separation for Ireland, and by any means possible: "Lest there might be a doubt in any mind, we will say that we accept the nationalism of '98, '48 and '67 as the true nationalism and Grattan's cry 'Live Ireland—perish the Empire!' as the watch-word of patriotism." This attitude put Sinn Fein, formally established as a political party in 1905, squarely in the nonsectarian, extremist tradition of Irish nationalism, as opposed to the more moderate constitutionalism of the Home Rulers. However, Griffith believed that the easiest way for Ireland to achieve independence was simply for the Irish M.P.s to withdraw from Parliament and establish themselves in Ireland as the true Irish Parliament, joined to Britain only by the crown.

Sinn Fein grew rapidly through a number of loosely coordinated nationalist societies in the early twentieth century. Its organizational structure from the beginning attracted the participation of members of the IRB. These militant nationalists in 1913 led the way in establishing a large paramilitary force—the Irish Volunteers. Originally headed by Eoin MacNeill, founder of the Gaelic League, the Irish Volunteers grew from 10,000 men to 180,000 by September 1914.

At about the same time, the urban working class of Dublin began to organize along militant nationalist lines. The central figures were James Larkin and James Connolly, two syndicalist union organizers who set up the Irish Transport Workers Union (TWU). By militant agitation and strikes, the Dublin workers won a number of concessions from their employers, but in 1913 they lost an extended and bitter conflict with the United Tramway Company of Dublin. The main British union council, the Trades Union Congress, which had its own battles to fight and which was leery of the syndicalists in both Britain and Ireland, failed to give sustained support to the Irish TWU. In reaction, the Irish workers became more nationalist than socialist in their outlook. In that heated atmosphere of both increasing class conflict and nationalist militancy, Connolly formed a small force to defend the union men against the police: the Irish Citizen Army. In 1914, the "Army" committed itself to a radical socialist and nationalist principle: "The ownership of Ireland, moral and material, is vested in the people of Ireland."

This was revolutionary talk. Against the whole militant nationalist movement there stood by 1914 an equally militant loyalist sentiment: Ulster Unionism. The Unionists of Ulster have constituted from the late nineteenth and early twentieth centuries to the present day one of the most durable pockets of political intransigence in British history. Ulster Unionism arose from the substantial number of Scottish Protestants first planted in Ulster in the seventeenth century. Though they amounted to about half the population of the nine counties of Ulster, these Scotch-Irish always believed that they might at any moment be drowned in the sea of Irish Catholics. They had placed their hopes of survival squarely on the shoulders of Britain after the Act of Union in 1801. When the first Home Rule bill was proposed in 1886, the Ulster Protestants rallied to the defense of the Union, because they thought that the old struggle between Catholics and Protestants for control over Ireland had been revived. The Protestant Orange Order became the heart and soul of Ulster Unionist resistance to Home Rule. To them, Home Rule meant Rome Rule. Even in the 1880s, then, many Ulster Unionists openly spoke of resisting Home Rule by force of arms. As one English Conservative declared in 1886, both as a warning and as a rallying cry: "Ulster will fight and Ulster will be right."

The determination of the Ulster Unionists to block any form of Irish national independence grew firmer after 1886. The growth of militant nationalism and the revival of Home Rule in the early 1900s stimulated them to organize the Ulster Unionist Council. Led by two utterly implacable politicians, James Craig (an Ulsterman) and Sir Edward Carson (a southern Irish Unionist), the Unionists readied themselves to fight Home Rule, if necessary by force of arms. In 1912, almost half a million Ulster Protestants signed a "Solemn League and Covenant" to use any and all means to defeat the creation of a Home Rule Parliament in Ireland. In 1913, the Ulster Unionist Council recruited a Unionist army of 100,000 men—the Ulster Volunteer Force. Thus the militancy of Irish nationalism, rooted in the soil of the Celtic revival, had provoked the fortress mentality of the Ulster Protestants. By 1914, with Home Rule about to be enacted, civil war in Ireland seemed inevitable. This impending disaster was a severe challenge to the British state and political system, which already were facing major crises at home and abroad.

Suggested Reading

Bew, Paul, *C. S. Parnell* (Dublin: Gill & Macmillan, 1980).

Brown, Malcolm, *The Politics of Irish Literature from Thomas Davis to W. B. Yeats* (London: Allen & Unwin, 1972).

Brown, Stewart J., *Thomas Chalmers and the Godly Commonwealth in Scotland* (Oxford: Oxford University Press, 1982).

Checkland, Sidney, and Olive Checkland, *Industry and Ethos: Scotland, 1832–1914* (London: E. Arnold, 1984).

Curtis, L. P., Jr., *Anglo-Saxons and Celts* (Bridgeport, Conn.: Conference on British Studies at the University of Bridgeport, 1968).

Davies, E. T., *Religion and Society in the Nineteenth Century* (A New History of Wales) (Llandybie, Dyfed: C. Davies, 1981).

Donaldson, Gordon, *Scotland: The Shaping of a Nation* (Newton Abbot: David & Charles, 1974).

Dunleavy, Janet, and Gareth Dunleavy, *Douglas Hyde: A Maker of Modern Ireland* (Berkeley: University of California Press, 1991).

Edwards, Owen Dudley, et al., *Celtic Nationalism* (New York: Barnes & Noble, 1968).

Foster, Roy, *W. B. Yeats: A Life*. 2 vols. (Oxford: Oxford University Press, 1197, 2003).

Hechter, Michael, *Internal Colonialism* (London: Routledge & Kegan Paul, 1975).

Howarth, Herbert, *The Irish Writers: Literature and Nationalism, 1880–1940* (London: Rockliff, 1958).

Jones, Gareth E., *Modern Wales* (Cambridge: Cambridge University Press, 1984).

Kee, Robert, *The Green Flag* (New York: Delacorte Press, 1972).

———, *The Laurel and the Ivy: The Story of Charles Stewart Parnell and Irish Nationalism* (London: Hamish Hamilton, 1993).

Kiberd, Declan, *Inventing Ireland* (London: Jonathan Cape, 1995).

Lee, Joseph, *The Modernization of Irish Society, 1848–1918* (Dublin: Gill & Macmillan, 1973).

Lyons, F. S. L., *Charles Stewart Parnell* (New York: Oxford University Press, 1977).

———, *Culture and Anarchy in Ireland, 1890–1939* (Oxford: Oxford University Press, 1979).

———, *Ireland Since the Famine* (London: Weidenfeld & Nicholson, 1971).

Morgan, Kenneth O., *Rebirth of a Nation: Wales, 1880–1890* (New York: Oxford University Press, 1981).

Morgan, Prys, and David Thomas, *Wales: The Shaping of a Nation* (Newton Abbot: Daivd & Charles, 1984).

O'Grada, Cormac, *Ireland: A New Economic History, 1780–1939* (New York: Oxford University Press, 1994).

Robbins, Keith, *Nineteenth-Century Britain: Integration and Diversity* (Oxford: Clarendon Press, 1988).

Smout, T. C., *A Century of the Scottish People, 1830–1950* (London: Collins, 1986).

Turner, Michael, *After the Famine: Irish Agriculture, 1850–1914* (Cambridge: Cambridge University Press, 1996).

Vaughan, W. E., ed., *Ireland Under the Union II: 1870–1921 (A New History of Ireland)* (New York: Oxford University Press, 1996).

———, *Landlords and Tenants in Mid-Victorian Ireland* (Oxford: Oxford University Press, 1994).

Williams, Gwyn, *When Was Wales?* (London: Black Raven Press, 1985).

Chapter 4

Politics and the State, 1867–1914

Although the British political system between 1867 and 1914 faced no gigantic events on the scale of the Industrial Revolution or the near-total war against the French Revolution and Napoleon, it nevertheless had to deal with major problems of long-term significance. Relative economic decline, the "rediscovery" of poverty, demands for a radically expanded electorate, class antagonism, the women's movement, and Irish Home Rule each challenged the British state in the late-Victorian and Edwardian periods—and sometimes all at once. The record of response was mixed: British politicians and statesmen responded to some of these issues effectively, but on others they moved ineffectively or not at all. Blockage of the legislative channels of Parliament seemed sometimes to become a chronic condition; at other times strong parliamentary majorities enabled one of the parties to legislate rapidly, resulting in an expanded role of the state, particularly in matters of social welfare. Through it all, the process of coping with the challenges of the period altered the political system in ways that no one in the 1860s could have anticipated: the "golden age" of the independent member of Parliament came to an end as extraparliamentary parties grew in importance; Ireland caused a realignment of parties; and the working class claimed direct representation in Parliament. By 1914 the mid-Victorian political balance and sense of consensus had frayed to the breaking point.

THE 1867 REFORM ACT AND THE STRUCTURE OF POLITICS

The British political system of the 1850s and 1860s was not, and was not supposed to be, democratic. It was intended to represent "stable," "responsible" individuals who had a stake in society. The Reform Act of 1832 had given the vote to about 800,000 men in England and Wales. By the 1860s, inflation, prosperity, and population growth had increased the number of electors to about 1 million in England and Wales and over 1.3 million in the United Kingdom as a whole—one in twenty-four of the population. The Reform Act had not abolished all small constituencies, nor had it eliminated "influence" and deference as major political factors. It *had* stimulated the development of extraparliamentary parties, but these remained small and under the thumb of the Liberal and Conservative parliamentary factions. Because neither the parties nor the cabinets of the day could exercise much discipline over the M.P.s, the years between 1832 and 1867 formed the golden age of the independent private member.

By the 1860s, however, the two parties had taken distinctive shapes. The Conservative party was the organ of the aristocracy and gentry and spoke for the preservation of the landed interest and the Church of England. Repeal of the Corn Law in 1846 had split the Peelites (Sir Robert Peel, who died in 1850, and his disciples) from the bulk of the Conservative party, and eventually the Peelites came to ally themselves with the Liberals. The Liberal party by the 1860s consisted of the Whig grandees, the Peelites, radicals like John Stuart Mill, and a number of middle-class commercial and industrial men. Outside Parliament, middle-class nonconformists and working-class artisans increasingly thought of themselves as radical allies of the Liberals. Generally speaking, the Liberals advocated "peace, retrenchment, and reform," but they were held together by the immensely popular Lord Palmerston, who spoke for popular patriotism and opposed extension of the franchise beyond the limits set in 1832.

Desire for parliamentary reform, however, had never died away either in the Liberal parliamentary party or in the country at large. It had been kept alive by ex-Chartists and by middle-class radicals who hoped that an additional dose of reform would destroy the aristocracy's grip on political power. John Bright, the Quaker whom Tennyson had called the "broad-brimmed hawker of holy things," argued that parliamentary reform would purify the state by checking the self-interest and irresponsibility of the aristocracy: "The class which has hitherto ruled this country has failed miserably. . . . If a class has failed, let us try the nation!" Although many of the governing elite would have rejected this moralistic cry against the aristocracy, they came around to reform as prosperity and social peace worked their magic. Even the prominent Whig Lord John Russell, known as "Finality Jack" in the 1830s, believed by the 1850s that progress in the economy and education had created more "responsible" men among the populace, and by the logic of 1832, responsible men were entitled to the vote.

The former Peelite William Gladstone, obviously a rising force in the Liberal party, reflected this shift in opinion. He was powerfully impressed by the Lancashire cotton workers' sober endurance of the hardships they suffered when the American Civil War denied raw cotton to British mills. In 1864, Gladstone declared that "every man who is not presumably incapacitated by some consideration of personal fitness or of political danger is morally entitled to come within the pale of the constitution." The death of Palmerston in 1865 unleashed the holders of such views.

Reformers in the Parliament of the 1860s thus were not moved by fear of revolution (as many had been in 1830–1832) but by the relative social peace of the time. Working-class reformers reinforced this spirit of accommodation by moderating their own claims. The main reform organization of working men, the Reform League, spoke for the comparatively well-off and "respectable" artisan elite, the same people who had successfully founded the moderate craft unions of the mid-Victorian years. They, too, sought limited extension of the franchise rather than universal suffrage, and they advocated it not as a right but as a privilege that had been earned. These working-class reformers cooperated readily with radical intellectuals and with provincial nonconformists like Bright on the objective of breaking the power of the landowners. Beyond this they had no agenda. As one radical journalist, John Morley, declared, the issue was between "brains and numbers on the one side and wealth, vested interest, rank and possessions on the other."

The growing consensus favoring reform set into operation the dynamics of party rivalry in the House of Commons. Because a reform act by the mid-1860s seemed inevitable, Liberal and Conservative leaders alike wanted to be able to take credit for it and tailor it for party advantage. The Liberal government of Lord John Russell (with Gladstone as leader of the House of Commons) introduced a moderate reform bill in 1866. A small number of the more cautious members of the Liberal party defected to the opposition, and the Conservatives, led by Benjamin Disraeli, opposed the bill in order to be able to seize the initiative themselves. This combination defeated the bill, and the Liberal cabinet resigned from office. Outside the House there were some popular demonstrations in favor of reform, including one that broke down railings in Hyde Park, but there was nothing like the dangerous popular movement of 1831.

The Conservative government that took office needed little pressure to sponsor a reform bill themselves. Although a minority of Conservatives believed that any extension of the franchise would create an inferior electorate, most thought that because reform could not be avoided, the Conservatives should take charge and pass a safe measure. Disraeli, the Conservative leader in the House of Commons, had more partisan reasons in mind. He believed that the Conservatives could survive in a more democratic future, but not if they condemned themselves to a role of sullen opposition to popular measures. He knew that the Conservatives' outlook and morale would brighten if he could give them the delightful experience of beating Gladstone. He also needed a victory to consolidate his own leadership of the Conservative party. Disraeli's objective, therefore, was to pass whatever reform bill he could. The details he cared little about; parliamentary victory was what counted.

Disraeli's brilliant management of his reform bill of 1867 steered the fine line between his own party, which opposed any extreme measure, and the radical wing of the Liberals, who would have defeated any moderate bill. His strategy was to introduce a moderate bill and then to accept radical amendments while taking care to defeat those presented by Gladstone. One by one, Disraeli accepted amendments that stripped away reservations, leaving an act that gave the vote to all urban householders. The Second Reform Act passed finally in August 1867. It was Disraeli's triumph; on returning home after victory in the wee hours of the morning, he found his wife had prepared for him a meat pie from the elegant shop Fortnum and Mason and a bottle of champagne. "Why, my dear," he said, "you are more like a mistress than a wife."

The Reform Act of 1867, and the accompanying redistribution of seats, did not usher in democracy or even universal manhood suffrage, but it did make for very substantial changes—"a leap in the dark," as one Conservative described it. The act expanded the electorate from 1.3 to 2.5 million, so that one in twelve of the population (or one of three adult males) had the vote. The artisanal stratum of the working class now for the first time formed the majority of borough voters. However, the well-to-do were protected by plural voting, for the act provided that a man could vote in every constituency in which he met the property qualification. Some wealthy property owners might cast as many as ten votes. (An amendment proposed by J. S. Mill to give votes to women was rejected.)

Nor did the act create equal-sized electoral districts, though it moved in that direction. The redistribution clauses abolished fifty-two very small or corrupt boroughs and gave about half of these to the largest towns and half to the counties. The Reform Act deliberately left landlord influence predominant in rural constituencies. Moreover, in order to protect the minority (that is, wealthy) voters in some urban constituencies, many large cities were given three seats and each voter was limited to only two votes; presumably, this would enable the minority to win one seat.

The Reform Act of 1867 left many features of the old electoral system in place, but it also led to major structural changes. After 1867, the rural and urban constituencies balanced each other, and about eighty-five seats were still controlled by patronage. Though the number of middle-class M.P.s increased, they did not form a majority until the 1880s. But in 1872, the secret ballot was introduced, and together with the Corrupt Practices Act of 1883 and the sheer size of most constituencies, the traditional expenditure of vast sums of money to bribe voters slowly came to an end. Then in 1884 and 1885, the dynamics of party rivalry produced further measures of reform and redistribution. The Third Reform Act (1884) extended the householder franchise from the boroughs to the counties, increasing the electorate to 5.7 million, or one in every six of the population. The Redistribution Act of 1885 met Conservative concerns by dividing the country generally into single-member constituencies of approximately equal size, an arrangement that preserved safe seats for the Tories. From 1884 to 1918, then, a householder franchise for males only, but not universal manhood suffrage, prevailed in Britain.

After 1867, party activism and party structures both expanded. The increase in the urban electorate prodded both parties to contest all constituencies in general elections. Moreover, the two parties found that they had to organize aggressively in each borough in order to win their share of the two or three seats. Full-time, professional party agents in each constituency now became the keys to electoral success. Local party organizations sprang up in most urban constituencies and after 1885 in all the rest. Supported by both politicians and party agents, these constituency associations engaged in recreational as well as electoral activities; thus in late-Victorian Britain, party politics in the form of picnics, football teams, and brass bands became an important part of popular culture.

Finally, as a result of the challenge presented by the massively enlarged electorate, extraparliamentary party "machines" were established. In the Conservative party the impetus came from the top down. As early as 1867, Tory politicos founded a federation of Conservative constituency organizations—the National Union of Conservative and Constitutional Associations. In addition the parliamentary leaders established the Conservative Central Office, headed by the very effective John

Gorst, to function as the party headquarters. This central bureaucracy controlled the National Union and also the Primrose League, a highly effective network of political clubs for party volunteer workers, including a large number of women. Neither the National Union nor the Primrose League presented a source of power rivaling the parliamentary leaders, but together with the Conservatives' superior wealth they provided a useful electoral instrument. Hence the Conservatives were able to appeal to the respectable middle class as well as to the landowners, and even to win consistently some 30 percent of working-class voters.

On the Liberal side, the party organization grew from the bottom up. Middle-class nonconformist grievances had produced a number of national, voluntary, single-issue organizations patterned on the old Anti–Corn Law League: the United Kingdom Alliance (temperance); the Peace Society (pacifism); the Liberation Society (disestablishment of the Church of England); and the National Education League (free, nonsectarian state education), among others. These radical nonconformist societies, with their main strength in the Midlands and North of England and in Scotland and Wales, were united by their common antipathy to Anglican landlords and by their underlying aim of turning Britain into a middle-class, nonconformist-style society. Their members were attracted naturally to the parliamentary Liberal party, which had maintained the traditions of parliamentary reform, civil liberties, free trade, and religious freedom. They also felt an instinctive admiration for the intensely religious and moralistic Liberal, Gladstone. Provincial middle-class nonconformity, therefore, in England as well as in Wales and Scotland, eventually attached itself to the parliamentary Liberal party.

In some urban constituencies, most notably in Birmingham, middle-class radicals sought to harness the power of these voluntary associations by founding local Liberal associations. These associations were able to attract the support of working-class members of the Reform League, respectable trade unions, and radical clubs. They spread rapidly in the 1870s. In 1877, these "caucuses," as they were called, joined to form the National Liberal Federation (NLF) led by Joseph Chamberlain, a Unitarian manufacturer and former radical mayor of Birmingham. Chamberlain sought to use the NLF to rid the Liberal party of the Whigs and capture it for the radicals. At the same time, however, the parliamentary party's central bureaucracy and national leader ship tried to use the NLF for their own purposes. This tension between the provincial radicals and the Liberal parliamentary leaders for control of the machine was one of the main themes in Liberal politics through 1886, when Gladstone and the parliamentary leadership won.

Although many British politicians and political observers expressed concern that the new extraparliamentary machines would dictate policy to the M.P.s, that never happened. Members of the traditional ruling elite feared that the development of party bureaucracies would transfer power from independent parliamentarians to professional politicians. But by 1900, the parliamentary parties had succeeded in bringing the machines under their own control. What *did* limit the independence of the ordinary M.P. was an in crease of party discipline in the House of Commons. The cause of this development was the public's rising expectation of parliamentary legislation and the corresponding need for cabinets to control business in the Commons more tightly and to marshal their parliamentary forces more efficiently. During the years between 1867 and 1900, the frequency of pure party votes grew rapidly. The day of the old-fashioned independent M.P., described by one Conservative as "the old judicial type of Member who sat rather loose to his party," was over. A new political structure had come into being: straight party votes in Parliament and mass politics in the country, with party machines controlled by the parliamentary leadership using professional organizers and volunteer party activists to mobilize party electoral forces.

GLADSTONE AND DISRAELI

Late-Victorian Britain was highly politicized, and everyone, whether in the Celtic countries or in England, seemed to be a partisan. In one of the delightfully satirical operettas that he wrote with Arthur Sullivan, W. S. Gilbert claimed

> That every boy and every gal
>> That's born into the world alive,
> Is either a little Liberal
>> Or else a little Conservative!

Daily newspapers like the *Times*, the *Daily Telegraph,* and the *Daily News* of London, as well as the *Manchester Guardian,* the *Leeds Mercury,* and the *Sheffield Independent*, gave very full coverage to political news and quoted parliamentary speeches at length. This politicization of literate Britain was a sign not only of the rise of parties but also of the classic duel between the two great party leaders of the period, Benjamin Disraeli and W. E. Gladstone. The public had seen nothing like their dramatic confrontations since the days of William Pitt the Younger and Charles James Fox in the last decades of the 1700s. Masters of parliamentary debate, these two giants of the House of Commons were enabled by the expanded electorate, the rise of the political press, and the shrinking of Britain by the railways to become *national* party symbols.

The two titans could hardly have been more different: it was as if a playful deity had designed each of them to challenge and irritate the other. Gladstone (1809–1898) was the model of Victorian religiosity and rectitude, a man who regarded his career in politics as God's calling. Underneath the surface, he was a man of prodigious energy and passion, so torn by self-doubt that he sometimes whipped himself for having experienced temptations of the flesh. The son of a wealthy Liverpool businessman, Gladstone combined traits of both Liverpool and Oxford: unparalleled mastery of government finance, a commitment to individual liberty, and a profound (if somewhat eccentric) devotion to the classics and theology. Gladstone had a strong and beautiful speaking voice, and he excelled in both parliamentary debate and platform oratory. He also had a strong sense of mission and personal destiny, which prompted one critic to say that although he did not

William E. Gladstone (1879). A man of unbending rectitude and greatest of Liberal statesmen, Gladstone was prime minister four times: 1868–1874, 1880–1885, 1886, and 1892–1894.

object to Gladstone's always having an ace up his sleeve, he *did* object to Gladstone's belief that God had put it there!

Gladstone's career was a long march from High Church Toryism to ardent Liberalism. His first speech in the House of Commons (1833) was a defense of his father's slave-holding interests in the West Indies. In the 1830s and 1840s, he distinguished himself by his overly complex and high-flying advocacy of the privileges of the established Church of England. But his severe sense of duty and public service made him a Peelite, and he never forgave Disraeli for his attacks on Peel in 1846. With the other Peelites, Gladstone drifted into anchorage in the Liberal party. His liberalism flowered in his advocacy of financial retrenchment, which he saw as limiting the power of the state, and in his emotional sympathy for oppressed nationalities abroad. To him, Britain should always act as a moral force for good in the world. His moralistic approach to politics attracted the nonconformists of England, Wales, and Scotland, to whom he became a heroic figure. Over time, Gladstone became convinced that the ordinary people had a greater capacity for virtuous public behavior than the landed elite, who, he believed, looked out only for their own self-interest. Politics to him became a choice between "the masses" versus "the classes."

Despite the fact that Disraeli outmaneuvered him in 1867, Gladstone and the Liberals won the first general election (1868) held after passage of the Second Reform Act. Gladstone became prime minister for the first of four times (1868–1874; 1880–1885; 1886; and 1892–1894). His first ministry was by far the most successful, for it rode the crest of a united party to act on many long-standing Liberal concerns. When Gladstone learned in 1868 that the queen would ask him to form a government, he responded, "My mission is to pacify Ireland." Two important pieces of Irish legislation followed: disestablishment of the Anglican Church of Ireland (1869) and a land act (1870) aimed at giving Irish tenants a degree of security of tenure. In addition, the Gladstone government rationalized the legal system, abolished purchase of commissions in the army, introduced competitive civil service exams, ended religious tests at Oxford and Cambridge, gave trade unions legal recognition for the first time, and established (by W. E. Forster's Education Act of 1870) the first state school system in England.

This was nineteenth-century Liberalism at its best, but each of these acts seemed to alienate one segment of Liberal support. In particular, Forster's Education Act infuriated militant nonconformists because it incorporated existing Anglican schools in the new state system. Moreover, some of the more cautious Whigs and middle-class men grew concerned about the government's activism, and they began a slow drift of propertied people away from Liberalism that was to go on for nearly fifty years. Thus the Liberals lost the general election of 1874, and Gladstone resigned from the leadership. What brought him back to power was a massive public outcry, led by the nonconformists, against Turkish atrocities on Bulgarian Christians (1876) and traditional British support of Turkey (see Chapter 5). Gladstone put himself in the lead of this moral opposition to power politics, and when the Liberals won the election of 1880, Gladstone again was the inevitable choice as prime minister.

Gladstone's second government (1880–1885) was not nearly as productive as the first. Plagued throughout by intractable problems in Ireland (raised by Parnell and the Home Rulers) and in the Empire, the government was able to carry little of the Liberal program except the Third Reform Act (1884). The government did not respond at all to Britain's long-term economic difficulties, for they were too committed to the existing economic system even to consider a change. Perhaps the major achievement of the government was the Irish Land Act of 1881, which (as we saw in Chapter 3) interfered with absolute rights of property in Ireland in order to give greater security to Irish tenants. But this legislation did not pacify the Home Rule movement, and the incessant demands by the Irish on the time of Parliament made radicals like Joseph Chamberlain impatient. By 1885, Chamberlain and his followers were glad to see the government fall, because its demise liberated them to carry out their long-desired assault on the Whigs. In this scenario, as we will see, the radicals forgot Gladstone.

Disraeli (1804–1881) served as a perfect foil for Gladstone throughout most of this period. The son of a Jewish man of letters, and himself an incurable romantic, Disraeli was the most improbable success story in Victorian political history. Though he was baptized as an Anglican at age thirteen, Disraeli was always proud of his Jewish heritage and was a courageous advocate of admitting Jews to Parliament (finally granted in 1858). This position was unpopular with the Conservative party, and Disraeli besides was not a member of the landed elite whom he sought to lead. Furthermore, Disraeli was much too flamboyant, too melodramatic, too openly ambitious to be attractive to Conservatives. They never really liked him, yet he had talents they could not do without after the Peelite split: he was devastating

Benjamin Disraeli. A novelist and romantic Tory of Jewish ancestry, Disraeli became leader of the Conservative Party and prime minister in 1874–1880.

in parliamentary debate, a master of political opportunism, and a magician of public gestures and symbols.

Disraeli had first made his reputation as a novelist. As a literary man he was not of the first rank, but his best novels (*Coningsby, Sybil,* and *Tancred*) deserve to be taken seriously. *Coningsby* (1844) was Disraeli's attack on the Whigs and an attempt to show that the Tories were England's natural, and best, rulers. In *Coningsby,* Disraeli asserted the romantic viewpoint of Young England: that there is a natural alliance between aristocracy and people. This theme he pushed even more effectively in *Sybil* (1845), which contends that England had become two nations, the Rich and the Poor. In *Tancred* (1847), Disraeli put forward religion as the solution to "the condition of England." But, afflicted as it is with Disraeli's vague and paradoxical views, *Tancred* is the least satisfying of the three novels.

Some historians have argued that in his novels Disraeli set out the themes for a "Tory Democracy" and then acted on them in 1867 and in his government of 1874–1880. Other historians have found little evidence for this view. Disraeli ran on a platform in 1874 of giving the people relief from "incessant and harassing legislation." He had no interest in legislative details and made little effort to lead his cabinet even by stating general principles. To be sure, his government was very successful in passing a number of pieces of social legislation, including legalization of picketing by trade unions (1875), extensions of the Factory Acts, a law to prevent adulteration of food and drugs, and permissive acts allowing towns to build working-class housing (1875) and to improve public health by cleaning up slum areas (1875). But most of these acts were due to the hard work of a middle-class Conservative cabinet member, R. A. Cross, who complained that he got little help from Disraeli. Yet one cannot deny that Disraeli helped his party, which might otherwise have faded along with the landed interest, survive in the new democratic age. He did so partly by showing the party how to win and partly by making it a comfortable refuge for the commercial and industrial men who, anxious about property, government interference, and public order, drifted away from the Liberals in the 1870s and 1880s.

HOME RULE AND BRITISH POLITICS

One of the principal sources of British concern about public order was Ireland, which continued to be afflicted with poor landlord-tenant relations and agrarian crime and to support militant nationalism. In the 1880s and 1890s, Irish issues continually intruded into British politics, not least because of the discipline and persistence of Parnell's Home Rule party. Though British politicians wanted to get on with "British" issues, Ireland seemed to take up most of their time. Irish issues like land reform and coercion raised the collective British blood pressure, and obstruction of the House of Commons by the Home Rulers in the 1880s forced the cabinet to take firmer control of the business of the House. Neither Gladstone's disestablishment of the Irish church (1869) nor his land reforms (1870 and 1881) pacified the country. By 1885, it seemed to most of the British that they could deal with the Irish only by resolute discipline in Parliament and coercion in Ireland, and for these purposes the Liberals and Conservatives would have to stand together.

Parnell, of course, sought to prevent just such cooperation. In the general election of 1885 (the first election held after passage of the Third Reform and Redistribution Acts), Parnell instructed the thousands of Irish voters living in Britain to throw their support to the Conservatives, his hope being that a close electoral finish would give him the balance of power between the two British parties. Presumably, he would be able to extract Home Rule from one of them. The election realized his strategy: the Liberals won 335 seats, the Conservatives 249. The Home Rulers, with eighty-six seats, could turn out of office any government formed by either party.

Gladstone, who was by then seventy-six years old and widely expected to retire from the Liberal leadership, thought that this constitutional predicament was intolerable. He concluded that the Irish nettle had to be grasped firmly and a measure of Home Rule enacted. Along with a number of other Liberals, he had realized that in governing Ireland the only alternative to granting Home Rule was more coercive acts, and he believed that long-term coercion was unacceptable to the Liberal conscience. In these views, Gladstone was in advance of most of propertied Britain, which, as an overwhelmingly Protestant nation, regarded with misgivings and even horror the possible rule in Ireland by the Catholic majority. As a High Church Anglican and as a cosmopolitan European, Gladstone had slowly come to accept the idea of Catholic rule in Ireland. Furthermore, as a moralistic Liberal, he believed that only the burdens of self-rule could teach responsibility to the Irish.

Gladstone, therefore, decided not to retire until the Irish question was settled. He preferred to let the Tories act, but when they refused, he was determined to try to pass Home Rule himself. His son let it be known that the "Grand Old Man" had been converted to Home Rule. This sensational political news won Gladstone the support of the Home Rulers, and he came back into office early in 1886 committed to try a Home Rule bill. The bill that he introduced in April 1886 (along with a bill to buy out the Irish landlords) convulsed British politics. It would have removed Irish representatives from the British Parliament and set up a subordinate Irish Parliament in Dublin to deal with strictly Irish matters. Gladstone, his followers among the Liberals, and the Parnellites argued that justice demanded passage of Home Rule, that the time had come to remove Ireland from British politics, and that a measure of local autonomy for Ireland would secure the Empire at its core. Opponents of the bill—including all of the Conservatives, most of the Whigs, and a few radicals led by Joseph Chamberlain—contended that Home Rule would turn Ireland over to people who were little better than criminals and who would persecute the Irish Protestant minority, despoil Irish property, and then separate Ireland completely from Britain. Home Rule thus would damage the Empire at its base.

British public opinion was as agitated about Home Rule as were the members of Parliament. Many men of property thought that if the Irish landowners were sacrificed to pacify an extreme, and often violent, movement, then no property was safe. Long-held British prejudice against Roman Catholics came into play, and the fact that the Home Rule bill made no allowances for Ulster Protestants roused fierce opposition. On the other hand, many radicals and laboring people in Britain felt strong sympathy for the Irish people, and they had little concern for the Irish landlords, whom they regarded as the cause of most of Ireland's problems in the first place.

After two months of impassioned debate, Gladstone's Home Rule bill was defeated in the House of Commons by thirty votes. More than ninety Liberals, most of them Whigs but also including Chamberlain and some radical M.P.s, voted against it and so departed from the party. In the subsequent general election of 1886 the "Unionist" alliance of Conservatives and Liberal Unionists won a major victory over Gladstone's Liberals and the Irish Home Rulers.

Home Rule thus caused a realignment of the British parties. Eventually, the Liberal Unionists merged into the Conservative party. At the same time, the Liberal party became more radical because the bulk of those remaining in the party consisted of the nonconformist radicals of England, Wales, and Scotland. The National Liberal Federation and the local Liberal associations, most of which were run by provincial middle-class radicals, remained loyal to Gladstone. Nonconformist radical power in the party now promoted to the official Liberal party platform standard middle-class nonconformist issues such as church disestablishment in Wales and Scotland, land reform (abolition of primogeniture and entail), the end of plural voting, and elective parish councils.

Gladstone and the Liberals campaigned hard for both Home Rule and the radical program between 1886 and 1892. Home Rule, however, was never very popular with the English electorate. When the Liberals won the general election of 1892, their margin was so narrow that Gladstone's fourth and last government (1892–1894) was dependent on the "Celtic fringe" and Home Rule support. Gladstone introduced his second Home Rule bill in 1893, and after a tedious repeat of all the arguments that had been heard for eight years, the bill passed the House of Commons, only to be summarily thrown out by the House of Lords. The Liberal government dithered between campaigning to reform the power of the Lords and trying to pass other items of their program. As Liberal morale faded, Gladstone resigned once and for all in 1894. Saddled with their commitment to Home Rule and their ineffectual record, the Liberals lost heavily in the general election of 1895. The Conservatives came into office and remained there for a decade of "firm government."

For almost all of the period between 1895 and 1905, the Liberals were a divided and unhappy party. To some Liberals, Irish Home Rule remained a moral crusade; to others, it was an electoral millstone around their necks, especially because the Home Rulers themselves were bitterly divided between Parnellites and anti-Parnellites. Some Liberals, including a few of the most visible national leaders like Lord Rosebery, H. H. Asquith, Sir Edward Grey, and R. B. Haldane, took up the cause of empire. Others opposed these "Liberal Imperialists" on behalf of the traditional Gladstonian commitment to a "little England." As we will see in Chapter 5, this disagreement became acute at the time of the Boer War in South Africa (1899–1902). Finally, the Liberals were divided between traditional believers in individualism, laissez-faire, and the nonconformist program on the one hand and the progressive New Liberals on the other. To many New Liberals, the commitment to Home Rule prevented the party from attending to a growing threat from the left: the desire among militant laboring men and socialists for an independent labor party.

THE RISE OF LABOUR

In the years after 1832, most British workers who had the vote supported the Liberal party. After the Reform Act of 1867, the Liberals could count on winning two-thirds of the greatly expanded working-class vote. The allegiance of trade union members to the Liberal party was especially strong, for these organized skilled workers regarded the middle-class nonconformists, who composed the backbone of the Liberal party, as their allies in the struggle against the Anglican landed elite. The Trades Union Congress (TUC), formed in 1868 by the mid-Victorian craft unions, was closely tied to the radical left of the Liberal coalition. In 1874, two trade unionists (both of them coal miners) won election to Parliament as Liberals. Working men thus had reason to hope not only that the Liberals would enact beneficial legislation but also that over time the Liberal party might evolve into a radical, antiaristocratic, working-class party.

Such an evolution did *not* occur; instead, by 1914 an independent working-class party had set up shop as a rival to the Liberals in claiming labor votes. Why did this happen? Was it an inevitable development? Certainly the Liberals always regarded themselves as a party that spoke for *both* the middle class and the working class. And there were few issues on which the Liberals differed from politically active working men. The working class in late-Victorian Britain, after all, did not want much in the way of legislation, because they knew that state intervention in the past rarely had favored the poor. But socialism and the New Unionism, two of the main developments in British society of the 1880s and 1890s, alike gave rise to the desire among working men to have their own *independent* representatives in Parliament. More generally, the revived class consciousness of the period—the strong sense of "them versus us"—generated the wish, not necessarily for new policies, but for independent working-class M.P.s.

The career of James Keir Hardie, perhaps the leading labor politician before 1900, reflected the growing working-class disaffection from the Liberals. Hardie was a Scottish coal miner, a romantic soul who in the 1880s converted to an ethical, non-Marxist brand of socialism. Like many miners in the 1880s, Hardie became an advocate of the eight-hour workday as a way of expanding employment and improving working conditions for miners. The refusal of one TUC official who sat as a Liberal M. P. to accept the eight-hour day earned a blast from Hardie in 1887. The next year, Hardie sought the support of his local Liberal association to contest a parliamentary by-election in Mid-Lanarkshire. He was turned down and therefore stood as a "Labour and Independent" candidate. He was defeated soundly; thereafter, Hardie spoke for establishment of independent labor representation at annual meetings of the TUC. He gradually won support as the New Unionists joined the organization. In 1892, Hardie won a parliamentary seat from the East End of London. He was the first independent labor M.P. and showed his affiliation by wearing a working man's cloth cap when he took his place.

Confrontations like Hardie's between working men and Liberal associations occurred with increasing frequency in the 1890s. Working-class leaders wanted to go beyond the role of giving support to the Liberal party. They wanted to represent working-class constituencies themselves. In theory, the Liberals could have agreed, but in practice, the wealthy commercial and industrial men who had founded and financed the Liberal associations wanted to keep the candidacies for themselves. Few of them liked the eight-hour day, practically none of them accepted socialism, and most of them had their defenses raised by the heated class antagonism of the day. Here was class consciousness asserting itself in unvarnished form.

The first effort by Hardie and other working-class leaders to establish an independent party for labor came in 1893. In the North of England, hard times in coal-mining and cotton-mill towns had spawned many labor clubs and working-class socialist societies. Representatives of these organizations, plus the Social Democratic Federation, the Fabian Society, and a few trade unions, met in Bradford in January 1893. They formed the Independent Labour Party (ILP), which vowed to "secure the collective ownership of the means of production, distribution, and exchange." This extreme policy proved too strong for most workers at the time. The ILP attracted a number of men and women passionately devoted to ethical socialism, people who were to serve for many years as the conscience of the British left; yet the ILP was too idealistic and its leaders too individualistic ever to become a mass party. Even the Fabians preferred for the time being to stay with permeation of the older parties. The foundation of an effective party for labor would depend on the trade unions.

Despite their traditional attachment to the Liberals, many trade unions began to move toward foundation of a labor party in the latter 1890s. Their motive was to defend themselves against the employers' counterattack on the New Unionism. Legal action and lockouts by the employers against the unions gradually persuaded trade union leaders that the Liberals, many of whose M.P.s were the very employers that they faced, would give the unions little satisfaction. Thus when in 1899 Hardie and the ILP urged the English and Scottish TUCs to endorse the idea of "united political action," the TUCs acted. In 1900, representatives of trade unions, the ILP, and a number of small socialist societies set up the Labour Representation Committee (the LRC), which eventually became the Labour party. Its founding resolution said nothing about socialism and little about policy: the LRC was simply to promote in Parliament the interests of labor.

The LRC could not automatically claim the allegiance of all trade unionists, still less the support of all working-class voters. Many of the biggest unions, including the coal miners, refused to affiliate. In the election of 1900, held in the middle of the Boer War, only two LRC candidates won seats in the House of Commons. But the Taff Vale decision of 1901 (see Chapter 1) convinced many trade unionists that labor power in Parliament was an immediate necessity. Over 120 unions now joined the 41 that had already affiliated with the LRC, and the party's electoral fund grew rapidly.

The potential electoral clout of the LRC concerned the Liberal party leadership. The Liberals did not wish to split working-class votes with the LRC and so give up seats to the Conservatives. The Liberal leader, Henry Campbell-Bannerman, and his chief whip, Herbert Gladstone, consequently struck an electoral bargain with the LRC's secretary, Ramsay MacDonald, in 1903. Gladstone and MacDonald agreed to prevent, where possible, Liberal and LRC candidates from contesting the same constituencies, in return for which Labour M.P.s would support a future Liberal government. This agreement allowed the LRC to win twenty-nine seats in the general election of 1906, which overall was a smashing victory for the Liberals. (Twenty-four other working men sat in the House as Liberals.) Shortly after the election, the LRC members of Parliament elected their own whips and took the name of "the Labour party."

Between 1906 and 1914, the existence of the Labour party caused much concern among provincial Liberal businessmen as they competed with the new party for the allegiance of the working class. As we will see in the next section, this was only one of several problems simultaneously troubling the Liberals. Yet the Labour party did not embark on any steady rise to power. The Liberal government, influenced by the New Liberals, passed much social legislation, which may have helped contain the advance of Labour. The Labour M.P.s decisively influenced only one piece of legislation, the Trades Disputes Act (1906), which reversed the Taff Vale decision, gave the unions legal immunity from suit by employers, and thereby sanctioned strikes and picketing. Clearly, the Liberal party held the initiative, and the Labour representatives seemed to serve only as a tail on the Liberal dog. The number of Labour M.P.s grew to forty-five by 1910, largely because the miners affiliated with the Labour party in 1909. But the general elections of 1910 reduced the number of Labour M.P.s to forty-two, and Labour morale sagged. In the country at large, however, two crucial developments were taking place: first, the number of union affiliations with the Labour party was growing along with union militancy; second, at the constituency level, the Liberal/Labour electoral pact was breaking down. Both trends promised big trouble for the Liberals, and at just the time when wealthy property owners were shifting from the Liberal to the Conservative party.

TRIUMPHS AND TRIALS OF LIBERALISM, 1906–1914

To the Liberals, the rise of Labour was like the defection of infantry battalions from the progressive army, which was locked in battle with the *real* enemy, Conservatism. Hence the formation of an independent Labour party helped make British politics in the decade before 1914 exceptionally frustrating and turbulent. Other forces—nationalist and Unionist emotions in Ireland, vigorous radicalism within the Liberal party itself, serious conflicts in industrial relations, an increasingly truculent Conservative party, and the militant tactics of the suffragettes—all contributed to political turmoil. The consensus of the mid-Victorian years seemed to be collapsing and the effectiveness of Parliament weakening. One distinguished historian, George Dangerfield, has labeled the period as "the strange death of liberal England"—not the death of the Liberal party but the end of a political culture in which Liberalism could flourish.

The Conservative party ruled Britain almost continuously from 1886 to 1905. The Conservatives, led by Robert Cecil, third marquess of Salisbury, attended mainly to foreign and imperial affairs, but they had successes on the domestic front as well, including (1) maintenance of the Union with Ireland, (2) the Local Government Act of 1888, which swept away hundreds of antique local jurisdictions and replaced them with elected county councils, (3) workmen's compensation (1897), and (4) an important education act (1902), whereby the state assured the financial viability of church schools and finally took some responsibility for secondary education. Popular concern about "national efficiency," the armed services, the Empire, and the defense of property worked to the benefit of the Conservatives, who were the party of Empire and private property. In the so-called khaki election of 1900, the Conservatives reaped the rewards of effective government and of Boer War patriotism by winning a big majority.

The Conservatives, however, were soon divided over an intensely emotional issue—tariff reform. Britain's economic troubles had raised interest in reestablishing tariffs as early as the 1880s when a "Fair Trade" movement attracted some Conservative manufacturers. But free trade held almost sacrosanct status in Britain, and neither party before 1900 was seriously willing to question the nation's fundamental economic arrangements. In 1903, however, Joseph Chamberlain (the

Joseph Chamberlain speaking in favor of tariff reform. The former leader of the radical wing of the Liberal party became a key figure in early twentieth-century conservatism. Here he argues that a tariff would not raise the cost of food significantly.

former radical and colonial secretary since 1895) set off a bomb by declaring himself in favor of a tariff duty on agricultural imports. Chamberlain proposed to give preferential treatment to the colonies on their farm exports to Britain and so to tie the Empire more closely together. Soon Chamberlain also converted to tariffs on manufactured goods, the intent being to protect British industry. Moreover, Chamberlain argued that money collected by the tariffs should be used to finance social reforms. Thus tariff reform was a bold and comprehensive package.

Arthur Balfour, who had succeeded his uncle, Lord Salisbury, as prime minister in 1902, was put in a tight spot by Chamberlain's proposal. The fervor of Chamberlain's tariff reform crusade was obvious, but Balfour knew that many Conservatives, including the youthful Winston Churchill, were devout free traders. Tariffs on farm imports were especially unpopular, since they would raise the price of food. Balfour took a middle position (retaliatory tariffs against countries that erected tariffs on British goods but no tariffs on agricultural products) that pleased no one. Eventually, Balfour shifted his position and committed the party to more thoroughgoing tariff reform, but by then Chamberlain had been removed from politics by a paralytic stroke and the Conservatives from office by electoral defeat.

The Liberal party rode the unpopularity of tariffs (their slogan being "big loaf" of cheap food versus the Tories' "little loaf") back into power. Nonconformist opposition to conservatism had also been roused by Balfour's Education Act of 1902, which, in establishing state responsibility for secondary schools, also had abolished the school boards set up in 1870 and gave local tax money to the Anglican schools. Liberal moralism had been further goaded by the government's approval of using Chinese coolie labor in South Africa after the Boer War. Together, these issues made for a Liberal landslide in the general election of 1906, when the Liberals, Labour, and Home Rulers won a majority of 355 over the Conservatives and Liberal Unionists.

This Liberal government had to cope with the simultaneous crises presented by industrial relations, Ireland, the suffragettes, and a rebellious Conservative aristocracy. The Liberals were very successful in social reforms, many of them inspired by the New Liberals, who wanted to avert the threat of Labour and among whom was H. H. Asquith, who served as chancellor of the Exchequer from 1906 to 1908 and then as prime minister after Campbell-Bannerman died. The first piece of social legislation was an act (1906) to permit local authorities to provide school meals for poor children. Next came old age pensions (1908), established in order to remove the stigma of pauperism from the growing number of workers who lived to old age. Third, the government in 1909 attacked the problem of unemployment by establishing labor exchanges, which to a degree improved the mobility of labor. Fourth, the Liberals also in 1909 passed the Trade Boards Act, setting up boards to fix wages in the so-called sweated industries like tailoring and lace making.

The most important piece of this burst of Liberal social legislation was the National Insurance Act of 1911. This was the work of David Lloyd George (1863–1945), a Welsh radical and energetic opportunist who became chancellor of the Exchequer in 1908. With Winston Churchill, who had come over to the Liberals because of the tariff issue, Lloyd George was a driving force for New Liberalism in the Asquith government. His National Insurance Act provided protection *outside* the Poor Law system against workers' sickness and unemployment in certain major industries. Both the unemployment and sickness benefits were built on the insurance principle: workers contributed from their pay while employed and received benefits while unemployed or ill. Employers and the state also made contributions. Lloyd George was able to overcome opposition from pressure groups like the friendly societies and trade unions, which in fact could not handle the massive problems of the day, by designating them as "approved societies" through which the act would operate.

The body of social legislation passed by the Liberals between 1906 and 1914 was very impressive, but it was not comprehensive and it did not erect a welfare state. The Liberal social reforms reflected a social democratic consensus that the state should ameliorate the worst *symptoms* of poverty and inequality, but they did little to attack the *roots* of the problem—unemployment, falling real wages, and the inability of workers in some industries to make a living wage. Still, the Liberal social legislation put the state on the road toward intervening to relieve social suffering.

That social reform effort involved crucial issues of finance, and Lloyd George decided to use the budget itself for social purposes. As Chancellor of the Exchequer, Lloyd George in 1909 boldly designed a budget aimed not only at financing the social programs (and, as Chapter 5 will show, a big naval program as well) but also at forcing the landlords to pay for what he and other radicals regarded as privileges. His budget of 1909 thus raised death duties (inheritance taxes on estates), increased the rate of graduation on income taxes (a principle first introduced in 1907), added a "supertax" on incomes over £5,000, and—most controversial of all—put taxes on land values. The tax rates of the Lloyd George budget by later standards would not be high, but the "People's Budget," as the Liberals called it, clearly endorsed the principle of transfer payments—that is, the wealthy paid taxes that were transferred to the poor through social programs.

Lloyd George's budget caused a major uproar. The Conservatives opposed it as "socialistic" and "revolutionary." The Liberals enthusiastically supported it as their alternative to tariff reform. The budget passed in the House of Commons, but the Conservatives used their huge permanent majority in the House of Lords to defeat it. The action of the Lords raised a serious constitutional issue: could the House of Lords, which was not responsible to the electorate, refuse supply (that is, funding) to the king's government? "That way," Asquith warned, "revolution lies." In December 1909 the Liberal majority in the Commons resolved that the rejection of the budget by the Lords was "a breach of the Constitution and a usurpation of the rights of the Commons" and then called a general election. The consequent election of January 1910 revolved around the issue of the budget versus tariffs. The Liberals won, though their majority was sharply reduced. The Lords accepted the verdict of the electorate and passed the budget.

The Liberals, however, by then were determined to curtail the power of the House of Lords, which had blocked or emasculated Liberal legislation as far back as the Home Rule bill of 1893. Ever since the Liberals had taken office in 1905, the Lords had consistently served Conservative interests. The upper house had become, Lloyd George said, "Mr. Balfour's poodle." In April 1910, therefore, Asquith introduced a reform that would end the Lords' authority over budgets and restrict their power over other bills to a two-year delay. The "Parliament Bill" readily passed in the Commons. Asquith knew that the Lords would reject it, entailing another general election, and he wanted King Edward VII (1901–1910) to promise to create enough Liberal peers to pass it if the Liberals won the election. However, the death of Edward VII and the succession of the cautious and dutiful George V delayed everything. Leaders of the two parties held futile constitutional conferences. Finally, in November 1910, George V agreed to create the Liberal peers if necessary, and a second general election of 1910 was held the next month. The result was

Emmeline Pankhurst being carried off to jail after a suffragette demonstration.

much the same as in January, and the Asquith government proceeded with the Parliament Bill.

The resistance of many Conservative Lords—and of Conservatives in general—now reached a fever pitch. "Ditchers"—Lords who would resist curtailment of their power to the last ditch—tussled with "hedgers"—those who would reluctantly accept some reforms in order to keep the social status of the peerage undiluted. The Liberals pressed on resolutely. Finally, when Asquith announced that the king had agreed to create a flock of Liberal peers, most of the Lords gave in: the bill reforming the Lords' power passed into law in August 1911.

In the meantime, the suffragettes were also applying intense pressure to the Liberal government. In retrospect, it seems clear that votes for women should have been part of the Liberals' historic mission, but a number of Liberals remained opposed, partly because they thought that women would tend to vote Conservative under the existing franchise. Moreover, the suffragettes alienated moderate men because they dared to reject the Victorian idea of "separate spheres" for men and women and even to attack the institution of marriage.

From 1905 on, Liberal politicians often had their public speeches disrupted by suffragettes. Spokesmen for the women presented a series of women's suffrage bills between 1905 and 1912, none of them accepted by the Liberal government. The Women's Social and Political Union (WSPU) staged giant demonstrations, sent delegations to Asquith, and then turned to smashing windows and defacing property. One woman set upon Winston Churchill with a horsewhip, and other ministers were assaulted. The home secretary had suffragettes arrested and countered their hunger strikes by force-feeding and the "Cat-and-Mouse" Act of 1913—that is, release and re-arrest. All of this pressure seems to have stiffened Asquith's own resolve against granting votes for women. Believing from the outset that women's suffrage might result in more votes for the Conservatives, Asquith decided that the women's violence must not be rewarded with the vote.

The Asquith government was more accommodating to the trade unionists, who were raising the heat in the nation at the same time as the suffragettes. The rise in prices, and the corresponding decline in the real wages, plus the militancy of the trade unions and stubbornness of most employers, generated violent disputes in industrial relations during the years 1910–1912. Already in 1907–1908, strikes in coal mining had led to legislation limiting the miners' workday to eight hours. Then in 1910, the miners of South Wales struck, and the consequent disorder required the government to dispatch troops to the area near Tonypandy. In the summer of 1911, a dockers' strike caused outbreaks of violence in London. Later that same summer railwaymen went on strike; troops were required to keep order in London, and several union members were killed. Keir Hardie declared: "The men who have been shot down have been murdered by the Government in the interests of the capitalist system." But the role of the government was not simply to send troops. Increasingly, the government was expected to mediate between employees and trade unionists. Likewise, the government sponsored legislation in 1911 for payment of M. P.s (a big help to the Labour party) and for allowing trade unions to contribute funds to the Labour party (provided only that union members be allowed to "contract out"). When early in 1912, the coal miners went on strike for a minimum wage, the Asquith cabinet rushed through emergency legislation to grant it. Nearly 41 million workdays were lost to strikes in 1912. And the situation promised to worsen: in 1913–1914, the miners, railwaymen, and dockers took up a proposal to form a "triple alliance" of mutual support in industrial disputes.

As if the obstreperous behavior of the Lords, suffragettes, and trade unionists was not enough, the Liberals now faced unreasonable and unconstitutional behavior by the Conservatives and Ulster Unionists over Irish Home Rule. Lurking behind the controversy over the House of Lords was the issue of Home Rule. The Conservatives knew that if the power of the upper House was limited, then Home Rule would be enacted; indeed, they suspected that the Home Rulers' support for Lloyd George's budget and Asquith's Parliament Bill had been bargained for by the Liberals. In this suspicion the Conservatives were generally correct. The Home Rulers had little leverage over the Liberal government until the two general elections of 1910 made the Liberals once again dependent on Home Rule votes in the Commons. By 1911, the Home Rulers were ready to insist that the Liberals fulfill their long-standing pledge to Home Rule. Asquith consequently introduced the third Home Rule bill in April 1912, and this time it would pass into law, since the Lords could only delay it for two years.

Their impending fate drove the Ulster Protestants to extremes of opposition. Under the leadership of Sir Edward Carson, a southern Ireland Unionist, and Sir

An Ulster Unionist demonstration. In the middle is the Unionist leader, Sir Edward Carson. The Ulster Protestant Unionists were implacably opposed to Home Rule for Ireland and would have opposed its implementation by force if necessary.

James Craig, an Ulsterman, Ulster Unionists prepared to resist Home Rule by all means necessary. In their belligerence, the Ulstermen were supported by Andrew Bonar Law, a Canadian of Scotch-Irish ancestry who had succeeded Balfour as leader of the Conservative party. "I can imagine," Law declared, "no length of resistance to which Ulster can go in which I should not be prepared to support them." This was to hint at civil war, which the Ulstermen meanwhile were preparing for. In September 1912 thousands of Ulster Protestants signed their "solemn League and Covenant" against Home Rule, and early the next year the Ulster leadership set to arming and drilling the Ulster Volunteer Force.

In southern Ireland, as we have seen, the Irish nationalists responded by forming their own force, the Irish Volunteers, which was secretly dominated by IRB men. At the same time, the Irish labor leader James Connolly formed the "Citizen Army" to protect his trade union during its lockout dispute with a Dublin tram company; soon the Citizen Army was supporting nationalist claims. By the end of 1913, Ireland seemed well on the way to civil war.

Asquith and his Liberal cabinet naturally felt less passionately about Home Rule than did the Irish nationalists; therefore, they were prepared to compromise by excluding Ulster (or parts of it) from the bill. John Redmond, the leader of the Home Rule party, believed that the Ulstermen were bluffing and thus pressured

Asquith to stand firm. But the Ulster Unionists were not bluffing. Asquith faced the real possibility of having to use British troops to force Home Rule on the most fanatically loyalist part of the Irish population, the Ulster Unionists. The Conservatives would give no support to the government on this issue because they were certain that the Home Rulers intended not to stop at provincial self-government but to take Ireland out of the United Kingdom altogether. The army itself was not reliable. In 1914, officers at the Curragh military post in Ireland resigned rather than prepare to march against Ulster. Asquith elected not to take firm action with the officers or with Ulster; always an indolent and somewhat indecisive man, Asquith felt he had no choice but to recognize the power of Ulster's claim.

Asquith's solution was to suggest an amendment allowing some Ulster counties to opt out of Home Rule for six years. Carson and others regarded this as only a "stay of execution." Despite Asquith's efforts at a last-minute conference with Carson, Law, and Redmond, he was never able to bring them into agreement. In the event, all such political maneuvering was overwhelmed by external events: shortly after the failure of the conference, Britain was enveloped by war in Europe. Home Rule was passed into law, but it was suspended for the duration of the war. For the time being, such divisive issues had to take second place to urgent matters requiring national unity: Ireland, labor unrest, women's suffrage, and Conservative obstruction all receded into the background. The First World War thus saved Britain, and the Liberal party, from bloody civil conflict, but at a price too horrible to contemplate.

Suggested Reading

Barrow, Logie, and Ian Bullock, *Democratic Ideas and the British Labour Movement, 1880–1914* (Cambridge: Cambridge University Press, 1996).

Bew, Paul, *Ideology and the Ulster Questions: Ulster Unionism and Irish Nationalism, 1912–1916* (Oxford: Oxford University Press, 1994).

Blake, Robert, *Disraeli* (New York: St. Martin's, 1967).

Blewett, Neal, *The Peers, the Parties, and the People* (London: Macmillan, 1972).

Brooks, David, *The Age of Upheaval: Edwardian Politics, 1899–1914* (Manchester: Manchester University Press, 1995).

Clarke, Peter, *Lancashire and the New Liberalism* (Cambridge: Cambridge University Press, 1971).

Coetzee, Franz, *For Party or Country: Nationalism and the Dilemmas of Popular Conservatism in Edwardian England* (New York: Oxford University Press, 1990).

Cowling, Maurice, *1867: Disraeli, Gladstone and Revolution* (Cambridge: Cambridge University Press, 1967).

Dangerfield, George, *The Strange Death of Liberal England* (New York: Smith & Haas, 1935).

Feuchtwanger, E. J., *Disraeli, Democracy and the Tory Party* (Oxford: Clarendon Press, 1968).

Gilbert, Bentley, *The Evolution of National Insurance in Great Britain* (London: Joseph, 1966).

———, *David Lloyd George: A Political Life: The Architect of Change, 1863–1912* (Columbus: Ohio State University Press, 1987).

Grigg, John, *Lloyd George: The People's Champion, 1902–11* (London: Methuen, 1978).

Hanham, H. J., *Elections and Party Management: Politics in the Time of Disraeli and Gladstone* (Hassocks, Sussex: Harvester Press, 1959).

Hawkins, Angus, *British Party Politics, 1852–1886* (New York: St. Martin's Press, 1998).

Heyck, Thomas William, *The Dimensions of British Radicalism: The Case of Ireland, 1874–1895* (Urbana: University of Illinois Press, 1974).

Jenkins, Roy, *Gladstone: A Biography* (New York: Random House, 1997).

Jenkins, T. A., *The Liberal Ascendancy, 1830–1886* (New York: St. Martin's Press, 1994).

Kent, Susan K., *Sex and Suffrage in Britain, 1860–1914* (Princeton, N.J.: Princeton University Press, 1987).

Lawrence, Jon, *Speaking for the People: Party, Language, and Popular Politics in England, 1867–1914* (Cambridge: Cambridge University Press, 1998).

Laybourn, Keith, *The Rise of Labour: The British Labour Party, 1890–1979* (London: Edward Arnold, 1990).

Magnus, Philip, *Gladstone* (London: Murray, 1954).

Marsh, Peter T., *Joseph Chamberlain: Entrepreneur in Politics* (New Haven: Yale University Press, 1994).

Matthew, H. C. G., *Gladstone, 1875–1898* (Oxford: Oxford University Press, 1995).

Mayhall, Laura Nym, *The Militant Suffrage Movement: Citizenship and Resistance in Britain, 1860–1930* (New York: Oxford University Press, 2003).

Pelling, Henry, *The Origins of the Labour Party* (Oxford: Clarendon Press, 1965).

———, *Popular Politics and Society in Late Victorian Britain* (London: Macmillan, 1979).

Powell, David, *The Edwardian Crisis, 1901–1914* (New York: St. Martin's Press, 1996).

Pugh, Martin, *The Making of Modern British Politics, 1867–1939* (Oxford: Basil Blackwell, 1982).

Purvis, June, *Emmeline Pankhurst: A Biography* (London: Routledge, 2002).

Rosen, Andrew, *Rise Up Women! The Militant Campaign of the Women's Social and Political Union* (London: Routledge & Kegan Paul, 1974).

Searle, G. R., *The Liberal Party: Triumph and Disintegration, 1886–1929* (New York: St. Martin's Press, 1992).

———, *A New England? Peace and War, 1886–1918* (Oxford: Oxford University Press, 2004).

Shannon, Richard, *The Age of Disraeli, 1868–1881: The Rise of Tory Democracy* (New York: Longmand, 1992).

———, *Gladstone and the Bulgarian Agitation, 1876* (Hassocks, U.K.: Harvester Press, 1975).

Smith, F. B., *The Making of the Second Reform Bill* (Cambridge: Cambridge University Press, 1966).

Stansky, Peter, *Gladstone: A Progress in Politics* (Boston: Little, Brown, 1979).

Ward, Paul, *Red Flag and Union Jack: Englishness, Patriotism, and the British Left, 1881–1924* (Rochester, NY: Boydell & Brewer, 1998).

Chapter 5

Empire and Diplomacy in the Age of Imperialism, 1870–1914

In matters of world power relationships, the years from 1870 to 1914 are rightly known as "the Age of Imperialism." During that half-century, the nations of Western Europe (and later the United States and Japan) expanded their imperial holdings around the globe, carving up Africa, seizing Pacific islands, and establishing claims in Asia. During this period European domination of the world reached its highest point. By any measure, Britain was the leading power in that imperial thrust. The British began the late-Victorian period with the biggest empire by far and then expanded fastest. The British Empire stood in 1914 as the largest empire the world had ever known. The British Empire, in fact, served as an inspiration— and source of envy—to the other Western nations.

Yet the same years from 1870 to 1914 also witnessed the beginning of the end of the *Pax Britannica,* for real British power eroded relative both to the power of other nations and to Britain's ability to fulfill its global commitments. In the early twentieth century, Britain consciously withdrew from its role as the world's policeman, at least in certain areas. Likewise, the erosion of British power ended Britain's "splendid isolation." These trends—imperial expansion and erosion of power— though apparently contradictory were in fact opposite sides of the same coin. Together, they explain how Britain drifted into a war in 1914 that was nearly to end Britain's status as a great power.

GREAT POWER RIVALRIES IN THE LATE NINETEENTH CENTURY

The international environment became much more difficult and dangerous for Britain in the years after 1870 than it had been for half a century. In part this was the result of political and economic development of other great powers on the European continent and overseas, and in part it was the consequence of national rivalries. In Europe, the major developments were the formation of united nation-states in Italy and Germany in 1870–1871. Italy was hampered by economic backwardness in its southern region and by imperfect national cohesion, but the new nation began to industrialize and by 1913 supported significant naval and military forces. Germany was a much more potent power. Germany industrialized at a very rapid rate after 1870, especially in coal, iron, steel, electricity, and industrial chemicals. By 1914, Germany accounted for an even larger share of world manufacturing output than Britain. German exports grew at a fast rate, and German products came into competition with British goods all around the world.

Of equal concern was the fact that Germany was a highly centralized, efficient, and militarized state. Drawing on a rapidly growing population of 49 million in 1890 (compared to 37.4 million for Britain) and on the Prussian military tradition, Germany was bound to play a central role in European affairs. Because the German Reich was born in a war with France, as a result of which Germany had annexed Alsace and Lorraine, the Germans were constantly concerned about the French desire for revenge. For this reason, the German chancellor, Bismarck, was careful not to irritate the British. In the 1870s, for instance, Bismarck discouraged German imperial expansion. But in the mid-1880s, for reasons partly political and partly commercial, Germany began to acquire colonies in Africa and the Pacific and to expand German influence in the Middle East. After Bismarck's dismissal from office in 1890, the German government became very aggressively imperialistic, believing that the superiority of German culture warranted imperial rule and the struggle for survival among the great powers demanded it.

Overseas, the international order was radically altered by the emergence of Japan and the United States. Japan, which for centuries had been an isolated and feudalistic country, modernized by strong state leadership after 1868. Consciously imitating the Western nations, Japan borrowed techniques from both the British navy and the German army. By 1895, Japan was a major power in the Far East. Its development, however, was dwarfed by that of the United States, which experienced unprecedented demographic, agricultural, and industrial growth after the end of the Civil War in 1865. By 1900, the United States produced more manufactured goods than any other nation, and by 1914 its national income was more than three times that of either Britain or Germany. Occupied through the 1880s with the task of filling up a continent, the United States began to assert itself overseas only toward the end of the 1890s. Even after the Spanish-American War, the United States preferred to act independently and to remain outside European entanglements. But by 1900, many Europeans, including British statesmen, believed that in the future giant states like the belatedly but rapidly industrializing Russia and the United States might dominate the world.

The great powers of Europe meanwhile formed an intricate and shifting system of alliances. The old "concert of Europe" was for all practical purposes dead, and each nation simply pursued its own interests and security vis-à-vis all the others. At the core of the alliance system were two sources of conflict: the hostility between France and Germany and the rivalry of Russia and Austria-Hungary for influence in the Balkans. The latter rivalry was made possible by the fact that Ottoman Turkey was such a decrepit empire that it could not control its Balkan provinces. As for the former problem, to protect Germany from French revenge, Bismarck sought to persuade the other European states that Germany had no territorial ambitions and to isolate the French by building alliances against them. Bismarck tried first a loose arrangement for mutual consultation among the three most conservative states, Germany, Austria-Hungary, and Russia (the Three Emperors' League, 1872). When that proved inadequate, he made a concrete military alliance with Austria-Hungary (the Dual Alliance, 1879), to which Italy was soon added (the Triple Alliance, 1882). To assure that Russia would not ally with France, Bismarck then negotiated a limited alliance with Russia (the Reinsurance Treaty, 1887).

The French all this time stewed in their bitterness against Germany. Though no longer the dominant nation on the Continent, France was still a great power. The French went to great lengths to field a huge conscript army—over half a million men before 1900. The French economy was modernizing at a moderate pace, and France enjoyed great stores of mobile capital. As the long-time rivals of Britain, the French were regarded by most Britons as the likeliest source of war. This feeling was aggravated by aggressive French imperialism in the 1880s and 1890s, when France acquired an empire in North and West Africa and in Indochina. But an empire was no substitute for power in Europe; consequently, the French persisted in their effort to find an ally against Germany. Finally, in the early 1890s they succeeded in reaching an understanding (*entente*) with Russia. This was made possible by the fact that in 1890, the new German emperor, William II, dismissed Bismarck from office and refused to renew the Reinsurance Treaty. Dismayed by the German government's behavior, the Russians turned to France and reached an understanding in 1894. Shortly afterward, the understanding developed into a military alliance.

The Franco-Russian alliance amounted to a diplomatic revolution. It not only broke France's diplomatic isolation but also realigned Russia, potentially the most powerful of all European nations. With a population four times as large as Britain's, Russia had a standing army in 1900 of more than a million men. Russia still was in many ways an antiquated state, for its economy was relatively backward and its peasantry and industrial population were impoverished. But the czar's government was driving Russia to great power status and was pushing to expand Russian power to the west, east, and south. Pan-Slavists in the government sought to expand Russian influence in the Balkans at the expense of the Ottoman Empire in Turkey, and the czar's regime also wanted to control the Straits at Constantinople between the Black Sea and the Mediterranean and to extend Russian power into Persia and Afghanistan. Such Russian pressures made for incessant clashes not only with the Turks but also with Austria-Hungary in Eastern Europe and with Britain in the Middle East. Thus for Great Britain, the Franco-Russian *entente* represented a combination of their two rivals of longest standing—a serious situation for a nation that was growing uneasy over imperial rivalries and relative economic decline.

BRITISH POWER AND INTERESTS IN THE LATE NINETEENTH CENTURY

Britain gradually became entrapped by these great power rivalries. In retrospect, it is clear that the late-Victorian years were a time of major changes in British power relationships. Britain was the greatest power on earth in 1870, and in many ways it retained that status through the end of the nineteenth century. The British Empire and industrial economy stood as the models to which the newly industrializing nations aspired. As the most mature industrial nation, Britain was the richest of all societies and therefore had the potential at least of wielding great military power. This fundamental strength enabled Britain to hold aloof from Continental alliances, preferring the luxury of acting independently. Yet, as we have seen, Britain's material power tended to erode, comparatively speaking, between 1870 and 1900, with the result that the British by 1900 were beginning to feel anxious about national security and the future of the Empire.

As we have observed, Britain led the world in industrial production in the early 1870s. The British produced more manufactured goods than the United States and Germany combined. They made more iron and steel, exported more goods, and consumed more energy than any other nation. That headstart inevitably declined as other nations like the United States and Germany industrialized, but Britain remained capable of supporting huge military and naval forces if they so chose. However, the British did not choose to maintain a large army. With an economy devoted to industry and overseas commerce, the British preferred to stay with their tried-and-true principles: free trade, overseas investment, low taxes, no conscription, and a small army. In the 1870s, the British army stood at about 200,000 men (130,000 at home and the rest in India)—a force smaller than those of Germany, France, or Russia. The Indian army, officered by the British, added another 200,000 men; it was this army that sustained British power in southern Asia and the Middle East.

The British navy, on the other hand, was by far the most powerful in the world. In the 1870s, the Royal Navy was larger than the next *three* (France, Russia, and the United States) navies combined. And, given the determination of the British to protect their Empire and far-flung trade, Britain regularly increased budgetary outlays on the navy. But the British faced two serious problems in maintaining naval predominance: one was that naval technology (iron and steel armored ships, steam power, screw propellers, and breech-loading naval guns) advanced rapidly, making old ships obsolete and raising the costs of new construction; the other was the decision by other industrializing powers to build modern navies of their own. The French built up their navy in the early 1880s, resulting in a significant "naval scare" in Britain. The British naval budget increased by more than 50 percent between 1882 and 1897 and promised to go up even more rapidly thereafter. Still, relative to the rest of the world, British naval strength decreased: in 1883, they had thirty-eight battleships and the rest of the world had forty; in 1897, they had sixty-two battleships but all the rest had ninety-six. This relative decline was masked by the absolute might of the British navy: for Queen Victoria's Diamond Jubilee in 1897, the Royal Navy gathered 165 warships for a review at Spithead, and none of these ships had to be withdrawn from a foreign assignment.

Naval superiority was closely tied to Britain's interests. The insularity of Britain was just as important as ever in assuring that the country was secure from invasion, provided that the navy controlled the Channel, the North Sea, and the eastern Atlantic. The British still had no territorial aims on the Continent and desired only that international trade be free. Overseas, the British needed to protect their Empire and the trade routes to it. India remained the prize possession in the Empire, and this meant that the trade routes between Britain and India around the Cape of Good Hope (at the tip of South Africa), or through the Mediterranean, then overland (to the Red Sea or Persian Gulf) were vital.

As in the first half of the century, the concern for India required the British to take a close interest in Turkey and in India's northwest frontier. Thus the Ottoman Empire was important to Britain both because several Turkish provinces, Mesopotamia, Iraq, Egypt, and part of Arabia, stood astride the routes from the Mediterranean to the Red Sea and the Persian Gulf, and because Turkey at Constantinople controlled access from the Black Sea to the Mediterranean, through the Straits of the Bosporus and Dardanelles. In 1875, Disraeli purchased for Britain a predominant holding in the Suez Canal (opened in 1869 to connect the Mediterranean and the Red Sea); thereafter, Britain gradually became more interested in Egypt itself than in Turkey. However, the British remained very concerned about Russian incursions into Turkey because they feared Russian ability to move its fleet from the Black Sea through the Straits. Meanwhile, the necessity of defending India's northwest frontier caused chronic confrontation with Russia, as Russian power expanded southward through Turkestan toward Afghanistan. Russia loomed as Britain's most serious rival.

Both Disraeli and Gladstone shared this general view of Britain's interests, but their styles of conducting foreign affairs differed widely. Disraeli thought that Britain in the 1860s had been ignored by the European powers and that he should assert British interests to ensure a hearing for Britain's views in the councils of the world. By this "Palmerstonian" attitude, the government need not make alliances with European nations, but it should forcefully protect Britain's national interests. This "power politics" approach shaped Disraeli's handling of the key external event of his time in office (1874–1880): a crisis in the Ottoman Empire. In 1876, Turkish troops and paramilitary forces massacred thousands of Christians in the Turkish province of Bulgaria. British nonconformists raised a moralistic outcry, but Disraeli was reluctant to press Turkey for reforms for fear of toppling the ramshackle regime. It was only after Russia intervened, defeated Turkey, and drew up a treaty (1878) seeming to threaten British interests that Disraeli acted vigorously. He sent a fleet to guard the Straits, called out the army reserves, and had Cyprus occupied. Finding an ally in Austria-Hungary, which also was concerned about Russian intrusion into the Balkans, Disraeli helped bring about the Congress of Berlin—a meeting of the European powers to revise the Russo-Turkish settlement. Disraeli returned from the Congress claiming "peace with honour": Russia was forced to give up much of its winnings, and Britain won possession of Cyprus and permission to protect the Straits from Russia.

Gladstone's approach was much more moralistic, and he adhered to the idea of the "concert of Europe" long after the concert had actually broken down. A devoted European, Gladstone preferred for Britain to act in accord with the other European states and even to insist when the British acted alone that they were really acting on behalf of Europe. His style in foreign affairs was exemplified by relations with Egypt. Because of the Suez Canal, Egypt was a major concern to all the European states, Britain most of all. Unfortunately, Egypt, which technically was a tributary to the Ottoman Empire, was internally unstable, and the khedive (governor) of Egypt got the country into debt with European financiers. The consequent truckling of the khedive to the European bondholders profoundly disturbed some nationalistic Egyptian army officers, who revolted against the khedive in 1881. The British and French grew worried about the Canal. Gladstone wished to act with the French to protect European interests in Egypt, but when the French withdrew, Gladstone had British military forces act independently, supposedly on behalf of Europe. In 1882, the British navy bombarded Alexandria, and the army then crushed the rebel Egyptian troops and occupied Egypt. In 1882, the British installed Sir Evelyn Baring in Egypt as consul-general; in effect he ruled Egypt until 1907.

Lord Salisbury, who succeeded Gladstone as prime minister in 1886 and dominated British external policy almost continuously until his retirement in 1902, was a sagacious pessimist and a pragmatic statesman. He realized that Britain's power relative to other nations' was beginning to deteriorate. He believed that Britain's continued greatness depended on expansion of the Empire, for the Empire provided "the necessary condition of that commercial prosperity and of that industrial activity which are the bread of life to millions of our people." But regarding Europe, Salisbury favored inactivity: as he said in 1887, "Whatever happens will be for the worse and therefore it is in our interest that as little should happen as possible." Concerned about the growth of the French and Russian navies, Salisbury's government in 1889 adopted the "two-power standard": Britain's navy would always be larger than those of the next two powers combined. Otherwise, Salisbury avoided broad permanent alliances while making agreements to settle specific issues. Thus he rejected the idea of an alliance with Germany but temporarily settled the dispute with Russia over Afghanistan and won the agreement of Austria and Italy to protect the eastern Mediterranean from Russia.

IMPERIAL EXPANSION, 1870–1900

Cautious and aloof as Britain stood in regard to Europe, the British were very active in expanding their formal Empire in the late nineteenth century. The Empire grew at an accelerated pace no matter what government, Conservative or Liberal, held office. Ironically, however, although British imperial expansion was undertaken in large part to shore up Britain's power in the world, it had the effect of overextending British resources and contributing to Britain's international isolation.

British imperialism in the late-Victorian years was, as some historians would say, "overdetermined"—that is, it had multiple causes, any one of which might have sufficed by itself. As we saw in Chapter 2, an imperial ideology composed of nationalistic pride, a sense of trusteeship, Social Darwinism, and racism took root in the decades after 1870. This ideology predisposed the British governing elite to expansive policies and decisions. Turbulence on the frontiers of the Empire continued to draw the British into annexations. Economics was crucial as the British sought to ensure their world trade position by staking out formal claims where informal control had once prevailed. Strategic or "geopolitical" reasoning was important in that the British—like the other European states—thought that they had to secure safe markets for what promised to be a highly competitive future. Generally speaking, late-Victorian British imperial expansion was driven by *anxiety* arising from a number of sources: (1) unification of Italy and Germany; (2) the industrialization of other nations; (3) the intrusion of European rivals into the colonial world; and (4) commercial rivalries that threatened to intensify.

Whatever the mix of causes in any particular case, the British gained a remarkable number and variety of colonies from the 1870s. These included, among others, Zanzibar (1870), Fiji Islands (1874), the Transvaal (1877, 1900), Cyprus (1878), Bechuanaland (South Africa, 1884), Somalia (East Africa, 1884), Kenya (1885), New Hebrides (South Pacific, 1887), Rhodesia (1888–1889), Uganda (1889), Sudan (1898), and Tonga (South Pacific, 1900). Many of these were acquired during the so-called scramble for Africa in the mid-1880s. Africa had been opened up to Europeans by explorers, merchants, and missionaries earlier in the century. In the 1880s there followed diplomats and soldiers; thus explorers like Dr. David Livingstone and H. M. Stanley captured the imagination of people at home, while the imperial ambitions of Britain, Belgium, France, and Germany brought about annexation of vast territories. The European states codified the partition of Africa at a congress in Berlin in 1884–1885, when they declared that any European nation could acquire a piece of Africa simply by occupying it and notifying the other powers.

Despite the public popularity of imperialism, most of the leading British statesmen of the period were reluctant imperialists. British officials knew that annexation of territory was expensive. They much preferred informal to formal control, and when forced to annex a piece of land they preferred protectorates and spheres of influence to direct rule, wherever possible. Gladstone and his Liberal party were positively hostile to imperial expansion, and Gladstone devoted his famous Midlothian electoral campaigns of 1879 and 1880 to a crusade against Disraeli's "forward policy." But neither Gladstone nor any other respectable politician opposed the Empire *itself*, and everyone agreed that the government had to protect what Britain already owned and even to secure, by force if necessary, British interests around the world. Consequently, as foreign pressure and British anxiety built up, expansion went forward like an irresistible force. The Liberals between 1880 and 1885 thus added territory at the rate of 87,000 square miles a year—a far faster pace than the Conservatives recorded between 1874 and 1880.

At the same time, the Empire was profitable for the officials who ran it— approximately six thousand people—and provided employment for the 120,000 troops who patrolled it. It was rightly observed that the Empire was a source of employment—"a vast system of outdoor relief"—for the landed class. Increasingly, families of the civilian and military rulers of the Empire formed a self-conscious element within the British ruling elite, with influence at home as well as overseas.

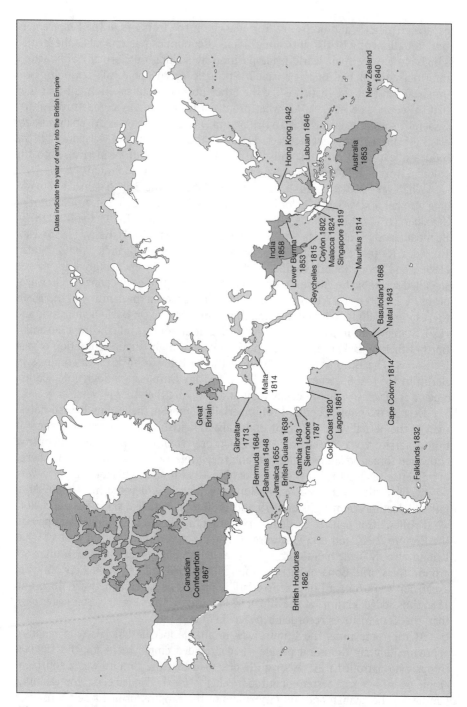

Dates indicate the year of entry into the British Empire

New Zealand 1840

Hong Kong 1842
Labuan 1846

Australia 1853

India 1858

Lower Burma 1853
Seychelles 1815
Ceylon 1802
Malacca 1824
Singapore 1819
Mauritius 1814

Basutoland 1868
Natal 1843

Cape Colony 1814

Malta 1814

Great Britain

Gibraltar 1713

Bermuda 1684
Bahamas 1648
Jamaica 1655
British Guiana 1638
Gambia 1843
Sierra Leone 1787
Gold Coast 1820
Lagos 1861

Falklands 1832

Canadian Confedertion 1867

British Honduras 1862

The growth of the British Empire, 1870–1920. Above, the British Empire in 1870

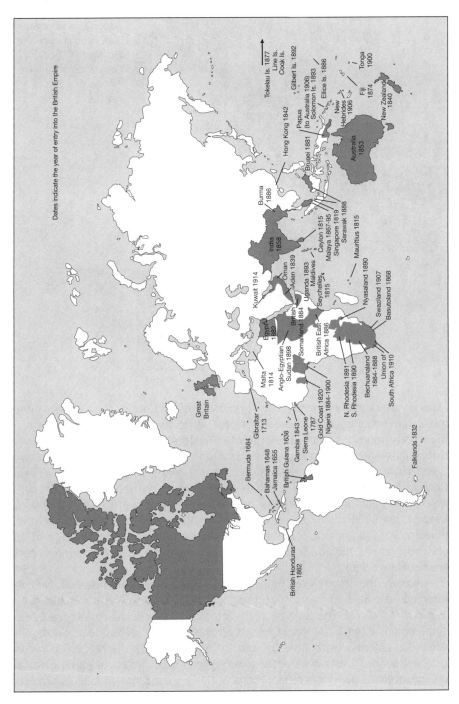

The British Empire in 1920

Imperial rivalry: the European powers and the United States show their envy over British imperial possessions.

Many investors and businessmen also profited from the Empire, most notably those involved in financing and developing colonial agriculture, mining, and public utilities. Their imperial profits went largely to investors from the upper class. But the British public at large had to pay the taxes that supported Britain's administration and defense of the colonies. Because even the white settlement colonies like Canada, Australia, and New Zealand were reluctant to share these costs, Britain's expenditures amounted to a subsidy paid to the colonials by the British taxpayers. In this sense, the British colonies exploited the Mother Country! India alone functioned as an ideal imperial possession: not only did India take an increasing portion of British exports, but also Indian taxpayers were required to pay for their own government and defense.

To make the Empire work more effectively in terms of both international politics and economic efficiency, a number of Britons from the 1870s on advocated imperial federation. The Empire in the late nineteenth century was a vast conglomeration of protectorates, Crown Colonies, spheres of influence, and self-governing colonies, with little to bind them together. The Imperial Federation League (founded 1884) was one prominent group that worked for closer political union (involving perhaps a rational constitution for the Empire) and for commercial unity. Joseph Chamberlain wanted to establish an imperial customs union, a huge free-trade area surrounded by a tariff wall; this lay behind his crusade for tariff reform after 1903. Yet the desire for imperial union came to little practical effect. The first Colonial Conferences were held in connection with Queen Victoria's jubilees in 1887 and 1897, but the colonial delegates who represented only the self-governing colonies would neither give up the autonomy they had won along with responsible government nor expose their own fledgling industries to British exports within a system of imperial free trade. They refused to contribute more to their own defense. It soon became apparent that the ties of empire between Britain and the self-governing colonies would be limited, as Lord Salisbury said, to "mutual good will, sympathy, and affection."

Meanwhile, the rapid colonial expansion of the European powers, including Britain, brought them into conflict with each other. Britain faced competition with Germany, for instance, in the Pacific, China, Southwest Africa, West Africa, and East Africa. In each case, German intrusion into the colonial scramble threatened some prior arrangements favoring British interests. In general, the British reacted by staking out their own claims and then reaching agreements with Germany by which each recognized the spheres of influence of the other. The most important example of this process occurred in East Africa, where the British thought that German imperialism threatened the headwaters of the Nile River—and therefore Egypt. To prevent that eventuality, the British claimed Uganda in 1888–1889, and in 1890 they traded to Germany the small North Sea island of Heligoland in return for German recognition of British control of Uganda.

British colonial conflict with the French promised to be more dangerous than rivalry with Germany. The French dreamed of establishing a North African empire across a broad belt of territory running east and west from the Sahara to the Red Sea. They were also angry about Britain's occupation of Egypt in 1882. For Britain, control of Egypt required control of the Nile south of Egypt; thus British and French interests clashed in the vast territory of the Sudan.

The British already had a major emotional investment in the Sudan. In the early 1880s, the Sudan was subordinate to Egypt, but the revolt of a puritanical Muslim sect led by Mohammed Ahmed ("The Mahdi") had ended effective Egyptian rule of the area. In 1884, Gladstone had recognized the collapse of Egyptian control in the Sudan and had sent a British general, Charles "Chinese" Gordon, to withdraw the last Egyptian forces from that desert wilderness. Alas, Gordon himself was a religious fanatic and a megalomaniac as well. He disobeyed his orders to withdraw, found himself besieged in Khartoum, and was slaughtered along with his garrison by the Mahdi in 1885. Gladstone came under fierce criticism by an outraged British public, but his government completed the withdrawal anyway—one of the few instances of a British decision to give up territory during the age of imperialism.

In the 1890s, the French sent an expedition under Captain Jean Marchand to occupy the Sudan. This roused the British lion to fresh action. Salisbury's government in 1898 dispatched a much larger force led by Sir Herbert Kitchener southward from Egypt. Kitchener's army took revenge on the Sudanese dervishes for Gordon's death, killing eleven thousand of them at Omdurman in less than five hours. According to Winston Churchill, who took part in the battle, it was "the most signal triumph ever gained by the arms of science over barbarians." Moving on up the Nile, Kitchener arrived at Fashoda a few days after Marchand. In Paris and London, tensions were high, and war was a distinct possibility. The French, however, were forced to withdraw, and they nursed their bitterness against Britain for half a decade.

THE SOUTH AFRICAN WAR, 1899–1902

The most serious colonial conflict Britain faced, however, was not with any European state but with the white settlers of Dutch descent in South Africa—the "Boers" or "Afrikaners." This conflict resulted in Britain's biggest war between the Crimean War and the First World War, and it revealed Britain's isolation and weakness. In this regard, as in the moral and political conflict it provoked at home, the Boer War was for Britain what Vietnam was later to be for the United States.

The conflict between Briton and Boer arose from different ideas of which white population should dominate southern Africa. The two peoples also differed in their views of the native African peoples: the British held a more paternalistic view and believed in theory at least that the black African could be "civilized," whereas the Boers believed that the Africans were an irretrievably "inferior" race. Racial views, however, did not prove to be the cause of war. The issue ultimately at stake was who would rule in the area. The British held two colonies in South Africa, the Cape Colony and Natal, and the British governor of the Cape Colony was also theoretically high commissioner over all the area. The Afrikaner farmers who had trekked from the Cape Colony in 1837–1838 had established two republics, the Orange Free State and the Transvaal. They were effectively independent of the British high commissioner, though the Boers knew that they would need British support if the Bantu peoples ever attacked them. To the west of the Boer republics lay Bechuanaland; to their north were the Matabele and Mashona peoples; and to their east was the well-organized Zulu military power.

British policy in South Africa had two principal goals: to keep safe the Cape route to India and to secure the Cape's hinterland. Conflict between the Africans and Boers made the hinterland insecure, and as British imperial ambitions heated up, they were increasingly inclined to take effective control of the whole area. In 1869, diamonds were discovered at Kimberley in Griqualand West, which both Britain and the Orange Free State claimed; the British annexed the territory. In 1877, an official of Disraeli's government annexed the Transvaal and got away with it, partly because the Transvaalers were concerned about the Zulus. In 1879, the long-expected war between the Zulus and the British broke out, and after one surprising loss in battle, the British crushed the Zulus at Ulundi. The destruction of Zulu power encouraged the Transvaalers to strive for independence. When it was not granted, the Transvaal revolted, dealing the redcoats a nasty defeat at Majuba Hill in 1881. Gladstone lived up to his moral opposition to the use of force for imperial expansion by giving independence to the Transvaal. But the settlement was left ambiguous, for the British still claimed "suzerainty"—an undefined degree of power—over all of southern Africa.

This shaky settlement between Britons and Boers was thrown into turmoil by the discovery of gold in Witwatersrand in the Transvaal in 1886. The gold mines, which were heavily taxed by the Afrikaner government, quickly turned the Transvaal into a prosperous state. By the 1890s, the Transvaal was buying modern weapons from abroad, mainly from Germany. These developments meant that one day the Transvaal instead of the Cape Colony might dominate southern Africa. At the same time, however, the gold attracted into the Transvaal thousands of English-speaking prospectors, who soon were as numerous as the Afrikaners themselves. The Transvaal government responded by denying the *uitlanders* (foreigners) political rights even while forcing them to pay taxes. In the minds of the British, the plight of the *uitlanders* offered a golden opportunity for overturning the Transvaal government.

Chief among the British imperialists who hoped to reannex the Transvaal was Cecil Rhodes, a self-made millionaire. Rhodes had parlayed his riches earned from the diamond and gold mines into political power in the Cape Colony. An Englishman who had originally come to South Africa for reasons of health, Rhodes indulged in fantastic dreams of British colonial dominion over all of Africa, much of the Middle East, the Pacific islands, and commercial settlements on the coasts of China and Japan. He even imagined that the United States could be recovered for the British Empire! To him Britain had to have a huge empire for markets and for employment of Britain's "surplus" population. "If you want to avoid civil war," he said, "you must become imperialists."

Among Rhodes's dreams was a British railway running through British territories from the Cape to Cairo. For him, then, the Orange Free State and the Transvaal stood as major obstacles. He had set out to circumscribe their influence, successfully urging on Britain the annexation of Bechuanaland in 1884 and sending troops from his British South Africa Company to occupy Matabeleland and Mashonaland in 1889. (The latter occupation soon became Rhodesia.) Now, in the 1890s, Rhodes sought to overturn the Transvaal government by instigating a rebellion of the *uitlanders*. In December 1895, with the tacit (and secret) approval of Chamberlain, the colonial secretary, Rhodes sent a column of his company's troops under Dr. Leander S. Jameson into the Transvaal. Unfortunately for Rhodes and the British, the Jameson raid failed because the *uitlanders* did not rise up, and only an official whitewash in Britain covered up Chamberlain's part in the sordid fiasco.

Rhodes found himself temporarily shelved by the Jameson disaster, but Chamberlain proved unrepentant. He and the British high commissioner in South Africa, Sir Alfred Milner, kept up the diplomatic pressure on the Transvaal. In 1899, the British preempted potential German support to the Transvaal by reaching an agreement with Germany over future division of the spoils if and when Portugal had to give up its colonies. In 1899, Milner moved British troops to the Transvaal borders.

Boer riflemen at the siege of Mafeking during the Boer War. Such troops punctured the pride of the vaunted British army.

When the Transvaal issued an ultimatum to Britain demanding withdrawal of the troops, Chamberlain and Milner had the war they wanted.

The South African War (1899–1902), however, did not proceed the way the British expected. British troops sailed for South Africa amid an outburst of popular patriotism. But the Boer army of less than 50,000 sharpshooters put up a spirited fight against the British army of some 400,000 men. The war passed through three phases. In the first (October 1899 to January 1900) the Boers inflicted several embarrassing defeats on stupidly commanded British forces, and they laid siege to Kimberley, Mafeking, and Ladysmith. In the second phase (the rest of 1900), the British, now effectively led by Field Marshall Lord Roberts and General Kitchener, defeated the Boer army and relieved the three besieged towns. By December 1900, the British thought the end of the war was in sight. In reality, it was only entering the third phase (1901–1902), in which the Boers resorted to hit-and-run guerrilla tactics. The British had no luck in cornering the Boer commandos and resorted to systematic sweeps through Boer territory to deny the support of the populace. British troops burned hundreds of farms and herded the population into concentration camps, in which about twenty thousand Afrikaners died of disease and malnutrition. Finally, the war closed with the Peace of Vereeniging in 1902, by which the Boers recognized British sovereignty, and the British promised eventually to restore self-government to the Boers. (The British promise was fulfilled in 1907, when the Orange Free State and the Transvaal recovered their autonomy within the British Empire. In 1910 the two Boer states joined the Cape Colony and Natal to form the Union of South Africa, a self-governing colony.)

Both abroad and at home the South African War, called the "Boer War" at the time, did Britain's reputation little good. The spectacle of Britain's inability to put down the little army of Afrikaner citizen-soldiers damaged Britain's image of invincibility in the minds of European statesmen. In Britain, the "pro-Boers," including the anti-imperialist section of the Liberal party led by the Gladstonian John Morley and the Welsh radical David Lloyd George, inveighed against the immorality of the whole affair. The pro-Boer Liberals differed sharply from the Liberal imperialists, who backed the war effort without flinching. The party leader, Henry Campbell-Bannerman, led a middle group of Liberals but came down on the side of the pro-Boers when he denounced the British scorched earth and concentration camp tactics as the "methods of Barbarism." The government won a big victory over the Liberals in the "khaki election" of 1900 when the war was going well, but in the long run the war eroded British confidence. Hence one important legacy of the South African War was the development of an anti-imperialist rationale, most notably expressed in *Imperialism: A Study* (1902), the potent critique of imperialism by the New Liberal theorist John A. Hobson. He argued that imperialism was not driven by noble motives but by the self-interest of a few overseas investors who manipulated public opinion and the British people as a whole. Hobson's book, of course, did not end the Empire or imperialism overnight, but it did contribute to the erosion of the imperial idea, which was gradually to fade in the twentieth century.

THE END OF ISOLATION

Weaknesses in Britain's military and international position exposed by the South African War had major repercussions. The South African War, in other words, brought to a head a number of concerns that had been growing since the 1870s about Britain's relative weakness in world affairs. On the one hand, the British were concerned about national defense and consequently reorganized and rebuilt their army and navy. On the other hand, the British began to feel strongly that as an isolated power they could no longer defend vital interests and therefore that alliances with other powers were needed.

Balfour's Conservative government (1902–1905) and its Liberal successors (1905–1914) alike sought to put British military forces on a sounder footing. As we will see in the next section, both Liberals and Conservatives engaged in a major buildup of the navy. Meanwhile, Chamberlain and other imperialists renewed their efforts to have the colonies take a share of Britain's heavy responsibilities. "The weary Titan," Chamberlain said in 1902, "staggers under the too vast orb of its fate." But the dominions (as the self-governing colonies were increasingly called) continued on the whole to refuse to contribute to Britain's military forces or to bind themselves in advance to support British foreign policy. The most that the British could accomplish was to set up in 1903 a Committee of Imperial Defense to improve consultations between Britain and the dominion governments. The Balfour government also set up for the first time in British history a general staff. Under Prime Minister Campbell-Bannerman, the Liberal secretary for war, R. B. Haldane, reorganized the army. He provided that six fully equipped divisions could be sent to Europe on short notice, backed the regular army with 300,000 well-trained "territorial" reservists, and promoted an Officer Training Corps in universities and public schools.

Britain, however, did not wish to become a thoroughly militarized society; hence the British recognized that the time had come to cut back on some commitments abroad. The tremendous growth of American power, for instance, meant that it was impossible for the British to contemplate a war in North America or to continue their dominant role in the waters of the Western Hemisphere. Hence the British from the 1890s on were inclined to settle their differences with the United States largely on American terms. Between 1895 and 1899, Britain and the United States settled a dispute over rival claims in Venezuela by agreeing to arbitration, Britain having recognized the validity of the Monroe Doctrine. The British then made no trouble for the United States during the Spanish-American War, and by the Hay-Pauncefote Treaty of 1901 the British conceded to America the right to build and control a canal across the Isthmus of Panama. Within a few years, Britain had withdrawn most of its warships from American waters and left the defense of British interests there to the United States navy.

Next came a treaty with Japan. Along with Britain and Russia, Japan had become one of the great powers in the Far East. By the early 1900s, Japan needed British neutrality in the likely event of a war with Russia over Korea or some other contested issue. The British for their part were gravely concerned about the Franco-Russian alliance of 1894, particularly in terms of naval strength, for in the Far East the combined French and Russian fleets would outnumber Britain's by a wide margin. If the British allied with Japan, they would win security in Asian waters and at the same time be enabled to strengthen the home fleet. In 1902, therefore, Britain and Japan pledged mutual aid should either be attacked by more than one power in Asia. By this treaty, the British gave up their cherished policy of isolation, which no longer seemed so splendid, and set terms in advance under which they would go to war.

Meanwhile, the Fashoda incident had finally taught both Britain and France that they needed to settle their colonial disputes. The French wished in particular to have a free hand in Morocco, and the British wanted to win recognition of their preeminence in Egypt. Like a treaty with Japan, a colonial agreement with France would greatly enhance British naval security. The outbreak of war between Japan and Russia in 1904 hurried Britain and French into agreement because neither Britain nor France wanted to be drawn into a Far Eastern war. King Edward VII contributed to Anglo-French friendship by his cosmopolitan manners in a visit to France. In April 1904, Britain signed an *entente* with France specifically covering colonial issues but opening the way for broader cooperation between these two ancient enemies.

Because France was already allied with Russia, a triangle of agreements could be completed among Britain, France, and Russia if the British could settle their differences with the Russians. As we have seen, Russia had long posed a serious threat to British interests in all the various aspects of "the Eastern Question" and specifically to British interests in Persia and Afghanistan and on the northwest frontier of India. As we will soon see, Britain was beginning to worry deeply about German intentions on the Continent and abroad. An understanding with Russia would bring relief to Britain whether in terms of the Eastern Question or of Germany. Thus after protracted discussions, Britain and Russia in 1907 reached a settlement of "colonial" disputes: Britain won Russian recognition of Afghanistan as a British sphere of influence; Russia won Britain's agreement not to annex Afghanistan outright; and the two powers divided Persia into zones of influence, Russian in the North and British in the South. By separate agreements, the British admitted that they would not resist eventual Russian control of Constantinople and the Straits, and the Russians recognized British control in the Persian Gulf. This settlement with another old rival completed Britain's diplomatic revolution: in place of isolation the British had now involved themselves in the European treaty system.

THE DRIFT INTO WAR, 1905–1914

Although the *entente* between Britain and Russia technically concerned colonial matters, the British statesmen who negotiated it had their eyes on Germany the whole time. By the early twentieth century, most British policymakers believed that Germany had become deliberately antagonistic toward Britain. For their part, many German statesmen thought that the British failed to recognize Germany's claim to a role in world affairs equal to their economic and cultural achievements. The rise of this Anglo-German antagonism was one of the key themes—perhaps an unavoidable one—in European history between 1890 and 1914. It explains how Britain's participation in the European treaty system, instead of keeping the British out of a general European war, eventually drew them into one.

The Anglo-German antagonism originated in the development of German rivalry to British supremacy in the world. As early as the 1870s members of the British ruling elite were expressing concern about the power of the German state, the superiority of the German educational system, and the growth of the German industrial economy. The British on the one hand tried to copy certain aspects of German culture, like research-oriented universities and a system of social security, and on the other hand they harbored deep resentment at Germany's rise in status. As we saw in Chapter 1, E. E. Williams argued in *Made in Germany* (1896) that German economic rivalry was "deliberate and deadly." Literary fantasies of German invasion of Britain became popular reading in Britain: *The Invasion of Dorking* (1871), *The Riddle of the Sands* (1903), and *The Invasion of 1910* (1906) to name a few. In the early 1900s this hostility toward Germany became entrenched among the permanent officials of the Foreign Office—most notably Eyre Crowe, the senior clerk, who was troubled by the essential role of force ("blood and iron") in the formation of Germany and by what he saw as the consistently anti-British stance of the German government. By 1907, his view that Britain must reassert its rights and power against Germany's policy of expansion was dominant in the policy-making circle of the British state.

Such a reading of German intentions since 1870 was not wholly true. Bismarck had wished to avoid alienating Britain and had regarded Germany as a satisfied power. Britain and Germany reached agreement in a number of colonial disputes.

The two nations even sporadically discussed the possibility of an alliance. Before the 1890s these discussions failed largely because the British did not wish to entangle themselves in alliances, and after 1890 the discussions failed mainly because the two powers had little to offer each other. Germany had needs on the Continent and Britain had needs overseas, and neither could do much to help the other. Chamberlain promoted an alliance with Germany in 1898–1899, but he hoped to win German support against Russia in the Far East, which the Germans had no interest in giving, and Lord Salisbury refused to commit Britain to the defense of Germany's interests in Europe. Similar inquiries into an Anglo-German alliance in 1901 also foundered. The result was only an increase of suspicion of Germany inside the British government.

The most important source of British antagonism toward Germany, however, was the rapid growth of the German navy. British power rested ultimately in the Royal Navy, and competition on the high seas appeared as a threat to Britain's most vital interest. Beginning in 1898, the Germans began building up their navy with the obvious intent of catching up with Britain. Inspired by the American Captain A. T. Mahan's *Influence of Sea Power upon History* (first published in 1890) and by the prevailing ideas of the day about the interrelationship of industry, colonies, and national power, Kaiser Wilhelm II and his chief naval planner, Admiral von Tirpitz, decided that a great navy was necessary for Germany to claim its rightful "place in the sun." Successive expansive German naval building programs inevitably threatened British maritime superiority, and Tirpitz aggravated the situation by concentrating a so-called risk fleet in the North Sea—a fleet that the British could not take the risk of failing to cover with its own fleet, and therefore a means of diverting British ships from other oceans. The British might have reached an alliance with Germany on condition that Germany cut back on naval construction. As late as 1912, R. B. Haldane appealed to the Germans on these terms. But the German emperor was adamant: Germany would have a big navy because all great nations do.

The British, however, would not and could not be outbuilt in ships by the Germans. The British, after all, did not have to maintain a large standing army as did the Germans, and thus they could devote their defense spending largely to the navy. As Lord Esher, government official and military reformer, said in 1912: "Whatever the cost may be, it is cheaper than a conscript army and an entangling alliance." The British steadily improved and increased the British fleet, adopting the dominant design of the day—the all-big-gun *Dreadnought* class of battleship—in 1906 and building twenty of them (against Germany's thirteen) by 1914.

At the same time as naval rivalry worsened relations between Britain and Germany, so also did German international behavior. After the British and French made their *entente cordiale* in 1904, the Germans hoped to break it down by diplomatic pressure. In 1905, Kaiser Wilhelm visited Morocco and demanded that the entente's Moroccan provisions be abandoned. But instead of crumpling British support for France, the Moroccan crisis strengthened it. At an international conference

British naval power at its peak: The Channel Squadron, *by E. de Martineau (1912).*

at Algeciras in 1906, the British stood by the French, and at the same time the two governments began to hold secret military staff talks that would eventually transform the nature of the *entente*. A second Moroccan crisis in 1911, caused by Germany's dispatch of a gun boat to Agadir in Morocco, had the same effect of driving Britain and France closer together.

The Anglo-French staff talks went on from 1905 to 1914. They were officially authorized by Sir Edward Grey, who was foreign secretary to both Campbell-Bannerman and Asquith from 1905 to 1914. Grey is not an easy figure for historians to analyze: a Liberal imperialist but not an ideologue, Grey was apparently a simple, aristocratic fisherman and birdwatcher, but underneath his Northumberland country gentleman's appearance, he was a clever and secretive diplomatist. Under the pressure of events—trades disputes, suffragettes, the revolt of the Lords, Irish nationalism, and the like—Asquith was content to leave foreign affairs to him, and Grey increasingly became pro-French and highly suspicious of Germany. He regarded the German naval buildup as proof of Germany's anti-British intent: "If the German Navy ever became superior to ours, the German Army can conquer this country. There is no corresponding risk of this kind to Germany: for however superior our fleet was, no naval victory would bring us nearer to Berlin."

Grey did not tell the cabinet of the staff talks until 1911 (although both prime ministers he served under knew of them), and even then he insisted that the discussions did *not* amount to a formal alliance with France. However, he did believe that the *entente cordiale* and the staff talks represented a moral commitment. That feeling was deepened in 1912 when by agreement France concentrated its fleet in the Mediterranean, and Britain removed most of its own Mediterranean fleet to the North Sea. Grey also believed that the British public would not stand by to see France defeated by Germany as in 1870, and he personally thought that the public was right in this view. Grey came to think that the defense of France was the defense of Britain because a Europe subservient to Germany would be intolerable to Britain. Yet he also believed—no doubt fooling himself on this point—that because Britain still had not signed a formal military and political alliance with France (or with Russia), Britain still retained freedom of action and could play the role of an honest broker. As events would finally teach Grey, he could not have it both ways.

By 1907, then, the states of Europe, including Britain, had locked themselves into a pair of antagonistic alliances—the Triple Alliance and the Triple *Entente*—which had the dangerous quality of intricate mechanisms: once one part was set in motion the other cogs and wheels would have to grind as well. Furthermore, each state was dependent on the others in its alliance and therefore on the weakest and least responsible partner. Germany was dependent on Austria-Hungary, even though the dual monarchy was deeply troubled by its unhappy ethnic groups and especially by the restlessness of the Slavic nationalities of southeastern Europe. Britain was dependent on Russia, even though Russian ambitions to be the protector of Balkan Slavic peoples threatened to clash with Austro-Hungarian interests. Further, the increase in armaments in all the states had created an atmosphere of fear and suspicion—not least in Britain and Germany. The alliance system and the armaments race together made all of the powers to varying degrees dependent on the advice of military and naval officers and on their tactical plans and timetables. The very internal dynamics of this system moved irresistibly toward war.

War between Austria-Hungary and Russia over some Balkan issue might have flared up on a number of occasions. In 1908, for instance, Austria annexed the Turkish province of Bosnia, which infuriated the Russians and their Balkan client state, Serbia. War was avoided only when the Russian foreign minister backed down. Then in October 1912, four Balkan states long at odds with Turkey—Serbia, Bulgaria, Greece, and Montenegro—formed an alliance, went to war with Turkey, and prepared to split up the winnings. Austria-Hungary and Russia felt they had to intervene, and the other great powers were barely able to enforce a settlement—which soon fell apart in a second Balkan war in 1913. That neither of these two wars resulted in a general conflict between the two alliances was due largely to the restraint exercised by Germany on Austria and by Britain on Russia. Unfortunately, such restraint was seen within each alliance as weakening that alliance and therefore as something that must not be tried again.

When, therefore, a Serbian nationalist assassinated the Austrian heir apparent, Archduke Franz Ferdinand, in Sarajevo (Bosnia) on June 28, 1914, the necessary restraint was missing. Three weeks later, in a move calculated to end the Serbian problem once and for all, Austria issued to Serbia an ultimatum that would have effectively destroyed Serbian independence. Already, the German government had resolved to back the Austrians' extreme measure and to support Austria if Russia then attacked. When the Russians began to mobilize their forces, various national war plans were set in motion. Germany declared war on Russia on August 1; because the German war plan—originally designed by Count von Schlieffen in 1892—specified that Germany must attack France through Belgium before turning on the much slower, more cumbersome Russian army, the Germans invaded Belgium on August 3.

The Austrian ultimatum to Serbia thus caused a Balkan war, and the alliance system turned it into a Continental war. What was Britain to do? The rapid march of events after June 28 caught the British politicians and public alike by surprise, for their attention was riveted on the converging crises of domestic politics—labor unrest, Home Rule, and Ulster resistance. Grey knew that if the Germans did not restrain Austria in their demands on Serbia then Europe would be "within measurable distance of a real Armageddon. " Yet he still thought that the *entente* with France and Russia did not *require* British military action. Once the cabinet began to focus on unfolding events in Europe, they were deeply divided as to whether Britain should intervene in the war. They did agree, however, that the British navy should defend the French coast from German attack. But when Germany invaded Belgium, the cabinet united quickly in favor of intervention; only two cabinet members resigned, John Morley and John Burns. The same feeling of sympathy for "little Belgium" also persuaded Parliament and public opinion that Britain must fight. Thus Britain entered the war with a high degree of unity: on August 4, crowds in Whitehall and Downing Street sang "God Save the King" as the time expired for a German reply to the British ultimatum. In subsequent days most politicians and newspapers pledged enthusiastic support of the war effort. Indeed, the outbreak of war to many Britons seemed a relief from the mounting strain of domestic conflict.

The German invasion of Belgium, therefore, was decisive for British opinion. Asquith and Grey did not need the Belgian issue to persuade themselves that Britain must intervene. They had come to believe that a German defeat of France would allow Germany not only to dominate the Continent but also to turn its massive resources to the construction of a larger navy. A German victory on the Continent would therefore be disastrous to British interests. As Grey told the cabinet, not only honor but also "substantial obligations of policy" required them to back the French. Grey had not been candid with either the cabinet or the House of Commons, but he was steady in his own views. Thus it was neither the *entente cordiale* nor Belgium that in *his* view ultimately required Britain's entry into the war, but Grey used those points effectively for his own purposes at the moment of crisis. If Asquith and Grey had known how terrible the war would be, and how destructive to British strength, they might have kept Britain out. But no European statesman anticipated how long and costly the war would be; none realized that it would change the world permanently.

Suggested Reading

Bates, Darrell, *The Fashoda Incident of 1898. Encounter on the Nile* (Oxford: Oxford University Press, 1984).

Beloff, Max, *Imperial Sunset, Vol. 1: Britain's Liberal Empire, 1897–1921* (London: Methuen, 1969).

Bourne, Kenneth, *The Foreign Policy of Victorian England, 1830–1902* (Oxford: Clarendon Press, 1970).

Brown, Judith M., and W. Roger Louis, eds., *The Twentieth Century*, vol. 4 of *The Oxford History of the British Empire*. ed. W. Roger Louis (Oxford: Oxford University Press, 1999).

Cox, Jeffrey, *Imperial Fault Lines: Christianity and Colonial Power in India, 1818–1940* (Stanford: Stanford University Press, 2002).

Friedberg, Aaron L., *The Weary Titan: Britain and the Experience of Relative Decline, 1895–1905* (Princeton: Princeton University Press, 1988).

Gilmour, David, *The Ruling Caste: Imperial Lives in the Victorian Raj* (London: John Murray, 2006).

Grenville, J. A. S., *Lord Salisbury and Foreign Policy* (London: University of London, Athlone Press, 1964).

Headrick, Daniel, *The Tools of Empire: Technology and European Imperialism in the Nineteenth Century* (New York: Oxford University Press, 1981).

Huttenback, Robert A., and Lance E. Davis, *Mammon and the Pursuit of Empire* (Cambridge: Cambridge University Press, 1986).

Kennedy, Paul M., *The Rise and Fall of British Naval Mastery* (London: Allen Lane, 1976).

———, *The Rise of the Anglo-German Antagonism, 1860–1014* (London: Allen & Unwin, 1980).

Krebs, Paula, *Gender, Race, and the Writing of Empire: Public Discourse and the Boer War* (Cambridge: Cambridge University Press, 1999).

Lowe, C. J., *The Reluctant Imperialists: British Foreign Policy, 1878–1902* (2 vols.) (London: Routledge & Kegan Paul, 1967).

Lowe, C. J., and M. L. Dockrill, *The Mirage of Power: British Foreign Policy, 1902–14* (London: Routledge & Kegan Paul, 1972).

Marder, A. J., *From the Dreadnought to Scapa Flow: The Royal Navy in the Fisher Era, 1904–1919* (5 vols.) (London: Oxford University Press, 1961–1970).

Nasson, Bill, *The South African War* (London: Hodder Arnold, 1999).

Packenham, Thomas, *The Boer War* (London: Weidenfield & Nicolson, 1979).

Porter, Bernard, *Britain, Europe and the World, 1850–1982* (London: Allen & Unwin, 1983).

———, *Critics of Empire* (London: Macmillian, 1968).

———, *The Lion's Share: A Short History of British Imperialism, 1859–1970* (London: Longman, 2004).

Price, Richard, *An Imperial War and the British Working Class* (London: Routledge & Kegan Paul, 1972).

Roberts, Brian, *Cecil Rhodes: Flawed Colossus* (London: Hamish Hamilton, 1987).

Robinson, Ronald E., and John Gallagher, *Africa and the Victorians* (New York: St. Martin's, 1961).

Rotberg, Robert I., *The Founder: Cecil Rhodes and the Pursuit of Power* (Oxford: Oxford University Press, 1988).

Spiers, E. M., *Haldane: An Army Reformer* (Edinburgh: Edinburgh University Press, 1981).

Steiner, Zara, *Britain and the Origins of the First World War* (New York: St. Martin's, 1977).

———, *The Foreign Office and Foreign Policy, 1885–1914* (London: Cambridge University Press, 1969).

Williamson, Samuel R., *The Politics of Grand Strategy: Britain and France Prepare for War, 1904–1914* (Cambridge, Mass., Harvard University Press, 1969).

Part II

An Age of
Total War

1914–1945

Chapter 6

The Great War, 1914–1918

Mass participation in world wars and the consequent losses in human and material resources were overarching themes in the history of Great Britain between 1914 and 1945. Two total wars, 1914–1918 and 1939–1945, stood as bookends around two decades of depression, and the depression itself was caused in large part by the damage done to the world economy by the first of these world wars. Seen in this light, the whole period of thirty-odd years after 1914 appear depressing and dispiriting. Yet in Britain this age of total war had paradoxical results: although the wars caused catastrophic losses in blood and treasure and accelerated the decline of British economic and political power in the world, they also contributed to the rapid advance of democracy and social welfare. The wars also called forth some of Britain's most gallant efforts. If this period encompassed Britain's lowest moments, it also included some of its finest hours.

The two world wars may well be seen by future historians as phases of the same conflict, a struggle by Britain and the Allies against Germany's bid for mastery over Europe. But from our relatively close vantage point, the First World War was a distinct, and distinctly terrible, historical event. It was known by contemporaries as "the Great War" because many Britons believed that it was a war to end all wars and because everyone recognized that it was an occurrence of cataclysmic proportions. As the first industrialized conflict, the Great War involved larger armies, more resources, more devastating machines, and more civilian effort than any war in European history. Though the British suffered less than the other great powers of Europe, they nevertheless became totally mobilized, sent abroad a huge army, and sustained losses unprecedented in British history. In a sense, in both material and psychological terms, they never completely recovered from it. As one Conservative politician wrote in 1921: "There are certain great historic events, like the Protestant Reformation and the French Revolution, that have altered mankind for good. The war was one of those far-reaching forces."

Sir Edward Grey observed on the evening of August 4, 1914, as time expired on Britain's ultimatum to Germany, "The lamps are going out all over Europe; we shall not see them lit again in our time." Given the tragedy of the next four years, this was a very prescient remark. Yet historians are not by any means agreed on the overall impact of the Great War on British history. Some say it was a "great discontinuity" that changed everything: it damaged Britain's economy beyond repair, destroyed Victorian confidence and conventional religious faith, killed the Liberal party while promoting Labour to take its place, advanced the cause of women, and introduced major elements of the welfare state. Other historians contend that the war only accelerated trends already in place and that such changes as occurred would have happened anyway. But to choose either of these interpretations at the expense of the other ignores two crucial points: (1) the war operated differentially on different trends—it accelerated some but delayed others; and (2) the urgent pressures of the war took long-term choices out of the hands of the policymakers who had to make decisions to further the immediate war effort, regardless of the long run. The Great War brought about an abrupt end to many Victorian institutions and practices, and the abruptness itself was a major feature of human experience.

THE COURSE OF WAR, 1914–1916

In August 1914, very few people in Britain expected a long war. Most expected the highly professional British Expeditionary Force (BEF), the result of Haldane's army reforms, to defeat the German thrust through Belgium. The BEF would take its place on the north (that is, left) end of the French defensive line and roll back the German army's advance in northern France and Flanders. As the BEF stopped the German right flank, the French would attack the German center in Lorraine. Together, the British and French would push the Germans out of France in a few months' time; meanwhile, the British navy would enforce a close blockade on German ports and defeat Tirpitz's High Seas fleet in one great battle. The Germans would soon be forced to ask for peace.

Unfortunately, the British plan went wrong from the beginning. The French offensive failed. The six divisions of the BEF (nearly ninety thousand men commanded by Sir John French) in northern France and Flanders were crumpled by the German onslaught. The British fought well at Mons (just across the border in Belgium) but were forced to retreat rapidly southward as the German offensive swung like a huge gate south and west toward Paris. The combined British and French armies were barely able to protect Paris, but then they managed to push the Germans back to a point about 50 miles from Paris. Next, in September 1914, the British and German armies tried to outflank each other by successive rapid moves to the north. These attempts failed, as the two armies soon reached the Channel coast. In October, the British tried to break through the German lines in Flanders, at the Belgian town of Ypres, but their attack ran headlong into a German offensive and failed. Thereafter, the war on the "Western Front" settled into a stalemate, and both sides began to entrench themselves.

By November 1914, the lines of trenches stretched 300 miles northward from the Swiss border through Flanders to the Channel. Between October 1914 and spring 1917, the front did not move more than 10 miles in either direction, even though each side hurled itself in massive, bloody assaults on the other. The weapons of defense—machine guns, barbed wire, and heavy artillery—held a great advantage over the offense. Deeply dug in and deployed in several parallel trench

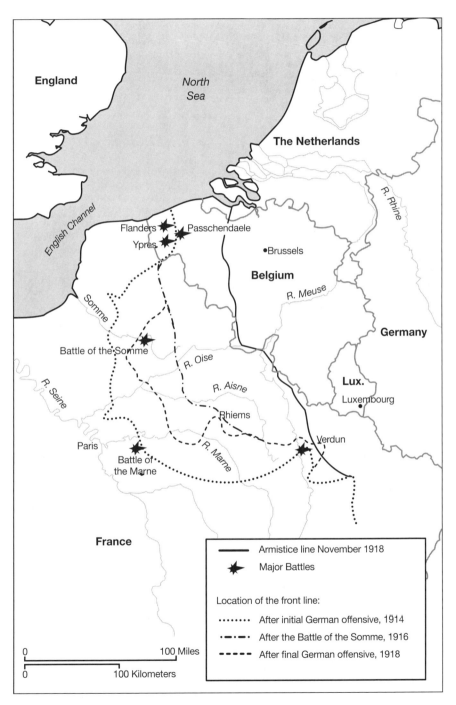

The Western Front during World War I

The famous recruiting poster of 1914, featuring Lord Kitchener: "Your Country Needs You."

lines from front line to rear areas, defensive forces could be made miserable but not crushed. Generals on both sides, however, cherished the dream of breaking through the enemy's defenses and so recovering a "war of movement." Thus the war in France became a series of alternating massive attacks and desperate defenses, as commanding generals sought to amass enough men and material for the one "knockout blow."

The British lost eighty-nine thousand men on the Western Front in 1914, which effectively destroyed their professional army. In late 1914 and early 1915, the British had to recruit a new army of some two million men. Cherishing its Liberal principles, the Asquith government relied entirely on volunteers. Conscription, the Liberals thought, would overstep the limits of government compulsion over the individual. The secretary for war appointed at the outbreak of the fighting, Lord Kitchener, was already a national hero. He made a personal appeal for volunteers and became the symbol of Britain's war effort when his imposing face appeared on a recruiting poster declaring "Your country needs YOU." Inspired by innocent patriotism, recruits came forward by the thousands, even though Kitchener did not at first have the means to train or equip them. The army had agreed that those who joined together would stay together in their units; hence the volunteers were organized into "Pals' Battalions" and kept their local and regional identity even when sent to the Western Front. Only partially trained, Kitchener's new army was dispatched to France in 1916. By the spring of 1916, the BEF stood at 1.5 million men—the largest government enterprise of any kind to that point in British history. At the same time, the British Empire also began to send forces—Indians, Canadians, Australians, and New Zealanders.

Until the new British army could be mobilized and trained, the French had to bear the brunt of the fighting against Germany. The BEF carried out two offensives in 1915, both of them failures. These futile assaults revealed severe shortages of artillery guns and shells. So serious was this "shell scandal," as we will see, that Lloyd George was made minister of munitions. Eventually, by his prodigious energy and unorthodox methods, Lloyd George corrected the munitions problem, although British troops suffered for more than a year from defective shells.

Kitchener and the government realized that the Allies for the time being would not be able to win a breakthrough in France. The alternative was to attack on some other front, preferably in an area where the German army was not so strong and where the British could take advantage of sea power. The area chosen—and enthusiastically promoted by the first lord of the admiralty, Winston Churchill—was the Gallipoli Peninsula on the Dardanelles Straits near Constantinople. The concept was that if the British could seize the Straits and take Constantinople, they could knock Turkey (a German ally) out of the war and bring aid to beleaguered Serbia and Russia. The government was soon embroiled in a bitter controversy over diverting troops from the Western Front to Gallipoli; hence they initially tried to force the Straits by ships alone. The purely naval attack in the Straits failed, however, as the British lost three battleships to Turkish mines. The government realized that only an amphibious assault on Gallipoli could succeed. Alas, the British invasion of Gallipoli (April 1915) was hastily planned and poorly supported. Despite backbreaking efforts by nearly half a million British, French, and Australian-New Zealand (ANZAC) troops, the Turks held firm, and the invasion ground to a halt in trench warfare. Finally, in December 1915, the Allied forces were withdrawn, the army having lost over 200,000 casualties.

In December 1915, Sir Douglas Haig replaced General French as commander of the BEF in France. Haig was a Lowland Scottish Presbyterian, with all the stolid, serious stubbornness of his breed. He was an unimaginative man, but he was courageous and determined. No one ever *looked* the part of a commanding general better than Haig, who was fit, erect, and handsome. Haig knew that his army would not be fully trained for an offensive until late summer of 1916. However, the French needed relief from German pressure because they were being drained dry by a German attack on Verdun. General Joffre, the French commander-in-chief, appealed to Haig for an early attack. Haig thus agreed to a massive assault in northern France, on the River Somme, even though his army was not yet up to the level of the German veterans they faced.

The Battle of the Somme (July 1–November 18, 1916) was one of the most terrible of the war and justifiably earned a place in British literary and popular culture alike for its horrors. Fourteen British and five French divisions attacked well-entrenched Germans along an 18-mile front. The assault was preceded by a week of artillery shelling, but the artillery failed both to cut the Germans' barbed wire and to crush their trenches. The British troops thus were caught in the open by murderous machine gun fire and artillery barrages. By the end of the first day, the British had suffered sixty thousand casualties, including twenty thousand dead. Attack followed counterattack for 140 days. By the time Haig shut down the offensive, the

British and imperial forces had lost 415,000 casualties—all for the advance of a few miles.

The year 1916 was equally frustrating for the navy. German submarines had made a close blockade of German ports untenable, but a more distant blockade sufficed. The Royal Navy swept the seas of the few German surface warships, cut off German shipping, and at the same time bottled up the German fleet. The British Grand Fleet still outnumbered the German High Seas Fleet by a substantial margin, but both sides desired a full-scale showdown between the main battle fleets. Neither, however, wished to fight except under favorable conditions. At last, at the end of May 1916, the German fleet emerged from port in an attempt to lure the British into a trap. The two fleets met in the North Sea off Jutland, and in a battle characterized by caution and confusion on both sides, dealt each other severe punishment. The Germans sank six British cruisers while losing one battleship and one cruiser and suffering major damage on a number of other large ships. The British evaded the trap and the Germans returned to port; they did not emerge again in force during the war.

The British commander at Jutland, Admiral Jellicoe, received much criticism for not pressing home the attack in the Nelson tradition. But as has often been observed, Jellicoe was the one man who could have lost the war in one afternoon. The strategic situation dictated "safety first" to Jellicoe, for as long as his Grand Fleet existed, the German fleet had to lie low, and as long as the German fleet was in port, the British could supply their troops in France and import materiel across the Atlantic. The best remark on Jutland was made by an American journalist: "The German Fleet has assaulted its jailer; but it is still in jail."

THE COMBAT EXPERIENCE

Combat under any conditions is bound to be a terrible experience, but warfare on the Western Front during the Great War was peculiarly horrifying. The experience of trench warfare was seared into the British psyche and became, as we will see in Chapter 8, an underlying nightmare in the modern imagination. The futility of even the bravest attacks, the impotence of individual efforts against the machines of war, the wasted landscape, the seeming inevitability of death were qualities that dominated the combat experience of millions of British soldiers.

Trench war was a new and unexpected kind of conflict. The Allies and Germans faced each other from their trenches, sometimes a mile or so apart, sometimes no more than 50 yards. In between the opposing trenches, "no-man's-land" was contested area, and even at "quiet" times the Allies and Germans crept out into no-man's-land to reconnoiter the enemy's position, listen to the unseen activities, carry out raids, and take prisoners. In their trenches near Ypres, the British lost seven thousand men a day even when they were not being attacked or attacking; staff officers called these losses "wastage." Trenches were dug in roughly parallel rows of three—the front or firing trench, backed up by support trenches. All were connected by communications trenches. The front trench normally was 6 to 8 feet

Trench warfare: a British trench at the Somme, 1916.

deep, with a "firing step" of a foot or two from which riflemen could fight. If one looked over the parapet of sandbags at the lip of the trench during daylight, he was sure to be cut down by a sniper. Thus life went on in what Professor Paul Fussell calls a "Troglodyte World"—men digging, burrowing, always moving out of sight in daytime and crawling out to patrol and fight only at night. The British trenches, unlike the German, tended to be wet, cold, and filthy, overrun with rats and often revealing the skeletons and rotting limbs of half-buried dead.

Both strategy and tactics on the Western Front were simple. Because the Germans occupied French territory, they had to be driven out; hence the British and French had to take the initiative. But industrial technology had given all the advantages to the defense. The machine gun was the new queen of battle, for it could from entrenched strong points, and with a minimum of tending by its operators, send an unbroken stream of bullets down the length of no-man's-land. In addition, the defense's heavy artillery could lay down precise barrages of high explosives and steel on the attacking troops. The only hope for attacking forces to have any chance against the enemy's trenches was for their own artillery to throw such a tremendous weight of shells on them that the machine guns would be destroyed and the defenders either killed or paralyzed by shock. Ideally, the attackers' artillery fire by the techniques of a "rolling barrage" could move steadily forward in front of them. In 1915 poison gas added its peculiar terror to the offensive technology. Attacking troops, therefore, could in theory go "over the top" of their own trench, quickly cross no-man's-land, and seize the enemy's trench by hand-to-hand fighting.

Attacking troops, however, normally found that the preliminary artillery bombardment did not work. Each side learned to dig bomb shelters at key points in their trenches. These dug-out rooms, sunk 20 feet or more into the ground and reinforced by timbers and concrete, gave protection to troops and machine guns from the bombardments. Battles thus became races once the opening artillery fire lifted: the attacking troops tried to cross no-man's-land—invariably a lunar landscape of shell craters, churned-up terrain, and barbed wire—before the machine gun crews dug their way out of shattered bomb shelters and ran up the steps to their gun emplacements. If the machine gun crews managed to set up their guns while the attackers were still in no-man's-land, they could cut them down like hay before a scythe.

The solution for trench warfare eventually would be the tank, a kind of self-propelled, armored, trench-crushing artillery piece. Unfortunately for the British, the engineers and armaments manufacturers were not able to develop and produce tanks quickly enough to have a decisive effect in the Great War. The British began experimenting with armored tractors in 1915, but after some early failures Kitchener's War Office gave up the idea. Thereafter, development of the tank was pushed by Winston Churchill, the immensely energetic first lord of the admiralty, until his resignation over Gallipoli in May 1916. Tanks were first committed to battle in September 1916, but they broke down too easily and the army never had enough of them.

The two greatest offensives in which the British were involved before 1918 illustrate these points: the Somme (1916) and Passchendaele (1917). The Battle of the Somme took place in what had been the rolling farmland of northern France. On most of the battlefield, the opposing trenches were only 500 yards apart, and the British believed that a preliminary barrage of seven days, in which 1.5 million shells would blast the German trenches, would enable the British troops to cross no-man's-land and simply occupy the German position. The British troops, however, were mostly volunteers of the "Pals' Battalions" and not well enough trained to do anything but walk across no-man's-land. Their company officers, many of them former public school boys, thought it was the duty of their working-class troops to do the killing, while they themselves walked in advance—and unarmed. As we have seen, the British artillery bombardment failed to cut the German wire or destroy their trenches. The German machine gunners won the race to their parapets and proceeded to mow down Kitchener's volunteers in waves. One British officer later surveying the field found "line after line of dead men lying where they had fallen." Most of the twenty thousand killed on that first day, a disproportionate number of whom were junior officers, died in the first hour.

Haig remained confident that he could find a way to break through the German line even after the Somme disaster. He rightly thought that the tank would provide the answer, but he overestimated the number that could be supplied. In the summer of 1917, Haig planned to use massed tanks to smash the German defense near Ypres in Belgium. To give the tanks a level field in which to maneuver, he would omit the usual preliminary bombardment. But production problems limited the number of tanks actually delivered to Haig; therefore, he decided to open with a bombardment after all. The shelling and an exceptionally heavy rain turned the battlefield into a treacherous bog. Into this nightmarish quagmire the British attacked in August 1917. The offensive was a total failure. The British suffered 250,000 casualties in four months, and the hideous mud took its own share of the victims. The British poet Siegfried Sassoon, who participated in the battle, wrote:

> . . . I died in hell
> (They called it Passchendaele) my wound was slight
> And I was hobbling back; and then a shell
> Burst slick upon the duckboards; so I fell
> Into the bottomless mud, and lost the light.

Said one staff officer on seeing the battlefield for the first time: "Good God, did we really send men to fight in that?"

The experience of trench warfare left permanent scars on the psyche of many a British "Tommy." It cruelly ended the high expectations and idealism with which so many marched off to war in 1914 and 1915 and replaced them with bitterness and a sense of irony. The young Cambridge poet Rupert Brooke expressed the early British enthusiasm for the war in "Peace" (1914):

> Now, God be thanked Who has matched us with His hour,
> And caught our youth, and wakened us from sleeping,
> With hand made sure, clear eye, and sharpened power,
> To turn, as swimmers into cleanness leaping.

But Brooke died of blood poisoning in 1915 on his way to Gallipoli. Soldiers discovered that the conventional reasons given for war were frauds—high patriotic ideals, religion, the flag—and that what kept them going was leadership, discipline, and loyalty to one's comrades.

The combatants felt separated by their experience from all other people, whether civilians or staff officers. Sassoon wrote:

> "Good-morning; good-morning"! The General said
> When we met him last week on our way to the line.
> Now the soldiers he smiled at are most of 'em dead,
> And we're cursing his staff for incompetent swine.

THE HOME FRONT

Idealism and enthusiasm for the war lasted longer at home than at the front. To be sure, there was from the beginning a significant antiwar movement in Britain. It never numbered more than a minority of intellectuals and political activists, but it included both Liberals and socialists who thought that Britain had no good reason to go to war or that the war had been caused by the international system itself, with its secret treaties, its bloated armaments, and its obsolete aristocratic wirepullers. Sylvia Pankhurst was a pacifist. Most of the Bloomsbury Group opposed the war, and Bertrand Russell lost his post at Cambridge and served a term in jail for his opposition. Ramsay MacDonald, chairman of the parliamentary Labour party, was forced by his party to resign his office because he opposed the war. A number of Liberals and socialists founded the Union of Democratic Control (UDC) to lobby for a negotiated end to the war and for open, democratic foreign affairs. Others founded the No-Conscription Fellowship to resist the introduction of a military draft. They became "conscientious objectors" to combat service; eventually over fifteen thousand men took this position, and over a third of them were imprisoned. On the whole, however, the vast majority of Britons supported the war effort. Only the Irish, as we will see in Chapter 7, proved less than enthusiastic.

Over time even ordinary patriotic civilians became frustrated by the lack of success on the Continent and at sea, and many finally gave in to dull despair because of the relentless flow of daily casualty lists. British civilians did receive occasional attacks from German warships and Zeppelins but all told suffered only 5,600 casualties from German action. But the British armed forces lost an average of 1,500 casualties *a day* for 4.5 years, and hardly a family was left unscathed. Added to the restrictions, shortages, and rationing brought on by the war, the casualty lists of husbands, fathers, sons, and lovers created an atmosphere of bleakness and exhaustion.

Public policy evolved from "business as usual" to massive state intervention in economy and society. To pay for the war, the base income tax was doubled in the first few months and then raised by another 40 percent within a year; the surtax also went up rapidly. Overall, the income tax went up by 500 percent during the war, and annual government expenditures increased by almost 700 percent. The government took the country off the gold standard right away and eventually adopted protective tariffs and took over the railways and shipping. The munitions crisis of 1915 led to government possession of the munitions factories and by 1918 to government ownership or control over coal mines, fuel oil refineries, and factories that produced airplanes, agricultural machinery, and industrial chemicals. All of this was done with the cooperation of big businessmen who accepted wartime "collectivism" in return for a government guarantee of profits. In the spring of 1918, the government adopted a national rationing scheme. By then, the government was buying and distributing over 90 percent of British imports.

The main mechanisms of government control were the three Defense of the Realm Acts (DORA) passed in 1914 and 1915. These extraordinary measures gave the government broad control over society, including the power to stop virtually any activity it pleased. Civil liberties as well as industry were thus subjected to government control. Eventually, DORA was used not only to direct the allocation of resources for industrial production but also to control the labor supply, restrict the consumption of certain goods, suspend holidays, and defend against leaks of national secrets. Yet, although some Liberals objected to DORA on grounds that the acts were illegitimate intrusions into individual lives, on the whole DORA was not abused by the government.

Undoubtedly the greatest intrusion by the government into private lives was conscription. Voluntary enlistment began to fall off in the middle of 1915, but the government knew that another two million men were available. Conservatives and other politicians anxious to press the war effort without restraint urged the introduction of conscription. Asquith resisted but finally had to give in. Parliament passed a measure providing for the draft of bachelors in January 1916. That act proved unable to supply enough bodies for the war's insatiable appetite, and by spring 1916 pressure was rising for general conscription. There was some public opposition from the No-Conscription Fellowship and from some Labourites, for a Labour conference had voted against compulsion earlier in 1916. But the demands of the army were irresistible; hence, in May 1916 an act made all men between the ages of eighteen and forty-one subject to conscription (later the upper limit was raised to age fifty-one). By the end of the war, six million of the ten million in that age group served in the armed forces—the highest rate of wartime participation in British history to that time.

The number of people who were in effect mobilized for the war effort was even greater. War production was almost as important as the fighting itself, which meant that the labor force had to be augmented and deployed effectively. Because many workers went into uniform at the same time as production was being stimulated, the demand for labor grew rapidly. Unemployment and underemployment, two of the chronic failings of the old economy, quickly disappeared. Workers held a strong position and consequently enjoyed higher wages. Prices also increased, and although wage increases overall more than compensated for prices, workers grew restless from time to time. Trade union officials reached an agreement with the government early in 1915 whereby the unions gave up for the duration of the war the right to strike and agreed to "dilution" (admission of unskilled or female workers into jobs formerly held by skilled male workers). However, an unofficial "shop steward" movement grew up in many areas—most notably on Clydeside in Scotland and in the coalfield of South Wales—to speak for ordinary workers' interests. Strikes did occasionally break out, and in general the government gave in.

Overall, labor benefited from the war effort. According to one estimate, employed British workers enjoyed by the 1920s a 25 percent increase in their standard of living. Moreover, the trade union movement won recognition and status by its cooperation with the government. Total union membership grew from 4 million in 1914 to 6.5 million in 1918. The expansion of union membership in turn greatly benefited the Labour party. Most of the members of the party supported the war effort, despite the internationalism of a few socialists. The Labour party cooperated with the government, and Labour leaders took government office for the first time. The party took advantage of its more favorable position to draft a new constitution early in 1918. This extended party membership beyond the unions and socialist societies to establish constituency organizations; it thereby created an effective national electoral machinery.

Women also benefited from participating in wartime mobilization. Thousands of women volunteered in auxiliary forces—the WAACS, the WRENS, and the WRAF. In addition, some 800,000 went to work in munitions industries and almost 1.5

million in clerical posts in both commercial and government offices. "Office girls," as they were called, became a permanent feature of the social landscape. Many of these working women migrated from one region to another to work: young women from Welsh mining communities to the munitions factories of the English Midlands, and village women to the offices of London and other urban centers. At the same time, thousands of women left domestic service, an occupation that had for many generations contributed to the subservience of women, to take industrial and commercial jobs offering better pay and more personal freedom. Many women thus enjoyed some liberation from old restrictions on women's economic and social roles and behavior. As they went to work in large numbers, women abandoned corsets, floor-length skirts, and prewar propriety. At the same time, the constant possibility of death for young men going off to the front encouraged young people to establish intimate relationships much more quickly. As one historian, Correlli Barnett, has written, "Love affairs with men so likely soon to die in battle made nonsense of Victorian ideas of female chastity."*

Women's contributions to the war effort were recognized by men. The consensus grew in male governing circles that women had earned a place in the constitution. J. L. Garvin, Conservative editor of the *Observer,* wrote in 1916:

> Time was when I thought that men alone maintained the State. Now I know that men alone could never have maintained it, and that henceforth the modern State must be dependent on men and women alike for the progressive strength and vitality of its whole organization.

This consensus was made more comfortable for men by the fact that the suffragettes put aside their agitation in order to show solidarity with the war effort. Indeed, Emmeline Pankhurst and the WSPU gave up their goal of eradicating "separate spheres" for men and women. In February 1918, when Parliament passed the Fourth (and greatest) Reform Act, granting the franchise to all men over twenty-one, it also granted the first installment of votes for women: women over thirty years who met a small property qualification got the vote. (All women over twenty-one finally received the vote in 1928.)

WARTIME POLITICS

The Great War put severe strain on the British political system. Speed of decision making and unity of effort were essential. It was impossible for Parliament to develop and oversee policies in these conditions; hence there was a significant shift of power to the cabinet and eventually to smaller councils within the cabinet. The office of prime minister became more important than ever. The public had little part to play in shaping policy. Even the general election that should have been held in 1915 was postponed for the duration. As time passed, the political parties put aside their normal adversarial role in favor of cooperation. Two different war coalitions were formed. In all these ways the British political system proved highly flex-

---

The Great War (New York Putnam, 1980), p. 46.

ible; yet the pressures of war split the Liberal party, which, as we will see in subsequent chapters, never recovered from its wounds.

Prime Minister Asquith was confident that he and his cabinet would be equal to the challenge of war, not least because they believed they had done everything possible to avoid it. Asquith did establish in 1915 a War Council, but he did not assign it executive responsibility. In general, he attempted to conduct the war through the cabinet, in which the most powerful figures were Kitchener, the secretary for war, who became the very image of the war effort; Winston Churchill, first lord of the admiralty, who had great initiative and imagination; and David Lloyd George, who increasingly impressed insiders with his energy and decisiveness. Asquith himself deferred in military and naval matters to the experts, especially Kitchener and Churchill, reserving for himself the role of chairman of the government.

Asquith had accomplished a great deal since becoming prime minister in 1908, for he had guided the Liberal government through exceptionally rough political waters. However, as one might have predicted by his indecisiveness in the crisis years of 1912-1914, Asquith in terms of both personality and methods proved unequal to the task of war. He was in some ways an extremely able man, with an impressive intellect and powerful debating skills. Under his leadership, the Liberal government had brought a unified Britain into the war; it successfully deployed the BEF and the Royal Navy; and it began the mobilization of the economy and the society for the war. But Asquith was more a mediator than a leader, a highly competent parliamentarian but one lacking in creative vision. He had little rapport with the public and presented an image of Olympian detachment. People who knew him thought he spent too much time socializing and playing bridge. It has to be admitted that he failed to act with enough speed and decisiveness and that he neglected to build an image to which either the public or the elite could rally.

As early as the winter of 1914 and the spring of 1915, the frustrations on the battlefield spread in parliamentary circles the attitude that Asquith was not forceful enough. The nationalistic Conservatives were especially eager for a more active government. The shell scandal of May 1915 revealed serious shortcomings in war production, and the Gallipoli disaster provoked the Conservatives to look for a scapegoat. The first sea lord, Sir John Fisher, a favorite of the Conservatives, resigned after a volcanic dispute with Churchill over the Dardanelles. Asquith met these problems by constructing a coalition government: he removed Churchill from the admiralty, brought several Conservatives and the leader of the parliamentary Labour party (Arthur Henderson) into the cabinet, and made Lloyd George head of a new ministry of munitions. This coalition lasted from May 1915 to December 1916.

Asquith's coalition brought him temporary political relief and set the production of munitions on the right track, but it otherwise failed to improve significantly the conduct of the war. By the spring of 1916, not only the Conservatives but also a Liberal "Ginger Group" were agitating for further change. Kitchener, who had little administrative ability, had become an embarrassment. Asquith reassigned most of Kitchener's duties to Sir William Robertson, chief of the imperial general staff, and he also appointed Haig commander of the BEF. (Kitchener was killed when a ship on which he was a passenger was torpedoed in June 1916.) But Asquith still deferred to his generals and failed to galvanize the cabinet into an effective executive. Worse yet, Asquith dragged his feet over the matter of conscription, and a rebellion in Ireland at Easter 1916 (see Chapter 7) damaged his authority.

Lloyd George meanwhile attracted much favorable attention by his success with the munitions industry. Some Conservatives thought that Lloyd George was unsuited for high office, both because he was of humble social origins and because he had in previous years distinguished himself by his Welsh radicalism and his opposition to the South African War. Others, however, were impressed by his driving force and his will to do the job at hand, whatever the methods required. Certain highly influential newspaper barons—including Sir Max Aitken (later Lord Beaverbrook), publisher of the *Daily Express*; Lord Northcliffe, jingoistic owner of the *Daily Mail* and the *Times*; and Geoffrey Robinson, editor of the *Times*—were pressing for reform of the executive and gradually turning to Lloyd George. The "Welsh Wizard" himself, a highly ambitious as well as a mercurial politician and administrator, was eager for change.

Finally, in December 1916, Lloyd George presented Asquith with a plan whereby a small, all-powerful war committee headed by himself would run the war while Asquith stayed on as a figurehead prime minister. Asquith had a momentous decision to make, and perhaps the patriotic gesture would have been to accept the plan. But Asquith was weary and discouraged, and he was grieving over the loss of his son Raymond on the Western Front. He could not accept the demotion and resigned. The Conservative leader, Bonar Law, was not able to gather the support necessary to form a government. The king, George V, therefore sent for Lloyd George, who became prime minister of a second coalition government as well as chair of a five-person war cabinet (composed of himself, three Conservatives, and one Labourite, Arthur Henderson).

Lloyd George's supercession of Asquith, and Asquith's reaction to it, fatally divided the Liberal party. Asquith never forgave Lloyd George for leading what he regarded as an unprincipled conspiracy. Yet it should be remembered that it was Asquith who had actually ended the Liberal government by forming a coalition in May 1915 and who now led about one hundred Liberal M.P.s into opposition. The war had split Liberalism in new ways; hence Asquith's Liberals came mainly from the left and center sections of the party, while Lloyd George's Liberals came from the right wing. Without the "Squiffies" (or "Wee Frees"), Lloyd George depended on Conservative support. The Liberal split hardened during the next two years as the Asquith Liberals regularly criticized Lloyd George. Asquith himself was ineffectual as leader of the opposition, since he wanted to be seen as supporting the war effort yet independent of the government. Deprived of a major segment of his party's support, Lloyd George increasingly looked to hard-driving businessmen to lead the war effort, and he slowly came around to the idea of establishing a new center party made up of Conservatives and right-wing Liberals. As we will see in subsequent chapters, this attempt by Lloyd George failed, but the Liberals were never able to recover their former position.

The Labour party meanwhile had been given a golden opportunity by the Liberal split to become the principal party of the left. Labour played its cards well and emerged at the end of the war in a vastly stronger position. As we have seen, the trade unions, which formed the basis of Labour electoral power, expanded greatly during the war. The new constitution of the Labour party also improved the party's electoral footing. The expansion of the franchise in 1918, by which Britain became a genuine democracy for the first time, made the working class overwhelmingly the majority of the electorate. The wartime expansion of state power accustomed British voters to "collectivist" (that is, state interventionist) action of a sort long advocated by the Fabian, state-socialist element of the Labour movement. Most important of all, the entry of Arthur Henderson into the cabinet (and other Labourites into lower-level government posts) helped voters in all social classes realize that a Labour party in power might not be such a frightening possibility. The Labour party participated in the war effort, but did not give up its independence. The Labour party generally supported the war, but had reservations about pressing it to the point of total defeat of Germany. They preferred an early peace to a "knock-out blow." Thus in September 1917, Henderson resigned from the Lloyd George coalition because he thought it important to attend an international socialist conference in Stockholm, which would also be attended by German socialists. The party supported Henderson's action and thereby affirmed its autonomy from Lloyd George's all-party government.

Lloyd George proved to be a leader of nearly superhuman energy and determination. He quickly assumed personal control over the war effort. Yet Lloyd George has never stood as high in the estimation of the British public as other great war leaders like the younger Pitt or Winston Churchill. Lloyd George was charming, uncannily sensitive to public opinion, and a superb manipulator of individuals and the press alike. He focused intently on his goals but was unscrupulous about his methods; thus he seemed willing to sacrifice the means for the end. Successively a Welsh radical, a pro-Boer, an aristocrat-bashing New Liberal, and now a ferocious war minister, Lloyd George appeared overly ambitious and unprincipled. He was highly partisan—a political fighter—but not a loyal party member. In 1910, during the impasse over the budget and reform of the House of Lords, Lloyd George had floated the idea of an all-party coalition government devoted to social reform and national defense. The conclusion seems inescapable that, as Lord Beaverbrook put it, "He did not seem to care which way he travelled, providing he was in the driver's seat."

Lloyd George's worst qualities would in peacetime rebound on him to isolate him on the periphery of politics. But during the war his best qualities came to the fore. He radically increased the amount and pace of governmental activity. His war cabinet of five proved a very flexible and effective instrument. Its members met approximately five hundred times in the next two years, ranging freely over all major issues and calling in other government officials and cabinet members as the need arose. Lloyd George enhanced its impact by creating a permanent cabinet secretariat, which coordinated the work of the whole ministry. To obtain information and advice on special topics, Lloyd George called on a group of private advisors

Brass hats and frock coats. From left to right: Albert Thomas, General Douglas Haig, General Joffre, and Prime Minister David Lloyd George.

housed in the garden of No. 10 Downing Street—his so-called Garden Suburb. He brought businessmen into the government. He recalled Churchill from political exile to take over the ministry of munitions. And he established and chaired the Imperial War Cabinet to coordinate the efforts of Britain and the dominions—and, when he saw fit, to circumvent his own war cabinet.

In the conduct of military and naval action, Lloyd George insisted on civilian control, but with only mixed results. He was able to impose his will on the admiralty on one crucial issue: in April 1917, he forced the navy to adopt the convoy system to protect Allied shipping from German submarines. This saved British food supplies. He was much less effective with the army. Lloyd George strongly favored an "eastern" strategy—attacking through Italy, the Balkans, or the Middle East. The top generals, Robertson and Haig, passionately believed in a "western" strategy—trying to defeat in France and Flanders the main concentration of the German army. This dispute between the "frock coats" and "brass hats" in 1917 went in favor of the generals. Only in 1918, when Lloyd George replaced Robertson as Chief of the Imperial General Staff (CIGS) with a more pliable officer, did he begin to win full control. Even so, Lloyd George was never sure enough of his politicial position to dismiss Haig; thus Haig controlled the war on land.

WAR'S END, 1917–1918

By the time Lloyd George became prime minister, the British realized that they were in for a long war that might well stretch into 1919 or 1920. Not just the armies but the entire societies of the combatant nations were involved. But 1917 on the whole went very poorly for Britain, with staggering losses and stalemate on the Western Front, a crisis at sea, and the collapse of their Russian ally. Indeed, the year between the spring of 1917 and the early summer of 1918 was the worst time of the war for the British. But the tide finally turned, not least because a great new ally, the United States, entered the war, and in 1918 the Western Front unexpectedly turned into a rout. The war was thus to end as abruptly as it had begun.

On the Western Front in 1917 the British launched new offenses but were thrown back. In the spring of that year, a new French commanding general, Nivelle, captured Lloyd George's imagination with promises of a lightning thrust and breakthrough. Haig was reluctant to cooperate, but the prime minister asserted some degree of control by subordinating him to Nivelle. The British part in the offensive was to be another assault in northern France, near Arras. But the Franco-British offensive initiated by Nivelle soon collapsed into the usual bloodletting and stalemate. Even so, Haig believed that he had learned how to achieve the ever-elusive breakthrough and now argued strenuously for a further British offensive in 1917. Another row between brass hats and frock coats ensued, and as usual the brass hats won. The terrible battle of Passchendaele (or Third Battle of Ypres) was the result: four months of murderous slogging, yielding 250,000 British casualties but no breakdown of the German defenses.

The war even went poorly for Britain on battlefields other than the Western Front. British and imperial troops had defended the Suez Canal and Basra near the Persian Gulf from seizure by Turkish armies since 1914. In 1916, the British army in Egypt took the Sinai Peninsula, and in 1917 it invaded Palestine (then a province of Turkey). The British objective was Jerusalem, but the Turks threw them back. It was not until December of 1917 that the British army, now commanded in the Middle East by General Sir Edmund Allenby, conquered Jerusalem. Meanwhile, British forces at Basra attempted to force their way up the Tigris River into Turkish Mesopotamia to Baghdad. Throughout 1915 and 1916 the British and Indian troops made little progress. Only by strong reinforcements and strenuous trench warfare in the desert were the British able to take Baghdad, which finally fell in March 1917.

Even so, the Turks remained in the war. In order to dislodge them from the Middle East, the British made momentous contradictory promises to various parties. To the Arab Sheraif Husain, the British promised independence for all Arab territories within the Ottoman Empire. To the European Zionist movement, in the so-called Balfour Declaration of November 1917, the British promised "a national home" for Jews in Palestine. And all the while, the British were making deals with the French to divide these territories among themselves. This tangled web of commitments would one day have serious consequences for the British and for the peoples of the area.

On the oceans, 1917 brought a major German submarine offensive. The Germans had discovered that the submarine was a near-perfect commerce raider: it could slip undetected out of safe ports to prey on merchant ships with little danger to itself. Neutral nations like the United States regarded U-boat warfare as unusually cruel, but the Germans through 1916 had tried to avoid sinking the ships of

The Passchendaele battlefield, Flanders, 1917.

neutral powers. Early in 1917, however, with their hard-pressed nation in need of a quick victory, the German leaders proclaimed unrestricted submarine warfare. American as well as British shipping to Britain would be cut off, and British industry would have to close down. The Germans knew that this submarine offensive was a big gamble, for it would provoke the United States into declaring war on Germany. The bet was that Britain might be defeated before the Americans mobilized their prodigious resources.

The gamble very nearly paid off. In the first month of unrestricted submarine warfare, the Germans sank over half a million tons of merchant shipping. The figure rose to almost 900,000 tons in May 1917. Admiral Jellicoe warned Lloyd George that "it is impossible for us to go on with the war if losses like this continue." But the British adopted the convoy system, whereby merchant ships crossed the Atlantic in groups protected by destroyers, like herds of sheep defended from wolves by shepherds. By September 1917, shipping losses to U-boats had fallen to a tolerable level, and the crisis passed.

The submarine offensive, moreover, had prodded the United States into entering the war on the side of the Allies. The United States declared war in April 1917 and began the massive job of preparing an expeditionary army. The American entry, however, was balanced by the Russian departure from the war. By early 1917, Russia, which had suffered huge losses of manpower on the Eastern Front, was wracked by food riots and demonstrations against the tsar's autocratic and inept government. In March 1917, Russia slid into revolution. The tsar abdicated and was replaced by a provisional social democratic government that tried to continue the

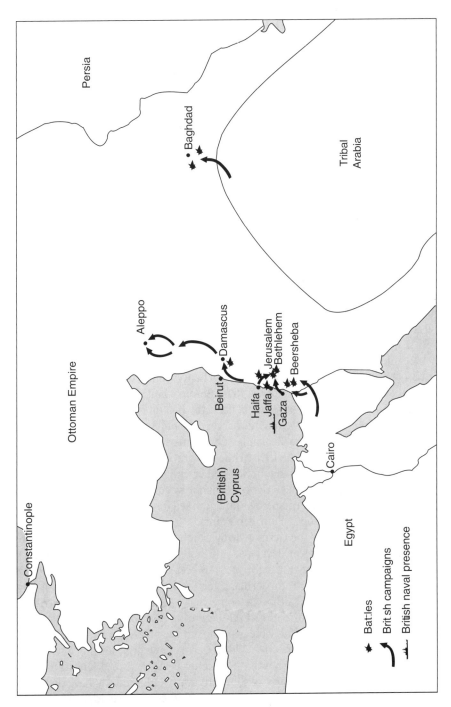

The Middle East during World War I

war effort. But a huge German offensive in September 1917 shattered the tottering Russian army, and in November the Bolsheviks (Communists) led by Lenin and Trotsky overthrew the provisional government. In December the new Bolshevik government made peace with Germany. By the Treaty of Brest Litovsk (made final in 1918), the Russians left the war and gave up vast territory, including Poland, the Baltic states, and much of the Ukraine. All told, Russia lost about one third of its population and one-half of its industry.

The departure of Russia from the war enabled the Germans to shift large numbers of troops from the Eastern to the Western Front, and to throw the German army into one last gigantic effort to defeat Britain and France before the Americans arrived. The German plan was to attack in northern France, divide the British army from the French, and then push the British northward to the Channel coast. The offensive came in March 1918 and almost succeeded. Lloyd George had prodded and cajoled the British and French military commanders to set up a joint command on the Western Front under the Frenchman General Foch. But coordination between Haig and his French counterpart remained poor, and the British defense nearly broke down before the German onslaught. The British army finally regrouped just east of Amiens and by mid-April fought the Germans to a standstill. Final German assaults came in May and June but got nowhere. Though the British did not know it, the failed German offensive of spring 1918 had exhausted the last German reserves of physical, psychological, and material resources.

In mid-summer 1918, with American troops now pouring into France, the British and French went on the offensive. The weakened German lines gave way. The British attacked just north of the River Somme, and with more than four hundred tanks they pushed the Germans back to their pre-spring position. Late in August, the British attacked again, now across the old Somme battlefield, and then the French, Australians, New Zealanders, and Americans took turns in launching assaults. By early autumn, with their armies reeling back to the German border, the German generals were panicking. In September, Bulgaria (a German ally) asked for peace, and British troops under General Allenby swept the Turks out of Palestine. On October 4, 1918, the German government asked for an armistice on the basis of President Woodrow Wilson's "Fourteen Points."

The rapid collapse of the German army caught the British, like the French, off guard. The British had never developed any systematic war aims. They wanted to end permanently the German naval rivalry, to keep a number of German colonies, and to collect reparations from Germany for the loss of merchant shipping. But Wilson's Fourteen Points, although somewhat vague, went beyond territorial rearrangements to argue for national self-determination and making "a world safe for democracy." While the Allies were working out the precise meaning of the Fourteen Points, the Great War drew to a close. Germany was not forced to surrender, even though the German army was thoroughly beaten; instead, an armistice (a cease fire) was signed. This way of ending the war would one day have disastrous repercussions. In any case, the glorious silence of peace returned to the world's battlefields on November 11, 1918.

COUNTING THE COST

To assess the impact of the Great War on Britain, one would have to investigate long-term political, social, economic, and even psychological trends. That investigation will be one of the purposes of the next several chapters. But even if we restrict our view to the short term, to the immediate consequences of the war, three questions of enormous complexity stand out: (I) What did the British gain from the war?; (2) What price did they pay?; and (3) Were the gains worth the costs?

In terms of power politics, the British gains were relatively small. They won Palestine, Trans-Jordan, and Iraq as "mandated" (that is, assigned as trusteeships) colonies from the Ottoman Empire. From Germany, Britain took Tanganyika, and other countries in the British Empire got Somoa, part of New Guinea, and German Southwest Africa. Britain eliminated the German navy as a rival, at least temporarily. Above all, the Germans were forced out of the Low Countries and France and were for the time being disarmed. More generally, Britain had avoided (again, temporarily) German domination of central and western Europe; thus they had protected what most British statesmen had long regarded as a vital British interest. The British, with France and Russia, were able to accomplish all this by mobilizing vast material, financial, and human resources without abandoning either the parliamentary system or the essentials of personal liberty and the rule of law.

Yet the price was fearful. The British lost 750,000 men in combat—about 9 percent of all men under the age of forty-five. (The Empire lost an additional 250,000 men killed.) Another 1.5 million Britons were wounded, thousands of whom remained invalids. The upper and middle classes lost more men proportionately than the working class, both because a higher percentage of upper-class men volunteered and because the leadership positions they assumed in the army and air force were very dangerous. About 12 percent of all men who served were killed, but over 15 percent of all army officers and 17 percent of all flying officers died. Over 19 percent of the Oxford students and graduates who served were killed, and 18 percent of those from Cambridge. This disproportionate loss of life among the elite gave Britain the sense that a whole generation had been lost.

How are the effects of such losses to be measured? The British losses in manpower were not as great as those of the other great powers (France lost 1.3 million and Germany more than 1.8 million.); still, the economic and social—not to mention the emotional—effects must have been severe for several generations. Certainly Britain in the 1920s and 1930s seemed to suffer from a lack of talent in politics and industry, even though the downturn of the demographic curve was soon righted. To give two concrete examples: thirty-five Fellows of the Royal Society, Britain's elite scientific academy, were killed, as were fifty-five members of the Royal Institute of Chemistry. Likewise, promising businessmen, professionals, scholars, workers, and politicians perished. These were arguably the most valuable of all of Britain's wasted resources.

The economic losses are almost as difficult to calculate. The war caused enormous dislocations in British industry. It destroyed shipping tonnage equal to 40 percent of the 1914 British total. It caused a huge proportion of Britain's industrial production to be directed toward armaments. It consumed and wasted capital at a fantastic pace. It caused some industries—like coal and steel—to be artificially built up, and others—like cotton textiles and railways—to be run down. Furthermore, the war severely damaged Britain's ability to earn invisible income, on which the economy had increasingly depended, and it disrupted the world's markets, diverted British efforts from foreign trade, and turned Britain from a creditor to a debtor nation. Britain lost major capital investments in Russia and elsewhere and sold off about £550 million of British assets in the United States. In addition, the British borrowed £1.4 billion to finance the war, most of it from the United States. Although Britain in turn loaned £1.7 billion to the Allies, much of that sum was never recovered.

At the same time, not all the economic consequences of the war were negative. The war stimulated expansion of new industries such as the automotive and aircraft industries, and it encouraged technological innovations in industries in which Britain had lagged before—machine tools, electrical power, artificial dyestuffs, petrochemicals, and metallurgy, to name a few. The war encouraged cooperation and rationalization (that is, merging of a number of companies in a given industry to form one or a few) in industry. There was a general opening of opinion among many manufacturers to improvement of production techniques.

All told, however, the British economic losses outweighed the gains by a wide margin. The destruction of resources, the loss of overseas wealth, the forced abandonment of foreign markets, the dislocation of the domestic economy—all proved to be a heavy burden in the subsequent decades. As we have seen, many old Victorian industries already, from the 1870s and 1880s, were beginning to face major problems. The Great War artificially propped up some but hastened the ruin of others, and it delivered a blow to Britain's position in world trade, both as a financier and as an exporter. In the 1920s, there was to be the beginnings of recovery and growth in new industries but not in the old; hence the war's economic effect in the most general terms was to serve as a watershed between the Victorian industrial economy and a newer, often troubled industrial economy.

In social terms, the war left a more mixed balance sheet, with the credits perhaps outweighing the debits. One of the great paradoxes of British history is that this most costly of wars had positive results for some segments of the society. The social structure itself emerged from the war unscathed, for Britain remained a sharply delineated class society. Nevertheless, the war, with its steeply graduated income taxes and high death duties, tended to diminish the gap between the upper classes and the working class. The war rapidly accelerated the trend set in motion by the late-Victorian agricultural depression: it brought many of the landed families down some notches from their customary rarefied economic position. Some businessmen did very well out of war contracts and investment in government securities, and in the House of Lords after 1918 there appeared the hard face of many a tough businessman. But other middle-class men, particularly from the lower levels of the class, suffered from high taxes and rising prices.

The working class, especially its heretofore unskilled and poorer sections, benefited from full employment and high wages. A sharp reduction in alcohol consumption and improved nutrition, both the results of government action, improved life expectancy in the working class. Trade union membership grew, and by 1920, 40 percent of working people belonged to unions. Thus the British working class as a result of the Great War became more homogeneous as well as better off.

As for the costs and benefits of the war on the status of women, in general, as we have seen, women's contributions to the war effort earned them wider opportunity for employment, more personal freedom, and the vote. In 1919, the Sex Disqualification (Removal) Act abolished *legal* barriers to women's advancement in the civil service and the professions. Also in 1919, the first woman M.P., Lady Astor, took a seat in the House of Commons. Yet the social gains for women were not unambiguous. The feminist movement gave up its attempts to abolish separate spheres for men and women, and after the war most "respectable" people believed that women should return to the home and leave the breadwinning to men. The number of women employed remained higher than in 1914, but women did not have access to top professional or commercial posts. Nor did they enjoy equal pay for equal work. As the historian Trevor Wilson has observed, the war left women "second-class citizens but had improved the quality of second-class travel."*

In sum, one can say that the British were on the winning side in the Great War and so preserved their status as a great power, but they found that the war had severely damaged their ability to behave as a great power. Further, the war accelerated certain improvements in status and standards of living for social groups that had enjoyed the least power in Victorian society. But these changes might have happened anyway, and in any case few of the British in 1919 would have said that these gains were worth the losses in blood and treasure. The young soldier-poet Wilfrid Gibson put it this way:

> We who are left, how shall we look again
> Happily on the sun, or feel the rain,
> Without remembering how they who went
> Ungrudgingly, and spent
> Their all for us, loved, too, the sun and rain?

Suggested Reading

Adams, R. J. Q., *Arms and the Wizard: Lloyd George and the Ministry of Munitions, 1915–1916* (London: Cassell, 1978).

Barnett, Correlli, *Britain and Her Army, 1509–1970* (London: Allen Lane, 1970).

———, *The Great War* (New York: Putnam, 1980).

Blake, Robert, *The Unknown Prime Minister: The Life and Times of Bonar Law* (London: Eyre & Spottiswoode, 1955).

Bourne, J. M., *Britain and the Great War, 1914–1918* (New York: Edward Arnold, 1990).

The Myriad Faces of War: Britain and The Great War, 1914–1918 (Cambridge: Polity Press, 1986), p. 728.

De Groot, Gerard J., *Blighty: British Society in the Era of The Great War* (New York: Addison Wesley Longman, 1996).

———, *Douglas Haig* (Winchester, N.H.: Unwin Hyman, 1988).

Ferguson, Niall, *The Pity of War* (London: Allen Lane, 1998).

Fussell, Paul, *The Great War and Modern Memory* (New York: Oxford University Press, 1975).

Gilbert, Bentley B., *David Lloyd George: A Political Life* (2 vols; Columbus: Ohio State University Press, 1987–1992).

Grigg, John, *Lloyd George from Peace to War, 1912–1916* (London: Methuen, 1985).

Hynes, Samuel, *A War Imagined: The First World War and English Culture* (New York: Atheneum, 1991).

Keegan, John, *The Face of Battle* (New York: Viking Press, 1976).

———, *The First World War* (New York: Alfred A. Knopf, 1998).

Kennedy, Paul, *The Rise and Fall of British Naval Mastery* (London: Allen Lane, 1976).

Koss, Stephen, *Asquith* (New York: St. Martin's, 1976).

Marder, A. J., *From the Dreadnought to Scapa Flow: The Royal Navy in the Fisher Era, 1904–1919* (5 vols.) (London: Oxford University Press, 1961–1970).

Marwick, Arthur, *Britain in the Century of Total War* (Boston: Little, Brown, 1968).

———, *The Deluge: British Society and the First World War* (London: Bodley Head, 1965).

Packer, Ian, *Lloyd George* (New York: St. Martin's Press, 1998).

Robb, George, *British Culture and the First World War* (New York: Palgrave, 2002).

Rothwell, V. H., *British War Aims and Peace Diplomacy, 1914–1918* (Oxford: Clarendon Press, 1971).

Scally, Robert, *The Origins of the Lloyd George Coalition: The Politics of Social Imperialism, 1900–1918* (Princeton, N.J.: Princeton University Press, 1975).

Schweitzer, Richard, *The Cross and the Trenches: Religious Faith Among British and American Great War Soldiers* (Wesport, CT: Praeger, 2003).

Steel, Nigel, and Peter Hart, *Passchendaele: The Sacrificial Ground* (London: Cassell, 2001).

Swartz, Marvin, *The Union of Democratic Control in British Politics During the First World War* (Oxford: Clarendon Press, 1971).

Tanner, Duncan, *Political Change and the Labour Party, 1900–1918* (Cambridge: Cambridge University Press, 1990).

Waites, Bernard, *A Class Society at War: England, 1914–1918* (Leamington Spa, U.K.: Berg, 1987).

Watson, Janet S. K., *Fighting Different Wars: Experience, Memory and the First World War in Britain* (Cambridge: Cambridge University Press, 2004).

Wilson, Trevor, *The Downfall of the Liberal Party, 1914–35* (London: Collins, 1966).

———, *The Myriad Faces of War: Britain and the Great War, 1914–1918* (Cambridge: Polity Press, 1986).

Winter, Jay M., *The Great War and the British People* (Cambridge, Mass.: Harvard University Press, 1986).

———, *Remembering War: The Great War between Memory and History in the Twentieth Century* (New Haven: Yale University Press, 2006).

———, *Socialism and the Challenge of War, 1912–18* (London: Gregg Revivals, 1993).

———, *World War I: The Experience* (London: Angus Publishing, 2006).

Woodward, E. L., *Great Britain and the War of 1914–1918* (London: Methuen, 1967).

Chapter 7

The War and the Celtic Countries: Ireland Leaves the Union, 1914–1923

The First World War challenged the British state to mobilize its people and its material resources on a massive scale. But as we have seen, the British state—officially the United Kingdom of Great Britain and Ireland—formally had existed only since 1801 and even by 1914 had not achieved complete integration or blending of its peoples. Indeed, the Great War broke out during the height of revival on the "Celtic fringe." The vital question was not only whether the British government would be able to gather and direct the money, matériel, and military forces necessary for the war effort but also whether the British state itself would hold together. In general, the answer to the second part of this vital question was "not completely": whereas Scotland and Wales rallied to the cause and became more "British" than ever, Ireland (or more accurately, the southern twenty-six counties) under the pressure and opportunities of the war broke with the Union.

THE IMPACT OF THE GREAT WAR ON SCOTLAND AND WALES

In Scotland and Wales, the national revivals had resulted in prevailing self-identities that were "British" as well as "Scottish" or "Welsh." The British part of these dual identities was reinforced by the war experience. In order to recruit men for military service and to rally support for the war effort, the government in London emphasized "Britain" rather than "England" in all its appeals and propaganda. Kitchener's famous recruiting poster, for instance, was meant for Britons in general. The men of Scotland and Wales volunteered for service at a rate at least equal to that in England: in all three countries (England, Scotland, Wales) the proportion of men who served was more than 40 percent of the male population between the ages of fifteen and forty-nine. Likewise, the casualty rates of Scottish and Welsh troops were about the same as those of English troops. The people of England, Scotland, and Wales bore the burdens of war equally.

The experience of war tended to break down regional horizons. The 650,000 men who served in the navy were organized without regard to regional origins. Englishmen, Scotsmen, and Welshmen sailed together as Britons. In the first years of the war, the army was different. Both because of long tradition and because of recruiting tactics, the British army was territorially organized. Scots were recruited into Scottish units (the Scots Guards, the Argyll and Sutherland Highlanders, and so on), and the Welsh into Welsh units (The Royal Welch Fusiliers, the Welsh Regiment, and so on). Officers, however, were generally assigned without reference to local origins. By the end of the war the rate of casualties and the need for rapid replacement had broken down the territorial purity of the enlisted ranks: Englishmen, Scotsmen, and Welshmen all served in the same units.

Likewise, military training moved thousands of men from one part of the British Isles to another. Scottish and Welsh soldiers trained in southern England, and English troops served in Scotland. Sometimes the results of this large-scale internal movement of soldiers had humorous results, as provincial men saw localities and heard accents other than their own for the first time. On one occasion, two English sentries in northern Scotland arrested a Gaelic-speaking woman, thinking that she was a German. On another occasion, an obviously bewildered group of Scottish troops at the Oxford railway station told a helpful inquirer, "We are going to Berlin. But we don't quite know at what junctions we are to change on the way." After the war, regional identities and loyalties were never the same again, and the sense of being part of one Britain was much stronger.

Yet the effects of the war were not homogeneous, because the economic conditions and the cultural revivals of Scotland and Wales were different. In Scotland, the economy suffered the same sort of dislocations as in the rest of Britain but with different social and political results. In the short run, the Great War vastly increased the demand for ships and munitions from the industrial area around Glasgow and the River Clyde. Clydeside became the chief munitions manufacturing center in Britain. The war also expanded production of certain specialized textiles like canvas for tenting and jute for sandbags. Unfortunately, this artificial demand only collapsed after the war. The war also deprived Scotland of its Continental markets for fish, and the Scots never gained them back. As a result of such disruptions, some 400,000 people emigrated from Scotland to England and overseas in the 1920s.

Meanwhile, the war radicalized a large segment of the Scottish working class. Shipyard and engineering workers on Clydeside were in a position to demand higher wages, and they sought to protect their status by resisting dilution of their ranks by unskilled laborers. Militant trade unionism, socialism, and even syndicalism took a strong hold. The shop steward movement, which grew up to replace the leadership of the official trade unions, gave the region the reputation of being "Red Clydeside." The Scottish working class even before 1914 had been turning in a militant direction because of unemployment and structural changes in industry. The war heightened this already growing class antagonism and therefore had the effect of breaking the long-standing Scottish working-class commitment to liberalism and the Liberal party. In the 1920s, the Scottish working class shifted heavily to Labour, and class loyalty tended to replace Scottish national loyalty.

The general trend in Wales was similar but not identical. Initially the war was very popular in Wales. Recruiting found an enthusiastic response, as the Welsh expressed their "British" identity and at the same time sympathized with "little Belgium" and "gallant little Serbia." Many Welsh nonconformist ministers preached anathema against the Germans, and local and national *eisteddfoddau* became patriotic celebrations. Lloyd George was able to work his fellow Welshmen into near hysteria for the war. Nevertheless, a few nonconformists remained pacifists, and the Welsh coal miners generally opposed conscription. These antiwar sentiments helped turn Wales from Liberal to Labour in the last years of the war.

Changes in the structure of Welsh society and economy caused by the war also helped erode Welsh liberalism. The Great War brought about a sudden decline of traditional Welsh landed society. Wartime demand raised prices for Welsh agricultural products like grain, milk, and livestock. This raised land values, but the government controlled rents. The tenants, consequently, fared better than the landlords in wartime conditions. Meanwhile, higher taxes—both income and inheritance duties—were squeezing the landlords. For these reasons, Welsh landlords in large numbers sold off their estates to tenant farmers. The long tradition of a dominant gentry in Wales came to an end, and thenceforward Wales was farmed by owner-occupiers. As the Welsh landlords faded from the scene, so also did one of the principal reasons for popular adherence to the Liberal party, which had for half a century given voice to opposition to landlordism in Wales.

The Great War also had a major impact on Welsh industry. It stimulated the expansion of heavy industries in South Wales, coal mining above all but also iron and steel. Industrial relations worsened as Welsh coal miners raised their demands for better pay and better treatment. The miners' ideology became more radical, with socialism and syndicalism becoming very strong. The news of the Russian Revolution in 1917 met widespread approval in South Wales. High rents and food shortages in 1918 further increased labor militancy. The resulting intense class consciousness—the Welsh equivalent of "Red Clydeside"—made impossible the traditional collaboration of Welsh laboring people with the Liberal party. As in Scotland, class consciousness replaced Welsh national consciousness.

Support for liberalism and the Liberals was being eroded by other forces. Disestablishment of the Anglican church in Wales was passed by the Liberals in 1914, though its implementation was suspended for the duration of the war. With disestablishment achieved, with the landlords selling out, and with Lloyd George ensconced in Downing Street, the future of Welsh Liberals must have seemed bright. But these achievements had exhausted the Welsh Liberal agenda; therefore, while the war was worsening class relations and accelerating a working-class trend toward Labour, the Liberals had nothing new to offer. Lloyd George was able to hold Wales for his personal branch of the Liberal party in 1918, but thereafter the Liberals in Wales collapsed.

IRELAND AND THE GREAT WAR, 1914–1916

The war had its most dramatic impact and caused the most damage to the United Kingdom in Ireland. As the war was breaking out, both the Irish nationalists and the Ulster Unionists were building large armed paramilitary forces, and they seemed to be heading for violent confrontation as the third Home Rule bill passed through its final stages into law. Over time, events related directly to the war made Home Rule obsolete and opened the way for the radical separatist brand of Irish nationalism. This was an ironic development because the war had delayed the confrontation between Irish nationalists and Unionists and because the war was to involve a smaller proportion of Irishmen than Englishmen, Scotsmen, or Welshmen. Yet the pressures of war strained the already weak ties of Catholic Ireland to England beyond the breaking point. England's difficulty, so the Irish nationalist saying went, was Ireland's opportunity.

On the day the war broke out in August 1914, the leader of the Home Rule party, John Redmond, made a dramatic pledge to the British Parliament. The Home Rulers, he declared, stood with Britain against German militarism in the hour of crisis. Let the Irish Volunteers and the Ulster Volunteers defend Ireland while the British army concentrated on the Germans in Flanders. The leader of Ulster Unionism, Sir Edward Carson, pledged the support of the Ulstermen. These two manifestos of Irish loyalty to Britain were well received by the British and Irish publics alike.

However, when Redmond took the additional step of urging the Irish Volunteers to enlist in the British army, he caused a serious split in Irish nationalist opinion. To the nationalists it was one thing to defend Ireland and another to fight for Britain in Europe. Why Redmond made his spontaneous plea is not clear; he may have wanted to win British gratitude so that at the war's end Home Rule would be implemented without the exclusion of any Ulster counties. Whatever his motive, the volunteers split apart, with about 110,000 remaining with Redmond and now calling themselves the National Volunteers, but with some 12,000 breaking away to form a new "Irish Volunteer" organization, a more militant and extremist force devoted to winning for Ireland more autonomy than simply Home Rule.

In subsequent months, Redmond recruited actively for the British armed forces. At first, Irishmen flocked to the colors. But as British losses on the Western Front mounted, and as the war settled into its bloody stalemate, Irish enlistments (at least outside of Ulster) fell off. In the end, about 112,000 Irishmen served in the British armed services during the war (about 60 percent of them Catholics and 40 percent Protestants), as compared to 688,000 Scotsmen, even though the Irish and Scottish populations were about the same size (about 4.5 million) in 1914. The British contributed to their problem of recruiting in Ireland by refusing to organize the southern Irish army units into an Irish corps with its own badges and symbols. Yet at the same time, the strongly unionist British high command allowed the Ulster Unionists to form their own purely Protestant division, the Red Hand of Ulster, which distinguished itself in many battles, including the Battle of the Somme, which afterwards was to loom large in Ulster Protestant hearts and minds.

The newly reformed Irish Volunteers meanwhile came under the secret control of the Irish Republican Brotherhood (IRB). This was the new generation of the old Fenian Brotherhood. The official head of the Irish Volunteers was Eoin MacNeill, the scholar of early Irish history and leader of the Gaelic League who had led the Volunteers before the split. MacNeill in 1913 had insisted that Irish nationalists form themselves into an armed force like the Ulster Volunteers, for he knew that one day Ireland might have to use force against Britain: *"They have rights who dare to maintain them."* But MacNeill also believed that a rebellion against Britain would be militarily and morally wrong unless there was a real chance for success. He believed that while at war Britain would use every ounce of its power to defeat a rebellion in the British Isles. The IRB men who penetrated the Volunteers felt differently: because of the war Britain would not be able to send enough troops to put down an insurrection in Ireland. This IRB determination to overthrow British rule before the war ended led to the great watershed in twentieth-century Irish history—the Easter Rebellion of 1916.

THE EASTER REBELLION, 1916

The chief IRB men who put themselves into leadership positions within the Irish Volunteers were Patrick Pearse, Thomas MacDonagh, and Joseph Mary Plunkett. All were poets and Gaelic enthusiasts, and all were motivated by romantic dreams of the Irish revolutionary tradition. Pearse was the most fiery and most important. Trained as a barrister but devoted to poetry, Pearse in 1908 had founded a school dedicated to educating Irish boys in Irish language and literature. Like others in the younger generation of Irish cultural nationalists, Pearse believed that the sordid mediocrity of modern civilization, typified by the unheroic post-Parnell Home Rule party, needed to be purged by sacrifice. Thus he greeted the Great War with twisted warmth: "The old heart of the earth needed to be warmed with the red wine of the battlefields." Deeply influenced by mystical Catholicism, Pearse by 1916 had concluded that Ireland needed a blood sacrifice—a rebellion that would fail in the short run but would redeem the honor of the Irish people in the long run. Pearse, in short, combined the myth of the army of the Gael with the sacrifice of Christ on the cross and so made ready to die for Ireland—and to take other, more innocent revolutionaries with him.

Pearse and the IRB were not the only Irishmen ready to rebel. James Connolly, the labor leader who headed the Citizen Army of two hundred men, believed that a rebellion *would* win, not least because as a socialist he thought the British government would not allow themselves to destroy private property in order to defeat the rebels. In the hours before the insurrection, Connolly too fell prey to the vision of noble sacrifice. Indeed, he vowed that this Citizen Army would fight even if the Irish Volunteers did not. Shortly before the rebellion began, he told a friend, apparently without regret, "We are going out to be slaughtered."

Another advocate of rebellion was Sir Roger Casement, an Anglo-Irish career foreign service officer and a passionate Irish nationalist. Casement already had arranged for the purchase of 1,500 rifles in Germany for the Volunteers in May–July of 1914. When the Great War broke out, Casement raised funds from the American-Irish nationalist organization, Clan na Gael, and returned to Germany for more military aid. Casement believed that Germany would want to weaken Britain by helping Ireland secure its independence. Unfortunately for the Irish rebels, Casement found the Germans skeptical and uncooperative. He was able to purchase from the Germans only twenty thousand rifles taken from the Russians on the Eastern Front.

Meanwhile, the IRB leaders set the date of the rising for Easter 1916. Knowing that MacNeill would oppose them, the IRB men kept their plans secret from him and his staff. What they planned to do was arrange for the Volunteers to turn out for training and drill on Easter Sunday, precipitate a rebellion, and then by presenting MacNeill with a fait accompli, force him to commit the Volunteers to the rebellion. Casement was to land with the purchased rifles and munitions just before the rising. To spur MacNeill into action, the IRB during the week before Easter forged a document that purported to be a British plan to disarm the Volunteers.

MacNeill suspected that scheming was going on behind his back, and four days before Easter he finally learned of the planned insurrection. Furious with the plotters, he cancelled the orders for the Volunteers' training exercises scheduled for Easter Sunday. Then when MacNeill heard that Casement was bringing arms from Germany, he reversed himself; but when on the day before Easter he learned that the ship carrying the rifles had been discovered and scuttled and that Casement had been arrested, he reversed himself again. MacNeill's final order against insurrection reached most of the Volunteers, but the IRB and Citizen Army leaders in Dublin—Pearse, Connolly, MacDonagh, Plunkett, and others—decided to go ahead with the rising on the day after Easter.

On Easter Monday some 1,600 men, including about 1,400 from the Volunteers and 200 from the Citizen Army, rebelled against British rule in Ireland by occupying major buildings in Dublin. Apparently they hoped that the nation would rise spontaneously to their support. They were sadly mistaken. The great majority of the Volunteers as well as the country as a whole remained quiet. The citizenry of Dublin looked on in amazement as bands of armed Volunteers seized the General Post Office (GPO) and several other buildings near the center of the city. Shortly after noon, Pearse appeared on the Post Office steps to proclaim the establishment of the provisional government of the "Irish Republic." The proclamation denounced British "usurpation" of power in Ireland and claimed "the allegiance of every Irishman and Irishwoman" (including those in Ulster). The new Republic combined the ideals of Young Ireland with those of socialism in ringing but ambiguous phrases: "We declare the right of the people of Ireland to the ownership of Ireland, and to the unfettered control of Irish destinies, to be sovereign and indefeasible."

The rebellion, as it turned out, lasted only a week. The people of Ireland did not rally to its support. Yet in the minds of some Irish nationalists to the present day, the Republic proclaimed at Easter 1916 remains the only legitimate Irish state. It holds a sacred status, hallowed by the blood of martyrs. Within a few days, the

The Easter Rebellion: figthing in the streets of Dublin.

British government had rushed thousands of troops to Dublin to support the Royal Irish Constabulary against the rebels. On Wednesday, the British began using artillery to blast the Republican strongholds. On Friday, the main rebel force was flushed from the burning GPO. On Saturday (April 29, 1916), Pearse surrendered, and other rebel commanders soon followed. The rising by then had cost the lives of 76 rebels, 300 civilians, and about 130 British soldiers and policemen.

THE ADVENT OF SINN FEIN

The early reaction of Irish public opinion toward the Easter rising was highly unfavorable, but the British proceeded to throw away their chance to consolidate the position of constitutional Irish nationalism. Ordinary Irish men and women, especially those of the middle class, continued to support the Home Rulers, who had roundly condemned the rising. The British military forces in Ireland set about rounding up the unconstitutional nationalists. They arrested about 3,500 men and women, of whom 170 were imprisoned and 1,800 interned in England. More important, the British, who had declared martial law in Ireland, tried and convicted the leaders of the rebellion before military courts. They executed fifteen of them, one after another, in a ten-day period in May 1916. (In addition, Casement was hanged in England later that August.) Pearse, MacDonagh, and Plunkett were among those shot, as was Connolly, who had been so badly wounded that he had to be strapped in a chair to face the firing squad.

Every volley from the firing squads moved Irish public opinion one more notch toward sympathy with the rebel nationalists. After executing fifteen, the British decided that enough was enough. This decision saved the lives of Countess Markiewicz, a passionate nationalist and feminist, and Eamon de Valera, the only rebel commander to escape execution. (The U.S. government had made representations on behalf of de Valera, who had been born in New York.) But the British cessation of the executions came too late: the dead rebel leaders had been made into martyrs and now joined the pantheon of sainted revolutionary nationalists from

Wolfe Tone to Thomas Davis. Moreover, Sinn Fein, although it had not as an organization participated in the rising, won political honor, whereas the Home Rulers lost credit. In both Britain and Ireland, the rebels were often called the "Sinn Fein Volunteers." From that point on, constitutional nationalism in Ireland was finished. As W. B. Yeats said in his great poem "Easter 1916":

I write it out in verse—
MacDonagh and MacBride
And Connolly and Pearse
Now and in time to be,
Wherever green is worn,
Are changed, changed utterly:
A terrible beauty is born.

With a view toward retaining Irish support for the war effort and toward placating public opinion in the United States, where Irish nationalism was a major political factor, Prime Minister Asquith deputed Lloyd George to find a quick solution to the Irish problem. Lloyd George probably was on an impossible mission, but he made the situation worse by his characteristic duplicity. He offered Redmond immediate implementation of Home Rule on condition of the temporary exclusion of six of the nine counties of Ulster. To Carson, on the other hand, Lloyd George promised permanent exclusion of the six counties. The contradiction between these promises was revealed in parliamentary debate, and the British Conservatives and Ulster Unionists rejected the arrangement anyway. Lloyd George's efforts at reconciliation thus failed, hammering one last nail in the Home Rulers' coffin.

Events in Ireland were now flowing strongly in favor of Sinn Fein. Under the leadership of Arthur Griffith, Sinn Fein had for more than a decade preached a separatist strategy whereby the Irish simply would refuse to cooperate with either the British Parliament or the British executive in Ireland. The IRB leaders who survived the Easter Rebellion now threw their support to Sinn Fein, which was a legal political organization, in order to take advantage of the disillusionment of the Irish public with the Home Rulers. De Valera even became president of Sinn Fein.

At the same time, the Lloyd George coalition (formed December 1916), faced with severe manpower problems on the battlefronts of the Great War, sought to apply conscription not only to England, Scotland, and Wales but also to Ireland. When in April 1918 the government decided it could delay Irish conscription no longer, Irish public opinion (except in Ulster) was solidly opposed. Even the Home Rulers opposed conscription, but because they had in 1914–1915 encouraged recruitment they now earned little credit. Sinn Fein, which led the anticonscription fight in Ireland, won yet more approval. The British responded by trying to suppress Sinn Fein, the Irish Volunteers, and even the Gaelic League. These steps proved unsuccessful. Sinn Fein's membership grew, and party candidates fared well in parliamentary by-elections. By the war's end in November 1918, Sinn Fein had become the most powerful political party in the southern twenty-six counties of Ireland outside Ulster.

In the British general election of December 1918, as we will see, Lloyd George's coalition, consisting of his segment of the Liberals and all the Conservatives, won a big victory over the Asquith Liberals and the Labour party. But in Ireland, the election was a resounding victory for Sinn Fein, which won seventy-three seats to six for the Home Rulers and twenty-six for the Unionists. The Sinn Fein victors, as they had promised, refused to take their seats in Parliament at Westminster. Instead, they gathered in Dublin, calling themselves the "Dáil Éireann," the Parliament of Ireland. By their theory, they constituted the Parliament of the Irish Republic, in theory the same Republic established by Pearse and the Easter Rebellion of 1916.

CIVIL WAR WITH BRITAIN AND THE TREATY OF 1921

The establishment of the Dáil Éireann soon led to a period of savage civil warfare in Ireland that was to last until 1923. There were two phases in the civil war: (1) 1919–1921, in which Irish nationalists fought the British, and (2) 1922–1923, in which factions of Irish nationalists fought each other. In these years of civil war, the twenty-six counties of southern Ireland won autonomy, but the six northeastern counties of Ulster were partitioned off. At the same time, habits of brutality and killing were formed that even today stain Irish events.

The first phase of this most "uncivil" conflict was a guerrilla war between Irish nationalists and the forces of Britain. It was the inevitable result of the Dáil's decision to establish a parallel governmental structure in Ireland as an alternative to British rule. The Dáil reaffirmed in 1918 the declaration of Irish independence proclaimed at Easter 1916, and it selected representatives to the peace conference that was to meet at Versailles. Furthermore, the Dáil set up an alternative court system, a land bank, and a board to settle disputes in industrial relations. In effect, two different governments, one British and one Irish, claimed sovereignty in Ireland. The British at first tried to ignore the Dáil's actions, but in January 1919 shooting started between the Irish Volunteers—who now called themselves the "Irish Republican Army," or IRA—and British police.

For the next two and a half years, the British and Irish engaged in a brutal conflict of terrorism and counterterrorism. The Dáil, with de Valera as its president, was on the run and met only in secret. The IRA was dominated by IRB men and operated outside the effective control of the Dáil. Given the vast superiority in numbers and armament of the British forces, the IRA had to adopt the hit-and-run tactics of guerrilla warfare. They wore civilian clothes and took refuge among the Irish populace, emerging to ambush military patrols and convoys and to assassinate enemy soldiers and spies. Led by Michael Collins, an extremely able and tough fighter, the IRA developed a ruthlessness and a fanaticism necessary for survival but poisonous to the humane qualities that would be necessary in peacetime.

The British fought fire with fire. Because they rejected acknowledgment of the Dáil's existence, the British refused to admit that they were embroiled in a true war in Ireland. To them it remained a police action but one conducted in conditions of open ferocity. Hence the government did not send the British army to Ireland but depended on the Royal Irish Constabulary and powerful supporting forces recruited in England. None of these elements exercised the discipline of the regular army. The supplementary forces, the so-called Black and Tans (from their dark green caps and tan uniforms) and Auxiliaries (or Auxis) were recruited from ex-army officers and enlisted men. In the face of IRA tactics, they engaged in ambushes, assassinations, torture, and reprisals. In order to deprive the guerrillas of popular support, these British forces took reprisals on whole Irish communities. Like their opponents, they often operated outside of control by their government, in this case London. And in 1920, the government itself sanctioned the practice of taking reprisals on Irish villages and communities. However, despite the fact that British forces outnumbered the IRA by fifty thousand to ten thousand, they were not able to win an outright victory.

British public opinion meanwhile became sickened by the killing in Ireland. By 1919 British opinion had finally accepted the idea of Home Rule for Ireland. Now, already weary of warfare and casualty lists, and having come to believe that they had fought the Great War for democracy and national self-determination, the British had no stomach for the seemingly endless brutalities in Ireland. Reprisals such as the sacking of the village of Balbriggen seemed indecent. Here appeared the British sense of fair play at its best. As the eminent writer G. K. Chesterton put it, "To burn down a factory and a row of shops because a comrade has been murdered is not self-defense—it is senseless revenge." Asquithian Liberals and Labourites urged an end to the fighting, as did an increasing number of nonconformists and Anglicans alike. Accommodation with Irish nationalism seemed the only acceptable policy for Britain—and the only way to maintain the unity of the British Empire.

Lloyd George responded to the growing antiwar sentiment by reviving Home Rule. In 1920 his coalition government, though it was dominated by Conservative Unionists, carried the Better Government of Ireland Act. It created a Home Rule Parliament for the twenty-six counties of nationalist Ireland and another one for the six northeastern counties of Ulster. In southern Ireland this act never came into operation, but it did in Ulster; thus it was the instrument by which Ireland was formally partitioned.

The Dáil and the IRA rejected the Better Government of Ireland Act on grounds that Home Rule was not enough for Ireland, and they continued fighting into 1921. Gradually, however, the IRA's resources became exhausted. By the summer of 1921, the IRA could command no more than five thousand guerrillas. Fortunately for them, had they but known it, the British also were approaching exhaustion, not of men and matériel but of willpower. Under pressure from public opinion at home and abroad, and especially in the United States, Lloyd George finally in July 1921 offered the Irish a truce and invited them to negotiate a treaty. The chief of the Imperial General Staff told Lloyd George that his only alternatives were "to go all out or to get out." And Lloyd George knew public opinion would not tolerate "going all out."

The peace negotiations between Britain and the Irish nationalists went through two stages. In the first, Lloyd George dealt with de Valera himself and offered limited "dominion status"—that is, southern Ireland would have self-government within the Empire like Canada or Australia—but the Irish dominion would have to recognize the partition of Ireland, contribute to the British war debt, and allow the British to keep military and naval bases in Ireland. De Valera said that he was no doctrinaire Republican but that these terms were not enough for Ireland.

In the second phase, de Valera stayed home and Lloyd George negotiated with a delegation from the Dáil, led by Michael Collins and Arthur Griffith. The Irish negotiators rejected mere Home Rule, and the British regarded full independence for Ireland (the "Republican" solution) as out of the question. The most the Irish could hope for was "external association," by which they would freely associate as a republic with the British Empire (or Commonwealth, as it was now coming to be called). What Lloyd George offered, however, was something less: dominion status, by which Ireland would have self-rule but would agree to allegiance to the British Crown as well as to membership in the Commonwealth. The Irish delegates insisted that the partition be ended, and they feared that the extreme nationalists in Dublin would never accept dominion status. After much tense negotiation, Lloyd George threatened to renew the war if the Irish delegates rejected his offer, and he was not bluffing; but he also suggested that a future boundary commission would so reduce the size of a separate Ulster that the partition would collapse. The Irish delegates felt that they had no choice and agreed to the treaty on December 6, 1921. Thus the Act of Union of 1800 and the United Kingdom of Great Britain and Ireland that it created were officially ended.

CIVIL WAR IN IRELAND, 1922–1923

The treaty closed an important chapter in Anglo-Irish relations, but it did not end the fighting in Ireland. When the treaty was debated in the Irish Dáil, it met strong opposition from the most militant nationalists. Many Republicans rejected dominion status because they would accept nothing less than the sacred Republic of 1916. De Valera did not insist on a republic, but he opposed the treaty on grounds that it did not go far enough toward real independence for Ireland. For him and others the symbolic matter of pledging allegiance to the British Crown was intolerable. The protreaty forces, led by the IRA commander, Michael Collins, argued that dominion status was all the Irish could get, that it represented a big advance over Home Rule, and that it would constitute a base from which Ireland could move toward full independence. After long and bitter debate, the Dáil approved the treaty by a narrow margin.

De Valera and a number of IRA commanders refused to accept the Dáil's verdict. De Valera resigned as president of the Dáil, and with his support the dissident IRA members took up arms against the treaty and the Dáil. Thus at the same time that the protreaty forces were assuming responsibility for governing Ireland, now known as the Irish Free State, they also had to fight a civil war against many of their

Eamon de Valera. The magnetic and somewhat mysterious Irish politican, a survivor of the Easter Rebellion, led the antitreaty forces within Irish nationalism.

former comrades-in-arms, who resisted the Free State on behalf of the now mythical Republic of 1916.

This phase of civil war in Ireland lasted from April 1922 until May 1923. The Free Staters won a general election in June 1922 over the antitreaty faction by nearly 80 percent to 20 percent; these figures suggest the relative size of the forces. But a majority of IRA heroes from the war against the British fought against the treaty. They claimed the title of "The IRA"—that is, that *they* were the true army of the 1916 Republic. Michael Collins led the protreaty army, which now had to face the same kind of guerrilla tactics that they themselves had once employed. Ambushes, assassinations, and military executions again prevailed in Ireland. The Free State, in fact, executed seventy-seven of the antitreaty guerrillas, including several of the most prominent commanders; this was three times as many executions as the British carried out between 1919 and 1921. Collins himself was killed in an IRA ambush.

The ruthlessness of the Free Staters and the impatience of most Irish civilians with the incessant killing finally persuaded the IRA that they could not win. Urged by de Valera to make their peace with the Free State, most of the IRA simply stopped fighting and turned in their arms but without surrendering. The IRA men, however, never gave up their view that the Republic of 1916 was the only true Irish state and therefore that the treaty, the Free State, and the partition of 1920–1921 were illegitimate. Almost to the present day, they and their descendants continued their often violent struggle to restore the Republic of 1916, which theoretically ruled a *united* Ireland.

Meanwhile, in the six counties of Northern Ireland (often mistakenly called simply "Ulster") the subordinate Parliament created by the Better Government of

Ireland Act of 1920 had come into existence. Ironically, then, the Ulster Protestant Unionists got exactly what they had resisted since 1886—Home Rule! The new Northern Ireland province of Great Britain was born in conditions of sectarian hatred and urban terrorism. The IRA in Ulster resisted the partition and the establishment of the Northern Ireland provincial government. However, the power of the Protestant Unionists, supported by the British government, was much too strong. The British government had drawn the boundary around Northern Ireland so as to exclude many Catholics and therefore to ensure a two-to-one majority of Protestant Unionists over the Catholic nationalist minority. Thus the IRA in the North had less support than in the twenty-six counties, and the nationalists in 1920–1921 had no chance either to thwart the will of the Unionists or to play an influential role in the formation of the provincial government and politics. Few of the Northern Ireland Catholics in fact wanted to play such a role, since most of them rejected the legitimacy of the province in the first place.

Taken as a whole, the years of passion and bloodshed in Ireland between 1916 and 1923 had established an autonomous dominion, but they had also partitioned the island and created a Unionist province in its most highly industrialized and prosperous region. It is hard to imagine that any of these events would have occurred but for the Great War. England's difficulty did prove to be Ireland's opportunity, but it also turned out to be the Home Rulers' catastrophe and a *united* Ireland's tragedy.

EPILOGUE: IRELAND, 1921–1939

In the two decades following the end of the civil war in 1923, the Irish Free State succeeded in establishing itself as a workable independent country, though one with more serious economic problems and a more stagnant society than the nationalists had anticipated. The treaty (and its partition) continued to be the dividing line not only in the island as a whole but also within southern Irish politics: parties aligned themselves mainly around the issue of whether the treaty was acceptable or not. The protreaty Free Staters organized themselves as the Cummann na nGaedheal party and ruled until 1932. They proved to be a conservative, right-of-center party in a society dominated by the Catholic middle class and the Catholic church. (In the 1930s, the Cummann na nGaedheal party merged with right-wing groups to form a new right-of-center party, Fine Gael ["Family of Gaels"], which still exists.) In 1925, the Boundary Commission called for by the treaty prepared to enlarge the borders of Northern Ireland rather than cut them back as Lloyd George had promised. The Cummann na nGaedheal government quickly accepted the existing boundary. This action gave the Republicans popular ground on which to criticize the founders of the Free State.

The Free State government, meanwhile, treated the IRA as a criminal organization and in 1921 formally outlawed it. The IRA for its part continued to regard the Free State as illegitimate, and Sinn Fein refused to participate in the Dáil. De Valera, however, did not wish to remain forever in the political wilderness, and in

1925 he organized a new political party, Fianna Fáil ("Warriors of Ireland"). He and the more moderate Republicans gradually moved back into more constitutional politics. In 1927, de Valera actually took his seat in the Dáil, while insisting that he had only signed the registry book (and in pencil at that) and not taken the oath. This highly complex, aloof, somewhat mysterious but charismatic man was a curious combination of romantic, Gaelic-League nationalist and pragmatic politician. He led Fianna Fáil to victory in 1932, and over the course of the next forty years made an indelible mark on Ireland.

In office in the 1930s, de Valera (1882–1975) led the Free State toward state action in social policies, in part to counter the effects of worldwide depression, and toward more complete separation from Britain. Fianna Fáil's social policies were not socialist, but they did commit significant funds to welfare benefits for the unemployed, widows, and orphans and to old-age pensions and housing construction. As for relations with Britain, de Valera openly criticized the partition, stopped the turnover of land purchase payments to Britain, and dropped the oath of allegiance. The British were not pleased, but they elected not to use force against the Free State.

In 1937, de Valera presented Ireland with a new constitution. It claimed that Ireland was "a sovereign, independent, democratic state"—a republic in all but name. The British already had given up the right of Parliament to legislate for the dominions by the Statute of Westminster (1931). Now, in 1937, de Valera's new Irish constitution set up a Parliament in Dublin of two houses, with a president as the head of state and a prime minister as chief executive. In many ways this constitution, which forms the basis for today's Irish Republic, showed the profound influence of the British example. But de Valera's constitution also claimed sovereignty over *all* of Ireland and by Article 44 recognized the "special position" of the Roman Catholic church as the religion of the majority of the Irish people. Both provisions, like de Valera's general "Irish-Ireland" outlook, were highly provocative to the Northern Ireland Protestants.

The relative political stability of the Free State after 1923 justified the predictions of generations of Irish nationalists: the Irish could in fact govern themselves responsibly. But in economy and society, autonomy did not work miracles. Ireland remained very much in the British economic orbit. Agriculture and industry alike were sluggish, and the Irish standard of living lagged behind that of Britain—indeed, behind that of Northern Ireland as well. Emigration continued to drain off many of the most talented young Irish men and women, so that in the 1920s, the population of the Free State fell below three million.

The Free State government vigorously tried to promote the Irish language, by preserving the Gaeltacht (the Irish-speaking conclave of the western counties) and by establishing Irish as the national language. Irish became the language of record in the courts and the Dáil's debates, for instance, and civil servants had to be competent in Irish. But the number and proportion of Irish speakers continued to decline because of the utility of English. Increasingly, the "Irish-Ireland" point of view came to be seen by progressive Irish men and women—and especially by literary intellectuals—as the outlook of a backward, provincial, exclusively Catholic section of the people. Certainly the Free State was built on a thoroughly conservative Catholic society. The population was 95 percent Catholic, and though the Catholics made no effort whatsoever to persecute the Protestant minority, the Catholic clergy and bishops dominated education, public morality, and to a significant degree social policy.

The degree to which the Free State was a Catholic country was not lost on the Unionists of Northern Ireland. These hard-bitten folk suffered from a severe case of "fortress mentality" in the first place. Even though the Protestants of Northern Ireland outnumbered the Catholics by 1 million to 500,000, they lived in fear that they would be swallowed up by Catholic nationalist Ireland. Union with Britain became their sacred principle. Furthermore, to protect themselves in their northern fastness, the Protestant Unionists built an authoritarian, bastardized parliamentary state in which the real power resided in the Orange Lodges, the militant Protestant clubs founded in the eighteenth century. Unified in a single, monolithic party, the Unionist party, the Northern Ireland Protestants reduced Catholics to second-class citizens. They abolished the proportional representation that the British had put in the Better Government of Ireland Act; they gerrymandered local government districts to deprive Catholics of influence in local government; they set up an exclusively Protestant (and habitually brutal) police force, the B-Specials; and wherever possible they discriminated against Catholics in housing, employment, and education. Working-class and upper-class Protestants cooperated in this mistreatment of the mostly working-class Catholic people of Northern Ireland. In Northern Ireland, religion and nationality were stronger than class consciousness.

The Catholics of Northern Ireland contributed to this situation by refusing to recognize the legitimate existence of the province. They typically gave their allegiance to Ireland—meaning a united, nationalist Ireland. In effect they withdrew from the politics of Northern Ireland until 1932, when their representatives first agreed to sit in the Northern Ireland Parliament at Stormont, near Belfast. Even then it was clear that the opposition in Northern Ireland, representing as it did the Catholic minority, would never be able to become the majority and form a government. In Northern Ireland, then, genuine parliamentary government could never work. All of this came into being with the knowledge and approval of the British government, which was only too happy to leave Northern Ireland to the Unionist majority and thus for the first time in more than a century get Ireland off the British political agenda.

Suggested Reading

Bowman, John, *De Valera and the Ulster Question, 1917–1973* (Oxford: Clarendon Press, 1982).

Boyce, D. G., *Englishmen and Irish Troubles: British Public Opinion and the Making of Irish Policy, 1918–22* (Cambridge, Mass.: MIT University Press, 1972).

Buckland, Patrick, *Irish Unionism* (2 vols.) (Dublin: Gill & Macmillan, 1972).

Coffey, Thomas M., *Agony at Easter* (New York: Macmillan, 1969).

Dangerfield, George, *The Damnable Question* (Boston: Little, Brown, 1976).

Devine, T. M., *The Scottish Nation: A History, 1700–2000* (New York: Viking, 1999).

Dunphy, Richard, *The Making of Fianna Fáil Power in Ireland, 1923–1948* (Oxford: Oxford University Press, 1995).

Elliott, Marianne, *The Catholics of Ulster* (London: Allen Lane, 2000).

English, Richard, *Armed Struggle: The History of the IRA* (New York: Oxford University Press, 2004).

Follis, Bryan A., *A State Under Siege: The Establishment of Northern Ireland, 1920–1925* (Oxford: Oxford University Press, 1995).

Hachey, Thomas E., Joseph M. Hernon, Jr., and Lawrence J. McCaffrey, *The Irish Experience* (Englewood Cliffs, N.J.: Prentice Hall, 1989).

Hachey, Thomas E., *Britain and Irish Separatism: From the Fenians to the Free State, 1867–1922* (Chicago: Rand McNally, 1977).

Hart, Peter, *The IRA at War, 1916–1923* (Oxford: Oxford University Press, 2003).

Harvie, Christopher, *No Gods and Precious Few Heroes: Scotland, 1914–1980* (Toronto: University of Toronto Press, 1981).

Hutchison, I. G. C., *A Political History of Scotland, 1832–1924* (Edinburgh: Donald, 1986).

Kee, Robert, *The Green Flag* (New York: Delacorte Press, 1972).

Lawlor, Sheila, *Britain and Ireland, 1914–23* (Dublin: Gill & Macmillan, 1983).

Lee, Joseph, *Ireland, 1912–1985: Politics and Society* (Cambridge: Cambridge University Press, 1989).

———, *The Modernization of Irish Society, 1848–1918* (Dublin: Gill & Macmillan, 1983).

Lenman, Bruce, *An Economic History of Modern Scotland, 1660–1976* (Hamden, Conn.: Archon Books, 1977).

Loughlin, James, *Ulster Unionism and British National Identity Since 1885* (London: Cassell Publishers, 1995).

Lyons, F. S. L., *Ireland Since the Famine* (London: Fontana, 1973).

Martin, F. X., ed., *Leaders and Men of the Easter Rising: Dublin 1916* (London: Mehtuen, 1967).

McCaffrey, Lawrence J., *Ireland from Colony to Nation State* (Englewood Cliffs, N.J.: Prentice-Hall, 1979).

Moran, Sean Farrell, *Patrick Pearse and the Politics of Redemption: The Mind of the Easter Rising, 1916* (Washington, D.C.: Catholic University of America Press, 1994).

Morgan, Kenneth O., *Rebirth of a Nation: Wales, 1880–1980* (New York: Oxford University Press, 1981).

Morgan, Prys, and David Thomas, *Wales: The Shaping of a Nation* (Newton Abbot: David & Charles, 1984).

Murphy, John A., *Ireland in the Twentieth Century* (Dublin: Gill & Macmillan, 1975).

Smout, T. C., *A Century of the Scottish People, 1830–1950* (London: Collins, 1986).

Townshend, Charles, *The British Campaign in Ireland, 1919–1921* (London: Oxford University Press, 1975).

Williams, Gwyn, *When Was Wales?* (London: Black Raven Press, 1985).

Chapter 8

Economy, Society, and Culture Between the Wars, 1919–1939

A leading historian once wrote that British culture after the Great War showed "evidence of minds scorched by war, and reacting against a nervous strain which was almost unbearable."* The same kind of thing might be said of the economy and society. Although there was a pervasive feeling by British politicians and businessmen that Britain should return as quickly as possible to the "normal" conditions that had prevailed before 1914, such a return proved impossible. Economy, society, and culture had been so altered that the Victorian and Edwardian "golden years" could never be recovered. Thus many features of British life after 1919 were clearly "modern," and the attempts to return to former conditions only multiplied the problems the nation faced. Yet the vestiges of nineteenth-century economic and social institutions continued to hang on. This quality of *insufficient* change led at least one veteran of trench warfare, the poet and novelist Robert Graves, to say "good-bye to all that" and emigrate. Interwar Britain was therefore what Professor Harold Perkin called a "halfway house"—a society halfway between Victorian ways, now often malfunctioning, and the ways of the post–World War II world.

THE BRITISH ECONOMY BETWEEN THE WARS

The Great War, as we saw in Chapter 6, caused enormous dislocations in the British economy. It had used up valuable capital, turned Britain into a debtor nation, eroded Britain's ability to earn income from invisible exports, disrupted world trade patterns, and caused some industries to be neglected. But the war had also stimulated the development of new industries and encouraged some rationalization of industry. Clearly, the United States had replaced Britain as the world's great economic power. Because the British economy was so heavily dependent on world trade, itself so radically disrupted by the war, the outlook for British recovery in 1920 was very bleak.

---

*E. L. Woodward, *Short Journey* (London: Faber and Faber, 1942), p. 122.

The British economy in the 1920s thus had to operate in world conditions over which Britain had little control. The United States and Japan had expanded their production enormously and taken over former British markets in Latin America and Asia, including even India. Dominions like Canada and Australia had increased their own industrial output and served less well as markets for British manufactures. The web of war debts and reparations skewed international trade. Moreover, most of the British export industries produced goods like textiles and coal in which Britain faced new, more technologically advanced overseas competition. Furthermore, these goods were to suffer a declining share of the world's markets because of new products like synthetic fabrics and petroleum. Finally, during the war, nations that had supplied primary products (foodstuffs and raw materials) had greatly increased their production, and this caused the price of primary products to fall. This situation was good for Britain as an importer of primary products, but it was also bad because it reduced the ability of primary producers around the world to buy manufactured articles from Britain.

With the benefit of hindsight, it is clear that the British after the Great War needed to move rapidly from wartime production and to shift resources of capital and labor away from the old staple industries (cotton, coal, iron) into newer industries that would be able to compete in world markets. Such a strategy was not seen clearly and in any case could not have been pursued by British politicians and businessmen, who alike wanted not to engage in rational state planning and direction of the economy but to remove the government as soon as possible from its economic role. This was a legacy of nineteenth-century liberalism. The Lloyd George cabinet did plan to demobilize troops rationally, by releasing workers in key occupations first, but protests and demobilization riots among the troops forced the government to adopt the simple principle of "first in, first out." Many ex-soldiers, including former officers, found it impossible to obtain work. Their discontent added to the severe labor unrest that already afflicted certain industrial areas like Clydeside (Scotland) and the coalfield of South Wales. The government also sought to end unpopular wartime controls as rapidly as possible: food rationing ended in 1919, and most of the economic regulations ended within two years. The government was pledged, as we will see in Chapter 9, to measures of social reform, but in its basic economic role, it sought to return to normalcy—that is, the noninterventionist state.

The government's policy of withdrawing from the economy seemed to be rewarded by a brief boom in 1919 and 1920. This "restocking" boom was caused by the desire of industries to replace worn-out machinery and to replenish stocks of consumer goods that had been depleted during the war. Unfortunately, the postwar boom misled many British industrialists and financiers as to the economic climate and encouraged them to invest in industries in which there was already too much productive capacity. It also encouraged the use of wartime profits in speculative buying and selling of companies, and like most bouts of company mergers, this one of the early 1920s left many firms with a massive burden of debt. When trade inevitably began to contract in 1921, these companies were forced either to cut wages, which caused serious problems in industrial relations, or to go out of business.

Britain thus slid into a depression in 1921, which though it had better and worse moments, lasted through the 1930s. The slump beginning in 1921 held on for most of the 1920s, and the economy was just beginning to emerge from it when the blizzard of worldwide depression struck in 1929. The worst years were 1929–1932. A recovery from that trough followed until 1937, when another downturn ensued, with yet another recovery only beginning when war broke out again in 1939. The economy overall continued to grow at a rate of about 2 percent a year, but the old staple industries suffered a major setback and, for the first time since the Industrial Revolution, contracted. Coal fell from its production peak of 287 million tons in 1913 to 227 million tons in 1938—a 21 percent decrease. Cotton textiles fell from 8 billion square yards to 3 billion—a 63 percent decrease. Shipbuilding dropped 69 percent between 1913 and 1938. Exports fell by 13 percent, and the imbalance between visible exports and imports worsened sharply, even as invisible earnings from overseas finance, brokerage, and investments declined. In the early 1930s, Britain suffered for the first time in the modern period (but not the last) a deficit in the balance of payments, and even a "run" on the gold and foreign reserves in the Bank of England (that is, foreign holders of pounds turned in huge amounts of them for gold and other currencies). Worst of all, the rate of unemployment was at least 10 percent every year between 1923 and 1939; in 1932, the worst year in these bleak times, it reached 22.5 percent.

The depression in the old staple industries represented the decline of the manufactures that had made Victorian Britain great. Whole geographical regions that had once been the scene of belching smokestacks and clanging factories now stood idle: South Wales, central and southeastern Scotland, the Belfast area of Northern Ireland, northeastern England, Cumberland, and parts of Lancashire. In South Wales, many mining towns had more than two-thirds of the work force unemployed. The shipbuilding town of Jarrow in Durham had an unemployment rate of 80 percent in the early 1930s. In the worst period, 1931–1932, 35 percent of British coal miners, 36 percent of pottery workers, 43 percent of cotton operatives, and 62 percent of ship builders were out of work. The novelist J. B. Priestley in 1933 found the industrial areas a dismal picture:

> . . . the industrial England of coal, iron, steel, cotton, wool, railways; of thousands of rows of little houses, all alike, sham Gothic churches, square-faced chapels, Town Halls, Mechanics' Institutes, mills, foundries, warehouses . . . railway stations, slag-heaps and 'tips,' dock roads . . . cindery waste ground, mill chimneys, slums, fried-fish shops, public houses with red blinds, bethels in corrugated iron, . . . a cynically devastated countryside, sooty dismal little towns, and sootier grim fortress-like cities. This England makes up the larger part of the Midlands and the North and exists everywhere; but it is not being added to and has no new life poured into it.

Could the decay of Britain's staple industries have been avoided in the 1920s and 1930s? Probably not, for the roots of decline in these industries lay partly, as we have seen, in patterns of trade and investment of the late nineteenth century; partly in the maturing of other industrial economies; and partly in the peculiar problems of the world economy after the Great War. But Britain aggravated the difficulties by mistaken policies. In 1925, for instance, the government decided to return to the gold standard at the prewar parity of $4.86 to the pound sterling. This was done to shore up Britain's position in international finance and to restore confidence in the British economy, but it overpriced British goods by 10 percent and thus made them less competitive in world markets. As we will see in Chapter 9, Britain went off the gold standard in 1932 to avoid a run on the pound and depletion of the Bank of England's gold reserves, but by then the damage to Britain's trade position had been done.

Moreover, orthodox economic theory, derived from the nineteenth-century Manchester School of classical economics and adhered to by almost all politicians, bankers, and academic economists during the interwar years, held (1) that the free market system was self-regulating, (2) that it would automatically adjust interest rates so as to maximize investment and production and thus bring about full employment, and (3) that the government must not intervene in the economy for fear of diverting capital, goods, and labor from "natural" rates of interest, prices, and wages. In Britain, this theory remained dominant until near the end of the thirties.

If the policymakers had listened to John Maynard Keynes (1883–1946), the brilliant Cambridge economist and member of the Bloomsbury Group, they might have concluded that the government should take responsibility for stimulating economic activity and increasing aggregate demand. In his pathbreaking work, *The General Theory of Employment, Interest, and Money*, Keynes contended that although market economies *are* self-regulating, they may reach equilibrium at low rates of investment and demand and a high rate of unemployment. In Britain's depression of the 1930s, the demand for goods was so low that industrialists had no incentive to borrow money from banks to expand production; instead they cut production and wages. Keynes believed that if the government pumped money into the economy (by investing in public works and by running a deficit), demand would be stimulated. As a result, businessmen would seek to invest in new factories and hire more workers. Wages would rise, and the demand for consumer goods would spiral upward. Thus deliberate "demand management" by the government could jolt the economy out of the doldrums.

By such policies alone, Keynes believed, capitalism could be saved from fascism or communism. But Keynes did not publish his great theoretical work supporting this view, *The General Theory*, until 1936; until then the majority of opinion held that he was preaching wasteful and irresponsible policies and therefore that the government could not intervene effectively.

At the same time, British governments between the wars were not completely inactive in economic policies. For one thing, all governments regardless of party affiliation sought to maintain the stability of sterling, and this goal seemed to them to require balanced budgets and maintenance (until 1932) of the gold standard. For another, in 1932 the government abandoned free trade, which had been enshrined in public policy since 1846, by passing the Import Duties Act and then opening trade negotiations with the dominions to establish a system of imperial tariff preferences. The government by these actions sought to protect British industry from foreign competition within the domestic market, to mark out the Empire as a safe haven for British goods, and to promote the "rationalization" (that is, streamlining) of British industries. The tariff was to have little effect, but its passage signified the end of one more aspect of the Victorian economic system.

The government promoted rationalization of industry in many ways. The theory was that British industry would fare better in world competition if the smaller, less efficient firms were either eliminated or swallowed up by larger companies. Such a movement, often called "concentration" as well as "rationalization," was already underway by the impetus of industry itself, as large companies amalgamated and bought out smaller ones. The formation of giant combines like Imperial Chemical Industries, Unilever, and Imperial Tobacco Company was typical of the concentration movement of the 1920s. By informal pressure and by parliamentary act, governments of the 1920s and 1930s helped foster such rationalization.

Concentration in the interwar period altered the structure of many industries. The 130 railway companies of 1914 were reduced to four regionally separate and noncompeting firms after 1921. The thirty-eight joint-stock banks were reduced to twelve in 1924, and of those, five dominated the rest. Iron and steel manufacturers entered a huge steel cartel after 1932. The myriad coal companies, long a problem in the mining industry, had been weeded out and joined in cartels by 1936. By 1939, the British economy, once one of the least amalgamated and centralized in the industrial world, had become one of the most highly concentrated, the one hundred largest companies by 1939 accounting for 26 percent of the nation's manufacturing output.

The restructuring of British industry also went forward during the interwar years by the development of new industries. Most of these produced light consumer goods as opposed to the heavy industry of the Victorian period, and most were located in the South and Southeast of England, near the huge consumer market of London, instead of in the old industrial centers of the North and Northwest. Chief among these new industries were electricity, rayon, and automobiles. Because of their early headstart in the use of steam and gas power, the British had lagged behind other advanced nations in electrical industries. During the 1920s and 1930s, however, the government's Central Electricity Board made great strides in concentrating the generation of electricity in a few efficient plants and in tying them together in a National Grid. These steps made electric power available to people in every region, and by 1938 there were nine million consumers of electricity. The country was flooded with electrical consumer products like irons, stoves, washing machines, vacuum cleaners, and radios. By 1937, for instance, approximately two million radios a year were sold. Meanwhile, the production of rayon (a cheap artificial fabric) expanded rapidly, at the expense of the cotton and woolen industries but to the advantage of consumers of inexpensive and lightweight clothing. The automotive industry, benefiting from wartime stimuli and mass-production techniques, rose to second place in the world (behind the United States). The British automotive industry by 1938 produced more than half a million vehicles a year and employed half a million workers. All of these new industries were part of a vast increase in the nationwide consumer-sales industry, with companies like Woolworth, Marks and Spencer, and Sainsbury opening stores in almost every locality.

How far the new industries were responsible for the overall record of growth in the 1920s and 1930s, and for the record of recovery in the later 1930s, is a matter for debate. Their mass-production techniques, "scientific" management (based on systematic time-and-motion studies), and economies of scale certainly made them more productive than most older firms, and they paved the way for the future. However, the new industries did not as yet constitute a majority of the industrial sector of the economy, and the rate of investment in British industry remained comparatively low. Probably the industry most responsible for recovery in the 1930s was building, for low interest rates (that is, cheap money for loans) encouraged a wave of home construction between 1932 and 1937, with a consequent demand for home appliances. Toward the end of the 1930s, rearmament, particularly in the aircraft industry, began to have a major effect on the economy. Thus the recovery, like the products of the new industries themselves, was built around the home market rather than foreign trade. This represented a significant shift in the shape of the British economy.

SOCIETY BETWEEN THE WARS

One of the paradoxes of the social history of interwar Britain is that the standard of living for most people continued to improve despite the depression. This was not true for the unemployed, but as we will see, the majority of people who sought work did find it. A visible index of the improved standard of living was the fact that shoeless, ragged children were now rarely to be seen. The main reason for the improvement of the material conditions of life for the employed population was that wages as well as salaries remained level after the sharp increase of the war years, while prices fell markedly. The cost of living declined by more than 20 percent between 1920 and 1938. This growth in real income enabled people to spend more for food and clothing. One estimate holds that per capita food consumption improved by more than 30 percent in the interwar years.

Other factors contributing to improved standards of living were education and some redistribution of wealth from the rich to the poor through governmental taxation and social services. In neither case were the steps taken radical, but they were significant. The spirit of social improvement generated by the war effort produced the Fisher Education Act of 1918, which at long last made free, compulsory education until age fourteen universal. The depression and consequent governmental concern with budgetary economy prevented full realization of the Fisher Act; nevertheless, public spending on education went up by 65 percent between 1920 and 1939, and by 1938 over two-thirds of all children between eleven and fourteen years of age were in secondary schools. Education beyond age fourteen remained woefully scarce for the working class. The middle and upper classes continued to fill up the fee-paid grammar (that is, college preparatory high) schools and the public (that is, expensive private boarding) schools. Although a number of provincial university colleges were added to the collection of red-brick universities, the British higher education system remained seriously underfunded and undersized. In 1938, only 2 percent of British nineteen-year-olds were enrolled in colleges and universities, and less than one-fourth of these were women.

The extension of state education after 1919 was not done for purposes of deliberate social engineering but for simple social justice. The same can be said of the transfer of incomes by the state from rich to poor. Graduated taxes, including both death duties and income taxes, remained relatively high after the First World War. Whereas the wealthiest people in Britain had paid income taxes at only an 8 percent rate in 1913, they paid at 42.5 percent in 1919 and 39.1 percent in 1938. Meanwhile, social benefits to the poor, including unemployment payments, old age pensions, medical insurance, and school medical treatments, grew from 4.2 percent of the gross national product in 1910 to 11.3 percent in 1938. For the first time the British working class collected more in social benefits from the state than they paid in taxes: by 1926, for instance, they enjoyed a net payback of 21 percent.

These improvements in standards of living did not eliminate class conflict, for Britain remained a severely class-ridden society, not least in its educational system. The improvements did, however, make some gains against poverty and narrowed the gap between rich and poor. Social investigators like Booth and Rowntree in the late nineteenth century had found that 30 percent of the population lived at or below the poverty level. But similar surveys between the wars (including some done by Rowntree himself) found that the number of impoverished had been reduced to 10 to 15 percent of the people. Moreover, the standard definition of poverty had been raised, from the inability to maintain physical efficiency to the inability to satisfy a wide range of human needs, including more for food, clothing, housing, heating, and lighting, and some for "extras" like beer, tobacco, and books.

Britain still was a nation of highly unequal incomes but not as unequal as in the previous century. A tiny minority of some two thousand families enjoyed average annual incomes of more than £40,000, whereas 88 percent of the population earned less than £250 a year. In between stood the middle and upper classes, who enjoyed between £650 and £10,000 a year. Doctors and barristers earned over £1,000 a year, and the rapidly growing class of professional managers of industry even more, whereas coal miners earned less than £150 and agricultural laborers, as ever the worst-paid group, less than £100. Still, the income pyramid thickened in its middle and bottom layers. In 1913, for example, the richest 10 percent of the population enjoyed 50 percent of the national income, but in 1938 the richest 10 percent took only 41 percent.

One of the main reasons that working-class incomes went further between the wars was that they were typically spread over fewer people. The practice of family limitation that had begun with the middle and upper classes in the 1870s had extended to the working class by the 1920s. Despite a decline in the death rate, therefore, a decreasing birth rate slowed the growth of the British population to less than one-half a percent a year. (Scotland, Ireland, and Wales grew even less fast than England, with the result that the British population increasingly resided in

England.) The average number of children per family fell from 3.4 in 1911 to 2.2 in 1931. As the number of large families decreased, the average wage-earner's pay packet had to support fewer people.

The desire of working people to maintain comparatively high standards of living underlay the practice of family limitation. The methods employed were numerous. Although the average age at marriage did not go up, by the 1930s two-thirds of married couples in Britain were using some form of birth control: abstinence, the safe period, coitus interruptus, diaphragms, and above all, condoms. Information about contraceptives became much more widely available, as social reformers who were concerned about the impoverishing effect of large families published cheap books and pamphlets and established a birth control movement. The information and technology of birth control were accompanied by a more liberal attitude toward sex. Dr. Marie Stopes, for example, published in 1918 two books (*Married Love* and *Wise Parenthood*) that together advocated sexual fulfillment in marriage as well as family planning. She helped found the National Birth Control Association in 1930, which became the Family Planning Association in 1939; it established clinics in most of the large cities.

There was a strong reaction among the public at large against feminism, because many people felt that peace and order in public life had to be founded upon a restoration of conventional relations between the sexes in private life; nevertheless, given the lower birth rate, smaller families, and the higher standard of living, the condition of women's lives was bound to improve. It is true that in general most women were turned out of wartime industrial jobs when the men returned to the work force in the early 1920s, and the percentage of women at work fell to the prewar level. Wage rates for women normally were only half of those paid to men, and the proportion of women workers organized in the trade unions was much lower than that of men. At the same time, however, the range of jobs open to women improved because of the growth of clerical, service, and "light industrial" work. Such work was rarely done by *married* women, for the assumption was still that a married woman's proper sphere was in the home. Even the civil service released women when they married. What made life better for the great majority of wives and mothers was the improved family income, family limitation, and the abandonment of prewar restrictions and inhibitions. The increased freedom for women was symbolized by the abandonment of the more formal and cumbersome Victorian fashions and adoption of lighter clothes, shorter hemlines, and even shorts for sporting activities like tennis and hiking.

British feminism had left behind its "heroic" phase of campaigning for the suffrage, but the British women's movement was now active and effective in a lower key. Cooperative guilds and women's institutes gave women the opportunity to learn about topics ranging from birth control and charitable activities to international politics. The Women's League of Health and Beauty promoted female athleticism. Mainstream feminism between the wars was divided between those who concentrated on improving women's position as mothers and those who focused on helping women achieve economic and professional independence. The Fabian

Women's Group campaigned for family allowances and a greater degree of economic independence for wives and mothers. The principal feminist organization of the time, the National Union of Societies for Equal Citizenship (NUSEC), likewise campaigned for reforms like family allowances and free birth control information that would improve the condition of life for women in the home, but it also advocated abolition of the marriage bar to work in the civil service.

Such activities by the women's movement chalked up an impressive record of accomplishment. As we have seen, the vote was granted to women over age thirty in 1918 and to all women in 1928. In addition the Sex Disqualification (Removal) Act of 1919 removed the legal prohibition of women entering the legal profession; the first woman M.P. (Nancy Astor) took her seat in the House of Commons in 1919; the first woman justice of the peace (J.P.) was appointed in 1920; women's rights in divorce were made equal to men's in 1923; and women won the right to hold and dispose of property on an equal basis with men in 1926.

For all the improvement in material standards of living, the most dramatic and memorable aspect of social life between the wars was unemployment. The unemployment rate averaged 10.6 percent in the 1920s and 16.1 percent in the 1930s. Its effect on communities in the old industrial areas was devastating and became engraved on the minds of the British working people. It was regional in its impact—the South and Southeast suffered relatively little—and it affected men over age forty-five more than younger ones because men over forty-five found it nearly impossible to get new jobs. J. B. Priestley observed that in hard-hit towns like Jarrow, thousands of workers seemed to spend their time just "hanging around"; the men, he wrote, "wore the drawn masks of prisoners of war." The coal miners, who formerly had been fairly well paid and were accustomed to prodigious labor, were perhaps the worst off, with their unemployment rate running 20 percent in the best years of the period and 40 percent in the worst. They found it miserable to be regarded as ineffectual or as layabouts; as one said,

> To men who had worked in the only industry they had known for anything
> from fifteen to fifty years, this was a new experience, of the most humiliat-
> ing and degrading kind.

There was simmering discontent but surprisingly little effective political action among the unemployed. The trade union movement was not organized or ideologically equipped to mobilize the jobless. Thus the National Unemployed Workers' Movement (NUWM) was formed in 1921 to give voice to the interests of the unemployed. The NUWM staged many demonstrations and hunger marches, but it was never able to organize more than 10 percent of the unemployed, partly because of the apathy and fatalism of the workers and partly because the NUWM was seen as tainted with communism. The most memorable of the hunger marches of the interwar years, a 300-mile march of two hundred men from Jarrow to London, was not an NUWM project. Though it stirred public emotion, the Jarrow workers' march accomplished nothing, except to get the marchers' unemployment allowances docked!

Unemployment in the 1930s: hunger marchers from Jarrow on the way to London.

The public payments of allowances to the unemployed became known as "the dole." The so-called means test by which the unemployed had to qualify for the dole became the aspect of the experience of unemployment they despised the most. By the 1920s, most British workers were covered by the unemployment insurance system introduced by Lloyd George in 1911 and expanded in subsequent years. Through it a worker earned unemployment payments for a maximum of fifteen weeks. Because many thousands of workers soon exceeded the covenanted fifteen weeks, the government, knowing that the Poor Law system could not cope with the vast numbers of jobless people, had to extend to them "uncovenanted" or "transitional" benefits. (In fact, the whole Poor Law structure was abolished in 1929–1930.) To receive these benefits, the dole, an applicant had to prove he was "actively seeking work," which many found humiliating. After the financial crisis of 1930–1931, the government set up the means test, which was applied to the applicant's entire household, to assure that his family was sufficiently impoverished to warrant the allowance. The unemployed person often had to submit to investigation of his house and home by prying officials, who wanted to know why certain pieces of furniture had not been sold, or how much money the family had in savings, or how much the children were contributing to the family income. In some cases, young people had to move out of the family home in order to prevent their own earnings from penalizing their parents. The means test understandably caused extremely hard feelings among the British working class—a legacy of bitterness that would affect post–World War II policies.

TRADE UNIONS, CLASS CONFLICT, AND THE GENERAL STRIKE OF 1926

British trade unions were thrown on the defensive during the interwar years. The Great War's demand for labor and the labor activism of 1919–1920 had expanded union membership to over 8 million, but because of the depression, union membership fell to 4.4 million in 1933, recovering only to 6.3 million in 1939. The wartime power of organized labor contributed to an increase in militancy over issues like dilution of the work force by unskilled laborers. That militancy was strengthened by the spread of socialism and syndicalism, especially after the Russian Revolution of 1917. Union militancy in 1919 coincided with problems of demobilization and return to a peacetime economy. The consequent struggle between workers and employers, which inevitably involved the government, marked the height of the wave of class conflict that had been building since the turn of the century. Strikes reached an unprecedented level in 1917–1922. Workers sought to win union recognition, to maintain the high wages they had won during the war, and to raise wages during the brief boom of 1919–1920. Moreover, these strikes were often accompanied by political demands for nationalization of the coal mines, railways, or banks. Once unemployment began to rise, however, the employers went on a counteroffensive. British industry averaged thirty-six million workdays lost to industrial conflict from 1919 through 1923.

The most severe problems were in the coal industry. This old industry was afflicted with a number of long-term problems: the existence of far too many small and inefficient coal companies; low productivity compared to other nations, due to inadequate investment in new technology and the exhaustion of relatively easily mined coal deposits; and a shrinking share of foreign markets. The government had nationalized the mines during the war, and the miners thought that permanent nationalization would eliminate many of the weaknesses of the industry. The miners also wanted higher wages and shorter hours, whereas the mine owners wanted to retain private ownership and cut wages in order to improve their competitive position. A series of disputes, strikes, and lockouts ensued between 1919 and 1925, culminating in the General Strike of 1926.

The narrative of events leading to the General Strike involves political history and will be covered in Chapter 9. What is important in this chapter is to understand the General Strike from the point of view of labor organization and morale. The miners had formed a "triple alliance" with the railwaymen and transport workers before the war. They called on their allies several times in the years between 1919 and 1926, sometimes with good effect but more often not. In particular the triple alliance failed in 1921, when the miners were locked out by the coal owners and forced to accept longer hours and wage reductions. When in 1925 foreign competition and the return to the gold standard brought about a crisis in the earnings of the British coal industry, the owners again tried to cut wages and to increase working hours. This time the miners appealed for help not to the triple alliance but to the Trades Union Congress (TUC). The TUC responded favorably, and emboldened by this support, the miners bargained stubbornly against the equally blunt determination of the mine owners. One government official said he would have thought the miners the stupidest men he had ever met, except that he had recently dealt with the owners.

Various efforts by the government to find a solution or to stall off the conflict failed, and on May 1, 1926, the miners were locked out by the owners. The TUC, though it had failed to make careful plans for a general strike, called on many of its unions to come out in support of the miners. The rate of support was very high: some 2.5 million workers struck. But this high union morale and solidarity lasted little more than a week. The government *had* made plans for the strike, and it stood firm, claiming that the General Strike was a threat to the constitution. It put into action its plans for moving essential supplies and services by volunteers, and it mobilized troops, warships, and auxiliary policemen. The middle and upper classes, including public school boys and Oxbridge undergraduates, rallied to the support of the government; for them the social order itself was at stake. There were some arrests and minor clashes, but the General Strike did not turn as ugly as it threatened to, and on one occasion police played a football match against strikers. The TUC never had any intention of overturning the constitution. Faced with the government's refusal to negotiate while the strike continued, and fearful of contributing to a revolutionary situation, the leaders of the TUC caved in. They called off the strike after nine days. The miners, feeling betrayed, remained locked out until the winter, when they too had to give in.

The unions' defeat in the General Strike contributed to a decline in union membership and morale. During the remainder of the 1920s and 1930s, the unions lost ground while trying to defend wages, working conditions, and their own legal status. In 1931, the low point of union membership, the unions included only about 25 percent of the work force. Meanwhile, the unions undertook some amalgamation, and the number of unions fell from over 1,200 in 1914 to about 780 in 1945. This development strengthened the official union movement but increased the degree of bureaucratization within the unions and therefore widened the separation of union leaders from their memberships. Consequently, the official trade unions in the 1930s reached an accommodation with the capitalist system, but their more militant members, led by the shop stewards, often engaged in unofficial ("wildcat") strike actions. These twin qualities of the organized labor movement— moderation by the official union leadership and militancy by some of the local rank-and-file members continued into the Second World War and postwar periods.

POPULAR CULTURE

Popular culture between the wars in Britain presents two strikingly different pictures: first, the misery and frustration of "life on the dole" for the unemployed;

The General Strike of 1926: armored cars and troops guard a food convoy in London.

second, the consumerism of mass culture built on the improved standards of living and smaller families of the employed.

As many contemporaries observed, it was possible for the unemployed to lose all ambition and to accustom themselves to living on the dole. But as "documentary" writers like George Orwell (in *The Road to Wigan Pier*) and Walter Greenwood (in *Love on the Dole*) showed, it was never easy. Life on the dole included living in overcrowded and squalid housing, wearing shabby clothes, searching daily for work, scrimping on twenty shillings a week, making miserable economies, gambling on horses or football pools in hopes of quick financial relief, and facing the inquisitorial Public Assistance Committee. There was not enough to eat, and people dropped from their diet expensive items like meat, vegetables, and dairy products, replacing them with "fillers" like potatoes, bread, margarine, and jam. A Sunday newspaper, an occasional movie, or a few hours at the pub were the only recreations. In some families, the long period of unemployment destroyed self-respect and pride in cleanliness and personal appearance. Young people in disturbing numbers turned to crime, and "adolescents" as a separate age group became a problem. But other families made heroic efforts to sustain the appearance of respectability. Some men stood every day in endless queues at the factory gates hoping for work. The Pilgrim Trust found that women were starving themselves "in order to feed and clothe the children reasonably well."

For those who enjoyed regular employment, the rise in real incomes meant better homes, less burdensome work, and the enjoyment of mass leisure activities of a kind once reserved to the rich. Slum clearance and house construction made significant advances between the wars. Toward the end of the war, Lloyd George's government pledged itself to "homes fit for heroes," and the Housing and Town Planning Act of 1919 and subsequent legislation helped local authorities build nearly two million houses for rent to working people. Private builders, mainly in the 1930s, constructed 2.5 million other homes. Many of the new houses built by local authorities were constructed on housing estates outside the cities, such as

Becontree, at Dagenham (outside London), and Kirkby, outside Liverpool. Nearly 20 percent of the working class was relocated to such "council housing." Although some critics feared that these new housing estates would destroy the community spirit of the old working-class neighborhoods, in fact the inhabitants quickly established vigorous communities in their new environs. The new council housing offered much improved space, privacy, light, heat, water, and sewerage, and their tenants on the whole preferred them to their former slum housing.

New consumer-oriented leisure activities came to take up a larger share of working-class time and income. As the average size of the British household declined, each family needed to spend less on necessities and had more to spend on leisure activities. Moreover, working people had more leisure time. The average work week fell from fifty-four hours to forty-eight, and the "weekend," with half a day free on Saturday and all day on Sunday, became the national norm. Further, there was an increase in the number of holidays. Legislation passed in 1871 had extended and rearranged the holiday calendar from the Victorian practice of allowing only four holidays a year. Between the wars, these official holidays tended to grow longer, and the custom of giving employees extended summer holidays with pay became established. By 1937, about three million workers enjoyed holidays with pay, and in 1938 the Holidays with Pay Act extended the privilege to eleven million more.

More leisure time and more money to spend generated consumer demand for a variety of leisure activities. Working people read more books, magazines, and newspapers than ever before, but they also took an interest in dance halls, gambling, movies, gardening, pigeon keeping, and professional sports (mainly football). The growth of holidays caused a boom in the holiday resort business. As early as the 1880s, better-off members of the working class were visiting seaside resorts like Blackpool, Southend, and Margate. By the late 1930s, such resorts received more than twenty million tourists a year, most of whom came by train and special motor buses. Probably about one-third of the population spent a holiday away from home each year. The resorts and campgrounds spun off many commercial activities to entertain the visitors: swimming pools, fairgrounds, hotels, pleasure piers, dance halls, and cinemas.

The principal new leisure-time activities of the interwar years sprang from new technologies: the cinema, radio, and automobile. Cinemas had become popular before the First World War; indeed, the wartime Ministry for Infomation used film for propaganda purposes. After the war, films became wildly popular, especially when "talkies" were introduced in 1927. The popularity of the cinema killed off the Victorian and Edwardian music halls. By 1939, there were almost five thousand cinema houses in Britain, and cinemas rivaled dance halls and pubs as the main forms of popular entertainment. By then, some twenty million tickets a week were being sold, and it has been estimated that in some towns 40 percent of the population went to a cinema at least once a week.

Radio was another Edwardian invention that received a major impetus from the war. The first regular programs were broadcast in 1922, and as sets became cheaper and more reliable, the number of licenses issued to private owners grew to more than eight million by the 1930s. By 1939, about three fourths of all British households had access to radios. In 1926, the British Broadcasting Corporation (BBC) was established as a public corporation, with control over all broadcasting in Britain. Using dictatorial authority, its first director-general, John Reith, committed the BBC to a policy of instruction as well as entertainment. "The preservation of a high moral tone," Reith declared, "is obviously of paramount importance." Otherwise, he said, Britain would have no more than the American system, with "no co-ordination, no standard, no guiding policy." Consequently, the BBC addressed the mass market by broadcasting dance bands, sporting events, and celebrities, and it also broadcast a heavy (and many said, humorless) diet of classical music, intellectual talks, serious drama, and news. Reith insisted on broadcasting only a nonregional, standard upper-class BBC diction and pronunciation, as well as a big dose of religious programming.

Neither the films nor the BBC was able to rival the newspaper press in mass communication and in molding popular taste and opinion. A newspaper press for the masses in Britain had its origins in the late-Victorian years, when the new state school system began to eliminate illiteracy. By the 1920s, most of the adult population were literate, although perhaps 20 percent must be regarded as only semiliterate and not able to follow a sustained argument or story. Given this level of literacy and the availability of spendable incomes, newspaper circulation grew rapidly. By 1939, almost 70 percent of the British people over sixteen read a daily national newspaper. These newspapers were run as giant business enterprises, and they engaged in ferocious commercial rivalry. As in business generally, concentration took place in the newspaper industry, and increasingly the popular newspapers were gathered into the hands of a few "press barons" and combines. The most famous press barons of the era were Lord Rothermere (Harold Harmsworth) and Lord Beaverbrook (Max Aitken), both of whom were fiercely ambitious and not shy about exercising their power in politics. The papers with the largest circulation, the *Daily Express* and the *Daily Herald*, sold more than two million copies a day each, whereas the so-called quality newspapers like the *Times* and the *Daily Telegraph* had circulations of far below a million. The style of the popular press, shaped by the simple desire to sell newspapers, ran to large headlines, eye-catching layouts, numerous photographs, short news stories, cartoon strips, crossword puzzles, advertisements, and games. In the view of some critics, the mass press was destructive of the genuine independence and self-taught wisdom of the working class. The papers, like the cinema, taught uniformity but not community; they homogenized the people into a mass of consumer-oriented individuals. In the words of the literary critic Richard Hoggart, the mass press helped teach the lesson that progress is nothing but "a seeking of material possessions."

As for automobiles, the British motor vehicle industry grew rapidly between the wars, but "motoring" remained largely a middle-class activity. Car ownership grew from about 100,000 in 1919 to 2 million in 1939. By the early 1930s mass-production techniques had driven down the price of a small Austin or Morris to between £100 and £200, which put them in the reach of most middle-class incomes but out of reach of all but the best-paid skilled workers in the working class. For the middle class, motoring became an immensely popular activity. Major highways were constructed, and repair garages, filling stations, and roadside cafes sprang up to cater to the newly mobile motoring public. By the 1930s, parts of England suffered from Sunday afternoon traffic jams. For J. B. Priestley, this represented the "new post-war England," a world of "arterial and by-pass roads, of filling stations and factories that look like exhibition buildings, of giant cinemas and dance-halls and cafes, bungalows with tiny garages"—a far cry from the old and decaying industrial areas of the country.

Popular culture between the wars was also notable for two aspects of ordinary life once important but now obviously in decline: drink and religion. The consumption of alcohol had fallen off sharply during the war, largely because of higher taxes on liquor and beer and shorter hours during which pubs could be open. Drinking never recovered during the interwar years. The pub was, to be sure, still a key feature of working-class communities, and respectable women now frequented them regularly, but men tended to spend more time with their families and less time in the pubs. Thus, while two vices, gambling and smoking, grew rapidly between the wars, drinking declined. One estimate is that expenditure on drink fell by more than 33 percent between 1919 and 1939, and the annual production of beer in the 1930s reached only half of the prewar level.

Organized religion in Britain had faced declining numbers since the beginning of the twentieth century. Between the religious census of 1851 and about 1880, absolute numbers of churchgoers increased, but the proportion of attenders as a percentage of the population leveled off. From the 1880s to 1914, church growth actually trailed behind population growth. The working class more than any other section of the country seemed to shy away from church membership and attendance, no doubt because they associated churches with the upper classes.

Just before and during the Great War, all of the main Protestant denominations suffered an absolute decline in numbers, perhaps in part due to the disillusionment with Christianity experienced by many soldiers in the face of the horrors of the Western Front. Roman Catholicism alone among the Christian denominations continued to grow, because its prominent role in Irish immigrant neighborhoods enabled it to hold the allegiance of its young people. The Protestant churches exerted themselves to reverse their decline in the 1920s and managed to increase their membership to a record level (in absolute numbers) of nearly six million in 1927. Thereafter, the increase in spendable income for employed workers, the growing participation in consumerism and material pleasures, and the competition from other leisure time activities drained people away from the Protestant churches. In 1941, fewer than five million Britons were active members of the Protestant denominations. Although many working-class people seem to have retained a vague belief in God and attended church to mark the major rites of passage in life (birth, marriage, and death), secularization—the removal of activities or ideas from the orbit of religion—was a main trend in popular culture.

HIGH CULTURE

The expansion of consumerism, the appearance of mass culture, and the decline of popular religiosity only confirmed the sense of crisis among high-brow intellectuals engendered by the war. The First World War permanently altered British *sensibility*. By "sensibility," students of literature mean the almost instinctive sense that cultivated people of a culture share about what is correct and incorrect, authentic and inauthentic, in literature and ideas. Major alterations of the British sensibility were already underway before the war, as the aesthetic and decadent movements and the Bloomsbury Group showed. But the war accelerated those changes and gave them a particular twist. The war for most British intellectuals caused a bitter disillusionment with Western civilization, for it seemed to make a mockery of all the conventional higher ideals of politics, society, and religion and demanded altogether new ways of expressing human experience.

This new sensibility was evident in the writings of the "war poets"—young men serving in the trenches who sought to express their outrage at the horrors to which ordinary human beings were subjected. The best of these poets—Siegfried Sassoon (who survived the war), Wilfred Owen (killed in 1918), and Isaac Rosenberg (also killed in 1918)—managed to avoid sentimentality and self-pity while describing the realities of the war of attrition in short, moving verses. This task required a new poetic diction as well as complete honesty. Here are two examples, the first from Sassoon's "Suicide in the Trenches":

> I knew a simple soldier boy
> Who grinned at life in empty joy,
> Slept soundly through the lonesome dark,
> And whistled early with the lark.
> In winter trenches cowed and glum,
> With cramps and lice and lack of rum,
> He put a bullet through his brain.
> No one spoke of him again.

And from Owen's "Dulce et Decorum Est," as the poet tells of a victim of gas:

> If you could hear, at every jolt, the blood
> Come gargling from the froth-corrupted lungs,
> Obscene as cancer, bitter as the cud
> Of vile, incurable sores on innocent tongues,–
> My friend, you would not tell with such high zest
> To children ardent for some glory,
> The old lie: Dulce et decorum est
> Pro patria mori.*

For the generation writing in the 1920s, disillusionment with grand ideals was the only valid outlook on the world and irony the only appropriate tone of voice. For example, in his autobiography (written when he was only thirty-four), Robert

---

*How sweet and noble it is to die for one's country.

Graves, who had served on the Western Front, describes his combat experiences in terms of unheroic irony. He explains that the only values that counted in the trenches were professional competence and loyalty to one's comrades. After the war, Graves felt alienated by British society, which seemed all too anxious to return to the prewar world. For writers like Graves, the brutal contrast between high hopes and reality, innocence and wisdom, allows only a posture of mocking humor. No longer could British poets indulge in high-flown words like *steed* or *charger, the foe*, or *the fallen*; only stark, plain words like *horse, the enemy*, and *the dead* would do. The war seemed to destroy the grounds for all values, yet it also seemed to polarize experience between friend and enemy, good and evil.

The war also encouraged a renewal of interest in the mystical, myth and ritual, and especially in myths of quest. This reaction can be seen in J. R. R. Tolkien's *The Lord of the Rings*, the mythical background for which Tolkien began composing under shellfire in the trenches, but usually the writers interested in mythical quests cast them in terms of a blasted and deformed world. The best monument of this turn of mind, and the greatest English poem of the interwar years, was T. S. Eliot's *The Waste Land* (1922). Eliot (1888–1965), an émigré from America, had not fought in the war and insisted that his poem concerned his own private experiences of despair and impotence and not those of the wartime generation. Nevertheless, *The Waste Land*, with its haunting lines echoing the legendary quest for the holy grail in a sterile and squalid world, seized the imagination of many of the young men and women to whom the war meant not only the creation of wasted landscapes but also the futility of Western civilization:

> What are the roots that clutch, what branches grow
> Out of this stony rubbish? Son of man,
> You cannot say, or guess, for you know only
> A heap of broken images, where the sun beats. . . .

Eliot was the preeminent "modern" poet and critic and therefore ranks with Virginia Woolf and the Irishmen Yeats and Joyce as one of the greatest contributors to the British "modernist" movement. Modernism, as we saw in Chapter 2, originated in the aesthetic and decadent movements of the late-Victorian and Edwardian years. It reached full flower in the 1920s and was to be a dominant intellectual force through the 1950s. Essentially, modernism was a repudiation of Victorian ideals and literary conventions. Modernists insisted that art is the highest activity in human life, and that art should not be bound by any requirement to be instructive or morally uplifting. Modernism was self consciously new and was devoted to experimentation and novelty in form and style. In the view of Eliot and his allies, a work of art must be regarded as "autonomous" (independent) from society, and even from the life of the artist who produced it. Yet it should also be understood as part of the tradition of Western art, seen not in historical terms but as a timeless storehouse of images, ideas, and associations.

Aestheticism, formalism, novelty, autonomy, and familiarity with the whole body of Western thought and literature were modernist qualities that, when combined with the modernists' ironic disapproval of the conditions of society and culture, made for very difficult and inaccessible poetry and fiction. It was the work of an alienated literary elite, most of whom thought that civilization was fragmenting and declining. Eliot himself found a basis for a more positive outlook when he reconverted to Christianity in 1927; thereafter, he declared himself "classicist in literature, royalist in politics, and Anglo-Catholic in religion," in short, an archconservative.

In the 1930s, modernism in Britain took a turn to the left. A younger generation of writers, who were born in the years between 1900 and 1914 and who came of age in the 1920s, rose to prominence. Chief among these were W. H. Auden, Cecil Day Lewis, Stephen Spender, and Christopher Isherwood. All of them grew up under the influence of *The Waste Land* and the doctrines of modernism, and all of them believed that Britain was in crisis, but they also believed that it was the obligation of the writer to respond to the crisis with socially responsible art. Working out that dilemma formed the main theme of their writing. Most of this so-called Auden generation were at the time socialists or communists, but their writings were not usually ideological. Poetry, Auden wrote in 1935, "is not concerned with telling people what to do, but with extending our knowledge of good and evil, perhaps making the necessity for action more urgent and its nature more clear, but only leading us to the point where it is possible for us to make a rational and moral choice."

The visual arts in Britain expressed the modernist commitment to novelty and formalism but without such a bleak view. British painting continued to lag behind that of the Continent. Postimpressionist painting had only been introduced to the British public in 1914, in an exhibition organized by the Bloomsbury Group's leading art critic, Roger Fry. Postimpressionist ideas influenced a number of British painters, but probably the ablest painter of the early twentieth century, Augustus John (1878–1961), could be regarded as "the last of the old masters." During the Great War, the insanely ruined quality of battlefield landscapes was effectively portrayed by the semi-abstract paintings of Paul Nash. But the only British painter of the interwar years who made significant contributions to artistic theory was Wyndham Lewis, who became an enthusiast of the formal abstractions of cubism and vorticism.

In architecture, an art form of necessity more closely tied to the tastes of the public, the vast majority of buildings continued to be designed in the traditional Classical, Gothic, or mock-Tudor styles. But modernism made some headway in the "Art Deco" style and in a few examples of the "international" style. The clean lines, the geometric formalism, and the decorative use of modern materials like chrome and plastic appeared in buildings like the cinemas of the Odeon chain, the Hoover factory at Perivale, and a number of London Underground stations designed by Frank Pick. The so-called modern or international style, which was borrowed from Continental innovators like Walter Gropius and Marcel Breuer, was more severely

Art deco: the Hoover building, Perivale, London, 1932. Modernism in architecture emphasized clean, geometric lines and functionalist design.

geometrical even than Art Deco. The modern style was aggressively antihistorical, devoid of ornamentation, convinced of the beauty of machines, and strongly influenced by cubism. It resulted in a number of boxlike, white, concrete, flat-roofed houses and school buildings—the forerunners of the post–World War II steel and glass functional architecture.

The modern style in architecture shows the ambivalence of the British modernist movement as a whole toward science and technology. Many modernist painters and architects were inspired by the orderliness of scientific logic and of modern technology. British philosophers like Bertrand Russell, Ludwig Wittgenstein (a transplanted Austrian), and A. J. Ayer provided the philosophical underpinnings of modernism. They admired natural science, and their highly abstract "logical positivism" saw the function of philosophy as simply the clarification of the logic of science. Yet many literary modernists stood in reaction against science and technology because they believed that science and technology had an increasingly important role in creating a society devoid of values and inhospitable to art.

Science, moreover, had risen in importance in British culture at the same time as serious literature seemed to be retiring to the periphery. The war of 1914–1918 was the first major conflict dominated by industrial technology. The British government at long last recognized the importance of scientific research to the national interest. In 1916, the Department of Scientific and Industrial Research (DSIR) was set up to fund research projects. Similarly, the Medical Research Committee, founded in 1913, was expanded rapidly in order to meet wartime demands in clinical medicine. Although government funding for science contracted after the war, direct government grants continued to be of considerable consequence, for instance in the development of radar in the 1930s. "Big science" had come to stay. Meanwhile, British universities, and especially Cambridge, now thoroughly professionalized and specialized, took a leading role in scientific research. Under the leadership of Ernest Rutherford, Cambridge's Cavendish Laboratory became a hotbed of discoveries in nuclear physics. Similarly, large British corporations in the electrical, chemical, and aircraft industries were beginning to establish laboratories and conduct their own research. In the nineteenth century, science had become professionalized; now it seemed to make a major claim on the resources of the society.

Finally, the decades between the wars witnessed the flowering of a remarkable renaissance of British music, which was to continue during and after the Second World War. During the nineteenth century, Britain had produced few significant composers, but in the twentieth century, and especially in the 1920s and 1930s, a number of major composers either reached maturity or began to produce important pieces. The earliest of these outstanding composers was Sir Edward Elgar (1857–1934), who wrote music expressing romantic and nationalistic sentiments before World War 1. In the 1920s and 1930s, Ralph Vaughan Williams (1872–1958) produced a large volume of work rooted in English folksongs and hymns and thereby capable of appealing to a very wide audience. Benjamin Britten (1913–1976) in the 1930s began to write major works that carried on the British choral tradition that reached back to the eighteenth century; his *War Requiem* (1962), first performed in the rebuilt Coventry Cathedral, tapped deep national emotions. As these three composers show, British music lagged behind the Continent in its formal theorizing. While the leading Continental composers (Stravinsky, Schoenberg, Webern, and Bartók) were engaged in radical experiments in musical forms, rhythms, and tonal relations, the British were more traditional and often built on romanticist themes, and this enabled them to establish contact with a broad public. At the same time, eminent conductors like Thomas Beecham and Malcolm Sargent, and new orchestras and the BBC, helped develop a wide national audience for classical music. Thus, while modernism was turning literature and painting inward toward an artistic elite, British music was sinking roots deep in the general public—a hopeful development in a time of difficulties and despair.

Suggested Reading

Alberti, Joanna, *Beyond Suffrage: Feminists in War and Peace, 1914–28* (New York: St. Martin's Press, 1989).

Aldcroft, Derek, *The Inter-War Economy: Britain, 1919–1939* (New York: Columbia University Press, 1970).

Banks, Olive, *The Politics of British Feminism, 1918–1970* (Aldershot: Edward Elgar Publishing, 1993).

Briggs, Asa, *History of Broadcasting in the United Kingdom* (2 vols.) (London: Oxford University Press, 1961–1979).

Brown, Callum G., *Religion and Society in Twentieth-Century Britain* (London: Pearson Longman, 2006).

Chisholm, Anne, and Michael Davie, *Beaverbrook: A Life* (London: Hutchinson, 1992).

Cronin, James E., *Labour and Society in Britain, 1918–1979* (New York: Schocken Books, 1984).

Cunningham, Valentine, *British Writers of the Thirties* (New York: Oxford University Press, 1990).

Fussell, Paul, *The Great War and Modern Memory* (New York: Oxford University Press, 1975).

Garside, W. R., *British Unemployment, 1919–1939* (Cambridge: Cambridge University Press, 1990).

Giles, Judy, *Women, Identity, and Private Life in Britain, 1900–1950* (New York: St. Martin's Press, 1995).

Glynn, Sean, and John Oxborrow, *Interwar Britain: A Social and Economic History* (London: Allen & Unwin, 1976).

Hall, Ruth, ed., *Dear Dr. Stopes: Sex in the 1920's* (Harmondsworth, Middlesex: Penguin, 1981).

Harrison, Charles, *English Art and Modernism, 1900–1039* (2nd ed.; New Haven: Yale University Press, 1994).

Hoggart, Richard, *The Uses of Literacy* (London: Chatto & Windus, 1957).

Hynes, Samuel, *The Auden Generation* (London: Bodley Head, 1976).

Laybourn, Keith, *Britain in the Breadline: A Social and Political History of Britain Between the Wars* (Wolfeboro Falls, N.H.: Alan Sutton, 1990).

———, *A History of British Trade Unionism: c. 1770–1990* (Wolfeboro Falls, N.H.: Alan Sutton, 1992).

LeMahieu, D. L., *A Culture for Democracy: Mass Communication and the Cultivated Mind in Britain Between the Wars* (Oxford: Clarendon Press, 1988).

Lewis, Jane, *Women in England, 1870–1950* (Brighton, Sussex: Wheatsheaf Books, 1984).

McKibbin, Ross, *Classes and Cultures: England, 1918–1951* (Oxford: Oxford University Press, 1998).

Orwell, George, *The Road to Wigan Pier* (London: V. Gollancz, 1937).

Perkin, Harold, *The Age of the Automobile* (London: Quarter Books, 1976).

———, *The Rise of Professional Society: England Since 1880* (London: Routledge, 1989).

Pugh, Martin, *Women and the Women's Movement in Britain, 1914–1999* (London: Palgrave Macmillan, 2000).

Roberts, Elizabeth, *A Woman's Place: An Oral History of Working-Class Women, 1890–1940* (Oxford: Basil Blackwell, 1984).

Saler, Michael T., *The Avant-Garde in Interwar England: Medieval Modernism and the London Underground* (New York: Oxford University Press, 1999).

Skidelsky, Robert, *John Maynard Keynes: A Biography* (3 vols.; London: Macmillan, 1983–2000).

Soloway, Richard A., *Birth Control and the Population Question in England, 1877–1930* (Chapel Hill: University of North Carolina Press, 1982).

———, *Democracy and Degeneration: Eugenics and the Declining Birthrate in Twentieth-Century Britain* (Chapel Hill, N.C.: University of North Carolina Press, 1990).

Stevenson, John, *British Society, 1914–45* (London: Allen Lane, 1984).

Chapter 9

Politics, Power, and the Coming of War, 1919–1939

In both domestic politics and foreign affairs, the 1920s and 1930s seem like decades of lost opportunities for Britain. The once great industrial giant staggered through twenty years of depression and unemployment, its resources stretched beyond their limit by overseas commitments, and finally let the triumph of 1918 slip away as war with Germany broke out again. The historian Charles Loch Mowat wrote that British politicians and statesmen between the wars were "pygmies" compared to the "giants" of the Edwardian and war years. There is much truth to this negative assessment, for in many instances British political leaders dithered and delayed, trying to muddle through times demanding urgent action. They showed little understanding of the tasks before the nation and seemed to blind themselves to pressing realities. Still, the British performance in politics, empire, and diplomacy between 1919 and 1939 was not a complete failure. The economic, political, and international problems confronting the British were of unprecedented scale, yet Britain came through them with its constitution and rule of law intact, with important advances in converting the Empire to a commonwealth, and with the social and intellectual foundations of the welfare state firmly established.

THE STRUCTURE OF POLITICS AND GOVERNMENT

The structures of British government and politics had undergone important changes since the nineteenth century and soon would experience more. Perhaps the most important development was the growth of the very size of government and the scope of its operations. The state was scaled back after the Great War, of course, but it never receded to its prewar size. Government expenditures reached 26.1 percent of the gross national product in 1930, more than twice the pre-1914 level. Government employees numbered almost 7 percent of the work force in 1931; the civil service alone employed 376,000 people, more than seven times as many as in 1880. Moreover, ever since the attempts of the Asquith government between 1908 and 1914 to settle industrial disputes, the state was expected to form one angle of a triangle of negotiation—the other angles being the trade unions and the major employers. Especially after the General Strike of 1926, this triangle of informal "corporatism" addressed many problems in industrial relations.

Constitutional arrangements had also changed. The power of the House of Lords, limited in 1911, declined further after the war, and from the 1920s on it was very unusual for a cabinet minister to come from the House of Lords. The war had increased the power of the cabinet and of the prime minister within it. The influence of the cabinet over the House of Commons was supreme, and the role of the prime minister was becoming more like the American presidency. In 1916, a cabinet secretariat had been established, which for the first time kept minutes of cabinet meetings and coordinated ministerial activities. This increased the efficiency of the executive and the control of the prime minister over his colleagues. After the war, some prime ministers like Stanley Baldwin sought to reduce the power of the prime minister, but they were in fact unable to do so. Parliament and the country alike expected prime ministers to play a dominant role in national affairs.

Meanwhile, true electoral democracy was achieved by 1930. The electorate was vastly expanded, and the nation was divided into electoral districts of nearly equal size, each returning one representative to the House of Commons. The Reform Act of 1918 increased the electorate from eight million to twenty-one million, of whom 40 percent were women. The Reform Act of 1928 added nine million more voters, and now 52 percent of the electorate were women. The sheer size of the electorate and legal limitations on the amount of money that could be spent in a campaign put a premium on efficient constituency organization and the work of party volunteers. This situation gave an advantage to the Conservatives and Labourites, for the Conservative party could rely on flocks of middle-class volunteers, and Labour had the trade unions for support. The Liberals, however, were badly divided: Asquith held control of the Liberal organization, but Lloyd George had most of the money, which he had raised as prime minister by selling peerages and other honors. Because the British electoral system ("first past the post") provided (and still does) that the winner of the plurality of votes in a constituency got the seat in Parliament, whereas the losers got nothing, it magnified divisions among party voters; hence the Liberals fared worse during the early 1920s in seats won than in popular votes received.

Political parties since the early nineteenth century in Britain had been an essential part of the constitution because of their ability to form and sustain governments and their efforts to educate the voting public. Two problems of the interwar years hampered the operation of this necessary part of the constitution: first, the continual sense of crisis sometimes seemed to demand that party rivalry be put aside in favor of coalitions; second, the rise of the Labour party, which was regarded by some people in the propertied classes as dangerous and illegitimate, put it in a position of power and influence. These problems gave party alignments an exceptional fluidity and overemphasized the need for political stability itself. All too often, politicians sought stability and tranquility and thus failed to put the real issues squarely before the public.

The Conservative party, once the organ of the landed classes, by the 1920s had become the party of industrial and financial as well as landed property. The drift of well-to-do middle-class people to the Conservatives had accelerated in the early 1900s, when fear of the spread of socialism pushed many businessmen into the

Conservative party, which they regarded as the best defense against the anticipated socialist assault on property. But the postwar Conservative party was not monolithic. Conservatives generally were strong imperialists and nationalists, and during the war they had insisted on aggressive pursuit of the war effort, conscription, and unconditional surrender. Some Conservatives, however, came to recognize that not every part of the Empire could be held in defiance of colonial nationalism. Likewise, the Conservatives on the whole believed in classical economics, laissez-faire, low taxation, and as little government as possible. Yet others still believed in state action to promote "national efficiency," and many accepted a modern version of the old idea of paternal obligations. Many Conservatives were fiercely antisocialist and saw in the Labour party the British toehold of Bolshevism. Others, including Baldwin, sought to diminish class conflict while defending the social order. In the 1930s, a number of young Conservatives, including the future prime minister Harold Macmillan, took a flexible approach to social welfare and advocated government spending and social services as a cure for depression. Most Conservatives between the wars favored protective tariffs, but a few, including many of the recent converts from the Liberal party, remained staunch free traders. Given these divisions, the strongest Conservative claim was simply that they were the party of safety and good sense.

The Gladstonian ideals of peace, retrenchment, and reform remained firmly embedded in the Liberal party, but the war had made them seem at least temporarily obsolete. Moreover, the energetic prosecution of the war effort by Lloyd George made many of the more pacifist and internationalist Liberals very uneasy. Lloyd George before 1916 had been the leader of the radical left wing of the party, but his Liberal supporters in the deposing of Asquith came from the party's right wing. Asquith proved to be an indolent leader of the anti-Lloyd George Liberals, formerly the party radicals. Liberals between the wars in general supported the free enterprise system, but they sought to make it work by using the state for humanitarian social welfare and even redistribution of "surplus" wealth. Electorally very ineffective, the Liberals after 1919 were the most intellectually innovative and progressive of the British parties. By 1929, Liberals like J. M. Keynes were advocating massive government spending on public works and deficit financing as a cure for depression and unemployment. Their problem was not in knowing what to do, but how to win the power to do it.

Whether the Liberals could have remained one of the two major parties after the split between Asquith and Lloyd George in 1916 is still an open question. There can be no doubt that the party was losing strength from both its left and right flanks before as well as during the war. Businessmen left the Liberal party for the Conservatives as their grievances were addressed and Britain increasingly became a middle-class nation. On the Liberal left, as we have seen, there was from 1900 strong continuity with the moderates of the Labour party on behalf of "progressivism." Many of these Liberal progressives, including a significant number of intellectuals like J. A. Hobson, H. W. Massingham, and R. B. Haldane, shifted to the Labour party after 1918 because they thought that Labour would be the most effective advocate of social reform. Similarly, many Liberal pacifist intellectuals, dismayed by Lloyd George, retreated to the Labour party, which despite its socialism seemed to be the best defender of Gladstonianism in external affairs. Many nonconformists, long the backbone of the Liberal party, shifted either to the Conservatives or to Labour as the political fires of nonconformity were dampened. The disestablishment of the church in Wales, which came into effect in 1920, was their last great political objective. At the same time, because the southern Irish counties were no longer represented in Parliament, the Liberals lost the eighty-odd votes in the House of Commons that the Home Rulers had long supplied. In short, drained of much of its traditional support, and hamstrung by the bitter division between Asquith and Lloyd George, the Liberals competed poorly for the allegiance of both middle-class and working-class voters. This was a recipe for disaster.

The Labour party, as we saw in Chapter 6, emerged much strengthened from the war. Its new constitution of 1918 proclaimed the purpose of creating a society based on cooperation rather than competition. Its famous Clause IV promised "to secure for the producers by hand or brain the full fruits of their industry, and the most equitable distribution thereof that may be possible upon the basis of the common ownership of the means of production." In actuality, however, the Labour party advocated only relatively moderate policies and was not an extreme socialist party. The constitution of 1918 made the party executive more dependent than ever on the trade unions, thus limiting the influence of socialist intellectuals. Clause IV, moreover, was written largely to separate the party from the Liberals. In practice, the Labour party favored nationalization of a few industries like coal and the railways, and it supported the principle of a minimum wage. Otherwise, its policies differed little from those of the more progressive Liberals: free trade, state welfare programs like unemployment and medical insurance, and orthodox (that is, balanced budget) governmental finance. The party had no solutions to the problems of industrial decay or unemployment.

Within the Labour party there was a wide range of socialist ideas. One of these was Christian Socialism, best expressed by the brilliant historian and social critic R. H. Tawney (1880–1962). Tawney was an upper-class intellectual deeply imbued with a sense of fellowship and social service. His socialist theory derived from applying Christian ethics to a capitalist society. Tawney believed that where capitalism went wrong was in its ethical basis, for it valued acquisitiveness and rewarded property owners more than their services entitled them to. In *The Acquisitive Society* (1920), Tawney argued for the reorganization of society according to professional function: property should be rewarded and given power according to performance of social service. Another brand of socialism prominent between the wars was Guild Socialism, articulated best by another historian and theoretician, G. D. H. Cole (1889–1959). Guild Socialism was the British equivalent of Continental syndicalism, which advocated rule of, for, and by trade unions, so that the state would wither away. Cole's Guild Socialism, inspired by the medieval guilds, was not so extreme as syndicalism, but it did advocate workers' control of industry through trade unions, direct action strikes, and the reduction of the state to the role of a voluntary association of consumers.

Neither Christian Socialism nor Guild Socialism had much to say about practical reform, for they looked to the general transformation of society. In this regard, they were at a disadvantage in competition with the pragmatic, reformist mainstream of middle-class British socialism, Fabianism. The Fabians, led more firmly than ever by Sidney and Beatrice Webb, remained democratic, gradualist, state socialists. They were given a boost by the growth of the state during the First World War. But even Fabianism had nothing to say about the problems of industrial decline, and its doctrine of governmental finance remained old-fashioned enough to please the strictest Gladstonian. Moreover, the Webbs discredited socialism to a degree by their lavish praise of the Soviet Union, which they visited in the 1930s. They overlooked the cruelty of Stalinism in their praise of Soviet bureaucracy. George Orwell's passionate depiction of the realities of poverty and unemployment, *The Road to Wigan Pier* (1937), called for a commonsensical socialism, but it also denounced the unrealistic crankiness of some forms of contemporary British socialism and the social-scientific coldness of Fabianism.

In Wales and Scotland, the replacement of the Liberals by Labour as the party of the left opened a gap in the political expression of nationalism. In Wales, the war and the postwar years witnessed a decline of nonconformity and the spread of socialism. The historic mission of liberalism seemed complete and the Liberal party obsolete. Welsh Liberals were demoralized by the split between Lloyd George and Asquith, and many Welsh Liberals felt betrayed by Lloyd George's cooperation with the Conservatives. The Labour party thus shouldered the Liberals aside, but as a class-based and centralized party Labour did not express Welsh nationalist feelings to the satisfaction of all former radicals. In 1925, a number of former Welsh radicals joined a few conservative romantics attracted to medievalism and Catholicism to form a new Welsh nationalist party, *Plaid Cymru*. The new party at first dedicated itself mainly to promoting the Welsh language and only later took up political autonomy for Wales. Strongly opposed by Lloyd George, Plaid Cymru remained tiny through the 1930s, but under the leadership of the passionate intellectual Saunders Lewis, it kept nationalism before the Welsh public.

In Scotland, the replacement of liberalism by Labour was less traumatic, perhaps because the leader of the Labour party in the 1920s, Ramsay MacDonald, was a Scot. But the Labour party in Scotland was split by a dispute between the militants of the old ILP and the moderates who made up the bulk of the party. Meanwhile, a Scottish literary renaissance in the 1920s promoted both political and cultural nationalism. Its greatest figure, the socialist and Scottish nationalist poet Hugh MacDiarmid (pen name of Christopher Murray Grieve), who was inspired by the modernism of Yeats and Joyce as well as the social criticism of Carlyle, sought to destroy Scottish parochialism while promoting a literature in the Scottish vernacular. Intellectuals of the literary renaissance and former members of the ILP joined to establish the foundations of the Scottish Nationalist Party (SNP) in 1928. Like Plaid Cymru, the SNP remained small through the 1930s.

Given the gravity of the depression in the 1920s and 1930s, it was inevitable that the Communist party on the one extreme and fascism on the other attracted some support. Many people, most of them intellectuals or militant labor organizers, thought that extreme social problems demanded extreme responses. The Communist Party of Great Britain was founded in 1920, in the first flowering of enthusiasm for the Bolshevik Revolution. But its revolutionary doctrine alienated the vast bulk of the British left. The Labour party consistently refused to have anything to do with it, and the TUC tried to ban Communists from the trade unions. At the time of the Spanish Civil War, however, a few leading intellectuals like Stephen Spender believed that the Communist party promised to be the best defense against fascism. Important as the Communist party became among certain intellectuals, its membership still never amounted to more than about five thousand people. Moderate democratic socialism and radicalism remained the mainstream of British progressivism.

As for fascism, it had a moment of notoriety in the 1930s but soon faded. In 1930, Sir Oswald Mosley, an upper-class member of the Labour government, revolted against his party because of its unimaginative response to economic and social crisis. Mosley was an energetic and ambitious convert to socialism who had adopted many Keynesian ideas. He developed a program of aggressive government action to direct the economy. When the Labour cabinet and then the party itself rejected his ideas, Mosley established a "New Party" and then the British Union of Fascists (BUF). His "blackshirts" (paramilitary party workers) and his own public posturing soon were imitating the Continental fascists, Hitler and Mussolini. There was some support for the BUF in the streets and a degree of sympathy for fascism in the upper class; however, the British public in general did not take to Mosley's antiparliamentary stance, and the BUF had little impact on politics.

THE LLOYD GEORGE GOVERNMENT, 1918–1922

The dominant figure in politics at the end of the war, and in a sense through the early 1930s, was David Lloyd George. Never a party loyalist, Lloyd George sought to continue his coalition government into peacetime. The war presented, he said, "an opportunity for reconstruction of industrial and economic conditions of this country such as has never been presented in the life of, probably, the world." The Labour party preferred to reestablish its independence from the coalition, but the Conservatives, hypnotized by Lloyd George's wartime leadership and anxious to keep an antisocialist alliance together, decided to stick with the coalition. A general election, the first since 1910, was called for 1918. Lloyd George and Bonar Law, the leader of the Conservative party, agreed to endorse some 600 candidates, about 150 of them Liberals who had supported Lloyd George. During the campaign, Lloyd George tried to emphasize reconstruction: Britain must be made a land "fit for heroes to live in." But victory over the Germans and the performance of Lloyd George himself stood uppermost in the voters' minds. They gave the coalition a landslide victory: 384 Conservatives, 136 Coalition Liberals, 33 Asquithians, and 59 Labourites. The Asquith Liberals were very bitter about the "coupon" of endorsement that Lloyd George and Law had issued, and as the second largest independent party, Labour now became the official opposition.

Lloyd George's first task was the peace negotiations in Paris. He had begun his electoral campaign as a moderate on the question of how to treat the Germans. During the campaign, however, he had succumbed to the vindictive spirit of the electorate. By the end he had promised to punish the kaiser and to collect "the uttermost farthing" in reparations. This political stance weighed heavily on him in Paris, for members of Parliament reminded him of it when they thought he was becoming too generous to the defeated foe.

Lloyd George joined the French premier, Georges Clemenceau, and the American president, Woodrow Wilson, to form the "Big Three" in Paris. The British delegation was highly competent, but the British had not made systematic plans for the postwar settlement. Lloyd George instinctively adopted the role of mediator between Clemenceau and Wilson; however, he was also bound by certain wartime agreements, by the imperial ambitions of some British statesmen, and by the expectations of the British public that the Germans would pay the cost of the war. Wilson sought to reach a comprehensive settlement of European boundaries by the principle of national self-determination and to provide for a new system of "open" diplomacy through a League of Nations. Clemenceau spoke for the French spirit of revenge and fear of German revival; thus he wanted Germany to acknowledge guilt for causing the war and to pay reparations for war damages. Furthermore, he sought to keep Germany disarmed and vulnerable to Allied forces and to assure that the League of Nations would enforce the peace settlement on the Germans. Clemenceau likewise desired to have an alliance for collective security with the British and Americans. Lloyd George thought that a healthy Germany was necessary for the recovery of Europe (and for British trade), and he saw the League as an agency for revising the details of the peace settlement. Yet Lloyd George accepted the French demand for an alliance, he agreed to a "war guilt" clause, and he insisted on elimination of the German navy and on an extremely high figure for reparations.

The Paris peace settlement, including the Treaty of Versailles between the Allies and Germany, gave the British much but not all that they wanted. Austria-Hungary was broken up, and Poland, Czechoslovakia, and Yugoslavia became independent. Germany remained intact but lost Alsace-Lorraine to France and territories in eastern Europe to newly created nations. Germany had to admit guilt and to accept payment of reparations to the Allies for an unspecified amount (set in 1921 at the enormous sum of $21 billion). The Saar industrial valley in Germany was to be occupied by the French for fifteen years, and the Rhineland was to be demilitarized. The German army was limited to 100,000 men, and certain types of armaments were forbidden. In addition, Britain won a mandate over German East Africa (Tanganyika), British colonies themselves picked up other German holdings, and Britain won the former Turkish territories of Palestine, Mesopotamia, and Trans-Jordan. Britain was thereby to remain the predominant power in the Middle East until after 1945.

Parliament ratified the Versailles Treaty almost unanimously, but when the United States rejected it as well as other European commitments, the British repudiated the military alliance with France. The Soviet Union had not been invited to Paris and stood outside the agreements. Indeed, during the negotiations themselves, the Allied powers, including Britain, sent troops to Russia in an abortive attempt to overthrow the Bolshevik government. Furthermore, as we will see in subsequent pages, a substantial portion of the British public soon turned against the Paris settlement. The complex structure put together in Paris began to come apart almost immediately.

Meanwhile, Lloyd George turned to domestic matters. Unfortunately, his plans for reconstruction ran afoul of postwar economic depression. The Fisher Education Act of 1918 set high goals for state education, the Addison Housing Act of 1919 stimulated the construction of 200,000 houses, and an act of 1920 extended unemployment insurance to eleven million additional workers. But the government's social programs felt the budgetary ax in 1920. Nor was Lloyd George able to solve the problem of the coal industry. Here his penchant for opportunism came to the fore. Agitation by the miners for better pay and shorter hours prodded him only into clever delaying action. He provided a government subsidy to wages and appointed a Royal Commission (the Sankey Commission) to report on the difficulties of the coal industry, but he then ignored its recommendations to nationalize coal royalties and amalgamate the smaller companies. Undoubtedly his most important achievement was the agreement with the Irish nationalists in 1921.

In 1918, Bonar Law had remarked that Lloyd George "can be Prime Minister for life if he likes." Yet by the middle of 1922, the enchantment of the Welsh magician over his coalition was decaying. His cabinet colleagues became restless under his one-man rule. The Irish treaty infuriated the die-hard unionists among the Conservatives. Lloyd George's blatant sale of peerages and knighthoods to men who contributed to his personal political fund offended Conservatives' sense of propriety. Coalition Liberals and Conservatives alike rejected his plan for "fusion" and formation of a new center party. Finally, his high-handed treatment of a crisis in the Middle East brought the discontent to a boil. In this so-called Chanak incident, Lloyd George's support for Greece in Asia Minor threatened to involve Britain in a war with the Turks. The matter was settled peaceably, but the Conservatives had had enough. In August 1922, Conservative M.P.s voted to withdraw from the coalition in favor of restoring the old party system. Lloyd George resigned his post that afternoon, and though no one expected it, he was never to hold office again.

MACDONALD AND BALDWIN

In the years between the fall of Lloyd George in 1922 and the premiership of Neville Chamberlain in 1931, the dominant figures in British politics were Ramsay MacDonald and Stanley Baldwin, two of the most puzzling characters in recent British history. Both were charming men and proponents of reconciliation in British society, but both were afflicted with intellectual softness and an inclination to inaction; hence they were responsible for drift in British policy. We will look at domestic policy first.

Ramsay MacDonald (1866–1937) was the leader of the Labour party from 1911 to 1914 and from 1922 to 1931, and he became the first Labour prime minister in 1924; yet at the end of his career he had earned the undying enmity of Labour party

Labour Prime Minister Ramsay MacDonald, with Margaret Bondfield, the first woman cabinet minister, 1929.

loyalists. MacDonald was the illegitimate son of Scottish peasants. Given an adequate elementary education, he became a clerk, a party activist, and an able administrator. He was handsome, a clever parliamentary tactician, and a gifted orator but was also rather reserved and overly sensitive to criticism. Over time, MacDonald developed an obtrusive vanity, and he felt more comfortable with members of the British elite than with members of his own party and class.

MacDonald was instrumental in the early development of the Labour party. A nondoctrinaire, ethical socialist, MacDonald was never a brilliant theorist but was a believer in organic social evolution. He thought that socialism would grow from social progress and prosperity, not the other way around. As secretary of the fledgling Labour party from 1900 to 1911, MacDonald negotiated the electoral alliance with the Liberals. Then as leader of the party after 1911 he helped persuade the radicals of the ILP to moderate their views and the trade unionists to think of the party as more than a union pressure group. In 1914, he opposed Britain's entry into World War I and resigned the leadership when the party voted to support the war effort. This gave him a reputation for radicalism and pacifism that he did not deserve. He returned to the leadership in 1922, thanks in large part to the votes of the militants like the Clydesiders. He was to disappoint them grievously.

The opportunity for MacDonald to form a Labour government came earlier than anyone expected—in 1924. The election of 1922 had confirmed Labour as the official opposition. In 1923, the Conservative prime minister, Baldwin, called a new general election on the issue of protective tariffs. The electorate still preferred free trade; hence the vote left the Conservatives as the largest party but denied them a majority. Labour won 191 seats and stood as the second largest party, even though the Liberals (reunited under Asquith) won 158 seats. Under the circumstances, several different governments might have been formed, and some politicians, like the violently anti-Bolshevik Winston Churchill, were desperate to keep Labour out. But Asquith decided to support a Labour government for at least a short while, for Labour and Liberals alike had supported free trade. Asquith said, "If a Labour Government is ever to be tried in this country, as it will be sooner or later, it could hardly be tried under safer conditions." In January 1924, therefore, King George V asked MacDonald to form a government, and he accepted.

The first Labour government was a tame affair. MacDonald and the other Labour leaders could have followed either of two strategies: to pursue moderate measures and thereby stay in office or to run up the flag of a thorough socialist program that would rally party enthusiasm but soon be defeated. MacDonald, who thought that the prime objective was to show that Labour could govern, chose the former. The government hoped to pass a few modest measures and to gain experience. During its nine months in office, the government passed one significant act, the Wheatley Housing Act of 1924, and MacDonald also impressed observers with his presence in foreign affairs. But the government had no solutions for unemployment and industrial conflict; thus MacDonald was happy to leave office by the end of the year. The issue that seemed likely to bring defeat was a commercial treaty that the government had negotiated with the Soviet Union. It received fierce criticism from the Conservatives, but before a vote was taken on it, the Labour government fell on a different issue. This was the "Campbell case," in which the Labour government had withdrawn prosecution of a Communist newspaperman named Campbell for allegedly inciting workers to mutiny. Although this was not a serious matter, MacDonald elected to resign when a vote in the House went against the government.

The subsequent election brought mixed results for Labour. The Labour party was soundly defeated, but the Liberals were annihilated. MacDonald lost the election but won a big battle in his long-term campaign to supplant the Liberals as the party of the left. Moreover, largely because he was Labour's only major talent as an orator and parliamentary politician, MacDonald retained leadership of the party.

In the election of 1929 MacDonald led Labour to victory: this time Labour won the most seats in the House of Commons (288, with Conservatives winning 261, and the Liberals only 59); yet again they had no absolute majority. MacDonald formed his second government, this one pledged to address unemployment and reduce international tension. Unfortunately, the catastrophic depression struck almost immediately. Unemployment jumped to two million by 1930, and the loss of tax revenue caused a major budget deficit. MacDonald and the mainstream of his party had no clue as to the solution to fundamental problems within the capitalist system. They believed that nothing important could be done, for they looked to the general transformation of society by socialism. Amid this crisis, the young Labour cabinet minister, Mosley (an impatient convert from Conservatism), proposed his Keynesian program of public works and deficit spending. When it was rejected, Mosley resigned from the government and went on to found the British Union of Fascists.

Meanwhile, the cabinet's dominant voice in economic matters belonged to the Chancellor of the Exchequer, Philip Snowden, a gaunt, fiery, teetotaler and one-time idealistic leader of the ILP. Snowden was an autocratic and dogmatic believer in Gladstonian finance: free trade and balanced budgets. Along with Treasury officials and city of London bankers, Snowden believed that the budget had to be balanced in order to protect the pound sterling. This was a strategy suited to defeat *inflation*, but the economy was suffering from radical *deflation*. In 1931, an official committee forecast that the budget deficit would reach £120 million and recommended massive budget cuts, much of which would come from unemployment benefits.

The question of budget cuts split the Labour cabinet and ended MacDonald's second government. MacDonald told the king that his divided government would have to resign. After consulting various political leaders, George V asked MacDonald to form a National Government with support from all three parties. MacDonald agreed, even though his cabinet had not been asked to vote on the matter. Only three members of the cabinet (including Snowden) agreed to serve with him, and the great majority of the Labour party angrily denounced MacDonald's decision. Soon there were accusations that MacDonald had conspired with the Conservatives and that he had given in to a "bankers' ramp." In fact, there had been no conspiracy. Instead, there was a failure of Labour ideas and a grievous lack of confidence by MacDonald in his colleagues.

MacDonald's National Government (1931–1935) was little more than a Conservative government in disguise. Baldwin was its dominant figure. The National Government immediately cut the budget and went off the gold standard, thereby ending the financial crisis, and in 1932, as we have seen, it abandoned free trade. Otherwise, its program was simply "Safety and the Union Jack." Its only contribution to economic recovery was to keep interest rates low, which encouraged borrowing and investment. MacDonald himself was increasingly inactive and irrelevant to his own cabinet. He resigned in 1935, and the National Government became what it had always been in actuality, a Conservative cabinet.

The new prime minister was Stanley Baldwin (1867–1947), who had already served as premier twice before, in 1923 and 1924–1929. Baldwin had risen to the leadership of the Tories, as he himself said, "by a succession of curious chances." Once a prosperous ironmaster, Baldwin put himself forward as a traditional country gentleman. Kindly and modest in personality, he had no political goal beyond preaching conciliation between industrialists and workers and keeping Lloyd George out of office. As a minister in Lloyd George's wartime coalition, Baldwin had been repulsed by the Welsh Wizard's free-wheeling and irreverent style, and he had helped lead the Conservative revolt against Lloyd George in 1922. In the subsequent Conservative government, Bonar Law served as prime minister until ill health forced him to resign in 1923. George V rather surprisingly summoned Baldwin to succeed Law instead of the arrogant aristocrat Lord Curzon, mainly on the grounds that the prime minister ought to come from the House of Commons.

Baldwin's first ministry (1923) was too short to be of much consequence, and

Conservative Prime Minister Stanley Baldwin, who liked to show the image of the country squire, in the garden of the prime minister's country residence, Chequers.

in his third (1935–1937) he was a spent force. But in his second administration (1924–1929), Baldwin had ample opportunity to act on his commitment to industrial conciliation and social harmony. He was a subtle politician but had little interest in legislation and was lucky to have as minister of health the remarkably diligent and efficient Neville Chamberlain, a son of the late Joseph Chamberlain. Neville Chamberlain was responsible for passing an impressive series of acts (twenty-one in all) of social reform. They included an extension of the old-age pension, unemployment insurance, and health insurance systems; creation of the Central Electricity Board and the BBC; support for construction of some 400,000 houses; and abolition of the old Poor Law unions. But it was Baldwin who took the lead in industrial relations, including the General Strike, and here his record fell short of his professed ideals.

Baldwin believed in capitalism, and he thought that the depression was a phase in the business cycle that had to work itself out. In the years leading up to the crisis of 1926, Baldwin refused to undertake reorganization of the coal industry or to persuade the coal owners to do it themselves. He allowed the return to the gold standard in 1925, which hurt the British coal industry by overpricing the product. Under the threat of a coal strike in 1925, Baldwin gave another temporary subsidy in aid of wages, as all British governments had done since the war, and appointed a new Royal Commission (the Samuel Commission). When it reported in 1926, Baldwin was unable to bring about the recommended restructuring of the coal industry or to persuade the miners to accept wage reductions. His government did prepare well for the expected strike. During the General Strike, Baldwin sought to separate the constitutional issues from the industrial ones. He insisted that the unions had no right to pressure the government, and in intense negotiations he pressured the leaders of the TUC, who were speaking for the strikers, to reject this potentially radical strategy. Thus Baldwin was seen by the public as ending the General Strike, but he failed to follow through with a settlement of the coal miners' claims. He had pledged to "ensure a square deal to secure even justice between man and man," but the miners eventually had to return to work on the employers' terms. And in 1927, he yielded to pressure from his party's right wing by passing an act prohibiting secondary strikes (strikes by unions not directly involved in the primary dispute) as well as strikes intended to coerce the government, and providing that a member of a trade union had to "contract in" (that is, positively give his or her consent) before any part of his or her union dues could be spent by the union's political fund.

In his third administration, Baldwin had to deal with another matter of constitutional importance—the abdication of a king. George V died in 1936 and was succeeded by Edward VIII. But Edward had been consorting with an American divorcee, Mrs. Wallis Simpson, and wished to marry her. Given the king's position as head of the Church of England, this was impossible. For once Baldwin was galvanized to decisive action. He refused to consider a "morganatic" marriage for Edward, whereby Mrs. Simpson would have become Edward's wife but not queen. Baldwin made it clear that if Edward insisted on marrying Mrs. Simpson he would have to abdicate. This he did, in December 1936. Edward's younger brother was proclaimed George VI. Baldwin retired after George's coronation in 1937, with the thanks of Britons ringing in his ears. Within two years, the consequences of his indecision and indolence, which characterized his foreign as well as domestic policies, had destroyed his reputation.

BRITISH POWER AND INTERESTS BETWEEN THE WARS

Baldwin's successor as prime minister was an altogether different kind of man: Neville Chamberlain, who was self-confident and decisive and who now focused exclusively on foreign affairs, with which Baldwin had always been uncomfortable. Chamberlain dominated his cabinet and conducted foreign policy practically alone. But before we judge his record in the international arena, we have to examine the context of British power and interests in which he operated.

Britain, of course, remained a great power in 1919. Given the collapse of Czarist Russia and the isolation of the Soviet Union, the withdrawal from Europe by the United States, and the Versailles Treaty's limitation of German armaments, Britain was arguably the strongest power in Europe and second only to the United States in the world as a whole. Nevertheless, scorched by war as the British psyche was, and distracted by the faltering economy, the British in the 1920s had little interest in maintaining great armaments or in involving themselves in Continental security arrangements. They did not even wish to pursue the traditional balance of power in Europe, since that policy was thought to have formed part of the discredited prewar diplomatic system. What might be called the "appeasement mentality" prevailed. Thus in 1919, the Lloyd George government established a "Ten-Year Rule," by which the armed forces were to assume each year that there would be no major war for the next ten years. The army and air force were allowed to languish. Even the navy was run down: naval estimates were cut by 85 percent by 1923. During the 1920s, the navy had only twenty battleships, all of them in the Atlantic and Mediterranean, with none for the key British naval base in the Far East, Singapore. Britain dropped the old treaty with Japan in 1922 at the insistence of the United States. Then by the Washington Naval Treaty of 1922, Britain accepted parity in battleships with the United States and a fixed ratio of capital ships with Japan, France, and Italy of 5:3:1.75:1.75. In 1930, the same 5:5:3 ratio among Britain, the United States, and Japan was extended to all ships.

Yet Britain's commitments remained huge. The British now accounted for only about 10 percent of the world's industrial output, but the British Empire encompassed 25 percent of the world's land surface. Excluding the socialists, most Britons between the wars believed that the Empire was more important than ever, but in fact it was of questionable value in terms of the economy as well as diplomatic and military power. From Africa to Egypt to Palestine to India, the British had to maintain military and naval forces as well as administrative structures, but this cumbersome imperial realm could not be readily mobilized for British objectives.

The dominions, for example, continued to develop their own independent policies and interests. They demanded to be represented at the Paris peace conference and were accepted as part of the British delegation. They became independent members of the League of Nations. During the Chanak crisis, the British government requested dominion military assistance, but except for New Zealand the dominions were far from enthusiastic about supporting a British matter that might involve them in war. From that time on, they insisted that they would have to be consulted before they would support British policy. Then the creation of the Irish Free State in 1921–1922 made it clear that dominion status would involve complete autonomy under the Crown. This was codified by an Imperial Conference in 1926 and clarified once and for all by the Statute of Westminster in 1931, which can be taken as the foundation of the British Commonwealth. In the following year, the National Government established a protective tariff and opened discussions with the dominions for a system of imperial tariff preferences. The Ottawa Commonwealth Conference of 1932 disappointed this hope, for although imperial preferences were accepted, the dominions rejected free trade within the Empire. The dominions did not wish to sacrifice their own interests for imperial economic union. All of these developments reflected credit on Britain's comparative flexibility in allowing self-government to the former colonies, but they also meant that only in extreme crisis could Britain hope to call on imperial support.

Even India was presenting major problems for British power. Nationalist agitation against British rule had long existed in India, and in the late nineteenth century the Indian National Congress had been established as an expression of middle-class Indian nationalism. In the 1890s a more popular protest entered the field, based on a Hindu revival and mass anti-Western conservatism. The Liberal government had attempted to conciliate Indian nationalism in 1907–1908 by allowing limited Indian participation in government at both the provincial and national lev-

Mahatma Gandhi, the leader of Indian nationalism and advocate of nonviolence and passive resistance to British rule, shown here in front of No. 10 Downing Street, London.

els. These reforms, however, were far from responsible government, and during the Great War the British promised additional measures in order to maintain Indian support. In these so-called Montagu-Chelmsford Reforms, implemented in the immediate postwar period, the British granted "dyarchy," a dual system of government at the provincial level in which the Indians had responsibility for certain functions, though not internal security. But this did not satisfy Indian nationalists. By the end of the war, Mahatma Gandhi's campaign of nonviolent noncooperation began to mobilize millions of Indians.

The nationalist agitation put enormous pressure on the British. In 1919, General Reginald Dyer's troops fired on a peaceful meeting at Amritsar and killed some four hundred demonstrators. British public opinion was passionately divided over the incident, but in general, despite the die-hard imperialism of a few Conservatives like Churchill, British will to rule India by force was dwindling. E. M. Forster's novel *A Passage to India* (1924) condemned British imperialism for its effects on Britons and Indians alike. Socialists and pacifists both opposed the use of force in the Empire. Many people in the British left supported the development of Indian self-government. Whereas imperialists were determined to hold out against colonial self-government, both the Labour and Liberal parties were more accommodating, and the Indian nationalist movement was irresistible. Ever the conciliator,

Baldwin accepted the idea of wider powers of Indian self-rule. The India Act of 1935, passed by the National Government, granted responsible government to the Indians at the provincial level and a partially elected legislature at the national level. Some British imperialists were furious: according to Churchill, the act marked "the definite decline, and even disappearance, of our authority in India."

Despite the alteration of empires around the world and the development of powers such as Japan and the United States, British foreign policy remained Euro-centered. The central problems for Britain were France, Russia, Germany, and the League of Nations. The French were desperate for security and depended on Britain to offset the potential power of a revengeful Germany. The British, however, did not share France's anti-German views, nor did the British wish to tie their hands by signing a mutual security treaty with the French. Instead, the British saw themselves as mediators between France and Germany and tended to think the French would be greater threats to peace than the Germans.

As for the Soviet Union, Conservatives (and many Liberals) in Britain regarded the Bolshevist government as an outlaw regime, especially because the Russians repudiated their war debt to Britain. There was a significant difference between parties: MacDonald's first Labour government attempted to establish normal relations with the Soviet Union, but as we have seen this was electorally unpopular, and Baldwin's government in 1925 abandoned the effort. MacDonald's second government managed to reestablish formal relations with Russia in 1929, yet Britain remained deeply suspicious of the Soviet government. Thus to many conservative Britons, the revival of Germany was necessary as a bulwark against the spread of communism.

Britain's attitude toward Germany was generally one of encouraging the restoration of Germany to a normal role in Europe. In 1919 Keynes had launched a severe attack on the Versailles settlement, *The Economic Consequences of the Peace,* in which he argued among other things that the reparations demanded of Germany were too high to allow for a stable central European economy. The British after 1919 tried in various ways to persuade the French not to demand too much from Germany. They declared that they would themselves ask for no more reparations from Germany than the Americans demanded in repayment of Britain's war debt. The British welcomed the Dawes Plan of 1924, whereby Germany's payments were stretched over a long period, and the Young Plan of 1929, whereby the payments were scaled down. When the Germans in 1925 sought to normalize relations with the Western powers by making permanent the German boundaries with France and Belgium, the British responded enthusiastically. By the Locarno agreement of that year, Baldwin's government guaranteed the Franco-German agreement, safe in the knowledge that it was not a genuine mutual-security treaty. Likewise, the British supported Germany's reentry into the League of Nations in 1926. They believed that Germany's legitimate grievances resulting from Versailles should be addressed. Such policies toward Germany, as we will see, lasted well into the 1930s.

As for the League, the British differed sharply from the French in their interpretation of its purpose. Whereas the French wanted to make the League a collective security agreement for enforcing compliance with the Treaty of Versailles, the British regarded it as a forum for airing international differences. The British defeated two French attempts to put muscle into the League—the Draft Treaty of Mutual Assistance (1923) and the Geneva Protocol (1924). Each in effect would have committed the League to action against an aggressor state. The British on the whole preferred disarmament agreements to the concept of action by the League, although the Labour party rather confusingly supported both. MacDonald, for instance, would accept no collective security agreement of any kind until disarmament had rendered it meaningless. The trouble with disarmament as a policy was that the great powers found it very hard to negotiate the necessarily complex multilateral agreements (the naval treaties were the only accomplishments), and each failure by the former Allies to agree to a disarmament formula only angered the Germans, who had been *forced* to disarm.

Rapidly evolving events of the early and mid-1930s exposed the weaknesses of British power and policies, and international affairs became more confusing as aggression itself increasingly appeared to be the enemy. In 1931, the Japanese invaded Manchuria, and the British did not lead the League toward halting the aggression. In 1933, economic depression and loathing for the Treaty of Versailles brought Adolf Hitler to power in Germany. He soon pulled out of a major disarmament conference in Geneva, for which the British had high hopes, even though Germany had already won preliminary approval of equal status in armaments, and then he withdrew from the League of Nations. In March 1935 Hitler announced that Germany would not adhere to the arms limitations of the treaty, and one year later he sent German troops back into the Rhineland, also in contravention of the treaty. In 1936, civil war broke out in Spain between the republic, supported by the left (liberals, socialists, and communists) and the rebels, supported by the right (monarchists, the church, and the fascists). The Spanish civil war deeply and emotionally divided British public opinion, and a number of British radicals and socialists volunteered for service with the republic. Baldwin's government pursued a policy of international "nonintervention," even though both Mussolini's Italy and Hitler's Germany actively supported the rebels and the Soviet Union actively supported the republic. This ineffectual policy satisfied no one in Britain.

In 1935, Italy invaded Abyssinia in direct contradiction of the charter of the League. British public opinion supported collective action of some kind by the League against Italy. In the general election of 1935, the National Government also supported League action but ruled out military force in favor of mild economic sanctions. The sanctions had no effect, and the British, mindful that they had no allies, sought to buy Mussolini's favor by proposing a partition of Abyssinia to his advantage. This backstairs betrayal outraged the British public and had to be dropped, along with the foreign secretary (Sir Samuel Hoare) who had made the offer. But nothing more was done for Abyssinia, and in 1936 Italy annexed it. The whole affair destroyed any hope for an effective League of Nations.

Meanwhile, Britain was taking the first halting steps toward rearmament. This was not done eagerly, partly because of financial considerations but mainly because public opinion seemed to be opposed. The British people desperately wanted to avoid war and understandably thought that armaments led to war. Vera Brittain's autobiography of her war years, *Testament of Youth* (1933), made a strong case for pacifism. In 1933 the Oxford Union voted in favor of the resolution "that this House will in no circumstance fight for its King and Country." A Labour party pacifist won a by-election in Fulham (London), also in 1933. A public opinion poll of June 1935 (the "Peace Ballot") showed that a huge majority of those consulted supported general disarmament, even though they contradictorily supported League sanctions that might lead to war. Baldwin later confessed that in 1933–1934 he could have won no support for a rearmament program. There was widespread fear of strategic bombing, fed by remarks such as Baldwin's that the "bomber will always get through." Yet rearmament did begin, and Baldwin was the key figure. The Ten-Year Rule was abandoned in 1932. Funds for the air force were increased in 1934 and decisively in 1935. Funding for the navy and army were sacrificed for air defense, and these services were still in poor shape in 1939, but the Royal Air Force (RAF) began to overcome the massive handicaps of design and production that had limited it. Perhaps most important, a government committee for scientific air defense research produced a system of radio direction finding—radar—by the mid-1930s.

CHAMBERLAIN AND THE COMING OF WAR, 1937–1939

When Neville Chamberlain became prime minister in 1937, he meant to put an end to what he rightly saw as drift in British foreign policy. It is thus a cruel irony that his good intentions ended in disaster. Chamberlain had served for a number of years under Baldwin, and he had concluded that Baldwin's relaxed style was inadequate. Furthermore, Chamberlain had great confidence in himself. A highly effective minister of health from 1924 to 1929 and a dominating chancellor of the Exchequer from 1931 to 1937, Chamberlain was experienced, clear minded, and logical, but also narrow and arrogant. He had a reserved, even bleak personality. "In manner he is glacial rather than genial," said one colleague. In his self-assurance, he was disdainful of many of the members of his government and chose to listen to only a select few. Unfortunately, he had poor understanding of human nature; hence he misread Hitler.

Chamberlain had no love for Nazism and knew that Hitler's regime was brutal. But Chamberlain as a good businessman did believe that all heads of state would know their own interests and thus could work out conflicting claims. He was concerned about the degenerating conditions of European relations and troubled about the slow pace of British rearmament, on which he had himself as Chancellor of the Exchequer under Baldwin kept a tight rein. Like many of Britain's military leaders, he was convinced of both Germany's military power and Britain's weakness. It has been argued that in his policy toward Germany after 1937—appeasement— he was buying time. Actually, he fashioned his policy because he thought it would work. He believed that Britain could and should deal independently with Germany because Russia was not trustworthy, because Britain had few interests in common with the small states of eastern Europe, and because an alliance with France would limit Britain's cherished freedom of action and provoke Germany besides.

Moreover, like the majority of British politicians and statesmen between the wars, Chamberlain thought that Germany had many legitimate grievances as a result of the Versailles Treaty. Therefore, although he knew he was bargaining with a weak hand, he thought he could reach an agreement with Hitler. Appeasement of Germany became his deliberate policy: "I do not see why we shouldn't say to Germany 'give us satisfactory assurances that you won't use force to deal with the Austrians and Czechoslovakians, and we will give you similar assurances that we won't use force to prevent the changes you want, if you can get them by peaceful means.' " Such a view might have been sensible with ordinary German statesmen, but it was based on a total misunderstanding of Hitler and his movement, as Chamberlain should have known from Hitler's book, *Mein Kampf*, as well as countless maniacal speeches by Hitler and his followers. Chamberlain's appeasement policy only persuaded Hitler that Britain was a weak, decadent nation.

Chamberlain did not brook any opposition to his policies from within his government. Critics like Sir Robert Vansittart, Philip Cunliffe-Lister (Lord Swinton), and Anthony Eden (foreign secretary in 1937) all were dismissed. He ignored the little band of Conservatives in Parliament led by Harold Macmillan, who raised the alarm about German militarism. The Labour party was divided and weak, unable to sort out its hostility to Nazism, its devotion to collective security, and its pacifism. Chamberlain's chief opponent was Winston Churchill, who had been attacking the government (not always fairly) about failure to rearm since 1933.

Churchill had gained much and varied experience in his long and remarkable career in Parliament and in cabinet office since before the Great War. Amazingly eloquent, energetic, and patriotic, Churchill had focused attention on himself at the Board of Trade, the Home Office, and the admiralty in the prewar Liberal government, as the author of the Gallipoli policy in 1915, and as a key member of the Lloyd George coalition. He had shifted his flag from the Liberals to the Conservatives, mainly because of his antisocialism, between 1922 and 1924 and then had served as Chancellor of the Exchequer under Baldwin from 1924 to 1929. Churchill took his outlook and policies not from social science but from his immersion in history. He held a "whiggish" view of English history, in which the main theme was the glorious, progressive evolution of English law and institutions. Churchill had no love for fascism but no concern about it as such; nor did he oppose aggression in itself. But as the descendant of the great duke of Marlborough, he feared the domination of the Continent by any one power, the latest example of which was German militarism.

Alas, Churchill had disqualified himself as a reliable witness by certain eccentric views in the 1920s. He was a fanatical anti-Bolshevist and tended to equate all forms of socialism with revolution. He had been a pugnacious antisyndicalist during the General Strike. He also was a die-hard imperialist who had opposed every step toward accommodation of Indian nationalism. To him dominion status for India was "a crime" and Gandhi a "naked fakir." Thus he had parted company with Baldwin over India in 1931 and resigned from the Tory front bench. He was not

Prime Minister Neville Chamberlain departing for Munich and a meeting with Hitler, September 1938. He returned to claim he had achieved "peace in our time."

invited to serve in the National Government. He had supported King Edward VIII in his desire to marry an American divorcee. To some degree he exaggerated the buildup of the German Luftwaffe, and he underestimated the rearmament steps of the British government. Not surprisingly, when he cried "wolf" about German rearmament from 1933, he won scant response.

The first major step taken by Hitler after Chamberlain became prime minister came in March 1938, when Germany annexed Austria following an intense propaganda and diplomatic campaign. Churchill was alarmed, but Chamberlain was not. Czechoslovakia was Hitler's obvious next target because the Versailles settlement had assigned a significant number of Germans to the new state. Chamberlain believed that Hitler wanted to take only Germans into the Reich, not other nationalities, and that this was a reasonable objective. Moreover, Chamberlain refused to make an alliance with France and Czechoslovakia on grounds that it would cause the Germans to feel encircled. He concluded that he should himself mediate the "Czechoslovakian problem" in order to avoid war—in other words, he would pressure the Czechs to grant the Germans living in Czechoslovakia (the Sudeten Germans) all of their demands for autonomy. When in September 1938 the claims of the Sudeten Germans, backed by Hitler, reached a crisis, Chamberlain flew to Germany to settle the matter with Hitler personally, without consulting the Czechs. In the course of three trips to Germany over a two-week period, he agreed to a plan whereby Germany won immediate occupation of all disputed Czech territories. During this "Munich Crisis," international tension was extremely high, and the fear of war with Germany pervaded Britain. Chamberlain spoke for many of his countrymen when he said in a radio broadcast:

> How horrible, fantastic, incredible it is that we should be digging trenches and trying on gas masks here because of a quarrel in a far-away country between people of whom we know nothing.

When he returned from Munich with the final agreement, which included a statement signed by himself and Hitler that Britain and Germany would never again go to war ("peace in our time"), the British public was wild with relief.

A minority of informed people, however, were humiliated by Britain's role in giving away a section of a sovereign nation, including a significant segment of that nation's defenses. Churchill called the Munich deal "a total and unmitigated defeat." When in March 1939 Hitler annexed the rest of Czechoslovakia, public and political opinion alike turned against Chamberlain. The Conservative party especially revolted in anger. Chamberlain now realized that opinion in the House of Commons demanded resolute resistance to Hitler; thus at the end of March he joined the French in declaring that if Poland, Hitler's apparent next target, were attacked Britain would go to war. However, Chamberlain still believed that peace with Hitler was possible, and besides the British and French had no real way of aiding the Poles. The only sensible tactic at the moment was to make an alliance with Russia for defense against Germany, but Chamberlain still profoundly distrusted the Soviets, and in addition the Poles themselves would allow no Russian troops on their territory. Italy and Germany signed a "Pact of Steel" in May 1939, and still the British delayed in reaching an agreement with the Russians. In August the Germans and Russians reached their own agreement, which opened the door to a German invasion of Poland. The attack came on September 1, 1939, and the British declared war on Germany on September 3. Only Mosley's British Union of Fascists protested, and their numbers were very small. Chamberlain said, "Everything I have worked for, everything I have hoped for, everything I have believed in during my public life, has crashed in ruins." Churchill, on the other hand, later wrote that "a very strong sense of calm came over me. . . . I felt a security of mind. . . . The glory of old England, peace-loving and ill-prepared as she was, but instant and fearless at the call of honour, thrilled my being and seemed to lift our fate to those spheres far removed from earthly facts and physical sensations."

As historians of Britain look back over the record of events between 1919 and 1939, their mood must be one of maddening frustration. Why did the British not recognize the danger presented by Hitler and take the forceful steps to stop him before war broke out? Why did the British remain so unprepared and seem to conduct their affairs with such naivete and lethargy? Why did they not stick to their tried-and-true policy of a balance of power in Europe? The answer in part lay in Britain's understandable revulsion of war after the horrors of 1914–1918. They wanted to avoid involvement in another war, and thus they shunned armaments and entangling alliances. They also did not have the economic power any longer to field massive armed forces without feeling the bite dearly. Troubled by decaying older industries and worldwide depression, the British believed that recovery would come through international conciliation and stability, not alliances and collective security. They failed to understand that Hitler was a new kind of force in the modern world, that he was driven by demons almost beyond the imagination of rational beings. One thing can be said for Chamberlain after all: his bending over backward to appease Hitler in September 1938 was an ultimate test that Hitler then failed for all Britons to see; thus when the British finally did decide to fight they knew it was a just war, and they came into the battle united.

Suggested Reading

Adams, R. J. Q., *Bonar Law* (Stanford: Stanford University Press, 1999).

———, *British Politics and Foreign Policy in the Age of Appeasement, 1935–39* (Stanford: Stanford University Press, 1993).

Blake, Robert, *The Unknown Prime Minister: The Life and Times of Andrew Boner Law, 1858–1923* (London: Eyre & Spottiswoode, 1955).

Cowling, Maurice, *The Impact of Hitler* (London: Cambridge University Press, 1975).

———, *The Impact of Labour, 1920–1924* (Cambridge: Cambridge University Press, 1971).

Dutton, David, *Neville Chamberlain* (New York: Oxford University Press, 2001).

Gilbert, Bentley, *British Social Policy, 1914–1939* (Ithaca, N.Y.: Cornell University Press, 1970).

Gilbert, Martin, *Winston S. Churchill* (8 vols.; vols. 4 and 5 cover 1916–1939) (London: Heinemann, 1966–1988).

Howell, David, *Macdonald's Party: Labour Identities and Crisis, 1922–1931* (New York: Oxford University Press, 2002).

James, Robert Rhodes, *The British Revolution, Vol. II: 1914–1939* (London: Hamilton, 1976–1977).

———, *Churchill: A Study in Failure, 1900–1939* (London: Weidenfeld & Nicolson, 1970).

Marquand, David, *Ramsay MacDonald* (London: Cape, 1977).

McCrillis, Neal R. *The British Conservative Party in the Age of Universal Suffrage* (Columbus: Ohio State University Press, 1998).

McDonough, Frank, *Neville Chamberlain, Appeasement and the British Road to War* (Manchester: Manchester University Press, 1998).

McKibbin, Ross, *The Evolution of the Labour Party* (Oxford: Clarendon Press, 1974).

Middlemas, Keith, *Diplomacy of Illusion: The British Government and Germany, 1937–39* (London: Weidenfeld & Nicolson, 1972).

———, *Politics in Industrial Society* (London: Deutsch, 1979).

Middlemas, Keith, and John Barnes, *Baldwin: A Biography* (London: Weidenfeld & Nicolson, 1969).

Morgan, Kenneth O., *Consensus and Disunity: The Lloyd George Government, 1918–1922* (Oxford: Clarendon Press, 1979).

Northedge, F. S., *The Troubled Giant: Britain Among the Powers, 1916–1939* (New York: Praeger, 1966).

Parker, R. A. C., *Churchill and Appeasement* (London: Macmillan, 2000).

Phillips, G. A., *The General Strike* (London: Weidenfeld & Nicolson, 1976).

Porter, Bernard, *Britain, Europe, and the World, 1850–1982* (London: Allen & Unwin, 1983).

Price, Christopher, *Britain, America and Rearmament in the 1930s* (New York: Palgrave, 2002).

Pugh, Martin, *The Making of Modern British Politics, 1867–1939* (Oxford: Basil Blackwell, 1982).

Skidelsky, Robert, *Oswald Mosley* (New York: Holt, Rinehart & Winston, 1975).

Chapter 10

Britain and World War II

When writing his justly famous history of World War II, Churchill designated 1940 for the British as "their finest hour." It is a label that should be applied to the whole of the British experience in the war, and it was true in more ways than one. The British people displayed admirable courage and fortitude throughout the war, summoning remarkable inner resources and willingness to sacrifice for the war effort. They also showed a sense of commonality and a commitment to social reconstruction that was doubly admirable in view of the class conflict and social disorders of the interwar period. As a direct result of the war effort, the British appeared to retain their status as a great power and build a welfare state that expressed a humanitarian public consensus until the 1970s. Time was to show that the former was illusory, but the latter was genuine.

STANDING ALONE, SEPTEMBER 1939 TO JUNE 1941

As World War II began, British efforts against Germany were ineffectual. The Chamberlain government realized that the British had no way to assist Poland, and the Germans (aided by the Russians, who invaded Poland from the east in order to claim their pickings) completed their conquest of that tragic nation by the end of September 1939. The Chamberlain government refused even to bomb Germany, for they still hoped to avoid an all-out war, and the French army stood still behind their defensive position facing Germany, the Maginot Line. In any case, the lack of British preparedness would have prevented an effective response to the new kind of warfare unleashed by the Germans—the *Blitzkrieg*, or lightning war. Adapted, ironically enough, from the ideas of British theorists who were ignored in Britain, *Blitzkrieg* emphasized speed and movement, with armored units (the *Panzer* divisions) backed up by tactical air support shocking the enemy and racing through gaps to disorganize and demoralize them. German tanks and screaming Stuka dive bombers soon earned a terrifying reputation among the Allies. Once Poland had been conquered, the Second World War assumed the same basic structure as the First—the Germans attacked rapidly in the west before turning on the Russians in the east—but *Blitzkrieg* revolutionized warfare itself. It took the British a year to learn the lesson and adjust.

As in the past, the British set high store by naval blockade, and the Royal Navy quickly assumed its positions covering German ports. Unfortunately the British reckoned without either German air power or Hitler's determination to establish *autarky* (that is, national economic self-sufficiency). German U-boats once again made close blockade impossible; thus although the Royal Navy did sweep the seas of German surface raiders, the U-boats endangered British shipping, including the most powerful warships. Submarines sank the aircraft carrier *Courageous* and the battleship *Royal Oak* in the first months of the war. Moreover, British ships proved to be very vulnerable to air attacks. Thus, when the British decided to aid Finland, which had been attacked by Russia in November 1939, and to cut off Germany's iron-ore shipments from Sweden in the process, they were unable to do so. Then, in a serious effort to stop the passage of the iron ore through Norway, the British decided to mine Norwegian waters and to occupy the port of Narvik. The Germans, however, outmaneuvered them with a quick seaborne and parachute invasion of Norway and Denmark in April 1940. The Royal Navy, under heavy air attack, was unable to prevent German landings or to support the British troops put ashore at Narvik. In June 1940, the British had to withdraw all their troops, and both Denmark and Norway were in German hands.

The Norwegian fiasco brought down the Chamberlain government. Chamberlain already was tainted by appeasement and was blamed in part for Britain's lack of preparedness. Moreover, his cabinet had not conducted the war with any drive or imagination. His foreign secretary, Lord Halifax, entertained hopes of settlement with Germany well into the spring of 1940. Backbench Conservative M.P.s grew angry with Chamberlain's ineffectiveness. In early May, when it was clear that the Norwegian campaign had gone sour, they revolted. L. S. Amery, who had been a critic of appeasement, attacked Chamberlain in the House of Commons, ending his speech with Cromwell's famous dismissal of the Rump Parliament following the seventeenth-century civil war: "You have sat here too long for any good you have been doing. Depart, I say, and let us have done with you. In the name of God, go!" When Chamberlain barely survived a Labour motion of censure, he resigned.

Winston Churchill succeeded Chamberlain, despite the fact that as first lord of the admiralty he had been largely responsible for the failure in Norway. Churchill by then had become the symbol of opposition to appeasement and the half-hearted war effort. On accepting the king's commission to form a government, Churchill later wrote,

> I was conscious of a profound sense of relief. At last I had the authority to give directions over the whole scene. I felt as if I were walking with Destiny, and that all my past life had been but a preparation for this hour and this trial. . . . I was sure I should not fail.

Churchill formed a National Government including Liberals and Labourites as well as Conservatives. It was an extremely able group. Clement Attlee, leader of the Labour party, became deputy prime minister; Ernest Bevin, secretary of the Transport and General Workers Union and chairman of the TUC, became minister of Labour and National Service; and Lord Beaverbrook served as minister for aircraft production. Churchill insisted on serving as minister of defense in a small inner war cabinet, and, later, becoming leader of the Conservative party. There would be no conflict between frock coats and brass hats in this war. Churchill from the outset took an active role in practically every aspect of the war effort, incessantly demanding more imagination and rapid action from his subordinates and urging the generals to take the offensive. But he was never able to dictate policy. "All I wanted was compliance with my wishes," he said, "after a reasonable discussion." Immediately after becoming prime minister, Churchill gave to the House of Commons the first of his magnificent wartime speeches that somehow said what the British people needed and wanted to hear. The new government had nothing to offer, he said, but "blood, toil, tears, and sweat." They had but one aim: "Victory—victory at all costs, victory in spite of all terror; victory, however long and hard the road may be."

The very day Churchill became prime minister, May 10, 1940, the Germans turned their *Blitzkrieg* to the west, invading Holland, Belgium, and France. The speed of their tank columns was too much for the old-fashioned Allied armies. Within three weeks the Dutch and Belgians had surrendered, and the German army had sped through France to the coast. The British Expeditionary Force (BEF) of ten divisions had been deployed in northern France on the Belgian frontier, but it was forced rapidly backward as the Germans broke the neighboring French defenses. In the midst of the rout, some British units fought well; however, by late May the BEF had retreated to a beachhead around Dunkirk on the English Channel, less than 30 miles from Dover. As the German tanks paused to allow the dive bombers to pound the beleaguered and exhausted troops, it looked as if the British would lose their entire army.

The evacuation of the BEF and some, at least, of the French army from Dunkirk was a miracle of improvisation. Between May 27 and June 4, while the RAF and the *Luftwaffe* fought overhead, some 850 British vessels took about 200,000 British and 140,000 French troops to safety in England. The navy, of course, carried the bulk of the troops, losing six destroyers in the process. In addition, hundreds of small private boats—tugs, yachts, fishing boats, ferries, coastal merchant vessels—made trip after trip into the cauldron and back. Dunkirk was a defeat, for thousands of British and French troops were left behind, and the BEF lost all of its tanks and heavy equipment. Yet the nucleus of the British army was saved to fight another day. In Britain Dunkirk was viewed as a glorious achievement. The "spirit of Dunkirk" signified high morale and resolution among all Britons and gave them confidence that however grim the military situation seemed they would not lose.

France capitulated to Germany on June 22, 1940. From that day for exactly one year, the British stood alone against German and Italian power. It must be remembered that Germany in 1940 was much more powerful than Britain, for Germany had a population of seventy million against Britain's forty-eight million and produced 50 percent more coal and steel and 75 percent more iron. The German army and air force were much larger than Britain's. The British could expect help from the dominions, which entered the war voluntarily, but they needed time to mobilize. Hence the British stood in greater danger even than in 1805, when Napoleon threatened to invade. In July, Hitler and his generals began planning operation "Sea

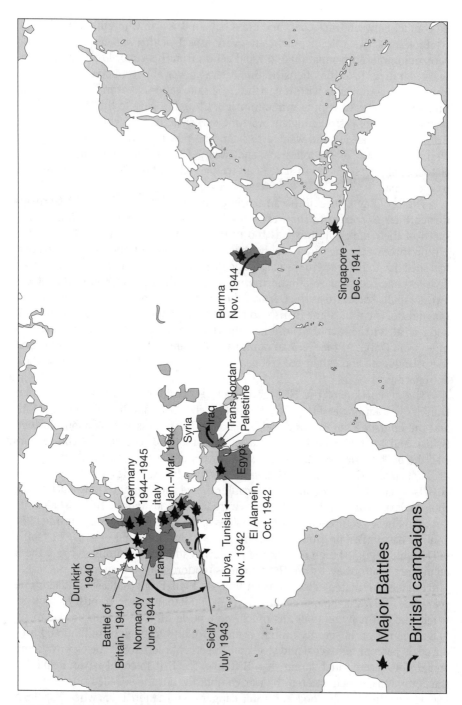

British involvement in World War II

British Spitfires taking off during the Battle of Britain, 1940.

Lion," the invasion of Britain. The German navy began collecting landing barges in the ports of France and the Low Countries. The Germans, however, knew that they would not be able to put the *Wehrmacht* (army) ashore unless the *Luftwaffe* controlled the skies; otherwise, the Royal Navy would destroy the invasion armada. Churchill in July 1940 had taken the "hateful" decision to destroy the French fleet at Oran to keep it from falling into German hands. Thus the Germans in the summer of 1940 opened their campaign against the RAF.

The struggle between the RAF and the *Luftwaffe*, the "Battle of Britain," the most dramatic battle of the war, lasted throughout August and September of 1940. The combatants were closely matched: the Germans had the advantage in number of aircraft, but the British fought over their own territory, which meant that their fighters could stay in combat longer and that they could recover at least some of their downed pilots. Furthermore, the British had radar, which allowed them to detect incoming German planes. Fortunately for the British, their rearmament in the mid-1930s had produced two fighter planes, the Spitfire and the Hurricane, which were the equal of the best German planes. The chief of British Fighter Command, Sir Hugh Dowding, had refused to waste these planes in the futile battle of France; thus when the Battle of Britain started, Fighter Command had some 690 first-class aircraft, whereas the Germans had about 1,000 plus 1,500 bombers. Every day the skies over southeastern England were filled with the vapor trails of airplanes in combat. The worst period of the battle came in late August, when the *Luftwaffe* concentrated on the British fighter bases. But then Hitler ordered the *Luftwaffe* to shift its attack to London, in retaliation for an RAF raid on Berlin. That switch gave some relief to Fighter Command. On September 15, the German air assault reached its climax, but the RAF beat it back. Finally, in October, Hitler cancelled the planning for Sea Lion. Of the British fighter pilots, Churchill said that "never in the field of human conflict was so much owed by so many to so few."

Prime Minister Winston Churchill inspecting air-raid damage to the House of Commons, London, during the Blitz, May 1941.

The Battle of Britain, however, was followed by a massive German bombing attack on British cities, above all on London. This "Blitz," as the British called it, went on from August 1940 to May 1941. Night after night German bombers appeared over London and other cities on the coasts and in the South and Midlands. The Blitz destroyed or damaged over three million homes, much of the City of London, the East End of London, the House of Commons, St. Paul's Cathedral, and Buckingham Palace. Coventry and Birmingham were severely bombed in November. About thirty thousand British civilians were killed, the majority of them in London. But in spite of the dire predictions made in the 1920s and 1930s, British morale was not broken, nor was production seriously damaged. Most Britons each day went about their business despite the nightly air raids, fires, and retreats to air raid shelters.

The RAF replied in kind, attempting to destroy German industrial production by long-range bombing. Unprotected by fighters over Germany, however, the slow British bombers were easy targets for antiaircraft guns and fighter planes. As losses grew, the RAF resorted to night bombing, which was too inaccurate to be very effective. The German populace, like the British themselves, did not wilt under long-range bombing, and German production went up steadily, reaching its peak in 1944. Strategic bombing, nevertheless, was one of the few ways the British had in 1940–1941 of taking the offensive against Germany. More than half of all British war production thus went to the construction of heavy bombers.

Meanwhile, the British were able to engage the Axis powers in the Mediterranean and Middle East, with mixed results. The British army faced large Italian forces in Abyssinia and North Africa and although badly outnumbered defeated

The most famous British photograph of World War II: St. Paul's Cathedral, London, sailing through the bombs during the Blitz, December 1940.

them in both places. Instead of consolidating their victory, however, the British (against Churchill's warnings) decided to aid the Greeks in their struggle against invading Italian forces. Hitler intervened to help the Italians in Greece just before the British arrived; hence the British troops came just as the Greek army was collapsing, and they had to be withdrawn in the spring of 1941 in a humiliating repeat of Dunkirk. The island of Crete fell to German paratroopers soon after. The Germans also intervened in North Africa, sending the Afrika Korps under General Erwin Rommel, the "Desert Fox," to aid the Italians. A master of tank warfare, Rommel drove the British back to Egypt and threatened the Suez Canal, which was the most important British possession in the region. For the next two years, the desert war against the Germans, in which columns of tanks operated like land-based fleets, was to dominate British warmaking, but it was never more than a sideshow for the Germans.

These were desperate times for the British. By early 1941, Britain had almost run out of financial resources. Churchill knew that without American help the British could not win, and he devoted much energy into coaxing the Americans into the fray. When the war broke out, isolationist opinion kept the United States neutral. However, after France fell and the Blitz was pounding London, American opinion shifted in Britain's favor. President Franklin Roosevelt strongly sympathized with Britain and realized that American security depended on Britain's survival. In November 1939, he put the sale of American arms on a cash-and-carry basis, which favored Britain. After the fall of France, he adopted the policy of giving all aid possible to Britain short of war. He traded fifty destroyers to Britain in return for rights to build bases in British colonies in the Western Hemisphere. In March 1941, Roosevelt proclaimed America the "arsenal of democracy," and through the Lend-Lease Program he pledged to sell, lend, or lease any supplies the British needed. In the process, the United States took most of Britain's gold reserves and foreign investments and restricted their exports. As Keynes said, "We threw good housekeeping to the winds. But we saved ourselves and helped to save the world."

THE TURN OF THE TIDE, JUNE 1941 TO JANUARY 1943

The nature of the war changed radically on June 22, 1941, when Hitler's forces invaded the Soviet Union. Apparently thinking that Britain was beaten and would have to make peace sooner or later, Hitler now decided to seize the rich agricultural and industrial regions of Russia west of the Urals. This area would form Germany's Continental empire. The British had tried to warn the Russians of the impending German invasion, but Stalin ignored them. The German attack took the Russians by surprise. By October the German army stood on the outskirts of Leningrad and Moscow. Churchill, the former rabid anti-Bolshevik, did not hesitate to pledge Britain's support to the Soviet Union. The one thing that now mattered was to defeat Nazi Germany. "If Hitler invaded Hell," he declared, "I would make at least a favourable reference to the Devil in the House of Commons." In July, Britain and Russia signed a formal alliance. Britain at last was no longer alone.

Given the initial success of the German army, however, Churchill's principal hope was still the United States. He met President Roosevelt at Placentia Bay, Newfoundland, in August 1941 to seek American help, especially in defending the British Empire in the Far East. Roosevelt refused Churchill's specific requests and resorted instead to a general statement of principles, the Atlantic Charter, that would be acceptable to the American electorate. But Churchill's problem of involving the Americans was solved by the Japanese, who attacked the American naval base at Pearl Harbor on December 7, 1941. The United States declared war on Japan the next day, and Churchill had issued a British declaration of war on Japan even before the American Congress could act. Hitler had signed an anti-Soviet pact with the Japanese in 1936, and in hopes of diverting American naval power away from the Atlantic, he had promised the Japanese to declare war on the United States if the Japanese attacked first. He kept his promise on December 11. Now there was a genuine worldwide war, and the Americans were totally committed on Britain's side. Churchill wrote: "So we had won after all! . . . England would live; the Commonwealth of Nations and the Empire would live."

In a major conference in Washington, D.C., during December 1941 and January 1942, Churchill and Roosevelt made their plans for the conduct of the war. Despite the fact that the British were now heavily dependent on their stronger partner, Churchill persuaded the Americans on his supreme principle of grand strategy: that Germany must be defeated before Japan. Further, the two allies formed an extremely close partnership, in which strategic decisions were to be made by a combined chiefs of staff operating under the basic decisions made by Churchill and Roosevelt themselves. This arrangement was made possible by the warm personal relationship between the prime minister and the president and by their common desire to avoid the divisions that had hampered the effectiveness of Britain and France in the First World War. No alliance like this had ever been made before.

The entry of the United States did not bring immediate relief to Britain. The end of 1941 and the beginning of 1942 instead brought disaster after disaster to British forces. In the Far East, much of the British Empire collapsed before the Japanese military onslaught. Since the First World War, the Japanese had concerned themselves with increasing their power and securing their economic future by expanding first into China and then into the southeastern Pacific, where Holland, France, and Britain had many colonies. The British between the wars had intended to make Singapore (Malaya) the key to defending their interests in the Far East, but they had not been able to provide adequate military or naval forces for its protection. Once World War II began, the British efforts in the Mediterranean and the Middle East deprived their Far Eastern forces of support. When the Japanese attacked the British colonies in December 1941, the British could resist only feebly. Hong Kong and British Borneo fell almost immediately. On December 10, Japanese airplanes sank two of Britain's mightiest warships, the *Prince of Wales* and the *Repulse*, which were helpless without air cover. The Japanese then advanced through Malaya in a brilliant campaign that repeatedly outmaneuvered the British. In February 1942, Singapore fell, and eighty thousand troops surrendered—the greatest single defeat in British military history.

Still the Japanese advanced. In Burma, the British resisted until May 1942 and then retreated into India, which now stood in peril of Japanese invasion. The Japanese took the Dutch East Indies and the Philippines from Holland and the United States and advanced against Ceylon and Australia. A small British naval force fended them off from Ceylon, but the Japanese bombed the the Australian town of Darwin. Only the American naval victory in the Coral Sea in May 1942 halted the Japanese advance.

Unable to fight on every front at once, the British had no choice but to leave the war in the Pacific to the American navy for the time being. The chief British concerns were North Africa and the supply lines across the Atlantic. In both areas the war slowly began to turn in favor of the British in late 1942 and early 1943. In North Africa, the British Eighth Army in June 1942 barely held off a German offensive at El Alamein, only 60 miles from Alexandria and the Canal. Churchill was anxious for the Eighth Army to take the offensive, and when his generals did not respond to his prodding he replaced them with the team that was to be successful during the rest of the war: General Harold Alexander, as supreme commander of the Middle Eastern theater, and General Bernard Montgomery, as commander of the Eighth Army. Montgomery was abrasive, egotistical, and self-confident to the point of arrogance. But he was a superbly methodical planner and a master of set-piece battles. In October 1942, after careful preparation, Montgomery launched his offensive at the second Battle of El Alamein. It was a great success, the first major British triumph in the war, and pushed the Germans out of Libya into Tunisia.

Victory bells rang out all over Britain. In November of 1942, combined British and American forces landed in Morocco and Algeria. The German forces were eventually trapped between the Allies advancing from the west and the Eighth Army from the east. About 100,000 worn-out German and Italian soldiers were forced to surrender in May 1943; North Africa was safe for the duration.

The Battle of the Atlantic was less dramatic than the events in North Africa but probably more important. Although the German navy never received from Hitler the number of U-boats it needed, the undersea fleet wreaked havoc with British shipping from 1940 through 1942. In April 1941, for instance, German U-boats sank almost 700,000 tons, which was more than the British could replace in a month. Three factors improved the situation for a time: the reintroduction of the convoy system, the reluctant cooperation of the RAF in long-range patrols, and the gradual assumption by the United States of antisubmarine work in the western Atlantic. In 1942, however, the Germans increased the number of U-boats and began to win the struggle again. At the same time, they made British attempts to supply Russia through the north Atlantic and the Arctic Ocean almost impossible. One convoy to the Russian port of Archangel lost twenty-four of forty ships. By March 1943, the British and Americans had nearly lost the battle. But the introduction of two new antisubmarine devices—"huff-duff" (high frequency direction finding) and small-scale radar (for use in airplanes and small warships)—made all the difference. In May 1943 the rate of submarine losses forced the Germans to suspend the U-boat campaign. The Battle of the Atlantic had at last been won by the Allies.

The most important turn of all came in the Soviet Union. The struggle there between the Germans and Russians was the biggest and costliest military conflict in human history. The Russians throughout faced about three-quarters of the total German army. But the Germans never were able to capture the major Russian cities, Leningrad, Moscow, and Stalingrad. The struggle for Stalingrad was the decisive battle of the war. By November 1942 the Germans were laying siege to the city. A battle of attrition even more brutal than Verdun ensued. Toward the end of November, the Russians finally broke through the German lines above and below the city and encircled the attacking German army. In January 1943, the entire German Sixth Army surrendered. Although heavy fighting in Russia and eastern Europe still lay ahead, the invincibility of the German army was broken. The tide of war had swung in favor of the Allies. Hitler told one of his generals, "The God of War has gone over to the other side."

THE WAR AT HOME

Even more than the Great War, the Second World War was a total war. It is safe to say that in one way or another, all of the British people became involved. Mobilization of the adult population was in theory complete. Civilian casualties were high; indeed, until late in 1941 more British civilians than military personnel died from enemy action. As a result, there was nothing like the split that opened during the First World War between those who served at the front and those who stayed home. Everyone was seen as pulling his or her weight and as sharing the misery caused by German arms. In Britain there was little opposition to the war, which was universally regarded as the most just of all conflicts. Some 60,000 men and 1,200 women did register as conscientious objectors, but they were pacifists and did not represent an alienated intelligentsia. The high degree of participation in the war eventually produced a strong sense of unity and a consensus favoring social reform.

The Blitz was the strongest unifier of all. Its worst period was from September 1940 through the summer of 1941, but German air raids went on throughout the war. In 1944, just when the British began to think they might be free from skyborne terror, the Germans launched pilotless rockets on Britain—the V1 "buzz bombs" or "doodlebugs" and the V2 ballistic missiles. Altogether, the Germans dropped more than 74,000 tons of bombs on Britain, or about 3.5 pounds per person. The British suffered about 300,000 civilian casualties. About two out of every seven houses were destroyed and two of every ten schools. Yet, although prewar experts had predicted that bombing would shatter the morale of any civilian population, German bombing did no such thing. People did feel stark terror, and the repeated nightly raids and scurrying to bomb shelters, back-garden dugouts, or the tube stations deprived people of sleep. Every minute spent under the rain of bombs, especially in the claustrophobic "Andersons," steel-framed family shelters measuring 6' x 6' x 4'6", seemed endless. Nevertheless, statistics on civilian mental disorder and drunkenness went down, and people willingly worked long hours and increased their productivity. People from all social classes shared bomb shelters, including the London tube stations. Thousands of civilians volunteered as air raid wardens and fire spotters. Factories reopened immediately after being hit, and shops in bombed districts took pride in prompt reopening, often with a kind of gallows humor: "More open than usual" was a common sign on shops that had lost their windows.

The experience of sharing the misery created a spirit of social unity. One observer wrote, "It is hard to persist in looking down upon, or resenting, a man who night after night is sharing the same dangers and doing exactly the same work as yourself." People in public became noticeably friendlier, and queuing became more courteous as rationing and shortages were shared equally. Although there was at first some resentment among the East Enders of London, whose neighborhoods initially received the heaviest bombing, many older men and women for decades afterwards remembered the war years as a time of exceptional decline of class antagonism. Evacuation of children from the inner cities had the same effect. In the first days of the war, more than 40 percent of all British children were removed from the cities to safety in the countryside. Many of them returned to their homes in subsequent weeks but moved out again during the Blitz. Many middle- and upper-class folks had never had close contact with urban working people, and some were repelled by the appearance and manners of the working-class children. Others, however, were shocked into a resolve for social reform.

Another important experience shared by the British people was contact with American troops. From January 1942, when the first American units landed in Britain, through the massive buildup leading to the invasion of the Continent in mid-1944, Britain was flooded with Americans. At one point, more than 1.5 million American soldiers and airmen were training in the English countryside, crowding the village pubs, and dominating the public places of London. They brought with them what was to the British lavish supplies of equipment, plus plenty of money to spend, cigarettes, candy bars, nylon stockings, American jazz, and other signs of the advanced civilization of the New World. It was not always easy for the more reserved Britons to accept the informal, garrulous, self-assertive style of the Yanks. Some Britons resented the fact that the American troops were popular with young British women. As the saying went, many of the British thought that the trouble with the Americans was that they were "over-paid, over-sexed, and over here." One British newspaper offered this helpful hint on understanding them:

> . . . like all children, they are very sensitive. They mistake our British reti-
> cence and reserve for the cold shoulder and positive dislike. They come
> from a land where everybody knows everybody, and everybody entertains
> everybody at sight. The contrast makes us seem unfriendly.

As was the case in the 1914–1918 war, the power of the British state expanded after 1939. An Emergency Powers Act was passed in 1939, and from 1941 the government took control over the economy. The government this time did not take ownership of coal mines and factories, but it directed production and distribution effectively through numerous controls and regulations. Keynesian strategies for planning and finance were adopted. The government even directed agriculture and increased the land under cultivation by 50 percent. War output went up dramatically, and eventually about 45 percent of the work force was employed in production of war-related goods and services. All food except bread and potatoes was rationed, and people shared the shortages equally by means of a point system that allowed some choice among scarce items. The government sponsored much scientific research, especially in electronics, aeronautical engineering, jet propulsion, medicine, and atomic energy. Some of the bigger projects proved to be beyond Britain's capacity once the basic discoveries had been made. For instance, some pharmaceuticals like penicillin had to be developed in the United States, and the atomic bomb also became an American project even though controlled nuclear fission was first accomplished by Rutherford at Cambridge in the 1930s. All of this huge growth of governmental activity was paid for by a combination of taxes (55 percent) and loans (45 percent). Inevitably taxes went up steeply: the standard rate of the income tax reached 50 percent and the top rate 97.5 percent.

The government mobilized almost the entire population over age eighteen. Conscription began in June 1939, this time with little dissent. Even women were conscripted, but they had a choice of the women's branches of the armed forces, civilian defense, or war work. Women returned to industry in large numbers, accounting for 34 percent of all workers in engineering and 62 percent in commerce. The Ministry of Labour had the power to draft workers into any industry but rarely had to use it. The minister of Labour, Ernest Bevin, was very successful in winning the cooperation of the trade unions, and thus compulsion was not necessary. Full employment was quickly attained, for war mobilization eradicated the twenty-year-old problem of insufficient work. Trade union membership climbed once again, from six million in 1939 to eight million in 1945. Because of the high demand for labor, wages went up by 80 percent during the war, whereas prices increased by only 31 percent. By 1945, real wages were up 50 percent over 1938.

As early as 1941, the high level of popular participation in the war effort, as well as the people's fortitude under the bombing, rationing, and shortages, began to inspire a strong feeling in favor of social reconstruction. The growth of the state made government planning and direction seem the obvious road for this social improvement. The Churchill government itself spoke of post-war social reconstruction as a way of showing the British public that the war was worth fighting. Members of all parties shared this sentiment, though Labour was the most outspoken. The most important result of this consensus was the appointment of an interdepartmental committee of civil servants chaired by William Beveridge, a long-time civil servant and social reformer of the pre-1914 New Liberal variety. Beveridge's report, published in December 1942, set the agenda for social reconstruction for the next decade.

The Beveridge Report was not a revolutionary document, but it caught the imagination of the British public. More than 600,000 of its various editions were sold in the first year. Beveridge called for extension and coordination of the British social services, which had been founded before 1914 and strengthened between 1919 and 1939, so that they would form a single comprehensive system. His principles were (1) financing of social services by the insurance principle, paid for by employers, employees, and the state; (2) a standard rate of contributions and benefits that would apply to all social classes, not just the poor; (3) a minimum subsistence for all, based on full employment, social security, family allowances, and a national health service. This plan, which was widely debated even before publication, quickly was taken by the public as the minimum acceptable program. The Labour party promptly endorsed it. However, Churchill and some Conservatives showed tepid interest at best. Churchill did not wish to rouse people's commitment to a plan that he feared could not be paid for, and he did not want to divert public attention from the war effort. The *Manchester Guardian* summarized his views as: "Eager reformers are asked to pipe down and trust the government." This was somewhat unfair, for in 1943 the government itself issued a series of "white papers" endorsing the gist of many of Beveridge's proposals, though with some reservations. In 1944, the government committed itself to maintaining full employment. In that same year, R. A. Butler, the Conservative minister for education, passed a major educational reform act (for details see Chapter 11). Whatever the government's achievements on the social front, its response was generally thought to be lukewarm; hence the Labour party reaped the greatest popular benefit from the Beveridge Report, though Beveridge was a Liberal, and his committee had been appointed by a government dominated by the Conservatives.

One cultural development of great importance was the establishment by the government of CEMA—the Council for Education in Music and the Arts. Total war might seem the worst possible time for cultural advance, but CEMA was the first effort by the British government to promote high culture directly—classical music, theater, painting—to the populace at large. Set up in 1940, CEMA took high-quality concerts, ballets, plays, and art exhibitions to the provinces. The popular response, especially to the music, was very positive. CEMA subsidized five major symphony orchestras. According to one observer, "Despite the blackout and general war-weariness, music has had in this country an extraordinary flowering." The arts, like social reform, were seen as an appropriate answer to German barbarianism, and CEMA made the privations of wartime a little easier to bear.

VICTORY, JANUARY 1943 TO AUGUST 1945

As American power built up at an accelerating pace, the likelihood of victory over Germany and Japan increased, but the role of Britain inevitably declined. Churchill continued to act as one of the "Big Three" with Roosevelt and Stalin, but increasingly he became a junior partner to the American president. Churchill's advice and counsel, which were based on more international experience than Roosevelt could summon, often proved invaluable; yet, gradually the American view of grand strategy came to govern the Allies' decisions. The partnership of Britain with the United States and the Soviet Union did finally bring complete victory but one tainted by political setbacks from Britain's point of view in both Europe and the Far East. Churchill put the theme for the last two years of the war acutely when he termed it "triumph and tragedy."

Once victory in North Africa was assured, Britain and the United States had to decide what steps to take next. Throughout the second half of 1942, the British and Americans debated the issue. The Russians naturally wanted the Western Allies to open a second front in France as soon as possible, in order to drain off some of the terrible German pressure on Soviet troops. The Americans, who were inclined to think in purely military terms, wanted to open a second front by means of a cross-channel invasion of France. They believed the military doctrine that the quickest way to victory was to close with the enemy's strongest forces and destroy them. Churchill and his generals, however, remembered the awful bloodletting of the First World War and Dunkirk as well. They preferred to attack on the periphery of Europe, on Germany's so-called soft underbelly, in Italy or the Balkans. The Russians later came to think that Churchill was stalling in order to let the Germans and Russians exhaust themselves against each other, but there is no evidence for this hypothesis. Churchill and his military advisers simply had grave doubts about the success of a frontal assault on the German forces, and they faced enormous logistical problems besides. Churchill's chief of the imperial general staff, Sir Alan Brooke, insisted that Italy be the next target. He got his way, and at the Casablanca Conference in January 1943, Churchill and Roosevelt decided on a landing in Sicily. This required postponement of a cross-channel invasion until 1944. Stalin was furious.

British and American forces landed in Sicily in July 1943, with General Alexander in command of the Allied forces. Sicily fell in slightly over a month. In early September the British and American forces crossed the Straits of Messina from Sicily into Italy. Already, Mussolini had fallen, and on September 8, Italy surrendered. However, Germany decided to defend Italy mile by mile, and the Allied supreme command withdrew some forces from Italy to Britain in order to begin preparing for the invasion of France. As a result, the joint British-American campaign found the going in Italy extremely tough. The Allies did not take Rome until June 1944 or clear Italy of German forces until the end of the war in Europe in May 1945. Throughout, the British Eighth Army fought with distinction. However, the overall value of the Italian campaign has always been questioned, for the Allies had to commit thirty divisions to the struggle, to only twenty-two for the Germans. The best that can be said for the Italian campaign is that to some degree it kept the Germans from strengthening their forces in France.

Churchill and Brooke continued to seek alternative strategies to a cross-channel invasion in 1943–1944. Churchill wanted to conduct a Mediterranean campaign, which could be built on British holdings at Gibraltar, Egypt, and Malta and which would shore up British power in the Middle East, increasingly important to Britain because of its oil reserves. He also had in mind a Balkan campaign, which would hit the Germans where they were weakest, and in 1944 he even considered an invasion of Austria and Hungary through the Adriatic. This would have the extra benefit of preempting Russian expansion in Eastern Europe. The British acted on their strategic preferences by aiding the Yugoslav partisans led by Marshal Tito, against the wishes of both Roosevelt and Stalin. The later independence of communist Yugoslavia from Russian dictatorship owed much to Britain.

The British, moreover, continued to invest heavily in the bombing of Germany. This RAF offensive remains one of the most controversial aspects of Britain's war effort. Both its effectiveness and its moral stance have been questioned, as they were during the war itself. The chief of Bomber Command, Sir Arthur Harris, believed that Germany could be defeated by "area bombing," which amounted to indiscriminate bombing of German cities. Although a few critics like Bishop George Bell openly condemned the policy, Churchill himself approved it. Despite serious losses of bombers and aircrews, Harris went ahead with the raids, some of which involved more than a thousand heavy bombers. In some instances, Bomber Command deliberately caused fire storms by means of incendiary bombs. Thus the RAF destroyed Hamburg in the summer of 1943 and Dresden in February of 1945, killing in the latter case 135,000 people. The German cities were not defenseless, for night-fighters took a fearful toll of British bombers. In the winter of 1943–1944 it appeared that the RAF had lost the battle over Germany. But the introduction of a long-range fighter plane into the American air force, which flew its missions in daylight, gave the Allies control over German air space. By mid-1944, the British and American air forces had created a severe oil shortage in Germany, and the RAF was making German troop movements in France nearly impossible. In these ways, the RAF ultimately contributed to the final Allied victory, though at a terrible price.

Meanwhile, Churchill and Brooke were pushed by the Russians and Americans into agreeing on a cross-channel invasion. This decision was made at the Teheran Conference in November 1943. Preparations on a colossal scale went forward in England. "Operation Overlord," the invasion of Normandy, was commanded by the American general Dwight Eisenhower, in recognition that the Americans would dominate the campaign on the Continent in both men and munitions. Sir Arthur Tedder of the RAF served as his deputy and General Montgomery as the commander of land forces in the invasion itself. All of southern England in early 1944 became a huge base and depot for the invasion troops: 3.5 million men, plus 6,800 ships and landing craft and 13,000 airplanes. The Allies took pains to deceive the Germans into thinking that the initial landing would come at Calais, while in actuality it was planned for Normandy, which is directly south across the Channel from Plymouth. On invasion day (called D-Day, June 6, 1944) five divisions went ashore—two American, two British, and one Canadian. The British and Canadians had been assigned the task of tying down the bulk of the German defenders. Hence they made slow progress and were able to take their main early objective, Caen, only after a month of severe combat. The invasion, nevertheless, was a success, and gradually the giant army gathered in England was sent across.

The Germans did not give up France without a desperate struggle. But the Americans broke out of the German defensive ring in Normandy in July and poured south and east through France. Paris was retaken in August. British forces on the Allied left wing took Belgium and much of Holland, where German resistance stiffened. The Germans launched a last-gasp counteroffensive in the Ardennes forest in December, in hopes of splitting the British from the Americans. The Americans contained the attack, however, and by the beginning of 1945 the Germans were being rolled back all along the front. Montgomery pushed for a single concentrated attack in the north, whereas Eisenhower insisted on moving forward at all points at once; the merits of the two tactics are still being debated. In any case, the Allies in March 1945 crossed the Rhine into Germany. The Russians, meanwhile, were pushing their way through Poland and Eastern Europe into Germany. Clearly, the end was near.

The time for postwar planning had come, and the grand alliance was beginning to show signs of stress. The British and Americans did not trust the intentions of the Russians, who were in fact determined to arrange a settlement of Central and Eastern Europe that would secure Russia from any further threat from Germany. The Western Allies for their part did not want to see any spread of communism into Europe, and Roosevelt in particular clung to Wilsonian ideals of democracy and national self-determination. Poland was a particular bone of contention, for hostility between the Poles and Russians was many centuries old, and rival Polish governments in exile existed in both Britain and the Soviet Union. Churchill wanted to keep the Russians out of the Mediterranean and to secure British influence there and in the Balkans. He was more willing than Roosevelt to engage in old-fashioned power politics. Roosevelt on the other hand leaned toward establishment of an organization of international cooperation. In October 1944, in a meeting with Stalin in Moscow, Churchill agreed that Russian influence would predominate in

Rumania, Bulgaria, and Hungary; that British influence would predominate in Greece; and that the two powers would share influence in Yugoslavia. Churchill expected as a matter of course that Britain would remain the paramount power in the Middle East. Early in 1945, Churchill urged Eisenhower to push as far into Eastern Europe as possible, in order for the Western Allies to have some bargaining power with the Russians, but the Americans preferred not to mix politics with military decisions.

This was the situation when the Big Three met at Yalta (in the Crimea) in February 1945. Poland and Germany were the main issues, and neither was settled satisfactorily. The brute fact was that the Russian army occupied Poland, and the Americans and British had no power over its fate, though they did secure Russian agreement on free elections for a postwar Poland and a sharing of power by both of the Polish governments in exile. As for Germany, the Russians would have been pleased to strip Germany of its industry to render it incapable of ever posing a military threat to Russia again, and to collect payment as far as possible for damages the Germans had done to western Russia. Churchill accepted the idea of German reparations, but he did not wish to render the Germans incapable of supporting themselves; otherwise, the beleaguered British would have to support a starving German populace in the region occupied by the British army. Churchill was more concerned with obtaining an occupation zone for the French, not out of generosity or because he liked the prickly leader of the revived French forces, General de Gaulle, but because Churchill now feared the withdrawal of the United States from Europe. This he got. In general, however, Britain simply did not carry the weight of the two world powers.

Churchill at Yalta still trusted Stalin to keep his commitments. But as the war drew toward a close, Churchill became more concerned about Russian domination of Eastern Europe. When the war in Europe ended with the suicide of Hitler and the surrender of Germany in May 1945, there was jubilation in Britain, but Churchill was already writing the Americans about the appearance of an "iron curtain" dividing the Russian sphere of Europe from Western Europe.

The war dragged on through the summer in the Far East. The British effort there had largely been restricted to India and Burma since 1942. Indian nationalism proved to be a severe trial for Britain during the war. The British viceroy in 1939 had simply declared that India was at war with Germany without consulting Indian leaders. The Indian army responded loyally, contributing 2.5 million men to the war effort, but nationalist opinion was decidedly negative. The Indian National Congress did not admire the Germans or Japanese, but they thought that India ought to be given responsible self-government before India supported Britain. Resignations by Indian provincial ministers, protests, riots, and a civil disobedience campaign led by Gandhi were endemic throughout the war. Some forty thousand defectors joined an "Indian National Army" to fight on the Japanese side. The British government in 1942 feared that the end of British rule in India was near. In that year, the cabinet sent Sir Stafford Cripps, a left-wing Labourite, to negotiate with the nationalists. Cripps promised Indian self-rule after the war. The nationalists,

Prime Minister Winston Churchill, President Franklin Roosevelt, and Premier Joseph Stalin at Yalta, February 1945.

who wanted the British to quit India immediately, refused the offer. Gandhi called it "a post-dated cheque drawn on a crashing bank." Only the revival of American and British military fortunes in the Far Eastern theater after 1943 enabled the British to maintain the status quo in India—temporarily.

In Burma, the British army and the Indian army scored a major victory over the Japanese. The Anglo-Indian forces, commanded by General William Slim, recovered from the losses of 1941–1942, defended northeast India from invasion in a desperate struggle, and then fought a brilliant campaign to retake Burma. The Burmese campaign was fought under the most difficult jungle and mountain conditions. The British soldiers in Burma thought that they were forgotten by the public at home, but they completed their reconquest of Burma at almost the same time as the victory over Germany in May 1945. The British began to plan for the recapture of Malaya, but the Japanese, reeling from one American blow after another and suffering from a massive bombing campaign including the use of atomic bombs on Hiroshima and Nagasaki, surrendered in August 1945.

COUNTING THE COSTS

In the third century B.C., King Pyrrhus of Epirus scored a victory over the Romans so costly that he said another victory like it would destroy his kingdom. The British could have said the same for the Second World War. They emerged victorious from the war, or at least on the winning side, having fought for more than six years, and they appeared in some respects to be a great power still. But the costs were enormous. Some 300,000 British servicemen were killed, less than half the 1914–1918 total. But 60,000 civilians and 35,000 merchant seamen, plus 200,000 British Empire troops also lost their lives. In addition, the British lost, as we have seen, a great many buildings to German bombs, including about 3.75 million houses destroyed or damaged and 20 percent of all schools. One estimate is that overall the British lost or used up about 10 percent of their total national wealth.

Terrible as these figures are, they show only the visible losses. To finance the purchase of munitions the British sold off almost all of their overseas investments (about £1.5 billion), and they used up about two-thirds of their gold reserves. The British position in the world economy had depended heavily on these, because income from foreign investments had been crucial in making up the gap between imports and exports and because the gold reserves had backed the huge volume of sterling currency held by the dominions and other countries in the "sterling area," a prime bloc for British trade. The British borrowed heavily during the war, and the national debt grew by about 700 percent. They now had enormous needs for reconstruction; hence they would have to borrow even more from abroad, because the Americans ended Lend-Lease immediately on Japan's surrender. Domestic industry had been run down, and exports in 1945 stood at less than one-third of the 1939 level. Britain now stood as the major debtor nation in the world, with heavy obligations to countries in the sterling area but with seriously reduced means of earning the necessary money.

The war had shown clearly that the British economy would not be able to sustain Britain's position as one of the three or four great world powers. By 1943, for example, both the Germans and the Russians were spending almost 25 percent more on armaments than the British, and the Americans were spending more than three times as much as the British without really straining. The British industrial sector, highly mobilized for war, reached its peak in 1942–1943, but by 1944 American war production was already 600 percent higher. The result of Britain's dependency on the United States was obvious in terms of British status as a great power, as Churchill noted at Teheran in 1943:

> I realised at Teheran for the first time what a small nation we are. There I sat with the great Russian bear on one side of me, with paws outstretched, and on the other side the great American buffalo, and between the two sat the poor little English donkey who was the only one of the three, who knew the right way home.

To be sure, the British Empire was restored in 1945, but it was restored largely because of the efforts of the Soviet Union and the United States, neither of whom approved of it. Both the dominions and the colonies had responded gallantly to Britain's need during the war—except for the Irish Free State, which remained neutral—but the war frayed the delicate bonds that held the Empire together. The loss of the colonies in the Far East, and especially the supposedly mighty Singapore base, to the Japanese in 1941–1942 was a psychological blow to Britain and a lift for colonial nationalists in Africa, Asia, and the Western Hemisphere. Australia and New Zealand recognized that their survival depended on themselves and the Americans, not the British. Moreover, Britain had to make promises for self-government or new constitutions all around the Empire: India, of course, but also the Gold Coast (Ghana), Nigeria, Kenya, Ceylon, Malta, Jamaica, Trinidad, and British Guiana. The new United Nations and the American policy of global free trade would alike present problems for the unity and effectiveness of the Empire. As Churchill said in December 1941, the British Empire would survive, but it survived radically transformed.

The survival of Britain itself and the defeat of fascism, Nazism, and Japanese militarism were the great positive achievements of the war. They were in fact Britain's only war aims. In addition, the war stimulated the growth and technological advance of newer industries like aircraft, motor vehicles, electronics, and chemicals. Agriculture grew because of both intensive mechanization and improved fertilization. Moreover, the wartime economy raised average real wages and set the stage for major improvements in the standard of living. The war stimulated feelings of social solidarity, revealed weaknesses in the social system, and encouraged the desire for social improvement. Furthermore, the war showed that state intervention and regulation could bring about positive changes. It led the British to accept Keynesian economics all at once. Most of these trends toward a welfare state were already evident before 1939, but World War II accelerated them. All in all, it was an impressive achievement by the British and in sum made for their finest hour.

Churchill never had any doubt that the British war aims were worth the cost of total effort and the expenditure of practically every last farthing. Perhaps a more cold-blooded calculation might have led the British to settle with Hitler after the fall of France, in hopes of saving the resources of Britain and the Empire while Germany and the Soviet Union drained themselves of lifeblood in their titanic struggle for Central and Eastern Europe. However, it is difficult to imagine that the British could have remained aloof from the conflict permanently or that any decent nation could have tolerated the insane brutality and anti-Semitism of the Nazi regime. In any case, the Japanese attack on the British Empire in the Far East would have involved Britain in a world war whatever the situation in Europe, and that war would have led to British dependency on America. Under the circumstances, Churchill made the right basic decisions, and though he may be faulted for mistakes of judgment on particular matters, his inspirational leadership of the nation in the darkest moments must rank as one of the most heroic feats of courage and will in British history. If the British victory in the end was Pyrrhic, that was the consequence of factors beyond Churchill's, and Britain's, control.

Suggested Reading

Addison, Paul, *The Road to 1945: British Politics and the Second World War* (London: Cape, 1975).

Bayly, Christopher, and Tim Harper, *Forgotten Armies: The Fall of British Asia, 1941–1945* (London: Penguin, 2005).

Best, Geoffrey, *Churchill: A Study in Greatness* (London: Hambledon, 2001).

Brooke, Stephen, *Labour's War: The Labour Party During the Second World War* (Oxford: Oxford University Press, 1992).

Bullock, Alan, *The Life and Times of Ernest Bevin* (3 vols.) (London: Heinemann, 1960–1983).

Calder, Angus, *The People's War* (London: Cape, 1969).

Churchill, Winston S., *The Second World War* (6 vols.) (Boston: Houghton Mifflin, 1948–1953).

Fraser, David, *Alanbrooke* (London: Collins, 1982).

Gilbert, Martin, *Churchill: A Life* (New York: Henry Holt & Co., 1991).

———, *Winston S. Churchill* (vols. 6 and 7 cover 1939–1945) (London: Heinemann, 1966–1988).

Gowing, Margaret, *Britain and Atomic Energy, 1939–1945* (London: Macmillan, 1964).

Harrisson, Tom, *Living Through the Blitz* (New York: Schocken Books, 1976).

Hinton, James, *Women, Social Leadership, and the Second World War: Continuities of Class* (New York: Oxford University Press, 2002).

Jackson, Ashley, *The British Empire and the Second World War* (London: Hambledon Continuum, 2006).

Jefferys, Kevin, *The Churchill Coalition and Wartime Politics, 1940–1945* (Manchester: Manchester University Press, 1991).

Jenkins, Roy, *Churchill: A Biography* (New York: Farrar, Straus and Giroux, 2002).

Kennedy, Paul, *The Rise and Fall of British Naval Mastery* (London: Allen Lane, 1976).

Lee, J. M., *The Churchill Coalition* (Hamden, Conn.: Archon Books, 1980).

Longmate, Norman, *Bombers: The RAF Offensive Against Germany, 1939–1945* (London: Hutchinson, 1983).

Louis, W. R., *Imperialism at Bay: The United States and the Decolonization of the British Empire, 1941–1945* (New York: Oxford University Press, 1978).

Marwick, Arthur, *Britain in the Century of Total War* (Boston: Little, Brown, 1968).

McKercher, B. J. C., *Transition of Power: Britain's Loss of Global Pre-eminence to the United States, 1930–1945* (Cambridge: Cambridge University Press, 1999).

Milward, A. S., *War, Economy, and Society, 1939–1945* (London: Allen Lane, 1977).

Morgan, David, and Mary Evans, *The Battle for Britain: Citizenship and Ideology in the Second World War* (London: Routledge, Chapman & Hall, 1993).

Rose, Sonya O., *Which People's War? National Identity and Citizenship in Wartime Britain, 1939–1945* (New York: Oxford University Press, 2003).

Smith, Harold L., *Britain in the Second World War: A Social History* (Manchester: Manchester University Press, 1996).

Stansky, Peter, and William Abrahams, *London's Burning: Life, Death, and Art in the Second World War* (Stanford: Stanford University Press, 1994).

Terraine, John, *The Right of the Line: The Royal Air Force in the European War, 1939–1945* (London: Hodder & Stoughton, 1985).

Thorne, Christopher, *Allies of a Kind: The United States, Britain and the War Against Japan, 1941–45* (New York: Oxford University Press, 1978).

Woodward, E. L., *British Foreign Policy in the Second World War* (London: H.M.S.O., 1970–1976).

Part III

Britain in the Postwar World

1945–2000

New counties of the British Isles: County Boundaries Established by Parliament in 1972

Chapter 11

Welfare, Affluence, and Consensus, 1945–1970

In the years since 1945, three themes have stood out in British history: (1) the creation of a welfare state built on a remarkable political consensus; (2) the faltering performance of the British economy; and (3) the decline of Britain from the status of a great world and imperial power to that of a middle rank European nation. These themes were, as one would expect, deeply interrelated. With the benefit of hindsight, which is always twenty-twenty, one might argue that the British could have done better in any one of these areas. But it is important to remember that the British have not been able to act entirely as they pleased, for they have been limited by institutions and attitudes inherited from the past and by forces in the world beyond their control. In recent decades, observers have frequently asked, "What's wrong with Britain?" Yet one might just as well ask, "What's right with Britain?" For on the whole, the British have achieved a comparatively decent, civil, humane society. If their recent history holds warnings for nations like the United States, it also serves as an admirable model.

The period from 1945 to the present is too close for historians to see the structure sharply. However, with regard to domestic matters, it seems reasonable to view the period as broken into two chronological parts: first, a time of consensus, from 1945 to about 1975; and second, a period during which the consensus was broken, from 1975 to the present. Immediately after 1945, there emerged in Britain a consensus involving a commitment to full employment, a comprehensive system of state-sponsored social welfare, nationalization of certain industries, and governmental management of economic demand by Keynesian techniques. This consensus coincided with, and contributed to, a period of consumer affluence. Consumer prosperity had major effects on British society and culture, but it was built on the shaky grounds of a British industry that was not very competitive in the increasingly harsh world economy.

BUILDING THE WELFARE STATE, 1945–1951

As the Second World War drew to a close, the British political parties began looking toward a fresh general election, the last having occurred in 1935. The

Clement Attlee, soon to be prime minister, and the Labour party celebrate their electoral victory, 1945.

Labour party was anxious to compete as an independent party, and many Conservatives wanted an early election in order to cash in on Churchill's immense personal prestige. No one wanted to repeat the experience of the Lloyd George coalition. Churchill himself wanted to delay until the end of the war but gave into pressure and set the election for July 1945. This decision was to have surprising consequences.

Churchill dominated the campaign, but the Labour party exploited popular belief that they would deal with peacetime issues better than the Conservatives. Public attention was shifting strongly to domestic concerns. Labour candidates embraced full employment and the Beveridge Report, whereas the Conservatives were more cautious in their promises. Labour meanwhile benefited from the participation of men like Attlee and Bevin in the wartime coalition and from the growth of the trade unions to more than eight million members. Churchill did not benefit his party when in a radio broadcast he said that a Labour government would introduce something like the Gestapo into Britain. He made funny remarks about the modest Attlee (whom he called "a sheep in sheep's clothing"), but these did not sit well with an electorate that appreciated Attlee's role in the war coalition. The British public profoundly admired Churchill's wartime leadership, but they separated that genuine emotion from their sense of political interests. Most of the voters wanted to correct the ills of the 1930s by means of programs and planning conceived during the war. Thus Labour won a major victory in the election, with 393 seats to 210 Conservatives and only 12 Liberals. Labour won not only the great majority of working-class votes but also about a third of those cast by the middle class.

The Labour party that came into office in 1945 was strongly reformist but not revolutionary. The party had been founded as a nonrevolutionary alliance of trades unionists and democratic socialists. Its most fervent element, the ILP, was an undogmatic collection of ethical socialists. Its principal theorists, the Fabians, were gradualist utilitarians. Its main electoral force, the trade unionists, were essentially devoted to defending the position of working people within the capitalist system. The party in the latter 1930s had set aside its vaguely utopian socialism and pacifism in favor of detailed plans for reform, Keynesian economics, and a realistic foreign policy. The cabinet formed in 1945 was led by men who had learned their politics during the early years of the century: Clement Attlee (1883–1967), the prime minister, had served in Parliament since 1922 and was uncharismatic but efficient and a good chairman of the cabinet; Ernest Bevin (1881–1951), foreign secretary, had an imposing stature and an aggressive personality, but he had made his name largely as a trade union leader and spokesman; Herbert Morrison (1888–1965), lord president of the council, had long been prominent in local government and in effect was a British-style political boss; and Aneurin Bevan (1897–1960), minister of health, was a former coal miner and passionate spokesman for the miners of South Wales. Of the leaders Bevan was the only representative of the party's left wing. All of these men had powerful memories of the 1930s and were determined to prevent a repeat of its poverty and unemployment.

The Attlee government's years in office from 1945 to 1951 formed one of the most productive legislative periods in British history. In six busy years, the Labour government established the superstructure of the welfare state, which in more or less modified form stands in place today. It also nationalized a number of major industries, all of which remained in state hands until the 1980s.

The welfare state consisted of government efforts to maintain full employment plus a comprehensive system of social services. Its purpose was not social revolution but assurance that henceforward no one would fall below a minimum standard of living and that everyone would have equality of opportunity. Its goals arose from a consensus that began building in the 1930s and reached maturity during the war. Both parties had committed themselves to full employment by 1945. To sustain full employment, the Labour party adopted Keynes's ideas of using the government's budget to manage demand and keeping interest rates low to encourage investment. (The Conservatives would do likewise until 1979.)

It is uncertain how far these economic policies were effective in the late 1940s, because the general increase in demand for industrial and consumer goods and the serious shortage of labor together kept the employment rate in Britain at close to 100 percent. Both factors were beyond the control of the government. What the Labour government contributed beyond its basic fiscal policy was negotiation of a massive loan from the United States. Because the Americans cut off Lend-Lease in

1945, with British industry in disarray and the country deeply in debt, the British were desperately in need of help. The government sent Keynes to the United States to seek a grant or loan in the fall of 1945. He found that the Americans drove a hard bargain; the British had to settle for a $3.75 billion loan, repayable at 2 percent over fifty years. Moreover, the British had to agree to give up their imperial trade arrangements in favor of multilateral free trade and to allow sterling to be freely convertible (that is, exchangeable) into gold and other currencies in 1947. (The British also received a smaller loan, on more favorable terms, from Canada.) The American loan received strong criticism from both the extreme left and the extreme right in Britain, and the convertibility provision, as we will see, caused severe hardship. But in the short run the loan enabled the British economy to begin to rebuild, employment to rise, and the Labour government to construct the welfare system.

The government's objective in its social legislation was to provide a *universal* system of social services for all British citizens "from the cradle to the grave." The system would make for equality of opportunity on the one hand and assistance with social problems like illness and old age on the other. The government would not prohibit individuals from buying services like insurance and schooling privately, but the state's social services were to be as good as money could buy, so that wealth would no longer command superior social security. That the government fell short of these noble goals should not be surprising; what is surprising is how close to their target they came.

The welfare legislation had four major elements: (1) comprehensive social insurance; (2) a national health service; (3) state-supported housing construction; and (4) public education. The principal legislation for social security (old age and unemployment benefits) was the National Insurance Act of 1946. This act established a contributory system whereby people paid a flat rate to buy insurance against those times when they could not work. The National Assistance Act of 1948 completed the system by including those who somehow did not qualify for social insurance—and abolished the vestiges of the 1834 Poor Law to boot. The idea of a "dole"—something for nothing—was abolished. Much modified, this system remains in place today. The system in theory assured that all citizens would have a minimum standard of living. However, the rate of benefits was specifically set in the act, and the benefits have inevitably failed to keep up with the cost of living. Although they have repeatedly been revised upward they have not always provided the desired minimum standard of living. The insurance system has not been self-supporting, and it has had to be subsidized by the Treasury. Moreover, certain pockets of poverty have proved to be stubborn, and recent governments have tended to focus on them rather than try to maintain a universal minimum. Nevertheless, it is clear that the system of social security has mitigated the severity of old age and unemployment, even as the age structure of the population has grown older and the rate of unemployment in the 1980s reached a level not seen since the 1930s.

All parties supported the National Insurance Act. Such was not the case with the National Health Service. This proved to be the most popular part of the Labour party's program, but the Conservatives had strong reservations about it. Health insurance in Britain dates from Lloyd George's National Insurance Act of 1911, and public health services were much expanded by the Emergency Medical Services of World War II, but in 1945 health insurance covered only about half of the population and did not extend to either hospitals or specialists. Doctors and hospitals tended to be centered in the prosperous South and Southeast of England. Hospitals—voluntary (that is, independent) and local authority—varied widely in quality. The rich had access to much better medical care than the poor. The Labour minister of health, Bevan, was determined to establish a medical system that made no distinction between rich and poor; thus he resolutely rejected the idea of a public medical service open only to people with incomes below a certain level. "The essence of the satisfactory health service," he declared, "is that the rich and poor are treated alike, that poverty is not a disability and wealth is not an advantage." His solution, embodied in the National Health Act of 1946, was to nationalize the hospitals, organize them around twenty regional schools of medicine, and establish a national doctors' service. The public was entitled to free medical care, either with a physician or in a hospital if necessary. Doctors could join the National Health Service (NHS) or not as they pleased; those that did were paid a basic salary plus a capitation fee for each patient on their lists. A doctor joining the National Health Service could also maintain a private practice if he or she desired. Patients remained free to choose the doctor they preferred, but through incentives the government distributed doctors more evenly around the country.

The Conservative party resisted nationalization of the hospitals, and the British Medical Association (BMA) feared loss of their independence and their personal relations with their patients. Bevan pointed out the advantage of improved state support of hospitals and medical training, and after lengthy negotiations with the BMA, he was able to launch the National Health Service in 1948. Most of the doctors joined, and by 1950, 97 percent of the population registered as patients. People flocked to their doctors' offices, many seeking eyeglasses and dentures they had never been able to afford. Within a decade, the number of hospital patients had risen by 30 percent. Waiting lists for noncritical surgery and other treatment quickly formed; they remain a major concern and have, especially from the 1980s, spurred the foundation of new private hospitals and the purchase of private care by those who can afford to "jump the queue." The cost of the NHS also went up, at first because of inflation and then from the 1970s because of the rising level of medical technology. The nation, as we will see, was hard-pressed economically and financially, and the government was not able to invest in hospital construction and improvement to the extent it had hoped. In the early 1950s, charges had to be set for eyeglasses and prescriptions. From time to time, British doctors have become unhappy with their rate of pay under the NHS, and significant numbers have emigrated to the United States before the government of the day could respond. Nevertheless, for all its problems, the NHS has provided good medical care free of charge to the entire population. It remains the boldest achievement of the British welfare state and the one that the populace would least readily give up.

Housing was the part of welfare provision that the British people wanted most urgently in 1945. Churchill's government had forecast a long-term need for three to four million new houses. The Labour government simply was not able to provide funds for new housing on that scale, but they made a start. The responsible minister, Bevan, elected to work through state subsidies to local authorities, leaving it to them to contract for new construction. Between 1945 and 1951, 1.5 million new houses were built, but because of the population increase and the formation of new households (both the results of the postwar baby boom), the demand for new houses ran ahead of the ability to build them; thus the need for houses was as great in 1951 as it had been in 1945.

In regard to education, the main legislation, Butler's Education Act of 1944, had been passed before Labour came into office. Labour's job was to implement it. The act of 1944 provided for secondary education for all to the age of fifteen—a great step, though probably seventy-five years too late. As implemented, this meant that all schoolchildren had to take an examination at age eleven (the dreaded "eleven-plus"), which determined whether they would be placed in a college-prep type high school (the grammar schools), a technical high school (few of which were actually provided), or the ordinary high school leading to employment (the secondary modern schools). This tripartite system was not a great success. Not only did the eleven-plus exam terrorize many ambitious households, it also failed to make the kinds of distinctions in ability that it was supposed to. Moreover, it did not democratize education or open British society to merit as the Labour party had hoped. Middle-class children on the whole did better than working-class children, who came from families that normally did not cultivate academic achievement. Butler's Education Act left the elite public schools untouched, and the Labour party did not have the nerve to attack them. Thus the new educational structure, which existed until the 1970s, increased social mobility for some working-class children but not as many as expected; on the whole it helped preserve the class system.

At the same time, the British university system remained relatively small. During the 1950s, the state increased its funding to the universities, so that in 1957 nearly 70 percent of university funds came from the government, and 75 percent of all university students held public grants paying for both their fees and their "maintenance" (room and board). That support made it possible for a British student to go to any university to which he or she was admitted. The problem was that the number of spaces available was very small. In the 1950s and 1960s, the number of universities in Britain grew from seventeen to forty-four, as the new "Plate-Glass" universities like Sussex, Essex, and Lancaster were built and certain technical colleges were raised to university status. The number of full-time students grew from 83,000 to more than 200,000 in 1968 (and 460,000 in the 1970s). Yet until the 1990s the proportion of the British population of college age who attended a university never went above about 8 percent, which was a figure below that of European countries and far below that of the United States. The British university system in the welfare state was less elitist than in the nineteenth or early twentieth centuries, but it remained closed to the bulk of the population.

The Labour party's record in social legislation was thus very impressive, and its supporters greeted it with idealism and hope. But the welfare state fell short of creating a classless society. At the time the legislation was enacted, some critics on the far left argued that the welfare state was a betrayal of true socialism, and some on the far right contended that it was too expensive and too corrosive of the necessary disciplines of work and thrift. As we will see, both critiques, especially that from the right, gained ground in the 1970s. Criticism and defense of the welfare state are thus part and parcel of current politics. From the historian's perspective, what can be said is that the welfare legislation was a significant but reasonable extension of earlier structures, that it was a humane response to the problems of the interwar years, and that it flowed along lines of state intervention emphasized by the necessities of the two world wars.

The Labour party in 1945 set high priority to nationalization of certain industries as well as to welfare reform. They believed that selective nationalization would enable the state to run these industries more efficiently than private enterprise, provide more ample capital investment, manage the industries for the benefit of society rather than for the profit of the capitalist, and improve industrial relations. They also believed that control over "the commanding heights of the economy" would enable the state to plan and direct the economy as a whole. In fact, however, the government for the most part nationalized only the older, more troubled industries, and they never decided for certain whether the principal objective of nationalization was to be greater efficiency or social service. Several industries, including the Central Electricity Board and British Overseas Airways Corporation (BOAC), had been nationalized before 1940. Now, in 1945, the Labour party nationalized the Bank of England, but this was mainly symbolic, for the bank already functioned as an arm of the state. Then came nationalization of the coal mines (1947), the railways (1947), trucking (1947), and electrical and gas distribution (1948). The iron and steel industry was nationalized after much controversy in 1949; it was the only one that was fairly healthy at the time. (It was denationalized, renationalized, and denationalized again in subsequent years.)

The method of nationalization chosen in each case was neither syndicalism nor Guild Socialism but rather the public corporation. Share owners were bought out, and the nationalized industries were put under the control of appointed boards responsible to a government minister, who in turn was responsible to Parliament. The chair of the board in most cases operated as an independent chief executive officer. The managerial force generally came from the ranks of the industries themselves; hence to the workers, the "bosses" looked the same as before. Nor did industrial relations improve. Few workers were appointed to the governing boards, and anyone who was came to be regarded, as Attlee said, "as a bosses' man." The history of each nationalized industry was different, but in general it cannot be argued that they functioned as well as Labour hoped. It is true that they brought about useful rationalization of the industries. Yet, management and workers remained remote from each other. The nation was too strapped financially to provide the capital that the industries needed; thus they did not become paragons of productivity. They were run at a loss to keep prices and fares down or to keep staffing levels high. Because they tended to be troubled industries, they did not provide a means of directing the whole economy. Whether the nationalized industries would have performed better if they had remained in private hands cannot be known; what is known is that where they brought about increases in production they did not come up to the growth standards of either Western Europe or Japan, and when efforts were made to denationalize road haulage in 1953 and steel in 1954 there was no strong buyers' demand for either.

THE ECONOMY FROM AUSTERITY TO AFFLUENCE, 1945–1970

Labour carried out its program of welfare and nationalization in conditions of extreme austerity. Bomb damage, run-down factories, used-up investments abroad, and foreign debt all made for grim times in which the privations and controls suffered by the people during the war had to be continued. Regulations requiring governmental permission or licenses controlled practically every enterprise, from equipping a shop to purchasing a new bathroom sink. Food rationing remained in place; indeed, rations sank to below their wartime level, and even bread had to be rationed in 1946. Because popular demand for consumer goods was very high, the government had to keep taxes up in order to suppress inflation of prices. The bitterly cold winter of 1946–1947 revealed a shortage of coal. Further, because British exports had collapsed during the war, the nation faced a serious balance of payments problem. The Labour government gave high priority to building up the export industries and restricting imports. Even so, a shortage of dollars and the convertibility of sterling, dictated by the American loan, caused a balance of payments and sterling crisis in 1947. Only the arrival from America of $3.2 billion (more than any other nation received) in Marshall Plan aid saved Britain from further cuts in rations, high unemployment, and an end to the house construction program.

Gradually, economic conditions turned for the better. The export campaign was successful, especially in the automobile industry. Between 1946 and 1950, British exports rose by 77 percent. Bread was derationed in 1948, followed by flour, eggs, and soap in 1950. Even so, some foodstuffs were rationed until 1954 and coal until 1958. In 1951, in order to mark the end of austerity and to celebrate the hard-won accomplishments of the British people, the government staged the "Festival of Britain," with exhibition halls to display British products and the new Royal Festival Hall on the south bank of the Thames for concerts. Unlike the Crystal Palace exhibition of 1851, the Festival of Britain was not international, or even imperial, but was purely British—a celebration of the material pleasures that the populace could soon hope to enjoy. In 1952, the coronation of Queen Elizabeth II, who succeeded her father, George VI, likewise marked the beginning of a new, more affluent time. It even gave rise to talk of a "New Elizabethan Age."

The period of postwar affluence in Britain lasted from the early 1950s to the early 1970s. Its positive features were full employment, fairly strong economic growth, and a consumer boom. Despite continuing popular fear that 1930s-level unemployment might reappear at any moment, the number of jobless people never rose above a million between 1945 and the early 1970s. So strong was employment that "full employment" came to be defined as an economy with only a 2 percent unemployment rate—a concept that was beyond the fondest hopes of interwar economists. The causes of full employment over the two decades of the 1950s and 1960s were (1) the postwar rebuilding from wartime destruction and expansion of exports; (2) low interest rates inspired by Keynesian financial policies; and (3) the influence of the huge American economic expansion. As the American economy grew, it pulled much of the world economy with it. In Britain, full employment allowed wages to rise, and although wages pushed prices up with them, real earnings improved for Britons by 80 percent between 1950 and 1970.

The high rate of employment and increasing real wages together generated a long consumer boom—the most notable in British history up to that point in time. People were weary of hardship and deprivation, which for many families had lasted since 1919, and they were eager to take advantage of consumer pleasures. Domestic demand soared for telephones, televisions, vacuum cleaners, washing machines, refrigerators, and the like. Installment buying, which had first become common between the wars, now broke down old standards of prudence and thrift. No doubt the welfare state enabled families to ignore saving for a rainy day. By the early 1970s half of British households owned their own homes, half had cars, two-thirds had washing machines, three-fourths had refrigerators, and nine-tenths had televisions. As Prime Minister Macmillan was to say, "Most of our people have never had it so good."

The booming domestic consumer market, plus considerable success in exports overseas, contributed to vigorous economic growth. The total of goods and services produced at home (the GDP) grew by an annual average of 2.7 percent in the 1950s and almost 3 percent in the 1960s. This was a better record for the British economy than at any time since the 1870s. The industries that carried the growth were new ones—automotive, electronics, aircraft, and industrial chemicals. The old staples of coal, iron, textiles, and shipbuilding continued to recede into the background. Both the growth record and the new industries were encouraging; yet British growth was only mediocre compared to that in the United States, Western Europe, and Japan. In the 1950s and 1960s, for instance, British output rose by about 60 percent, but that of West Germany shot up by 250 percent and Japan by 300 percent. The British share of world trade in manufactured goods fell from 22.8 percent in 1938, to 19.8 percent in 1955, and to 10.8 percent in 1970. Britain lost overseas markets to more efficient industrial powers and even began to be crowded out of significant sectors of the domestic market. In these facts and figures lay a crucial story for post–World War II Britain: British economic growth was good but not good enough.

The British age of affluence, therefore, involved not only welfare, full employment, and a consumer boom but also the short-term problem of chronic balance of payments crises and the long-term problem of inadequate productivity. These problems of the 1950s and 1960s grew to crisis proportions in the 1970s. Some detailed analysis is therefore necessary. Given the sensible decision after 1945 by the Labour government not to shut Britain off from the rest of the world and run a self-sufficient "fortress" economy, the British had to import large quantities of food-stuffs and raw materials every day. In addition, the demand for consumer goods—mainly American goods in the 1950s and 1960s but increasingly European and Japanese—contributed mightily to the import bill. As in the nineteenth century, the British had to pay for imports by a combination of visible exports (manufactured goods, mostly) and invisible income. The British achievement in exporting manufactured goods between 1950 and 1970 was much better than between 1919 and 1939, though not as strong as it needed to be. In no year between 1945 and 1975 did British exports alone pay for imports. Meanwhile, invisible income from foreign investments, brokerage of foreign trade, international insurance, shipping, and so on, had been radically reduced by the two world wars and by the emergence of the United States as the world's financial power. Thus from 1950 to 1970 the British experienced recurring shortfalls in the balance of payments.

Balance of payments deficits meant that Britain faced serious problems in paying for its imports. These difficulties were aggravated both by threats to the value of sterling and by the various governments' (Labour and Conservative alike) efforts to preserve it. Whenever the balance of payments fell into deficit, it meant that businessmen around the world were accumulating excess pounds whose value was being drained by inflation; thus holders of sterling around the world periodically rushed to trade their pounds for gold or other currencies—normally the dollar. Since the British had created the Sterling Area in 1939, and now sustained it as a symbol of British power, many countries held vast quantities of sterling as reserves (backing) for their own currencies. The British felt responsible, therefore, to maintain the convertibility of sterling at a high value. As balance of payments deficits reached crisis levels, the government of the moment either had to devalue sterling (which it did twice) or clamp down on imports and dampen domestic consumer demand.

The periodic restriction of imports trapped both Labour and Conservative governments into a cycle of policies called "stop-go." All the cabinets of the 1950s and 1960s wanted to let the British consumers have the goods they desired and to encourage the economy to grow. Hence in the "go" phase of the cycle, they eased import restrictions, provided cheap money for investments, and encouraged installment buying. But as the economy heated up, it increased inflation, sucked in imports, created a balance of payments deficit, and caused the government to adopt "stop" measures: import restrictions, tight money, and controls on installment buying. Stop-go made for an uncertain economic environment and discouraged investment and production.

Stop-go, however, was not the underlying problem of the British economy. Inadequate industrial production was the fundamental long-term flaw. British industry in the 1950s and 1960s (and as we will see in Chapter 14, in the 1970s and 1980s as well) neither captured enough foreign markets nor held a sufficient share of the domestic market to enable Britain to pay its way. The explanations for this failure—or "British disease," as it has been called—are hotly controversial. The trade unions blamed incompetent management, and management in turn blamed the trade unions. Both are probably correct. In addition, economists tend to cite purely economic factors, whereas social and cultural observers emphasize factors in British society beyond the market itself; again, both are probably correct. In general one may say with confidence that (1) British economic troubles began in the last quarter of the nineteenth century and were seriously aggravated by the two world wars; (2) British industrial relations in the post–World War II period were poor; (3) the level of investment was low; and (4) British culture discouraged aggressive business practices.

To elaborate, we have already seen that Britain in the late nineteenth century grew less fast than newly industrializing nations and that the British tended to retreat into imperialism and dependence on invisible earnings rather than face hard competition. The two world wars injured British industrial capacity while dealing a blow to the traditional British success in foreign trade and investment. Poor labor-management relations, which hampered British productivity and which afflicted British industry through the 1980s, grew out of the long history of class conflict. Even in the 1950s and 1960s, management and trade unionists viewed each other with suspicion and thus tended to escalate every dispute, no matter how trivial, into a battle in the class war. British executives, who were no longer the owner-operators of the nineteenth-century type but salaried professional managers, were aloof from the workers. Heaven forbid that they eat in the workers' canteens! They normally were dismissive of workers' demands.

The workers for their part assumed that company profits in some vague way represented exploitation, and they displayed an "instrumental" attitude toward their work. Thus they showed little company loyalty and regarded their jobs as a necessary evil for earning enough money to pay for consumer pleasures. Moreover, the British trade union movement remained both highly bureaucratized and highly fragmented. Union officials had relatively little control over their workers, who looked to shop stewards for leadership; and the multiplicity of unions within any one industry (or company) caused much scuffling among the unions for jurisdiction as well as hypersensitivity about gradations in pay. Finally, British trade unionists were scarred by the experience of unemployment in the 1930s. In the postwar period they fought to keep high manning levels (overmanning and feather-bedding, according to managers) and absurdly restrictive job descriptions. For all these reasons, reform of the trade unions and of the legal structure that controlled their activities became an important issue from the late 1960s. Meanwhile, the restrictiveness and conservatism of the unions often minimized the productive advantages of such investment as management attempted.

Investment in British industry was low for many reasons. The stop-go policy cycles discouraged long-term investments, as did poor industrial relations. Government research and development funds, which were ample, were directed largely toward military projects. The welfare state removed an incentive for private savings, and the population as a whole seemed to prefer social security and satisfaction of immediate consumer desires to investment for the future—a problem faced by every mature industrial society. In general, the rate of return was not high enough to induce people to invest in British industry; hence Britain in the 1950s and 1960s actually had a net *outflow* of capital. This was an old feature of the British economy but one that the nation could no longer afford.

British business practices were wedded to the past and not sufficiently innovative, especially in design, marketing, and customer services. Too many British managers looked back to the past, when British industry had everything its own way. An American think tank, the Brookings Institution, concluded in 1968 that British managers tended to be amateurish and lethargic. An "old-boy" network and social status prevailed in recruitment and promotion of the managerial class. Britain had no business schools until the 1960s, and engineering (unlike pure science) remained a relatively low-status profession. Moreover, the old landed ideal, with its prejudice against hard work and commercial profit, softened the drive of British businessmen. An American diplomat in 1955 noticed

> a sense of doubt concerning the social utility of industry and the legitimacy
> of profit, a sort of industrial inferiority complex often suffered by business
> leaders themselves. . . . In the extreme, some British industrialists seem
> almost ashamed of their vocation, looking on their jobs as a necessary evil
> or—in the case of family businesses—an inherited "white man's burden."

The traditional British sense of their nation as the countryside—typified by stately homes and the Lake District—directed the energies of British executives toward acquiring landed estates and retiring from the commercial fray. The ablest young people studied the arts subjects and entered the professions (law, medicine, academe, the civil service) rather than industry. In fact, the more the professions dominated British society, the less the nation valued profit and production.

The age of affluence in Britain, then, was marked by economic growth and consumer prosperity but also by increasing competitive shortcomings in the world economy. The quality of life as well as the quantity of life was never higher for most people, but both in retrospect were enjoyed on borrowed time. As Prime Minister Edward Heath was to say in 1973,

> The alternative to expansion is not, as some occasionally seem to suppose,
> an England of quiet market towns linked only by trains puffing slowly and
> peacefully through green meadows. The alternative is slums, dangerous
> roads, old factories, cramped schools, stunted lives.

AFFLUENT SOCIETY

To the ordinary British citizen of the 1950s and 1960s, the great new fact of life was a higher standard of living. The welfare state assisted the majority of the population by its "transfer payments"; thus most people received from social services more than they paid in through taxes. Moreover, as we have seen, average income went up faster than prices, and families were able to buy homes, automobiles, televisions, and the like. These material comforts took less work to purchase: the average work week fell to less than forty-five hours, and most people had three weeks' holiday a year. The standard life-style became more "privatized"—that is, it centered on the home and revolved around activities like watching television, gardening, and working on do-it-yourself projects on the house or car.

Superficially, the new affluence tended to diminish class differences. Working people could now afford mass-produced clothes that resembled the finery of the upper classes. In fact, in the 1960s, "classless" clothes like blue jeans and T-shirts became the fashion for middle-class youth. Working-class and middle-class people became more alike in material comforts and leisure activities. Middle-class families could no longer afford servants, and many working-class families could have homes, cars, and holidays. As the number of professional administrators in the society grew, there was some increase in upward social mobility for working-class boys. White-collar workers, who occupied a middle ground between workers and managers, increased as a percentage of the work force. The distribution of incomes became somewhat less unequal: by one account the richest 1 percent of the population owned 43 percent of all wealth in 1954 but only 30 percent in 1972.

Nevertheless, class and class consciousness remained the keys to British social structure and social relations. "Embourgeoisement"—the conversion of working people to middle-class attitudes—was much talked about in the 1950s, but it never really came about. One major poll in 1972 showed that 95 percent of the British people identified themselves with some social class. In general in such polls about two thirds said they were working class, slightly less than one third said they were middle class, and 1 percent said they were upper class. People's sense of what they could aspire to also revealed the continuing realities of class divisions. For most working people, hard manual labor with no real possibility of promotion was reality. Middle-class people could aspire to "get another couple of notches up," as one chemist put it, and "send the boys to boarding school." Middle-class and professional men and women had job security and rising promotion (and salary) scales, whereas working-class people were stuck with the same jobs and faced layoffs whenever times were bad. Upper-class types still enjoyed a graceful and comfortable life. As one upper-class Labour cabinet minister, Richard Crossman, put it, "Ann and I have a facility of freedom and an amplitude of life . . . which cuts us off from the vast mass of people."

The solidarity of the working class was shown by the power of the trade unions. The years of full employment encouraged trade union membership among workers, especially males. In 1971, 58 percent of all male employees belonged to unions. (The respective figure for women was 32 percent, because the union leadership continued to think of their organizations as male institutions.) Overall, union membership reached 44 percent of the total work force, which was the highest level in British history except for the unusual years of 1919-1920. "White-collar" unions among administrative personnel became important for the first time. The number of strikes averaged about 2,500 a year, causing the annual loss of some three million workdays. As we will see, industrial conflict got worse, not better, in the late

1960s and early 1970s, and this was eventually to help bring the age of consensus to an end.

Meanwhile, a new division was emerging in British society: race. After World War II, the number of immigrants into Britain from the Commonwealth, as the Empire was now called, grew rapidly. Both "push" and "pull" forces were involved. Colonial peoples from the West Indies, Africa, India, and Pakistan came to Britain seeking better jobs and wider opportunities, and sometimes they were fleeing from postcolonial political troubles. The British government and employers encouraged them to come in the 1940s and 1950s because of the labor shortage. Labour also was idealistic about the Commonwealth: in 1948 the Labour government adopted the British Nationality Act, which allowed citizens of the Commonwealth to come to Britain with full rights of British citizenship. By 1951, the black population of Britain had doubled to 200,000, and in 1961 alone, 113,000 "colored" (including blacks, Indians, and Pakistanis) immigrants arrived. The immigrants did not disperse evenly across the country but concentrated in a few urban areas, notably London, Birmingham, and Bradford. Because the British were accustomed to a relatively homogeneous population, many of them did not readily accept the newcomers. As early as 1958 the Notting Hill area of London suffered serious race riots. Pressure quickly built for legislation to limit immigration. A law was passed in 1962 establishing a quota system. Further restrictions followed in 1965, along with Britain's first Race Relations Act. Although racial discrimination was thereby banned, serious racial prejudice and tensions continued to exist. As we will see, race and immigration became important political issues in the 1960s.

The effects of the affluent society on women were decisive in favor of normalizing work outside the home and creating a greater degree of equality with men. It is important to remember that most women in Britain had always worked and that economic necessity had from the nineteenth century led many women to take jobs outside the home. The proportion of women in the work force was very stable (at about 30 percent) from 1851 to 1951. Likewise, the percentage of women who worked *outside* the home stood at about 35 percent between 1851 and 1951. Not even the two world wars, which had temporarily drawn large numbers of women into industry, significantly altered these long-term figures. What *had* changed between 1914 and the 1950s was a greater *diversity* of jobs held by women and an increase of *middle-class* women in gainful employment. Thus in the early years of the twentieth century, about 40 percent of all working women were in domestic service, but by 1951 only 23 percent were; in the 1950s over 32 percent were employed as clerks and secretaries in business and commerce.

After World War II, the number of *married* women working outside the home increased radically, and in the 1950s and 1960s the proportion of the total female population who were employed went up as well. In 1931, work was still for single women, but in 1951 the proportion of working women who were married reached 40 percent and in 1961 over 50 percent. Women as a proportion of the labor force now grew to about 35 percent, when 42 percent of all women were employed. Women flowed into office jobs, retail clerks' positions, and teaching, and in lesser numbers into the professions. This amounted to a social revolution, which occurred despite the assumption by Beveridge and other founders of the welfare state that the woman's proper place was in the home with the children.

The causes of these increases were both demographic and economic. The average age at marriage was declining, but the birth rate remained low. Hence married women on average in Britain now spent only four years in pregnancy and caring for infants, as compared to fifteen years in the late nineteenth century. They were much more inclined in the 1950s and 1960s to return to work once their children reached school age. Middle-class inhibitions against female employment had long since disappeared. Moreover, the ever-growing expectations of material goods by families drew women into employment, at the same time as domestic labor-saving devices made it possible.

The rising number of women at work contributed to expansion of equality for women, though complete equality, whether formal or informal, was not attained. Employment gave a growing number of women a sense of economic and psychological independence, especially because female employment was no longer concentrated in subservient fields like domestic service. The women's liberation movement, which as we will see in the next section became highly influential in the 1960s, both expressed and advanced the sense of women's independence. The results of the movement were significant: the Divorce Reform Act (1969) made irretrievable breakdown of the marriage the sole ground of divorce, and one that was equally open to women and men; the Matrimonial Property Act (1970) recognized women's contributions to marital property in kind as well as in money; and the Equal Pay Act (1970) established the principle of equal pay for equal work.

No doubt most of these steps were thwarted to a degree in practice. And in informal terms the advance of equality for women was slower. In some British homes, men in the 1960s helped more in housework and childrearing, but this was more true of middle-class families than those of either the rich or the working class. "Separate spheres" still existed, though in a changed form: men tended to wash dishes, repair the house, and tend the garden, and women did the shopping, cooking, and child care—while *also* holding down a job outside the home. Men still got the lion's share of higher education: in the 1960s only about a quarter of university students were female. And something of the old double standard continued to exist in matters of sex. In a survey completed in 1969, for example, 63 percent of the women reported that they were virgins at the time of their marriage, as compared to only 26 percent of the men.

Affluence had as big an impact on the lives of young people as on women. The youth of Britain had more money, more freedom to spend it, and more to spend it on than ever before in British history. Teenagers, in fact, enjoyed more disposable income than any other age group. Inevitably, they came to dominate a major segment of the consumer market. This revolved around clothes, records, radios, record players, and other items subject to commercialized trends in fashion. From 1950 Britain experienced waves of youth-oriented fashions: in the 1950s, the "Teddy Boys" affected Edwardian-style suits; in the 1960s came hippies, miniskirts, hotpants, and the boutiques of King's Road and Carnaby Street; in the 1970s followed "skinheads" and "punks." Throughout the period "youth" tended to become almost

The Beatles: John Lennon, Paul McCartney, George Harrison, and Ringo Starr.

a separate social class, knit together by fashion and pop music. Rock 'n' roll, introduced into Britain by the American group Bill Haley and the Comets in the 1950s, became a major feature of popular culture. Bands like the Beatles in the 1960s, the Rolling Stones and the Sex Pistols in the 1970s, and the Police and Boy George in the 1980s, expressed the age-old rebelliousness of young people in a new, highly marketable form and gave them a culture—complete with heroes, icons, rituals, and discourse—closed to their elders, to whom its attractions remained an unpleasant mystery.

The advent of youth culture coincided with the growth of what was called "permissiveness." The relative independence of young people from parental control was one of many causes of this permissiveness in Britain. Another was the long decline of Christianity, which gradually loosened the hold of Victorian morality on the middle class and the "respectable" working class. (The aristocracy and the nonrespectable stratum of the poor had always indulged in permissive behavior.) The rapid expansion of the universities took many thousands of young people away from home to institutions that were not interested in acting in *loco parentis* (in place of the parents). This bred a number of student "revolutionaries" who sought to accelerate the pace of social change, democratize the universities, and destroy the capitalism whose affluence and welfare state made it possible for them to attend universities in the first place. Their ideology was part uninhibited personal pleasure, part idealistic socialism, and part hostility to authority; it peaked between 1967 and

1970 in numerous protests and sit-ins. A fourth cause of permissiveness was the improvement and spread of contraception, including "the pill," which was introduced in the 1960s and which had a major impact on sexual attitudes and behavior. Finally, there was affluence itself, which gave people, young and old alike, greater freedom from the traditional discipline of economic survival and encouraged immediate gratification of personal desires.

To conventional Britons, the consequences of permissiveness were clear: sex, drugs, and crime. There was enough evidence in each case to make the proposition plausible. One indication that Victorian morality regarding sex was eroding was the acquittal on charges of obscenity in 1960 of the publisher of D. H. Lawrence's sexually frank novel *Lady Chatterley's Lover*. Another was passage in 1967 of laws making it easier to obtain an abortion and decriminalizing homosexual acts between consenting adults. In addition, by 1970, three-fifths of all couples were using contraceptives, and 20 percent of all married women were taking the pill. Women in greater numbers assumed that sex was something for them as well as for men to enjoy. The frequency of premarital sex increased, as the "sexual revolution" of the Western world occurred even in Britain: at one university in 1970, almost all the girls surveyed said that they were virgins when they arrived but that by their third year less than half were. The number of illegitimate births went up by 60 percent between 1950 and 1970, even though the number of abortions tripled in the five years after passage of the Abortion Act of 1967. Censorship of sexual material in the theater ended and became less strict over such material in films.

Drug use was a key feature of youth culture, but it was not restricted to young people by any means. Drugs were available by prescription through the National Health Service. In the 1950s the users were mainly middle-aged and elderly people, who took them as sleeping pills, tranquilizers, and antidepressants. In the 1960s, however, young people in large numbers began taking nonprescription amphetamines, heroin, cannabis, and LSD. In Britain, hashish (from the cannabis plant) became the preferred drug, though the Beatles' hit song "Lucy in the Sky with Diamonds" was thought to be a tribute to LSD. A law was passed in 1964 making possession of nonprescription drugs illegal, but it had little effect.

The crime rate in Britain went up from the late 1950s about 11 percent a year. Between 1951 and 1972, cases of crimes against property tripled, and cases of assault increased tenfold. The highest rates of increase were for people under twenty-one years of age. Britain remained much more peaceful and law-abiding than the United States; however, the number of police officers had to increase by almost 40 percent and police officers more frequently had to carry arms. The reasons for the increase in crime are not certain. Many conventional folk blamed the courts for "coddling" criminals and for abolishing the death penalty in 1965. Probably the actual culprit was affluence itself, along with its spin-off, self-indulgence. As standards of material acquisition went up, so also did the gap between those who could buy the goods and those who could not. Advertisements made consumer goods infinitely desirable; perhaps this incited some have-nots to crime. In the words of one official report:

The material revolution is plain to see. At one and the same time, it has provided more desirable objects, greater opportunity for acquiring them illegally, and considerable chances of immunity from the undesirable consequences of so doing.

THE CULTURE OF AUSTERITY AND AFFLUENCE

High culture in Britain from 1945 to the 1970s was exceptionally vigorous. The Labour government intended to promote the "quality" as well as the "quantity" of life and therefore renamed the wartime CEMA as the Arts Council, giving it funding to support the arts, which it has done with distinction. But this was only a relatively small factor in creating conditions for cultural and intellectual vitality. Of greater consequence was the sense that between 1945 and 1951 Britain had experienced a sharp break with history. This notion simultaneously caused regret, high hopes, and disillusionment. World War II was seen as decisive not only for the defeat of Germany but also for the cooperation between the Soviet Union and the West. The hopefulness of that cooperation soon collapsed in the bitterness of the Cold War. Likewise, the use of atomic bombs in 1945, and the subsequent proliferation of atomic weapons, cast a pall on victory itself. The welfare state gave reason for celebration by the idealistic left, but its shortcomings spurred the elaboration of strong critiques, including some from extreme socialists. The sense of a clean break with the past gave rise to ideas of liberation—in social thought, in theology, and in feminism—but each generated strong reactions.

More than ever, the universities served as the locales for intellectual life in Britain. Not only natural scientists, social scientists, and humanistic scholars found their outlets for teaching and research in the universities, but also a growing number of novelists, poets, and critics. This was not entirely healthy, for the specialization encouraged by universities made a holistic view of life and the world nearly impossible. In 1959, the eminent scientific administrator and novelist, C. P. Snow, called attention to the fragmentation of high culture in his famous "Two Cultures" lecture at Cambridge. He argued that scientists knew little about literature and literary folk knew nothing about modern science and that this was a regrettable fact since the world needed an integrated vision of things from its intellectuals. Revelation of the split in culture was shocking enough, and then Snow was fiercely attacked by the leading Cambridge literary critic, F. R. Leavis, for preferring the scientists to the literary intellectuals. The two men proceeded to show by their dispute that the divide between the two cultures was all too real. At its base the debate was about industrialization and whether the kind of society it created was morally superior to the preindustrial world: Snow said yes and Leavis said no. This was a theme that ran throughout the period.

Meanwhile, the writers who reacted most sensationally to the materialism of Britain in the age of the welfare state and affluence were the novelists and playwrights known as "the Angry Young Men." They included Kingsley Amis, John Braine, Alan Sillitoe, and John Osborne. Most of them were from the working class, and all of them opposed the materialism of British life and expressed a pervasive restlessness and purposelessness. They were angry because things had not changed enough despite the war and welfare: snobbery, class divisions, conventional morality, and traditional institutions like the monarchy and the church still remained. Amis satirized academic life in his novel *Lucky Jim* (1954). Braine attacked the cynical scramble for corporate power in *Room at the Top* (1957). Sillitoe's *Saturday Night and Sunday Morning* (1958) revealed the mindless pleasure-seeking of a young factory worker, who lives only for his weekends of drinking and womanizing and who is unconscious of the Labour party's long struggle to attain the welfare state. Most famous of all was Osborne's play, *Look Back in Anger* (1956), in which the hero rages against conventional pieties, the lack of "commitment" among those around him, and his own powerlessness. The Angry Young Men were the precursors of the student revolt of the 1960s, but they thought, as Osborne put it, "There aren't any good, brave causes left." All they could do was use their anger to try to make other people feel things more intensely.

Other intellectuals in the 1950s and 1960s found a channel for their criticism of modern life in campaigns for *liberation*—the sense that the time had come to liberate the British people from obsolete or oppressive attitudes and institutions. One of the most important of these liberationist movements was the New Left. This grew out of university-based Marxism in the 1950s and produced the *New Left Review* in 1960 as well as three major socialist thinkers: Richard Hoggart, Raymond Williams, and E. P. Thompson. All three of them turned away from Stalinism and a clanking, deterministic type of Marxism toward a more subtle and humane form looking back to Marx's early writings on alienation. On this basis they offered a radical critique of British society and culture. Hoggart criticized the mass media for eroding the ability of the working class to sustain its own authentic perspective on life and work. Williams explored the social foundations of literary culture, which he saw as now regrettably separate from the lives of ordinary people. He explained that the idea of "culture" itself had developed as a moral reaction against capitalist industrialism but had turned in self defense away from involvement with society. Thompson, the most influential thinker in the British New Left, was a social historian and polemicist of great passion and insight. He showed in *The Making of the English Working Class* (1963) how the English laboring poor had made themselves into a new community—the working class—during the period of the Industrial Revolution. His sense of people's active role in forming their own lives led him to battle Continental, Stalinist-style Marxists and to engage in the crusade against nuclear weapons.

A second intellectual movement for liberation was feminism. British feminists of the 1950s and 1960s, many of whom were associated with the New Left, realized that the advances toward equality for women had not gone far enough. By the 1970s, many also felt that the sexual revolution had resulted in the sexual objectification of women, and that society's norms and expectations for women were too limiting. Hence they consciously tried to resurrect the "heroic" militancy of the pre-1914 suffragettes and to eradicate the deep cultural roots of the oppression of females. They established strong movements against rape and wife battering. The two leading British feminists were Doris Lessing and Germaine Greer. Lessing, a socialist and a psychological novelist of great power, wrote of the difficulties women faced in attaining psychic wholeness in a society dominated by men. For her, liberation lay in self-understanding and the integration of personality. Greer, the ablest feminist polemicist, argued that the new objective of the women's movement had to be a revolution in gender relations. In *The Female Eunuch* (1970) Greer channeled her anger into an attack on gender stereotypes and on the means of their social construction. Greer contended that in capitalist society women were taught to be both the big spenders and the emblems of big spending; thus they were made into servile and thoughtless sex objects. She also delivered smashing assaults on Freudian psychoanalysis, myths of love and marriage, popular romance fiction, and the image of the female in male literature. Amid all these ideas was work for a generation of feminists.

In theology, the quest for liberation took the form of rejection of "old-fashioned" ideas of God and Christ. These were regarded by liberal Christian theologians as outdated and therefore obstacles to faith. They should be replaced, the liberals thought, by the idea of God as a force working *within* creation. The best-known expression of these views in Britain was *Honest to God* (1963) by Bishop John Robinson. He put forward an existentialist theology, declaring that God is not "up there" or "out there" but is the very "ground of our being." Moreover, Christians must find Christ in the hungry and needy of the world. *Honest to God* sold 350,000 copies in its first year, but it caused a storm of controversy. It may have driven away as many people from Christianity as it attracted. Christian church membership, especially in the Protestant denominations, continued to decline in Britain. By the 1970s, only 5.5 million Britons (including those in Northern Ireland) were active members of Protestant churches, and 5.3 million were practicing Roman Catholics.

Liberationism took a very different form in the ideas of environmentalists and opponents to economic growth. Many of these notions, best seen in the works of the economists Ezra Mishan and E. F. Schumacher, were based in romanticism and religion—in the ideas that there are higher values than materialism and that humanity should practice proper stewardship over God's creation instead of exploiting and wasting it. Schumacher's best-seller, *Small Is Beautiful* (1973), drew attention to the destruction of the world ecosystem by rampant greed and technology. Schumacher urged that people liberate themselves from false assumptions that all economic growth is good and that bigger technology is better. They must understand that from recognition of limits on human desire comes wisdom. Perhaps it can be argued that as a citizen of a country afflicted by low growth, Schumacher was making a virtue of necessity. Yet his solutions—"Buddhist economics," reverence for creation, and appropriate technology—were (and are) eminently sensible.

In imaginative literature, novelists and poets expressed very different reactions to the postwar world, but all in one way or another expressed profound alienation. Doris Lessing contended that capitalism was making life "petty and frustrating"

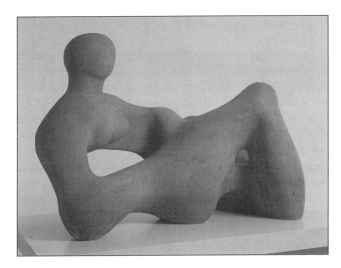

Recumbent Figure,
by Henry Moore,
1938.

while debasing popular culture. George Orwell, who had been an ardent if cantankerous socialist before the war, now expressed grave doubts about the leviathan states created by total war. In *1984* (1949), Orwell painted a bleak picture of a world dominated by warring, mind-warping superpowers and warned against the totalitarianism of communism. He became the most widely read of all serious writers in the English language. Evelyn Waugh, a prominent satirist during the interwar period, now expressed archconservative disgust for the modern world; as he says of one character in *The Ordeal of Gilbert Pinfold* (1957), "He abhorred plastics, Picasso, sunbathing and jazz—everything in fact that had happened in his own lifetime." Joyce Cary, in novels like *The Horse's Mouth* (1944) and *Not Honour More* (1955) displayed a wonderful ability to imagine a wide range of characters and celebrated through them the free imagination, which clashes tragically or humorously with the established order of things. Graham Greene, like Waugh a convert to Catholicism, expressed a somber sense of the imperatives and dilemmas of religion and morality in the bleak conditions of decolonization, wartime, and the Cold War.

The writing styles of the two ablest British poets (other than the Scotsman Hugh MacDiarmid) of the period were quite different from each other. Philip Larkin believed in clear, accessible, technically proficient poetry that adhered to traditional rhyme and meter. A poet with a mundane view of life, Larkin took as his themes the distance between hope and reality, the deceptiveness of choice, and the certainty of old age and death. Ted Hughes (1930–1998) was a poet of violent emotions and seeming admiration of violence. His poetry reveals an awareness that in the modern world miracles and madness are scarcely distinguishable. Hughes admired the capacity of animals to do what humans can not—to see clearly—thus the hawk

Effortlessly at height hangs his still eye.
His wings hold all creation in a weightless quiet
Steady as a hallucination in the streaming air.

Hughes was made poet laureate in 1984; he died in 1998 and was succeeded by Andrew Motion.

In the visual arts, two figures stood out (and still do): the painter Francis Bacon and the sculptor Henry Moore. Bacon (1909–1992) was a self-taught artist who mysteriously combined expressionism, cubism, and realism in deeply disturbing—even unnerving—paintings. Bacon did not care at all what people thought of his work and made no effort to make his paintings beautiful. Yet his images of monstrous, half-human creatures, often crouched in tortured postures, are not easily forgotten. Somehow they express the horror and violence that are part of the modern world. Moore's work is equally powerful, but it emphasizes formal qualities and is less disturbing than Bacon's. Moore was strongly influenced in the 1920s by pre-Columbian Mexican sculpture and in later years by England's rolling landscape. His massive works are not realistic, but they do abstract the essence of real objects, whether they be reclining female figures, helmeted heads, or atomic explosions. They give a sense of solidity and order that is missing from many of the other products of British high culture since 1945.

Suggested Reading

Aldgate, Anthony, *Censorship and the Permissive Society: British Cinema and Theater, 1955–1965* (Oxford: Oxford University Press, 1995).

Alford, B. W., *British Economic Performance Since 1945* (London: Macmillan, 1988).

Benson, John, *The Rise of Consumer Society in Britain, 1880–1980* (New York: Longman, 1994).

Bernstein, George, *The Myth of Decline: The Rise of Britain since 1945* (London: Pimlico, 2004).

Bogdanor, Vernon, and Robert Skidelsky, eds., *The Age of Affluence, 1951–1964* (London: Macmillan, 1970).

Brookshire, Jerry, *Clement Attlee* (Manchester: Manchester University Press, 1996).

Burk, Kathleen, ed., *The British Isles since 1945* (Oxford: Oxford University Press, 2003).

Caine, Barbara, *English Feminism, 1780–1980* (Oxford: Oxford University Press, 1997).

Cairncross, Alec, *The British Economy Since 1945: Economic Policy and Performance, 1945–1995* (2nd ed.; Oxford: Blackwell Publishers, 1995).

Chick, Martin, *Industrial Policy in Britain, 1945–1951* (Cambridge: Cambridge University Press, 1998).

Cronin, James E., *Labour and Society in Britain, 1918–1979* (New York: Schocken Books, 1984).

Davies, Christie, *Permissive Britain: Social Change in the Sixties and Seventies* (London: Pitman, 1975).

Deakin, Nicolas, *Colour, Citizenship and British Society* (London: Panther Books, 1970).

Eatwell, John, *Whatever Happened to Britain? The Economics of Decline* (London: Duckworth [BBC], 1982).

Ford, Boris, *The Cambridge Guide to the Arts in Britain, vol. 9: Since the Second World War* (Cambridge: Cambridge University Press, 1988–1990).

Goldthorpe, John H., *Social Mobility and Class Structure in Modern Britain* (Oxford: Clarendon Press, 1980).

Hennessy, Peter, *Having It So Good: Britain in the 1950s* (London: Allen Lane, 2006).

————, *Never Again: Britain, 1945–1951* (New York: Pantheon, 1994).

Laybourn, Keith, *The Evolution of British Social Policy and the Welfare State, c. 1800–1993* (Keele: Keele University Press, 1995).

Lowe, Rodney, *The Welfare State in Britain Since 1945* (New York: St. Martin's Press, 1993).

Marwick, Arthur, *British Society Since 1945* (London: Allen Lane, 1982).

————, *Culture in Britain since 1945* (Oxford: Blackwell, 1991).

Morgan, Kenneth O., *Labour In Power, 1945–1951* (Oxford: Clarendon Press, 1984).

Noble, Trevor, *Modern Britain: Structure and Change* (London: B. T. Batsford, 1975).

Pearce, Robert, *Attlee* (New York: Longman, 1997).

Pelling, Henry, *The Labour Governments, 1945–51* (New York: St. Martin's, 1984).

Perkin, Harold, *The Rise of Professional Society: England Since 1880* (London: Routledge, 1989).

Prochaska, Frank, *Royal Bounty: The Making of a Welfare Monarchy* (New Haven: Yale University Press, 1996).

Rowbotham, Sheila, *The Past Is Before Us: Feminism in Action Since the 1960's* (London: Pandora, 1989).

Sinfield, Alan, ed., *Society and Literature, 1945–1970* (New York: Holmes & Meier, 1983).

Sissons, Michael, and Philip French, eds., *The Age of Austerity, 1945–1951* (London: Hodder & Stoughton, 1963).

Smith, Harold, L. ed., *British Feminism in the Twentieth Century* (Amherst: University of Massachusetts Press, 1990).

Tiratsoo, Nick, ed., *The Attlee Years* (London: Pinter Publishers, 1991).

Tomlinson, Jim, *Democratic Socialism and Economic Policy: The Attlee Years, 1945–1951* (Cambridge: Cambridge University Press, 1997).

Veldman, Meredith, *Fantasy, the Bomb, and the Greening of Britain: Romantic Protest, 1945–1980* (New York: Cambridge University Press, 1994).

Welsby, Paul, *History of the Church of England, 1945–1980* (London: Oxford University Press, 1984).

Wiener, Martin, *English Culture and the Decline of the Industrial Spirit, 1850–1980* (Cambridge: Cambridge University Press, 1981).

Chapter 12

Illusions of Power: Politics and Foreign Relations, 1945–1970

In British political history, the 1950s and early 1960s are often thought of as "the Age of Consensus" because both major parties accepted full employment, the welfare state, and management of the economy. Political differences between the parties seemed to shrink, so that there was as much dispute *within* each party as there was *between* the parties. Some political observers began to speak of "the end of ideology" and "the end of politics," for government increasingly seemed to be a matter of fine-tuning by experts. Yet one might say that consensus included political failure as well as achievement, because neither party was able to solve the long-term problems of the British economy, and each was in turn driven to adopt the same policies to cope with short-term crises. The power of the British government over fundamental economic troubles was thus illusory, and the political consensus gradually broke apart. Moreover, illusions of power overseas contributed to that essential weakness. One after another, Labour and Conservative cabinets found that they had to give up their illusions of power, withdraw from Britain's traditional worldwide commitments, and move toward a wholly new reorientation of Britain's role in the world.

THE STRUCTURE OF GOVERNMENT AND POLITICS

As a result of the two world wars and changing assumptions about the role of the state in society, the scope of the government was much larger after 1945 than ever before in peacetime. The Civil Service itself grew to include some 750,000 people. Counting the nationalized industries, probably 25 percent of the entire work force was employed by the state. Public expenditure, not counting the nationalized industries, reached 41 percent of the gross national product (GNP) in the 1950s and 1960s. Taxes rose to about 35 to 40 percent of the GNP. The government, as we have seen, assumed leadership in maintaining a minimum standard of living for all citizens and in managing, if not planning, the economy. The expansion of the state in Britain, as in every Western industrial nation, seemed irresistible.

The Civil Service was a key element in the state. It provided the continuity and experience that allowed the various ministries to accomplish their plans. Having developed high professional standards in the late nineteenth century, the British Civil Service in its enlarged postwar condition remained efficient and incorruptible. Its power lay in its expertise. The civil servant's role was to advise government ministers and then carry out their decisions. In this role, the civil servants were supposed to be impartial, but the Labour governments often complained that they showed a Tory bias. There was some truth to this accusation, not because the Civil Service was deliberately partisan but because it was recruited from a narrow upper-class base. In the 1950s and 1960s, 85 percent of the civil servants were graduates of Oxford and Cambridge. They instinctively expressed traditional upper-class views and argued for "the way things have always been done." Even an official committee established in 1965 was unable to change these views.

The constitution itself underwent a number of changes that reflected the increased scope and complexity of government as well as further democratization of the electorate. The key to the unwritten British constitution after 1945 remained the unlimited power of Parliament. The actions of Parliament were (and are) not limited by any higher law, written code, or judgments by the courts. Nevertheless, the role of Parliament in governing the country, and the particular parts played by its two houses, changed to a degree. The power of the House of Lords, already restricted in 1911, was further limited in 1948 to delaying legislation for only one year. In 1958, legislation provided for the appointment of *life* peers and peeresses. (Titles of life peers are not inherited.) This meant not only that women for the first time sat in the upper house but also that people of experience and achievement could invigorate its deliberations. Since 1958 most "creations" have been life peers. The Labour party expressed some interest in reconstituting the House of Lords or abolishing it altogether (as we shall see, the government of Tony Blair after 1997 was to eliminate most of the hereditary peers from the House of Lords); but in fact the peers played a useful role in dealing with potentially divisive moral issues like drugs, divorce, and abortion. In 1963, an act was passed allowing peers to renounce their titles in order to sit in the House of Commons, where the real political power rests.

The power of the House of Commons over the Lords was (and is) supreme, yet the Commons itself declined in practical authority after 1945. The reasons for that decline were the increase in the power of the electorate on the one hand and that of the prime minister and cabinet on the other. Both of these trends had been developing for a long time. The electorate, which included from 1971 all males and females over the age of eighteen, had clearly become the source of ultimate political decisions. Parties appealed to the voters on the basis of coherent programs, advertising, and the mass media. This in effect limited the freedom of action of the House of Commons itself, for M.P.s were limited by the pledges made in the campaigns. Moreover, the prime minister and the government tended to appeal directly to the voters, using Parliament to register decisions made by the electorate. The cabinet subjected the M.P.s to tight discipline and completely dominated the agenda of the House of Commons. The House of Commons could (and can) still set the outer limits of the government's actions and serve as a national sounding board; otherwise, since 1945 it has played an almost automatic, even ritualistic, role in national policy-making.

The growth of the power of the prime minister was much discussed in the 1960s, when it seemed to many observers that the prime ministers were becoming more and more like American presidents. Some critics held that the prime minister's authority had grown relative to both the House of Commons and the cabinet. But what in fact grew was the power of the executive itself, not necessarily that of the prime minister. Some prime ministers since 1945 have dominated their cabinets by force of will and personality (like Macmillan, Thatcher, and Blair), but others have acted in the more old-fashioned role of chairperson of the cabinet (like Attlee). The prime minister's main weapons since 1945 have been the power over ministerial appointments, including the right to appoint and fire cabinet ministers, to set the agenda of cabinet meetings, and to command the attention of the mass media. Yet these powers do not amount to "presidential" authority, for the prime minister is constrained to a degree by the need to satisfy cabinet colleagues and the wishes of his or her party.

Unofficial interest (or pressure) groups played a major role in British government after World War II. Interest groups have multiplied enormously since the days of the Anti–Corn Law League. They first became vital to British government during and after the First World War, and since 1945 they have become even more so. Many of them were economic producers' groups like the Confederation of British Industry, the National Union of Manufacturers, the British Iron and Steel Federation, the Cake and Biscuit Alliance, and hundreds of others. The trade unions, and above all the Trade Union Congress, also served as powerful interest groups. There were (and are) numerous professional associations like the British Medical Association and the National Union of Teachers. In addition, there are hundreds of voluntary associations that concern themselves with special interests such as old age, poverty, civil liberties, and penal reform. The very complexity of industrial society has called these interest groups into being, and the expanded power of the state over economic and social affairs has drawn them into constant contact with departments of the government. They act at all levels—on the parties, on Parliament, on the executive, and on the Civil Service. Because of their expertise, as well as their lobbying, they have influenced most legislation since 1945. Because pressure groups act behind the scenes, they are not often seen as what they have in fact become—an essential part of the British governmental machine. In the years since 1945, Britain became a *quasi-corporatist state*, in the sense that much crucial decision making was made through consultations among politicians, civil servants, and these extraparliamentary bodies.

It remained the case, however, that the most important elements in the British structure of government and politics between 1945 and 1970 were the political parties. Parliamentary government was party government. Moreover, in the postwar period the party system was dominated to an unusual degree by the two major parties—Labour and Conservative. Britain had been famous for a two-party system, yet throughout the century between 1845 and 1945 there actually were important third and fourth parties—the Home Rulers, then Labour, and finally the Liberals themselves. After 1945, however, the Labour and Conservative parties together won on average 91 percent of the popular vote and 95 percent of the seats in the House of Commons. Why this domination? For one thing, both parties were "national" in that they organized the politics of every region except Northern Ireland; this reflected the high degree of political integration of the British Isles since 1919. The class system and the "first-past-the-post" electoral arrangements (that is, the system whereby the candidate winning the most votes in a constituency wins the seat and the other candidates win nothing, no matter how many votes they earn) favored the division of the electorate into only two blocs. Furthermore, two-party dominance depended on affluence and consensus; as we will see in Chapter 14, it was to fragment when the Age of Affluence crumbled.

The Labour party, rooted in the working class and especially the trade unions, was the party of the left and center-left. In theory it had a more democratic structure than the Conservative party. The annual party Conference voted on a long list of issues and was thereby supposed to direct the actions of the Labour M.P.s. The National Executive Council (NEC), elected by Conference, was to exercise continual supervision over the Parliamentary Labour Party (PLP). In actuality, the party's M.P.s before 1914 had found that they needed to exercise their own sense of priorities in the tumble and flow of parliamentary life. By 1945 the brute fact of having become one of the two parties that alternated in forming governments had expanded the prestige and power of the party leader over both the NEC and the Conference. In 1945, the chairman of the NEC peppered Attlee with directions about the electoral campaign, and Attlee showed who was boss by a blunt remark: "A period of silence on your part would be welcome. " Yet the Labour party leadership after 1945 could not dictate policy to Conference and remained dependent on the trade unions. The unions provided more than half of Labour party funds. A law of 1913 had allowed the unions to collect a political levy from all members who did not "opt out." In reaction against the General Strike, Baldwin's government in 1927 required the unions to collect political funds only from those who "opted in," but the Labour government in 1946 reversed that, restoring the "opting out" provision. Moreover, the trade union leaders were entitled to cast ballots at the annual party Conference by the "bloc vote," which meant that the union's entire vote went to the majority position no matter how narrow the majority. This gave the biggest unions (the transport workers, the municipal employees, and the miners) decisive power in both the Conference and the NEC. Although the Labour party leaders had to take a broader view of national affairs than simply trade union interests, and although they themselves were less and less likely to come from the working class, they could not defy strongly held union policies.

The Conservative party, occupying the center-right and right of the political spectrum, depended on the votes of the middle class, three-fourths of whom voted Tory. The party leadership in Parliament dominated the party Conference and reflected a higher economic and social status than even the party voters and activists. The parliamentary leadership wrote the party platforms and in effect required the annual Conference to ratify them. Until 1965, the party leader was selected not by Conference but by mysterious consultations among the top few parliamentary figures; after 1965, Conference won the right to elect the leader but still exercised little control over him or her. Conservative M.P.s were overwhelmingly drawn from the ranks of wealthy company owners and directors and professionals, whereas almost half of the Labour M.P.s were trade unionists. Two-thirds of the postwar Tory M.P.s had gone to the exclusive public schools and about one-third to "Oxbridge" (Oxford or Cambridge). The Conservative Conference, meanwhile, reflected that part of middle-class Britain that had a foot in the countryside. As the *Economist* observed in 1957: "There they were—the clergyman's wife, the small employer, the retired service officer, the county lady—the softly respectable representatives of suburban and rural but not industrial England." Given this social composition, it is remarkable that the Conservative party managed to win about one-third of the working-class votes in each election.

Of the other British political parties, only the Liberals had significant national appeal. As we will see in Chapter 13, the party structure in Northern Ireland differed from that in the rest of Britain. In England, Scotland, and Wales, the Communist party, the National Front (extreme right-wing nationalists), Plaid Cymru (the Welsh Nationalist Party), and the Scottish National Party all were active between 1945 and 1970 but together claimed less than 2 percent of the total vote. The Liberals, meanwhile, who had been reduced to less than 7 percent of the vote in 1935, now found that their popular support gyrated between about 2.5 percent and 9 percent, even though many of the fundamental ideas behind the welfare state were Liberal in origin. The Liberals elected as many as twelve M.P.s and as few as six. The class alignment of British politics had crowded the Liberals out, and many Liberal voters between 1945 and 1970 were either disgruntled Labourites or Conservatives, temporarily voting Liberal to protest some decision by their parties. This does not mean that British politics were polarized between left and right. There was in fact a broad band of moderate "center" opinion in the British electorate, but this center bloc was effectively claimed by the Labour and Conservative parties. This was the electoral meaning of consensus.

DECLINE OF THE LABOUR GOVERNMENT, 1945–1951

In view of the big majority won by the Labour party in 1945 and the subsequent legislative success of the Attlee government, Labour might have been expected to rule for a very long time. This proved not to be the case. The party exhausted its program and began to suffer serious internal divisions.

By 1948 the Labour government had completed the construction of its welfare system and carried out most of its nationalization of industry. Iron and steel were nationalized in 1949, but this project caused more controversy than any other step in nationalization. Plans to nationalize sugar and other industries roused little support, though the left wing of the Labour party was anxious to proceed with them. The government's program of economic austerity had become unpopular, and the public wanted to get rid of wartime controls. Thus in the election of 1950, the government's majority was sharply reduced. As the party's morale sagged, the government was torn by a hot dispute between the left-wingers, led by Aneurin Bevan, and the moderates, led by Herbert Morrison, over proposals to nationalize more industries and to cut some social programs. More ominously, defense spending, which the moderates supported and the left opposed, began to encroach on expenditures for the welfare state, especially the National Health Service.

The problem of defense spending in 1950–1951 is a reminder that the Labour government did not operate in an international vacuum. The British emerged from World War II with the *appearance* and the *habits* of a world power. These trapped the Attlee government into relatively conventional approaches to foreign and imperial affairs. The British were among the victors in the war and occupied the most industrialized part of Germany. Attlee in 1945 met with Truman and Stalin as if an equal. The Empire-Commonwealth was at least superficially intact; it seemed the best opportunity for expanding British trade, and it gave the British some hope that they could continue to deal with the United States and the Soviet Union on equal terms. But in fact, as the Attlee government soon realized, the British could no longer keep all their commitments around the world. The question was where to withdraw and where to hold on.

In retrospect, one might well argue that the government should have radically altered the role of Britain in the world, dropped the pretense (and expense) of being a world power, abandoned old imperial connections, and settled for being a European nation of medium size. But Europe lay devastated by the war, while more than half of Britain's exports went to the Commonwealth. Furthermore, sentimental ties to Britain's old transoceanic role were powerful. The Labour party thought that to jettison the underdeveloped colonies in Africa and elsewhere would be unfair to the colonial peoples. Thus Labour adopted the policy of "trusteeship" for the dependent colonies—a policy of economic and political development that looked forward to a distant future for colonial self-government. This way the British could retain the economic value of the colonies while making some gestures toward idealism. But trusteeship required the British to retain military and naval bases, army garrisons, police forces, and administrative personnel overseas. To keep up these forces, together with the half million occupying troops in Germany, the British committed themselves to conscription and to substantial foreign military expenditures.

The atomic bomb, like the Commonwealth, was seen as a way to maintain great power status. In particular, the Labour government thought that the bomb would impress the Americans, give the British some influence over United States policy, and restrain the Russians. The British government, cut off from American nuclear secrets in 1946, decided formally (but without telling Parliament) to construct a bomb in 1947. They accomplished the task in 1952. They also set out to develop their own delivery system of strategic bombers. For all these reasons, British expenditures on defense were the third highest in the world, behind only the United States and the Soviet Union, and remained so throughout the period from 1945 to 1970.

In some areas, however, the Attlee government realized that they could not retain control of their possessions. The prime examples were India, Pakistan, Burma, and Ceylon. During the war, Indian nationalists had made it plain that the days of the British *raj* (rule) were numbered. The Labour cabinet agreed, for Labour had been committed to Indian independence since the 1930s. Hugh Dalton, the chancellor of the Exchequer, said in 1946 that "if you are in a place where you are not wanted, and where you have not got the force, or perhaps the will, to squash those who don't want you, the only thing to do is to come out." In 1946, "communal" violence—riots and killings between India's Muslim and Hindu communities—showed that Britain no longer actually controlled the country. The problem was that although all Indian nationalists demanded independence from Britain, the Muslim minority wanted a separate Muslim state (Pakistan), and the Hindu majority wanted a unified India. The British preferred a federation for all India but were unable to impose this solution. Therefore, amid terrible scenes of communal bloodshed, the British simply declared in 1947 that India would become independent the next year. In actuality, the last British viceroy, Lord Mountbatten, found that the date had to be advanced. In August 1947, both India and Pakistan became independent, and both opted to remain as republics within the Commonwealth. Burma and Ceylon followed soon after.

The departure from India meant that the British no longer had their old strategic interest in keeping the Middle Eastern routes to India. But the Middle East now assumed a new value for Britain: oil. Britain after 1945 imported more than three-fourths of its oil from the Persian Gulf region through the Suez Canal. The British needed to protect their oil interests in the Middle East while cutting their other commitments in the region. In particular, the British wanted to retain paramount interest in Iraq, which protected the eastern approaches to the Canal; Iran, Saudi Arabia, Kuwait, Oman, and what became the United Arab Emirates, which together produced most of Britain's oil; and Aden, which controlled the Red Sea entrance to the Canal. On the other hand, the British in 1947 gave up to the United States their role of supporting the governments of Greece and Turkey. And in 1948 they abandoned their mandated territory, Palestine, to the rival claimants in the area, the Arabs and the Jews.

The British role in the Palestine Mandate for thirty years had been a source of confusion and violence. The Lloyd George government in 1917 had promised the European Zionists to create a "national home" for the Jews in Palestine, while honoring the rights of the Palestinian Arabs. However, the British during World War I also encouraged their Arab allies to revolt against Turkish rule, and they set up friendly Arab kings in Saudi Arabia, Iraq, and Jordan during the interwar years. The Arabs believed that Britain had promised to support Arab rule in Palestine. The British disputed this view, but whatever the merits of the various arguments, the Arabs hotly opposed Jewish immigration into Palestine, which after World War II threatened to become a flood. The British were made to realize that they could not keep their conflicting commitments. They tried to limit Jewish immigration but won no gratitude from the Arabs. After 1945, Palestine dissolved into a triangular

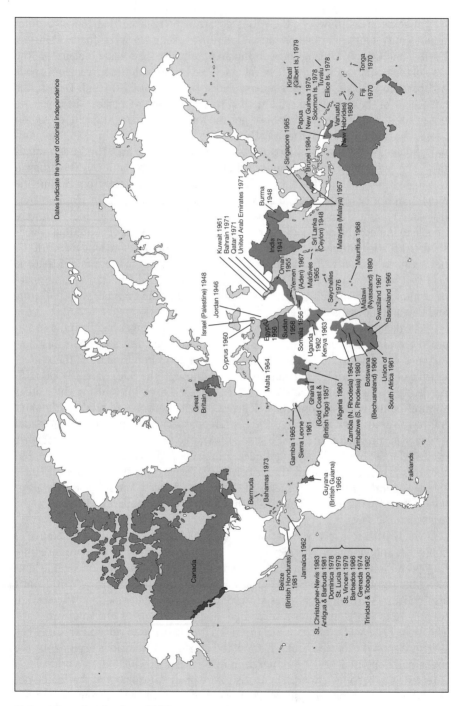

Dates indicate the year of colonial independence

Kiribati (Gilbert Is.) 1979
Tonga 1970
Papua New Guinea 1975
Solomon Is. 1978
Tuvalu
Ellice Is. 1978
Fiji 1970
Vanuatu (New Hebrides) 1980
Singapore 1965
Brunei 1984
Burma 1948
Kuwait 1961
Bahrain 1971
Qatar 1971
United Arab Emirates 1971
India 1947
Sri Lanka (Ceylon) 1948
Malaysia (Malaya) 1957
Mauritius 1968
Oman 1955
Yemen (Aden) 1967
Maldives 1965
Seychelles 1976
Israel (Palestine) 1948
Jordan 1946
Cyprus 1960
Egypt 1956
Sudan 1956
Somalia 1960
Uganda 1962
Kenya 1963
Malawi (Nyasaland) 1890
Swaziland 1967
Basutoland 1966
Botswana (Bechuanaland) 1966
Union of South Africa 1961
Malta 1964
Great Britain
Ghana (Gold Coast & British Togo) 1957
Nigeria 1960
Zambia (N. Rhodesia) 1964
Zimbabwe (S. Rhodesia) 1980
Gambia 1965
Sierra Leone 1961
Guyana (British Guiana) 1966
Falklands
Bermuda
Bahamas 1973
Canada
Belize (British Honduras) 1981
Jamaica 1962
St. Christopher-Nevis 1983
Antigua & Barbuda 1981
Dominica 1978
St. Lucia 1979
St. Vincent 1979
Barbados 1966
Grenada 1974
Trinidad & Tobago 1962

Retreat from Empire from 1945

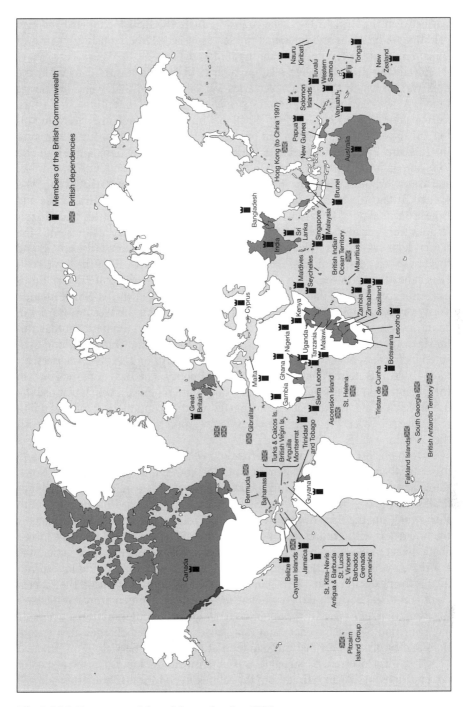

The British Commonwealth and Dependencies, 1990

war between the British, Jews, and Arabs. In 1948, the British simply abandoned Palestine to the Arabs and Jews, and the Jews succeeded in establishing their own state in most of the territory west of the Jordan river.

Meanwhile, British foreign relations after 1945 were increasingly shaped by the Cold War, in which the main adversaries were the United States and the Soviet Union. As we have seen, Churchill's suspicions of Soviet intentions in Eastern Europe grew during 1944 and 1945. In 1946, Churchill declared in a speech in Fulton, Missouri, that an "iron curtain has descended across the Continent" because the Russians intended to dominate the Eastern European nations. American and Russian relations rapidly worsened in disagreements over Poland, Czechoslovakia, and Germany, among others. Rejecting the appeals of Labour's left wing, who wanted Britain to stand aside from the polarization of world politics, Attlee and Ernest Bevin aligned Britain with the United States. Although Attlee and his colleagues were socialists, they had no use for communism. They also resented the Soviet demands for the industrial machinery in Britain's sector of Germany, and they saw Soviet domination of Eastern Europe as a threat to all of the Continent. Hence the Attlee government took a leading part in the formation of Western European alliances, first in the Brussels pact of 1947 and then in the North Atlantic Treaty Organization (NATO) in 1949. NATO bound Britain, the Western European countries, Greece, Turkey, the United States, and Canada to automatic mutual military assistance. This was an unprecedented step for Britain, which had long treasured its freedom of action in Europe. Likewise, the British accepted American air force bases in Britain—another unprecedented policy. The British participated in the Organization for European Economic Cooperation (OEEC), which planned the use of Marshall aid. In other developments toward the economic and political union of Europe, however, the British stood aside on grounds that their future lay with the Commonwealth.

The high cost of participating in the Cold War came home to the Labour party in 1950, when the Korean War broke out. The communist government of North Korea invaded South Korea in June of that year, expecting a quick victory and unification of the country. The United States immediately decided to come to South Korea's aid, and the British, who had Munich in mind, felt that they had to support the Americans with ground troops as well as naval and air power. British concern about Soviet military strength in Eastern Europe was increasing at the same time. For these reasons, the Attlee government doubled its estimates for military spending for the next three years. This renewed the left-right dispute within the government, for Attlee, Bevin, and their allies believed that social expenditures would have to be cut in order to pay for the defense spending. Aneurin Bevan heatedly resisted any reduction of social services and especially the proposed charges on prescriptions and eyeglasses provided through the National Health Service.

This intragovernment struggle was intensified by a personal struggle for power. Cripps and Bevin retired from the cabinet in poor health, and Attlee himself was ill and weary. Bevan hoped to assume the party leadership, but he was challenged by Hugh Gaitskell, an intellectual of the party's center who became chancellor of the Exchequer in 1950. The Bevan-Gaitskell rivalry was to last for more than five years. In 1951, in protest against the government's priorities, Bevan and two colleagues resigned from office. The government obviously was stumbling, and in hopes of obtaining a bigger majority in Parliament, Attlee called a general election. The country, however, was tired of austerity and controls and perceived Labour as having run out of ideas. The Conservative party accepted the welfare state but promised a return to more free enterprise. The Conservatives also successfully put themselves forward as the natural party of government. The election of 1951 gave the Conservatives a small majority, and Churchill at age seventy-seven formed his second government.

THE TORY YEARS, 1951–1964

The Conservative victory in 1951 led to thirteen consecutive years in office. This was not due to Churchill's preeminence. The hero of the Second World War was in poor health and losing his ability to keep on top of affairs. He retired in 1955 and died in 1965. Meanwhile, the Conservative party after 1951 reaped the benefits of good luck as well as administrative talent. While the Conservatives worked to show that they could administer the welfare state more efficiently than Labour, the Labour party agonized over its left-right split. Moreover, favorable trends in the world economy contributed to Britain's prosperity and gave the Conservatives an electoral advantage. Thus, although the Conservatives struggled initially with the nation's balance of payments problem, in 1952 a fall in world commodity prices temporarily benefited Britain's balance of trade. Churchill's government was able to carry out a "bonfire of controls" and to preside over the beginnings of a period of economic growth that lasted through the 1960s. The consumer prosperity of the 1950s and early 1960s enabled the Conservatives to take credit for what seemed to be economic success and to ride out political disasters at home and abroad.

All of the Conservative prime ministers between 1951 and 1964 accepted the national consensus on full employment, the welfare state, and the managed economy. Churchill (1951–1955) took little interest in domestic affairs and left them to his able Chancellor of the Exchequer, R. A. Butler. The continuity of Butler's policies with those of his Labour predecessor, Gaitskell, gave rise to the term *Butskellism*. Anthony Eden (1955–1957) occupied himself almost completely with foreign affairs, but he reflected a traditional Conservative commitment to Disraelian "Tory Democracy":

> We are not a party of unbridled, brutal capitalism, and never have been. Although we believe in personal responsibility and personal initiative in business, we are not the political children of the laissez-faire school. We opposed them decade after decade.

Eden's successor, Harold Macmillan (1957–1963), who seemed to rule with unflappable ease, had worked to commit the Tory party to social reform in the 1930s and remained a believer in Butskellism and managed economic expansion. Finally, Sir Alec Douglas-Home (1963–1964), though not a skilled economic manager, nevertheless represented the old paternalist tradition of the landed gentry and aristocracy.

Prime Minister Harold Macmillan in his favorite habitat, on a grouse-shoot, 1959.

Conservative domestic accomplishments were impressive. The Tories oversaw a long period of full employment and economic growth that only gradually showed itself to be inadequate by comparison to Western Europe and the United States. In the early 1950s, they denationalized the iron and steel and the road haulage industries, ended food rationing, and abandoned many wartime controls. They created the Independent Television Authority in 1954 to provide some private competition to the BBC. They financed the construction of more than 600,000 new houses and sponsored a major expansion of the educational system, most notably at the university level. In 1961, Macmillan's government set up the National Economic Development Council ("Neddy"), which attempted to go beyond management to economic planning. It was to bring together government, business, and union leaders and to make expert projections on growth and modernization.

Overseas, too, the Conservatives observed the postwar consensus, because they had to cope with the same shrinking of British power that had shaped Labour's policies. As the traditional party of imperialism, the Conservatives did not face withdrawal from British commitments happily. They kept defense spending relatively high, even though the British economic base was falling behind that of other Western nations and Japan. Yet even the high expenditures on defense could not keep the military forces at a high level of readiness on all fronts at once. The British army, radically cut from its 1945 level, was overstretched by the commitment to NATO on the European continent and to policing duties from Malaya to Egypt. The Royal Navy's *share* of defense spending went up throughout the 1950s and 1960s, but the real ability of the navy to protect the Commonwealth and transport army units to trouble spots declined along with British economic clout in the world.

The Conservatives sought to compensate for the decline in military force by building a British hydrogen bomb as well as an independent delivery system. This was immensely expensive, but Conservative defense planners, like their Labour predecessors, thought that possession of the H-bomb would give Britain vast power more cheaply than conventional forces and provide a degree of influence with the United States, which was rapidly developing a huge nuclear armory to deter the Soviet Union. Macmillan, who hoped that the British would be able to play the role of the Greeks to the American Romans, said:

> The independent [nuclear power] gives us a better position in the world, it gives us a better position with respect to the United States. It puts us where we ought to be, in the position of a Great Power.

The British tested their first H-bomb in 1957. It is doubtful, however, whether the bomb added to British power. As a government white paper recognized in 1957, the Soviet Union could annihilate Britain with only ten H-bombs. Furthermore, the bomb was useless in defense of the colonies against nationalist guerrillas. Nor could Britain hope to keep up with America and Russia in developing delivery systems. The last British effort to build a ballistic missile ("Blue Streak") had to be cancelled in 1960, and the British had to depend on the United States for delivery systems—first "Skybolt," which the Americans cancelled in 1961, and thereafter Polaris submarines. Meanwhile, Britain was actually protected from the Soviet Union by the American nuclear umbrella, which had key bases in Britain. Nuclear weapons thus made Britain more, not less, dependent on the United States.

From the Conservative point of view, the biggest benefit of nuclear weapons may have come in domestic politics. This was because the Labour party was severely divided over nuclear armaments. In the early 1950s various groups in the left-wing of the Labour party began to agitate against the H-bomb. In 1958 anti-bomb activists founded the Campaign for Nuclear Disarmament (CND) to urge Britain to drop out of the nuclear arms race. CND was a broad middle-class movement, with strong roots in the Christian churches, but it included many Labour as well as Liberal intellectuals, among them Bertrand Russell, John Braine, Alan Sillitoe, Doris Lessing, and Henry Moore. CND's annual marches from the atomic research station at Aldermaston to Trafalgar Square in London attracted the support of thousands of idealists as well as much attention from TV and newspapers. For the marchers, CND represented a reassertion of British moral leadership in the world at a time when British political leadership was declining.

The Labour party, which was already torn between Gaitskellites and Bevanites over the future of socialism, found its internal dispute aggravated by the nuclear issue. Bevan and the left insisted on further nationalization of industry and

Campaign for Nuclear Disarmament march from London to Aldermaston (site of the British nuclear weapons research station), 1972.

a commitment to socialist direction of the economy; Gaitskell and the right resisted more nationalization and advocated a strong private sector in a mixed economy. Gaitskell was able to carry the majority of the party for his moderate policies and after Attlee's retirement in 1955 to win the party leadership. CND, however, exercised much influence with the left wing. Many Bevanites wanted the party to adopt the policy of unilateral nuclear disarmament. Gaitskell stoutly opposed this on grounds that it would require Britain to renege on most of its existing treaties and split with the United States. Bevan himself eventually supported Gaitskell on this issue; he shocked his supporters in 1957 when he rejected unilateralism because it would abandon British influence and send future British foreign secretaries "naked into the conference chamber." Nevertheless, the Labour unilateralists won their point in the Party Conference of 1960. Gaitskell, having vowed to "fight and fight and fight again" managed to reverse the decision in 1961. This swing of the policy pendulum shows that the Labour party was too divided to take advantage of its electoral opportunities.

SUEZ AND AFTER

The best of those opportunities came as a result of a disastrous effort by Eden's government in 1956 to retain by force British control over the Suez Canal. "Suez," as the incident became known, both shocked idealistic Britons and revealed the truth about British weakness. The background to this sorry episode began in 1953, when Britain's puppet ruler in Egypt, the bloated and corrupt King Farouk, was overthrown by nationalists in the Egyptian army led by Colonel Gamal Abdel Nasser. Nasser increased long-standing Egyptian pressure on the British to give up their control over the Suez Canal. Egyptian relations with Britain and the United States worsened, and in 1956 the Americans attempted to keep the Egyptians in line by backing out on a loan to build a huge dam on the Nile at Aswan. In July 1956 Nasser nationalized the Suez Canal Company in order to use Canal revenues to finance the dam. The British saw this act not only as a test of British power but also as a danger to British oil supplies from the Middle East.

The British prime minister, Anthony Eden, overreacted to Nasser's seizure of the Canal Company. Eden had much experience in foreign affairs and had been Churchill's heir-apparent since 1945. Strikingly handsome and well spoken, Eden seemed the perfect product of Britain's "natural" ruling elite. Yet he proved to be brittle and inept in the Egyptian crisis. Eden personalized Britain's struggle with Nasser, whom he wrongly equated with Hitler. "Nasser's got to go," he declared, "it's either me or Nasser." Thus Eden began to plot with the French government to use force against the Egyptians. The United States opposed the use of force in this circumstance, yet Eden misinterpreted some remarks by the American secretary of state, John Foster Dulles, and assumed that he had American support. In October 1956, the British and French brought Israel into their conspiracy: the Israelis would attack Egypt, and the British and French would then intervene, allegedly to separate Egyptian and Israeli forces but actually to occupy the Canal Zone. On October 31, the Franco-British invasion began, and despite the slowness of their forces, the British and French achieved their immediate military objectives, though not before the Egyptians blocked the Canal.

The Eden government, however, was not able to keep its winnings. Nasser was not thrown out of office, and he roused world opinion against this recurrence of European imperialism. Meanwhile, British public opinion expressed outrage at the Suez operation. The Labour party had a field day in Parliament, and most newspapers opposed the naked use of force. Worst of all, the United States government made its displeasure known. They encouraged a run on the pound sterling and blocked efforts by the British to borrow from the International Monetary Fund. This left the British no choice but to withdraw from Suez. By the end of December, all British and French forces had left Egypt. This disaster symbolized the end of British influence as a world power. Eden, who already was a very sick man, resigned from office in January 1957.

Strangely, the Suez catastrophe brought about neither a Labour government nor a fundamental reconsideration of British foreign and defense policies. Eden was succeeded by Harold Macmillan, who turned out to be one of the most effective peacetime prime ministers in the twentieth century. With great talents for parliamentary maneuvering and public persuasion, and with a remarkable ability to project a calm, masterful image, Macmillan restored the morale of the Tory party and rode out the political storm. He also restored close relations with the United States.

Queen Elizabeth in Ghana, 1961. At Her Majesty's right is Ghana's prime minister, Kwame Nkrumah. Ghana was the first of many former African colonies to win its independence.

He enjoyed genuine friendships with Presidents Dwight Eisenhower and John F. Kennedy. He rightly regarded the "special relationship" with America as vital if the British were to maintain their commitments in the Far East, the Middle East, and Africa. In each of these areas, the forces eroding British power were relentless. The Macmillan government's close ties with the United States allowed the British to buy time. Whether this was a wise strategy for the long run is open to question for, as Macmillan admitted in 1960, the "winds of change" were blowing too strongly for Britain to resist.

Despite the Conservatives' efforts to hold on, the parade of British colonies winning independence gathered speed in the 1950s and 1960s. The story in each colony was different, but generally the pattern was for the British to try to keep control in the face of indigenous nationalism, and when that became impossible, to give the colonial government over to local conservative groups favorable to British interests. Only when forced to did the British hand over authority to radical nationalists. Ghana was one major example. There had been strong nationalist movements in Ghana and Nigeria since 1945, and the British had imprisoned the leading Ghanaian nationalist, Kwame Nkrumah. In 1952, however, Ghana won responsible government, for elections showed that the nationalists spoke for the colony. Nkrumah became the new Ghanaian prime minister. On the other hand, the British fought a successful war against communist guerrillas in Malaya between 1948 and 1955 and then turned the government over to locals friendly to Britain. In Cyprus, the British gave way before Greek nationalists. In Kenya, African nationalists waged the ferocious "Mau Mau" terrorist campaign against British troops and white settlers. The British finally granted independence to Kenya in 1963, with the radical nationalist Jomo Kenyatta assuming power in the new country.

In south-central Africa, the British sought to sustain their influence and protect the white settlers there by setting up a bogus federation of Northern Rhodesia, Southern Rhodesia, and Nyasaland. They hoped that the whites of Southern Rhodesia would control the whole. But the huge black majorities of Northern Rhodesia and Nyasaland refused to accept this neocolonial arrangement. In 1963, after years of bloody demonstrations, riots, killings, and repression, Northern Rhodesia and Nyasaland left the Federation. By then the march of colonies to independence was a stampede: in 1960, British Somaliland, Cyprus, and Nigeria; in 1961, Sierra Leone, the Cameroons, and Tanganyika; in 1962, Jamaica, Trinidad and Tobago, and Uganda; in 1963, Singapore, Malaysia, and Kenya; in 1964, Nyasaland, Malta, and Northern Rhodesia (Zambia); in 1965, Gambia. More were to follow, so that by the 1970s British colonial holdings included little more than Gibraltar, Hong Kong, and the Falkland Islands.

Macmillan's government, meanwhile, was increasingly troubled by the chronic problems of relatively inefficient industrial production and deficits in the balance of payments. By 1960 it was clear that the Commonwealth was *not* developing into an effective economic unit. Macmillan, along with many big businessmen, government economic experts, and the Foreign Office, began to consider a momentous decision: to join the "Common Market" or European Economic Community (the EEC). The British, as we have seen, stood aloof from the EEC when it was first formed, but the explosive growth of Western Europe now suggested that Britain's future might be brighter in association with Europe, especially if the British could also keep such beneficial arrangements with the Commonwealth as they had. Those favoring an application to join the EEC argued that it would open up a vast "domestic" market for British industry and expose British companies to strong competition that would force them to become more efficient. In short, membership in the Common Market would give the British economy a healthy jolt that it needed to break out of the stop-go cycle.

Not surprisingly the proposal for such a major shift in Britain's policies and orientation toward the world roused strenuous opposition. The far right of the Conservative party opposed joining the EEC because of their British nationalism and their sentimental ties to the Commonwealth. The Labour left opposed entry because they thought that the Common Market was a capitalist institution founded to perpetuate capitalism, the Cold War, and the arms race. Some of the more moderate Labourites, including Gaitskell, were concerned about the specific terms of entry and feared that membership might mean, as Gaitskell warned, "the end of Britain as an independent state."

In the end, the House of Commons voted in favor of applying for entry to the EEC by an overwhelming majority. The British thus applied for membership in 1961. The French president, Charles de Gaulle, however, was deeply suspicious of the British application. The EEC was constructed in such a way as to be very favorable to the French economy, and he did not want the British to spoil these arrangements. Moreover, he believed that the British were not really ready to break their ties with the Commonwealth and the United States. He did not want Britain to serve as a Trojan horse inside the walls of the EEC for Commonwealth and American interests. After protracted negotiations, de Gaulle vetoed British entry. This was an obstacle that not even "Supermac" could overcome.

LABOUR'S RECOVERY AND FALL, 1964–1970

De Gaulle's rejection of the Conservatives' application to join the EEC left Macmillan without any significant constructive policy, but it was not this that brought his government down. Instead, it was a tawdry scandal involving a member of his government. John Profumo, secretary of state for war, was exposed by the press for having an affair with a model named Christine Keeler, who was having another affair at the same time with the Russian naval attaché. This revelation came hard on the heels of several other security lapses, including the defection to the Soviet Union of Kim Philby, a British Secret Service officer who had been spying for Russia for many years. Macmillan resigned in 1963; referring to Keeler and her flatmate, Macmillan said he had been "brought down by two tarts." He was succeeded not by R. A. Butler as expected but by the Scottish aristocrat Sir Alec Douglas-Home (formerly the fourteenth earl of Home).

The Labour party, meanwhile, was papering over the dispute between its left and right wings. Gaitskell died in 1963. To succeed him as party leader, the Labour M.P.s elected Harold Wilson, who won support from both left and right wingers. Wilson was a nonideological technocrat. He had attended Oxford as a scholarship boy and had become an academic economist. He had worked as a government statistician during the war, entered the House of Commons in 1945, and became the youngest cabinet minister in 1947. Wilson had resigned from the cabinet with Bevan in 1951, thereby winning the reputation of being a left-winger. In fact, however, Wilson believed in blurring ideological issues in favor of party unity. He was by nature a manipulator and compromiser—a born politician.

By law, Douglas-Home had to call an election no later than 1964. In the electoral contest of that year, he proved to he an ineffective campaigner, ill at ease in television appearances and uncomfortable with domestic issues. He lost some credibility when he said he "did his sums with matchsticks." Wilson, on the other hand, was a clever speaker, excellent on television, and obviously a master of facts and figures. He spoke frequently of modernizing Britain, emphasizing not socialism but science, technology, and efficiency. He promised to spur a second industrial revolution and to transform Britain by "the white heat of technological change." The result was a narrow victory for Labour, which won 44 percent of the popular vote and thirteen more seats than the Tories, but only four more seats than Tories and Liberals combined.

The Conservative defeat led not only to the selection of a new party leader but also to a change in the party constitution. Douglas-Home was no match for Wilson in parliamentary debate, and he gave up the leadership in 1965. The Conservatives understood that the secret consultations by which they traditionally had found a leader would no longer do. They now resorted to a formal election by the Conserv-

Labour Prime Minister Harold Wilson, at one time thought to be a leader of the Labour left, later considered a technocrat and opportunist.

ative M.P.s. The winner in 1965 was Edward Heath, a self-made man rather than an heir to broad acres—and like Wilson, a technocrat. His election was the beginning of a historic shift of the Tory leadership to the middle-class businessmen who now made up the bulk of the party supporters.

Harold Wilson's government from 1964 to 1970 proved to be extremely frustrating to the members of his own party. Among the reasons for this disappointment were the expectations that Wilson raised by his technocratic rhetoric and by his own self-image. Wilson liked to appear the economic expert and to compare himself to the late John F. Kennedy. In reality, he exercised no more power over the economy than his predecessors and fell far short of Kennedy in style and glamour. He also tried to take a presidential approach to governing, largely ignoring the senior civil servants and his own cabinet officers. He relied instead on a "kitchen cabinet" that included some friends, a pair of academic economists, and Marcia Williams, his political secretary. His cabinet consequently rarely discussed significant policies and turned into a sullen and quarrelsome group.

More important in causing the troubles of the Wilson government were the economic problems it inherited. Wilson failed to attack the country's underlying weaknesses in industrial production and became trapped by the twin symptoms of the "British disease," inflation and balance of payments deficits. Faced with a rapidly escalating balance of payments deficit in 1964–1965, Wilson might have devalued the pound in order to make British goods cheaper for overseas customers. He decided instead that it was vital for the Labour government to maintain the confidence of the financial community. Therefore, he adopted a series of stopgap measures to slow imports: budget cuts, import surcharges, restrictions on install-ment buying, and increases in the interest rate. In 1965, he set up the National Board for Prices and Incomes (NBPI), which was to urge (not force) companies and unions alike to hold back price and wage increases until justified by improvements in productivity. Later the same year, the NBPI was given authority to *enforce* its wage and price judgments, but it was only partly successful. In 1965 the Wilson government also published a "National Plan," which declared that economic growth should be 3.8 percent per year. This was futile for the simple reason that the economy did not respond to government goals as if they were commands.

Wilson's economic measures in 1964 and 1965 earned the government enough support to warrant a fresh general election. In the election of 1966, the Labour party won a majority of ninety-six seats over all other parties combined. Yet the brute facts of economics continued to bear down, and by mid-1966 a mounting trade deficit caused another sterling crisis. Wilson attempted to improve British industrial efficiency by renationalizing the steel industry, by establishing the Indus-trial Reorganization Corporation (IRC) to bring about mergers of smaller compa-nies into bigger ones, and by levying the Selective Employment Tax to direct work-ers into industry. None of these plans worked. In 1967, Wilson admitted defeat and devalued the pound by 14 percent. This was only one of three crushing blows his government received in the years between 1967 and 1969.

The second blow was rejection of a new application to join the Common Mar-ket. Wilson had never been enthusiastic about joining the EEC. But by 1967, Wil-son and other influential members of his government had come to the conclusion that the National Plan would not work and that Britain was running out of options. Wilson realized that for Britain to remain outside the Common Market entailed an uncomfortable dependency on the United States. Furthermore, he hoped that membership would increase the efficiency and technological progress of British industry and attract investment into Britain. In May 1967, therefore, Britain made its second bid to join the EEC—now since the Brussels Treaty of 1965, known as the EC (European Community). Unfortunately, General de Gaulle still distrusted British intentions, and now he was concerned about British economic weakness as well. He vetoed the British application in November 1967.

Wilson's third major defeat was the collapse of his policy for improving indus-trial relations. British industry, as we have seen, had long been hobbled by conflict between workers and management. In the latter half of the 1960s, as prices rose, so did workers' demands for higher pay, and so also did the number and severity of strikes. The number of strikes, for instance, rose by almost 50 percent between 1967 and 1969. Britain's record in strikes was by then worse than that of any major industrial nation except the United States. Most of the British strikes were unoffi-cial, many of them were the result of interunion jurisdictional disputes, others arose from workers' desire to maintain traditional wage differential or work rules, and some involved secondary strikes and boycotts. A Royal Commission (the Dono-van Commission) in 1968 recommended certain changes in trade union law to bring strikes under control. The Labour government did not want to go as far as the Donovan Commission proposals but recognized that some changes were necessary. Its response, laid out in a white paper entitled *In Place of Strife*, called for reforms including removal of legal immunity from unofficial strikes and mandatory votes by a union's membership when the leaders of that union considered calling a strike. The union movement rose up in protest, and the Labour government, dependent as it was on trade union support, gave way to pressure. Wilson withdrew his bill and substituted for it an ineffective agreement with the TUC to discourage strikes.

The Wilson government was hardly more effective in foreign and imperial affairs. Wilson declared in 1965 that "Britain is a world power, a world influence or she is nothing." In fact, economic weakness continued to make Britain subservient to American policy. Wilson maintained the British nuclear force (Polaris submarines, purchased from the United States). Moreover, Wilson was dragged into support of American policy in Vietnam, which escalated into a major war in 1965. Wilson and his cabinet to a degree shared the American concern about communist expansion in Southeast Asia, but the left wing of the Labour party was very unhappy about supporting the United States. Wilson could only try to walk a tightrope between his own party's criticism of the Vietnam War and American power to strangle the pound sterling. His solution was to attempt to mediate between the United States and the Soviet Union, but this laudable intention came to nothing because British power over the situation was an illusion.

Dependence on America also caused the Wilson government trouble on the issue of maintaining military bases east of Suez. Until the mid-1960s, despite the departure from India, Britain kept a significant military and naval presence in the Far East, the Indian Ocean, and the Persian Gulf. In addition to Hong Kong and Singapore, the British set high store by their base at Aden on the southern tip of the Arabian peninsula. The United States, which formerly had been hostile to the British Empire, now pressed the British to keep up their worldwide commitments in order to help counter the expansion of Russian power. The British, however, could no longer afford the military forces necessary to maintain a role east of Suez, and holding on to Aden involved Britain in a struggle with Arab nationalists in Yemen (which claimed Aden) and in Aden itself. In 1967, after a vigorous parliamentary debate, the Wilson government decided to end British commitments east of Suez and thus to pull out of Singapore, the Indian Ocean, Aden, and the Persian Gulf. The Americans and the conservative Arab sheikdoms were unhappy with the British decision, but increasingly Wilson and his successors focused their defense strategies on Europe.

The ineffectualness of Wilson's government was revealed most clearly in the matter of Rhodesian independence. When the Central African Confederation broke up, the white minority population of Southern Rhodesia was left in control of the country. They composed less than 5 percent of the Rhodesian population. The British did not try to force majority rule on Rhodesia, which was still formally a British colony, but they did press the whites to make progress in that direction. In 1965, resentful of British pressure and persuaded that they could defend their minority rule better on their own, the white government of Rhodesia declared independence from Britain. Already, in 1961, South Africa had left the Commonwealth on the same issue. The new black and brown nations in the Commonwealth urged the British not to yield to the white Rhodesians; the very existence of the Commonwealth was threatened. Wilson refused to recognize Rhodesian independence without Rhodesian commitment to progress toward majority rule. However, because he renounced the use of force on Rhodesia, he had little bargaining power. He met with the Rhodesian leader, Ian Smith, on board British warships in 1966 and 1968, but not even these impressive settings intimidated the stubborn Smith. Rhodesia thus made good its unilateral declaration of independence. Wilson managed to hold the Commonwealth together, but his Rhodesian failure severely damaged Britain's standing with the non-European nationalities of the Commonwealth and the developing world.

THE GENERAL ELECTION OF 1970

Despite the reversals suffered by many of his key policies, Wilson seemed to enjoy substantial public support. He was justifiably criticized for sacrificing long-term strategies for short-term tactics; nevertheless, he stood higher in public opinion polls than the Conservative leader, Edward Heath, not least because Heath was seen as something of a cold fish. Thus when early in 1970 the balance of payments showed a temporary improvement, Wilson called a general election. During the campaign, the Conservatives attacked Labour's record on the economy without offering much of a program of their own. Wilson was thrown on the defensive and was hurt by his government's lack of success abroad and by the increasing number of strikes, rising inflation, and growing unemployment at home. The electoral swing against Labour surprised all observers, and the Conservatives won a majority of thirty seats over all other parties.

The election of 1970 seemed at the time simply the result of a natural swing of the pendulum against the ruling party and toward its opponents. In retrospect, however, the election revealed that the postwar consensus was beginning to unravel. The turnout of voters was comparatively light—only 72 percent of the eligible voters went to the polls, a very low total for Britain. There was little enthusiasm for either major party. Labour party membership, which had peaked in 1957, had declined and now included only slightly more than half of all trade unionists. Within the working class, disillusionment with the party was very strong, for Wilson had inspired and then disappointed such high hopes. Many young working people were drifting away to the New Left and other socialist groups. In the Conservative party, the far right, led by Enoch Powell, expressed restlessness with Heath and the mainline Conservatives, on grounds that the party leaders were not sufficiently opposed to immigration and the "permissive society" and not enthusiastic enough about free enterprise. In these shifts of attitudes, born in the atmosphere of decline and economic malaise, were the beginnings of the polarization that was to mark the 1970s and 1980s.

Suggested Reading

Bartlett, C. J., *The Long Retreat: A Short History of British Defense Policy, 1945–70* (London: Macmillan, 1972).

———, *"The Special Relationship": A Political History of Anglo-American Relations Since 1945* (New York: Longman, 1992).

Beloff, Max, *Imperial Sunset, vol. 2: Dream of Commonwealth* (Dobbs Ferry, N.Y.: Sheridan House, 1989).

Black, Lawrence, *The Political Culture of the Left in Affluent Britain, 1951–1964* (New York: Palgrave, 2003).

Brown, Judith M., and W. Roger Louis, eds., *The Twentieth Century,* vol. 2 of *The Oxford History of the British Empire,* ed. W. Roger Louis (Oxford: Oxford University Press, 2000).

Cain, P. J., and A. G. Hopkins, *British Imperialism: Crisis and Deconstruction, 1914–1990* (New York: Longman, 1993).

Carlton, David, *Anthony Eden: A Biography* (London: Allen Lane, 1981).

Cook, Hera, *The Long Sexual Revolution: Women, Sex, and Contraception, 1800–1975* (Oxford: Oxford University Press, 2004).

Crossman, R. H. S., *Diaries of a Cabinet Minister* (3 vols.) (London: Hamilton, Cape, 1975–1977).

Deighton, Anna, *The Impossible Peace: Britain, the Division of Germany, and the Origins of the Cold War* (Oxford: Oxford University Press, 1990).

Dockrill, Saki, *Britain's Retreat from East of Suez: The Choice Between Empire and the World? 1945–1968* (New York: Palgrave, 2002).

Foot, Michael, *Aneurin Bevan, 1945–60* (London: Macgibbon & Kee, 1962–1973).

Horne, Alastair, *Macmillan* (2 vols.) (London: Macmillan, 1988–1989).

Howard, Anthony, *RAB: The Life of R. A. Butler* (London: Cape, 1987).

Howe, Stephen, *Anticolonialism, in British Politics: The Left and the End of Empire, 1918, 1961, 1964* (Oxford: Oxford University Press, 1993).

Judd, Denis, *The Lion and the Tiger: The Rise and Fall of the British Raj* (Oxford: Oxford University Press, 2004).

Larres, Klaus, *Churchill's Cold War: The Politics of Personal Diplomacy* (New Haven: Yale University Press, 2002).

Lewis, Roy, *Enoch Powell: Principle in Politics* (London: Cassell, 1979).

Mackintosh, John P., ed., *British Prime Ministers in the Twentieth Century, Vol. II: Churchill to Callaghan* (London: Weidenfeld & Nicolson, 1977–1978).

McIntyre, David W., *British Decolonization: When, Why, and How Did the British Empire Fall?* (New York: St. Martin's Press, 1998).

Morgan, Kenneth O., *The People's Peace: British History, 1945–1989* (Oxford: Oxford University Press, 1990).

Navias, Martin S., *Nuclear Weapons and British Strategic Planning, 1955–1958* (Oxford: Oxford University Press, 1991).

Northedge, F. S., *Descent from Power: British Foreign Policy, 1945–73* (London: Allen & Unwin 1974).

Pelling, Henry, *Britain and the Marshall Plan* (New York: St. Martin's Press, 1988).

Porter, Bernard, *The Lion's Share: A Short History of British Imperialism, 1850–1970* (London: Longman, 2004).

Ramsden, John, *The Age of Churchill and Eden, 1940–1957* (London: Longman, 1995).

Reynolds, David, *Britannia Overruled: British Policy and World Power in the Twentieth Century* (New York: Longman, 1991).

Rhodes James, Robert, *Ambitions and Realities: British Politics, 1964–70* (London: Weidenfeld & Nicolson, 1972).

———, *Anthony Eden* (London: Weidenfeld and Nicolson, 1986).

Roth, Andrew, *Enoch Powell: Tory Tribune* (London: Macdonald and Co., 1970).

Rothwell, Victor, *Anthony Eden: A Political Biography* (Manchester: Manchester University Press, 1991).

Sandbrook, Dominic, *Never Had It So Good: A History of Britain from Suez to the Beatles* (London: Little Brown, 2005).

Schenck, Catherine R., *Britain and the Sterling Area: from Devaluation to Convertibility in the 1950s* (New York: Routledge, 1994).

Thomas, Hugh, *The Suez Affair* (London: Weidenfeld & Nicolson, 1967).

Thorpe, Andrew, *A History of the British Labour Party* (New York: St. Martin's Press, 2001).

Turner, John, *Macmillan* (New York: Longman, 1994).

Weiler, Peter, *Ernest Bevin* (Manchester: Manchester University Press, 1993).

Williams, Philip M., *Hugh Gaitskell* (London: Cape, 1979).

Wilson, Elizabeth, *Only Halfway to Paradise: Women in Postwar Britain, 1945–1968* (London: Tavistock, 1980).

Young, John, *Britain and the World in the Twentieth Century* (London: Arnold, 1997).

———, *Winston Churchill's Last Campaign: Britain and the Cold War, 1951–1958* (Oxford: Oxford University Press, 1996).

Chapter 13

Economic Decline, Nationality, and Devolution: The Celtic Countries, 1945–1989

In the 1970s and 1980s it became clear that Britain is a *multinational* state—that is, in terms of government Britain is a single unit, with decision making highly centralized in London, yet in terms of culture and identity it includes a number of distinct regions that qualify to greater or lesser degrees as nations (or peoples with common cultures): the English, Welsh, Scots, Northern Ireland Protestants, and Northern Ireland Catholics. England is the dominant region by far; therefore, the English saw little distinction between "English" and "British." In the Celtic countries, the dual identity developed in the nineteenth century has experienced crosscutting influences. Northern Ireland, as we will see, was a special case, but economic prosperity and the welfare state seemed to be drawing Wales and Scotland in the 1950s and 1960s more closely into the English/British core. Centralization was the main theme in British economics, politics, and government. But in the latter 1960s and 1970s, as economic troubles mounted and the Empire shrank, Celtic national identities reasserted themselves. For a time, the unity of Britain itself seemed to be threatened, and this threat contributed to the end of the consensus that had prevailed since 1945.

WALES

It is important to remember that Wales has been fully integrated with England since the 1500s. Unlike the Scots, the Welsh retained no legal system, schools, or church of their own on which they could focus their sense of Welsh identity. Welsh national identity thus was a matter of language, culture, and religious nonconformity. During the nineteenth century, it was closely tied to popular hostility to the big landlords and was expressed by liberalism and the Liberal party. Industrialization had drawn a dense concentration of Welsh speakers to South Wales and thereby for a time had strengthened the hold of the language. By the twentieth century, however, migration of English and Scottish people into South Wales and the strong ties of Welsh industry to the British economy combined to reduce the proportion of Welsh speakers in the population and thus weaken the sense of distinctive Welsh identity. By 1931, only 31 percent of the Welsh spoke Welsh. In the depression decades after 1918, class identity was more important than Welsh identity in Wales.

The Labour party, as we have seen, dominated Welsh politics after 1918. It inherited the Liberals' role of speaking for Welsh interests, but it was ambivalent about Welsh nationalism. Labour not only was the party of the whole British working class but also it depended on the trade unions, which saw themselves as nation-wide British organizations. The Labour party in the 1920s routinely endorsed the principle of Home Rule for Wales but in fact showed little interest in it. After World War II, the Labour party was a powerful *centralizing* force everywhere in Britain because it believed in democratic central planning. Labourites, including many Welsh Labour M.P.s, believed rightly that real social progress had been achieved by the welfare state. They were reluctant to see further progress for all the British people diminished by proposals for national self-government in Wales.

According to the Labour and Conservative parties alike, the major problem in Wales after 1945 was to restructure the Welsh economy. Wales had become almost totally dependent on the iron and coal industries, both of which had declined since World War I. The South Wales coal mines were old, deep, and inefficient, and the iron and steel mills suffered from backward technology and embittered industrial relations. The solution was to diversify; therefore, the post–World War II Labour government and its Conservative successors sponsored the development of new industries in Wales—clothing, toys, bicycles, vacuum cleaners, synthetic fabrics, oil refineries, and potato chips—in addition to investing in giant new steel mills. The coal mining industry was deliberately contracted. By 1979, there were only 30,000 coal miners in Wales, compared to 136,000 in 1938.

The restructuring of the Welsh economy was only partly successful. Although Wales benefited from the general economic expansion of the 1950s and 1960s, Wales remained a "special area"—a relatively depressed region. Rural Wales continued to lose population as Welsh farming became mechanized. Tourism in the scenic areas proved insufficient to hold young people who earlier would have gone into farming or rural crafts. The closure of coal pits, the failure of the new steel works to compete in world markets, and the rural depopulation all contributed to unemployment that was higher in Wales than in Britain as a whole. By the 1970s, Wales was a classic case of industrial decline.

In 1974, coal became crucial to Britain again. The Arab-Israeli war of 1973 provoked an Arab embargo on oil exports to the West. Oil prices jumped 300 percent in early 1974, and the demand for coal soared. British coal miners, including those of Wales, seized the opportunity to claim wage increases. The result, however, was not a recovery of the coal industry in Wales or anywhere else in Britain, but a protracted strike, bitter confrontation between the government and the coal miners (to be discussed in Chapter 14), and polarization in British politics. The Welsh coal industry continued to contract, so that in the latter 1970s, the unemployment rate in South Wales climbed toward double digits.

Meanwhile, the traditional popular culture of Wales was also changing. Rural small-town Wales was disappearing. Nonconformity was losing its hold on the Welsh people, and although Wales in general held to its religious roots more firmly than did England, the chapel and Sabbatarianism (the idea that Sundays should be devoted to God and not recreation or work) were fading before the new consumerist and permissive culture. Some Welsh towns now voted to keep cinemas open on Sundays, and industrial South Wales even elected to allow pubs to do business on Sundays. More seriously, the Welsh language continued to decline: 28 percent of the people spoke Welsh in 1951, but only 20 percent in 1971. Especially disturbing to Welsh nationalists was the fact that only a small number of Welsh children were learning Welsh, even though Welsh was taught as an elective in all primary schools and some high schools. The *eisteddfod*, with its celebration of Welsh-language poetry and singing, continued to flourish, as did Welsh history and literature in the University of Wales. High culture generally was vibrant, although the most famous of the Welsh poets, Dylan Thomas, wrote in English. It was traditional popular culture that was endangered, for as an official report of 1967 said, widespread speaking of Welsh was needed to protect the distinct cultural and social values of Wales.

Concern about economic troubles, cultural decay, and the decline of Welsh-speaking caused a revival of Welsh political nationalism in the 1960s. In 1945, Welsh nationalism seemed dead. The Labour party dominated Welsh politics and stood for centralized policies and national integration of Britain through balanced regional development. The Conservatives, who opposed any kind of separatist movement in Britain, did establish a minister of Welsh affairs, and both Labour and Tory governments set up various Welsh advisory councils, most of them economic. But these were meant to give British ministers more information about Wales, not autonomy to Wales. Neither party made more than cosmetic efforts to satisfy Welsh interest in self-government.

Plaid Cymru (the Welsh Nationalist Party) in 1945 remained small, with strength only among academics and in the rural Welsh-speaking areas. It managed to get 250,000 signatures on a petition for a Welsh Parliament in 1956, but the party's membership in 1959 was still only about seventy-five thousand. However, by the late 1950s Plaid Cymru was beginning to grow because of the unpopularity of decisions made in London, and in the 1960s its growth accelerated because of concern about the language. The leading advocate of Welsh nationalism, J. Saunders Lewis, came out of retirement in 1962 to lead a crusade to save Welsh. Young militants in the language movement adopted the tactics of mass demonstrations and sit-ins. A few extremists imitated the Irish Republican Army and set off bombs in public buildings. By the late 1960s, Welsh nationalism was in full flower, and Plaid Cymru presented a real threat to Labour's political domination in Wales. Plaid Cymru won its first parliamentary seat in 1966 and in the early 1970s took ten more.

As Plaid Cymru's appeal spread even to the Welsh working class, who increasingly voted nationalist in protest against their economic plight, the Labour party naturally tried to pacify nationalist sentiment. The Wilson government set up the Welsh Office, headed by a secretary of state, in 1964. It then passed the Welsh language Act of 1967, which gave Welsh "equal validity" with English in Wales. In the 1970s BBC television for Wales began broadcasting a substantial number of programs each week in Welsh. And as unemployment in the South Wales coalfield went up to 10 percent, Labour began to consider establishing some form of Welsh provincial government. This proved to be a very controversial issue in Labour circles. The Labour cabinet rejected a plan for a Welsh legislative council in 1966 but created a Royal Commission (the Crowther Commission) in 1969 to consider the whole constitution. "Devolution"—the idea of devolving some degree of autonomy on Wales and Scotland—came to the forefront of British politics.

Always reluctant supporters of regional autonomy, Wilson's government favored only an elected Welsh regional council with modest executive, no legislative, authority. Labour's limited plan did not satisfy Welsh nationalists, but it roused all the old unionist passions of British patriots; thus devolution had a very rocky road in British politics. Some Welsh nationalists began to dream of an independent Wales that would prosper on oil refining revenues while the rest of Britain sank into poverty. In the general election of February 1974 (the narrative of which will be given in Chapter 14), Wilson was returned to office with a minority government, but for the first time since 1945 Labour failed to win 50 percent of the Welsh vote. Labour now had to act on devolution. A Labour white paper of September 1974 called for elected assemblies in both Wales and Scotland, the Welsh assembly to have no legislative, only executive, powers. The issue split the Labour party, for many Labourites remained devoted to centralized socialist planning. Conservative opposition to devolution was solid. Wilson decided that the way to paper over the division within his party while doing something to placate Welsh (and Scottish) nationalism was to introduce a devolution bill for both Wales and Scotland, but on condition that if it passed, referendums in both Wales and Scotland would be held *before* the bill was formally enacted. Moreover, in each of the referendums, at least 40 percent of the *total eligible* electorate would have to vote "yes" for the bill to go into effect, regardless of the majority of those actually voting. Eventually, separate devolution bills for Wales and Scotland were introduced, both with the referendum provision, and both were narrowly passed by Parliament in 1977.

As preparations for the referendums were made, the general issue of Welsh and Scottish autonomy roused much emotional controversy. In England and in Wales, some British patriots believed that Great Britain might be breaking up, whereas many Welsh nationalists believed that devolution was not enough. Certainly, a popular referendum on a parliamentary decision was a constitutional innovation, which to some observers seemed to strike a blow at the cherished tradition of parliamentary sovereignty. In Wales itself, the debate over devolution was, curiously enough, increasingly dominated by the opponents of Welsh nationalism, perhaps because the proposed Welsh assembly would have at least limited legislative authority. Many nationalists were lukewarm toward the bill, and English-speaking Welsh men and women feared that any Welsh assembly might fall under the sway of a romantic, backward-looking, Welsh-speaking minority. In the end, when the referendum was held in 1979, only 11.8 percent of the eligible voters cast ballots *for* devolution. Of those who actually voted, devolution lost by 20 percent to 80 percent. The devolution issue was dead for the time being in Wales, killed by concern among the vast majority of the population about the potentially disastrous economic and social effects of separation from Britain. Welsh nationalism, however, did not die out; it simply found different channels of expression: Welsh literature and language and a myriad of committees and councils set up by the government over time to administer Welsh economic, social, and cultural affairs. But as we will see, Wales suffered from economic and social disaster anyway.

SCOTLAND

The main themes in the history of Scotland after 1945 were similar to but not exactly like those in Wales. In Scotland, as in Wales, one key theme was the decline of heavy industry. Likewise, in Scottish politics the story was the erosion of Labour's position in the face of a revived nationalism. Scotland differed from Wales, however, in that North Sea oil made a much bigger impact north of the Tweed and in that the Scottish National Party (SNP) had somewhat more success than Plaid Cymru, even though the Scottish languages (Gaelic and Scots) had faded much more seriously than had Welsh. As a result of these and other factors, the vote on the devolution issue in Scotland differed sharply from that in Wales, though with much the same general outcome.

The central elements of the Scottish economy had long been agriculture, textile manufacturing, and heavy industries such as iron and steel, shipbuilding, and coal mining. The Scottish economy in the early twentieth century thus was roughly similar to that in Wales, but it was somewhat more diverse. These "staples" of the Scottish economy declined rapidly in the 1920s and 1930s; consequently, a steady stream of Scottish men and women migrated southward. During World War II, Scottish industry benefited from armaments and shipbuilding contracts, but many factories in other lines of work simply closed down. Thousands of young Scottish women, especially from the Highlands, were conscripted to work in munitions plants in the English Midlands. Although unemployment in Scotland disappeared during the war, Scotland became more dependent than ever on a few heavy industries. After 1945, as demand for British heavy industrial products shrank, the Scottish economy suffered severely.

The Attlee government, as we have seen, believed in regional planning and development. Yet its record in Scotland was not very successful, and the manufacturing lost during the war was not replaced. Hydroelectric plants were built in the Highlands, and agriculture in the Lowlands was improved by mechanization. But Scottish shipyards lost out in the worldwide competition to build the new-style gigantic container ships and oil tankers that shippers demanded after World War II. The Clydeside shipbuilding firms suffered from overly cautious management, obsolete design and marketing, and "bloody-minded" industrial relations. Scottish coal mining, like that of the Welsh, was hampered by the age and depth of the mines and the declining demand for coal in an age of cheap oil. By the end of the 1950s, the growth rate of the Scottish economy was only half that of the rest of Britain. In the 1960s, the Labour government of Harold Wilson invested heavily in the Scottish economy and promoted mergers of smaller companies into huge ones. Yet Scottish economic growth lagged and unemployment rose compared to Britain as a whole. Furthermore, with the decline and amalgamation in heavy industry went loss of control by Scots of their economy: by the late 1970s, only 41 percent of Scottish manufacturing was owned by Scots.

North Sea oil, however, provided a major growth industry for Scotland. Oil had been discovered in the North Sea off Holland in 1959. The first commercially sound oil field off the Scottish coast was discovered in 1970. Exploration and production proceeded rapidly after the Arab-Israeli war of 1973 sent oil prices skyward. Because almost all of the British-owned North Sea reserves were in fact off the northeastern coast of Scotland, the oil companies (most of them American) located their main shore operations in northeast Scotland. The huge production platforms, for example, were built there, and the oil was piped ashore for storage and refining there. The northeast of Scotland, as Professor Christopher Harvie has written, took on a "Yukon-like" atmosphere. Aberdeen became a boom town. By 1977, the North Sea field had reached full production, and in some ways Scotland was the main beneficiary.

This is not to say that the Scots were very happy about the way that the British government had handled the oil bonanza. Scotland suffered most of the environmental damage resulting from the oil boom. Moreover, the Scottish economy needed a long-term and well-planned infusion of capital as well as maximum return from the "high-tech" operations associated with commercial oil production. The British government, however, needed quick cash returns from the oil in order to take care of the balance of payments deficit. Thus, it neglected both to control the rate at which the oil was pumped up from the seafloor and to assure that Scotland got all of the exploration and production contracts. Most of the exploration rigs and supply ships, for example, were built abroad. Most grievously, from the Scottish point of view, the British government regarded the oil as British, not Scottish, and therefore did not turn the oil tax revenues over to Scotland. These policy issues all contributed to the revival of Scottish nationalism: "It's Scotland's Oil" became the slogan of the Scottish National Party.

As in Wales, the Labour party in 1945 had a firm grip on liberal-left voters in Scotland. Labour regularly won a majority of Scotland's parliamentary seats, with the Conservatives winning most of the rest and the Liberals a few. Yet as a centralizing party, Labour gave no more attention to Scottish problems than it did to Welsh problems. Throughout the 1950s and 1960s, Parliament spent little time on Scottish issues. Although the Labour governments of Attlee and Wilson invested more funds per capita in Scotland than in any other region of Britain, Labour was not seen by the Scots as "speaking for Scotland."

Especially from the mid-1960s on, many Scots wanted some party to speak for Scotland. Unlike the Welsh nationalists, who believed that a nationalist political

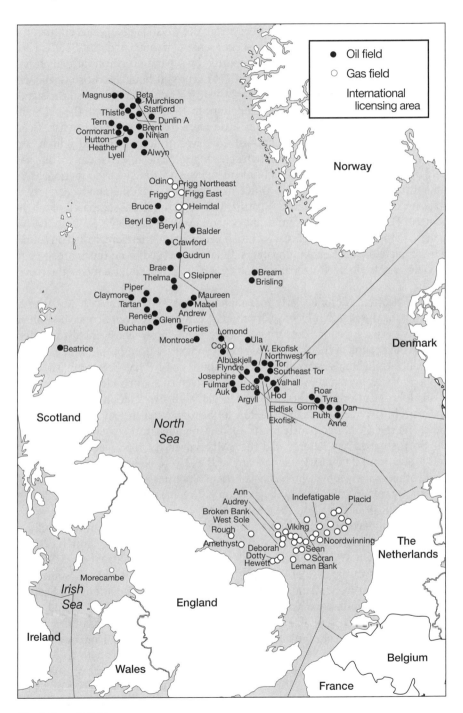

North Sea oil fields

movement was necessary to stop the erosion of the Welsh language and culture, the Scottish nationalists could draw on a secure sense of national identity. Scottish distinctness had been recognized and supported by separate institutions, which had been protected by the Treaty of Union in 1707. Thus, although Scottish Gaelic was spoken by only seventy thousand people in the Highlands and western islands (about 1.5 percent of the Scottish population) in 1960, and although the old Scots language of Robert Burns had become little more than a dialect of English, Scotland had its own judiciary, laws, administrative system, and established church. The Church of Scotland (or "kirk"), though suffering some decline in membership, had held up better than the Church of England and was a strong focus for national sentiment. Furthermore, a Scottish Office had existed since 1885 and a secretary of state for Scotland since 1926. A Scottish Grand Committee, composed of all the Scottish M.P.s, had exerted significant control over the details of Scottish legislation since the nineteenth century. Scottish nationalism, therefore, rested on sound, if incomplete, institutional foundations. What was needed, from the Scottish point of view, was a Home Rule Parliament by which Scots could control their own affairs.

The Scottish National Party rose rapidly in the 1960s because it was seen as speaking for the Scottish identity. Its support came partly from Scots who wanted a positive expression of Scottishness, partly from those who wanted to protect against the decline of the Scottish economy, and partly from people who were dissatisfied with Labour's centralizing orientation. The SNP had been founded in the 1930s but was overshadowed by World War II and Labour's electoral victory in 1945. John MacCormick, the SNP leader, gathered two million signatures on a covenant in 1947 demanding Home Rule for Scotland, but the covenant movement faded and the SNP fared poorly in the 1950s. Only toward the end of the 1950s, as the Scottish economy faltered, did the SNP recover. By 1968, party membership had grown from 2,000 to 100,000. Many of these were converts from Labour, but many others were people who had never been in politics at all. The SNP won a parliamentary seat in 1967, and in the election of October 1974, the SNP won 30 percent of the Scottish vote and eleven seats.

By 1970, devolution for Scotland had become a major issue. It attracted the support of a variety of Scots: the SNP, the Scottish New Left, the Church of Scotland, the Scottish TUC, and the Scottish Conservative party all supported Scottish Home Rule! As in the case of Wales, Prime Minister Wilson had to do something about devolution in Scotland. His solution was to support creation of a Scottish assembly with limited and vaguely defined legislative powers. In Scotland, as in Wales, Wilson's scheme deflated the Home Rule movement. It was criticized in Scotland by by prodevolutionists because it did not go far enough and by antidevolutionists because it would obviously lead to additional steps. Labour in Scotland was divided over the issue. Scottish Conservatives now united against devolution on the slogan "Scotland Says No." The SNP had argued that North Sea oil would make an independent Scotland viable—indeed, more prosperous than an aged and shrinking Britain—but Wilson's devolution bill did not give the Scottish assembly control over the oil. When the referendum was held, devolution won a majority of the votes cast, but only 32.9 percent of the total electorate voted yes, and 30.8 percent voted no.

The referendum killed devolution in Scotland just as it did in Wales. The SNP worked its revenge by helping to bring down the Labour government in 1979. In the subsequent general election of 1979, however, the SNP lost all but two seats, and as we will see the new Conservative government of Margaret Thatcher adopted policies that accelerated Scottish economic decline and drove Scottish unemployment up to depression levels.

IRELAND

Devolution had been tried in only one part of Britain—Northern Ireland—and there it was a disastrous failure. *Dominion status*, however, which gave much more extensive power than any devolution or Home Rule plan, was reasonably successful in the Irish Free State, the twenty-six counties of southern and western Ireland. As we saw in Chapter 7, the Free State, set up in 1921, proved capable of governing itself responsibly. Although it was not economically progressive, the Free State was a stable democracy. Under the leadership of the enigmatic but magnetic Eamon de Valera, the Free State moved toward full independent status, adopting in 1937 a new constitution that made Ireland an independent republic outside the Commonwealth in all but name. At the same time, however, de Valera's vision of a rural "Irish-Ireland" of virtuous small farmers contributed to both the stagnation and the obvious Catholicism of Free State society.

During World War II, the Irish Free State remained neutral despite heavy pressure from Churchill and the British government. The Free State's neutrality was extremely unpopular with Britons and Americans alike, for they believed that Ireland's neutrality posed a threat to Britain's survival and represented a betrayal of freedom. It is true that some Irish men and women admired Hitler's program of economic recovery in Germany and that IRA extremists believed as always that "England's difficulty is Ireland's opportunity." But the main reason for Irish neutrality was simply an Irish desire to assert genuine independence from Britain. As de Valera had once said, "Small states must not become the tools of any great powers." Hence formal neutrality from 1939 to 1945 was another step toward Irish independence; meanwhile, in private the Irish government leaned toward the British side. British planes were allowed to fly over Ireland, downed Allied pilots were returned to their British bases whereas downed German pilots were interned, and German submarine movements were reported to the British.

After the war, the move toward an Irish republic was irresistible. After all, neutrality during the war was incompatible with membership in the Commonwealth. De Valera's Fianna Fáil party had established a clear dominance in Irish politics, but the honor of proclaiming the Irish Republic went to the opposition. In the years from 1945 to 1948, a large number of Irish nationalists became discontented with Fianna Fáil's lack of a progressive program, and a new political party (Clann na

Poblachta, "Children of the Republic") was founded to express the combination of republicanism and social reform. The new party made inroads on Fianna Fáil's support. In 1948 a coalition of opposition parties was able to vote Fianna Fáil and de Valera out of office. The new prime minister, John A. Costello, decided to declare a republic outside the Commonwealth in order to "take the gun out of politics." Thus, the Republic of Ireland Act was passed by the Dáil (Irish Parliament) and came into effect at Easter 1949.

Attlee's government in London did not block the new Irish Republic, but clearly they were irritated. The British government in a sense tried to ignore the Irish move to republican status: the government declared that the Irish were a "nonforeign" people and gave them the same status in Britain as British subjects. The two countries maintained the existing system of trade preferences. This meant that Ireland, a nation of three million people, as opposed to the fifty million of Britain, remained firmly in Britain's economic orbit. At the same time the Attlee government reassured the anxiety-ridden Protestant Unionists of Northern Ireland that their province would not be undermined; thus, the British declared that "in no event will Northern Ireland or any part thereof cease to be a part of His Majesty's dominions and of the United Kingdom without the consent of the parliament of Northern Ireland." This declaration seemed to promise permanent British support for Protestant rule in Northern Ireland.

The new Irish Republic at first reflected the character of the Free State as it had emerged under de Valera. It was Gaelic, Catholic, and rural in its orientation. The government tried hard to protect the Irish language, both by preserving the "Gaeltacht" (the small, Gaelic-speaking area in the west of Ireland) and by requiring all students to study Irish in school. Irish was made *an* official language. As for Catholicism, Article 44 of de Valera's constitution of 1937 was incorporated by the Republic, and it acknowledged the "special position" of Roman Catholicism as the religion of the majority of the people. Legislation outlawed divorce and contraception. Even as an Irish welfare state began to emerge, the Catholic bishops played a major role in shaping public attitudes and policy. In 1951, for instance, the coalition government proposed a bill for pre- and postnatal health care for mothers and children. The bishops joined the Irish Medical Association in opposing the bill, their grounds being that it might lead to governmental policies on family and sex that were inconsistent with Catholic teaching.

In the latter 1950s, Ireland began to experience a degree of the economic growth and prosperity that swept through the Western world. De Valera in 1959 ascended to the nation's presidency, a nonpolitical position as head of state. His successor as prime minister and leader of Fianna Fáil was Sean Lemass. He committed the government to an extensive plan of economic expansion. Investment, tax incentives, and government direction of the economy were all brought into play. The significance of the government's role in the subsequent economic expansion is debatable, but the extent of growth is not. Production and living standards went up during the 1960s, and unemployment and emigration declined. New factories, housing developments, automobiles, and television became common features of Irish life. At the same time, national attitudes began to open up; the rather stagnant, closed, censorious quality of Irish culture began to break down. Secularization began to erode the authority of the Catholic church and to promote more cosmopolitan values. It was in that spirit of expansion that Ireland applied for, and was accepted to, membership in the European Common Market in 1973. Ireland thus by the 1970s still depended heavily on the British economy, but it had come a long way from the impoverished colony of 1800.

NORTHERN IRELAND: THE TRAGIC PROVINCE UNDER THE STORMONT REGIME

While the Free State was moving toward independence and progress, the province of Northern Ireland was acting out its tragic destiny. From the moment of its creation, Northern Ireland (the six northeastern counties of Ulster) was the scene of division, conflict, and violence. The Protestant majority systematically discriminated against the Catholic minority, who in turn withheld their loyalty from the province. Neither as a society nor as a political unit did Northern Ireland work; hence from the point of view of most observers Northern Ireland was Britain's most grievous failure of the recent past.

Many different explanations have been offered for the problems of Northern Ireland. The religious explanation, for example, is that in Northern Ireland Protestants and Catholics were locked in a religious war like those of the seventeenth century. There is some truth to this view, which explains why *Protestant* and *Catholic* are still useful terms for designating the contending parties. Yet theology is not what was at stake, and the social situation was more complex than a straightforward religious war. Most Catholics in Northern Ireland, for example, were (and are) in the working class, and although there was a substantial Protestant working class, most of the property owners were Protestant. Liberals and socialists tended to view Northern Ireland's conflict in terms of poor economic conditions: develop the economy and raise standards of living, they said, and the conflict would disappear. Again, there was something to this interpretation because unemployment and competition for jobs did aggravate tensions between the communities. But this cannot have been the whole story, for the simple reason that there were many more dimensions to the conflict than economics. Extreme Irish nationalists, including Marxists, blamed British imperialism for the troubles. They said that Britain held on to Northern Ireland for traditional colonialist motives and that if Britain had let the colony go, Northern Ireland would have reunited with the Republic and peace would have reigned. The problem with this interpretation is that the British no longer gained any material advantage from holding Northern Ireland, and the British public was obviously sick of the whole mess; further, the imperial interpretation neglected the majority of the Northern Ireland population, who did not want to be reunited with Ireland. They were (are are) the ones who insist most loudly on keeping the British connection. If the British had abandoned Northern Ireland, there would likely have been a bloodbath, and that was why the British remained.

The problem of Northern Ireland. Anti-Catholic graffiti in Belfast; "UVF" stands for Ulster Volunteer Force, a Protestant paramilitary group.

The official British interpretation was that the conflict arose from the agitation of a relatively few unrealistic and fanatical Irish nationalists, who in turn provoked extremism among Protestant Unionists. They believed that the great majority of people in Northern Ireland, Protestant and Catholics alike, wished to live in peace and prosperity. If the British army and police could eliminate the nationalist terrorists, then over time good sense and mutual trust between Protestants and Catholics would develop, and the nationalist desire to reunite with Ireland would fade away. Unfortunately, this interpretation failed to understand the depth of either Irish nationalist emotion among the Ulster Catholics or anxiety among the Ulster Protestants.

A more plausible interpretation than any of these is that Northern Ireland suffered from a *cultural conflict* (and still does): two cultures had come to exist in Ulster, and each felt threatened by the other. Religion was at the core of these two cultures, but more than religion was involved. Neither culture recognized the other as legitimate. One, that of the one-million-strong majority, was (and is) Protestant, unionist, and British; the other, that of the minority's half-million people was (and is) Catholic, nationalist, and Irish.

How did these two different cultures come to exist in Northern Ireland? It is important to remember that the Northern Ireland Protestants, many of whom are Presbyterians of some variety, descend from the settlers planted in Ulster by the English in the seventeenth century. The Protestant settlers included not only landowners but also tenant farmers and craftsmen. As a result, the Protestant community in Ulster in the twentieth century included both upper-class and working-class people. Many of the settler population by the end of the eighteenth century had come to feel a strong sense of Irish identity, but the events of 1798 frightened them into dependency on the Union and British power. The Home Rule movement of the late nineteenth and early twentieth centuries reinforced their fear of being swallowed up by a Catholic, nationalist Ireland. Hence their "fortress mentality" by 1914 had brought them near civil war. Although they had opposed Home Rule fanatically, they found themselves in possession of a separate Home Rule Parliament in the six most heavily Protestant counties of Ulster in 1920. Thus, the Northern Ireland province was born in conditions of fear and bigotry.

By the 1920s, the Protestants of Northern Ireland tended to be exceedingly narrow and belligerent people. Their two-to-one majority over the Catholics of Northern Ireland gave them little sense of security. As we saw in Chapter 7, they set up a structure of public oppression and private discrimination against the minority, while the British simply looked the other way. The Protestants were Unionists one and all, and they regarded the Catholic minority as subversive of the new province. To an extent, they were right, for the Catholic minority's sympathies lay with the Free State and Irish nationalism. Most Catholics of Northern Ireland did believe that Northern Ireland was an illegitimate province and that the Protestant Unionists were not genuinely Irish. As far as the Protestant Unionists were concerned, this minority disloyalty was made worse by the fact that the Free State (and its successor, the Republic) still claimed theoretical jurisdiction over all of Ulster.

The political and social arrangements of Northern Ireland set in concrete the conflicting cultural identities of the majority and minority. The provincial governmental institutions, which controlled the police, social welfare, education, and economy, were completely dominated by the Protestant Unionists. The so-called Stormont Parliament in 1929 abolished proportional representation, which was supposed to guarantee representation of the Catholic minority. The Unionist party regularly won at least two-thirds of the seats at Stormont and almost all of Northern Ireland's seats in the British Parliament. Local government was monopolized by the Unionists through gerrymandering of constituency boundaries. The Stormont Parliament passed a Special Powers Act in 1922, giving the government extraordinary authority to maintain public order and to put down Irish nationalist activity. The police (the Royal Ulster Constabulary and the B-Specials) were almost exclusively Protestant, as were the judges and magistrates.

Northern Ireland from the outset was a segregated society. One of the few things that Catholics and Protestants could agree on was that there would be no "mixed education." The state schools in the province, therefore, were (and are) almost exclusively Protestant, and Catholic children attended Catholic schools, which were themselves heavily supported by the Ulster government. The curricula of the two school systems—and above all the history taught in them—differed widely. Residential patterns became sharply segregated, partly by personal preference and partly because of Protestant intimidation. Protestants and Catholics came to display a strong sense of territoriality about their neighborhoods. Most marriages took place *within* the two religious groups. Social organizations from clubs to newspapers were entirely separate. Employers tended to hire only their fellow co-religionists, and because most big employers were Protestants this practice discriminated against Catholics. As one prominent Unionist said in 1933: "I would appeal to Loyalists, therefore, to employ good Protestant lads and lasses."

The result of this political and social segregation in Northern Ireland was that Protestants and Catholics developed very different views of themselves and their world. Protestant children learned British history and celebrated British heroes and holidays. Catholic children learned Irish history and drank in a powerful dose of Irish nationalist mythology in which the English are the villains. The Protestant Unionists believed (and still do) that because their ancestors came to Ulster as early as the seventeenth century, they have a right to be there. Further, they often considered themselves to be the only honest, hardworking, loyal part of the population, and that the Catholics were backward, superstitious, and treasonous. Ulster Catholics, on the other hand, identified themselves as Irish nationalists and the Protestant Unionists as British colonists. These different outlooks affected everyday life in Ulster. Every summer, when the Northern Ireland Protestants celebrated the great moments in their history—the anniversaries of the Battle of the Boyne and the relief of the Seige of Londonderry—they insisted on parading through Catholic neighborhoods, pounding their huge Lambeg drums and carrying banners with pictures of William of Orange ("Good King Billy") and Queen Victoria. The Catholic minority had to suffer this annual humiliation in silence, but they asserted their independence by flying the tricolor of the Irish Republic of 1916 at Eastertime.

During the 1950s and 1960s, a growing number of Ulster Catholics began to change their attitudes toward the Northern Ireland province. Partly because of the rise of ecumenism within the Roman Catholic church, and partly because they appreciated the benefits of the British welfare state, many Ulster Catholics began to consider reaching an accommodation with the Northern Ireland government. Many young Catholics had taken the opportunity of attending universities, and this experience widened their horizons. To a degree they were liberated from the mythology of "the Green Flag." Thus, although they did not abandon all hope of reuniting with the Republic, many Ulster Catholics began to think that they could benefit for the time being from winning full rights as citizens of Northern Ireland. They received encouragement in this shift of attitude by Sean Lemass's more flexible approach toward Northern Ireland and the partition of 1921.

Out of this changed atmosphere came the Northern Ireland civil rights movement. Beginning in 1967, civil rights activists marched and demonstrated for equal treatment in politics, employment, and the law. The movement was made up of middle-class people, mostly young men and women, whose political views ranged from liberal to radical socialist. Inspired by the American civil rights crusade, they believed in nonviolent tactics and adopted the American hymn "We Shall Overcome." Reunification with Ireland was not one of their goals, and many of the civil rights marchers had abandoned their childhood religious beliefs. At the same time, many of them, like the charismatic student radical leader Bernadette Devlin, had been raised in the Catholic community and educated in Catholic schools. As the Protestant Unionists instinctively recognized, the attitude toward Protestant Unionism, if not the program of the civil rights marchers, was Irish nationalist, and the Unionists knew that full civil rights for the minority inevitably would spell a reduction of their own power.

The Ulster Protestants reacted irrationally to the civil rights campaign. In 1968–1969, Protestant mobs attacked civil rights marchers and beat them with bricks, stones, and clubs in plain view of the television cameras. The police stood by and watched the mayhem or joined in it themselves. Early in 1969, for instance, a civil rights march from Belfast to Derry (the Catholic name for Londonderry) was broken up with shocking brutality by a Protestant crowd at Burntollet Bridge in Derry. When the Northern Ireland government at last began to grant some civil rights to Catholics, Protestant fanatics like the fundamentalist preacher Ian Paisley nearly went wild. Paisley believed that the civil rights movement was nothing more than a plot to reunite Ireland and subjugate the Ulster Protestants to the pope, who was in his view the Antichrist.

By the summer of 1969, the situation in Northern Ireland was sliding toward continual unbridled violence. In Belfast, people were killed in Protestant-Catholic riots. In Derry, Catholics of the poor Bogside neighborhood battled the police for three days. Finally, in August 1969, Wilson's Labour government sent the British army into Northern Ireland to restore the peace and to keep the Protestants and Catholics apart. The Catholic community welcomed the army as their defenders against the Protestant majority and their oppressive police force. Unfortunately, the arrival of the army coincided with the revival of the Irish Republican Army (IRA).

The IRA from 1921 had refused to accept the legitimacy of Northern Ireland. They believed in the continued mystical existence of the Irish Republic established at Easter 1916, and they believed that they were the rightful army of that sacred republic. To the extent that the Free State and the later Republic accepted in practice the partition of Ireland, the IRA regarded them as traitors. From time to time, the IRA had staged guerrilla war in Northern Ireland, but the Stormont government was too strong for them. Their latest campaign, from 1956 to 1962, had won little support from the Ulster Catholics. In the 1960s the IRA became more Marxist and focused on social and political grievances. When the Protestant mobs attacked the civil rights marchers and Catholic neighborhoods, the IRA was in no position to defend them. The bitter joke, which appeared as graffiti on Belfast walls, was that IRA stood for "I ran away."

In December 1969, the IRA split, and one faction renewed the old campaign of violence on behalf of Irish nationalism, abolition of the partition, and reunification of Ulster with Ireland. These IRA men, the "Provisionals," thought that the social and political posture of the IRA in the 1960s had been a mistake, for the real heritage of Irish nationalism stretching back to Wolfe Tone was simply to fight for an independent Ireland. The others, the "Officials," stood by the IRA policies of the 1960s, arguing that all of Ireland would have to become socialist before it could genuinely be free. Drawing on the support of the beleaguered Northern Irish Catholic community, the Provisional IRA began a savage campaign of shootings and bombings against the British army, the Ulster police, and Protestant paramilitary organizations.

The struggle in Northern Ireland rapidly escalated. Murder, assassinations, bombings, and "knee-cappings" (shooting victims in the knees) became the order of the day, as did death tolls of nonparticipants caught in the struggle. Many people in the Catholic community soon turned against the British army because the troops were enforcing laws that had been made by the Protestant majority and because the troops tried to flush the IRA out of its nests among the Catholic population. In July 1971, army troops killed two young Catholics in Derry, and when the Stormont government refused to investigate, the small delegation of Catholic representatives in the Stormont Parliament withdrew. Then in August 1971, the army and police began the tactics of "internment"—arrest and imprisonment without trial of IRA suspects and sympathizers. Internment camps were set up, and army and police officials apparently tortured some prisoners to get information. In August 1972, British troops fired on protestors demonstrating against internment; fourteen people were killed. This sealed the fate of the Stormont government, which plainly could neither maintain order nor claim the confidence of the Catholic community. In 1972, the British government suspended the Northern Ireland government and established direct rule of the province from London.

NORTHERN IRELAND UNDER DIRECT RULE, 1972–1989

The British now presided over a vicious three-sided war in Northern Ireland. On the first side was the British army, working with the police (organized in two overwhelmingly Protestant units, the Royal Ulster Constabulary and the Ulster Defence Regiment, the B-Specials having been disbanded), supposedly as a neutral force keeping the Ulster Protestants and Catholics from slaughtering each other. Increasingly, however, the army was drawn to the side of the Protestant majority. On the second side was the Provisional IRA and splinter groups like the Irish National Liberation Army (INLA). These guerrilla forces were, of course, illegal, but they had a legal front in the Ulster branch of the old Sinn Fein party. On the third side were the paramilitary forces of the Ulster Unionists—most notably, the Ulster Defence Association and the Ulster Volunteer Force (UVF). These Unionist forces were closely connected with the Unionist party and the Orange Lodges, and they often benefitted from official British Army intelligence, though this collusion was not known at the time. The spirit of this conflict was well expressed in a UVF declaration of 1966; "From this day we declare war against the IRA and its splinter groups. Known IRA men will be executed mercilessly and without hesitation." The violence inevitably spilled over to civilians thought to be sympathetic to one side or another—and to innocent bystanders as bombs went off in pubs and shopping districts. Between 1969 and mid-1976, over 1,500 people were killed in Northern Ireland, and between 1976 and 1989 some 1,500 more.

The British goal remained what it had long been: to get Irish troubles off the British political agenda. Throughout the period, therefore, the British hoped that conditions would improve so as to allow them to restore "devolved" government to Northern Ireland. But the British government now realized that devolution in Ulster would require that the Catholic minority have a voice in any provincial government. "Power sharing" became the accepted principle. Some moderates in the Catholic community, including the main opposition party, the Social Democratic and Labour Party (SDLP), approved of power sharing, but the IRA and most of the Protestant majority opposed it. The British pressed on with their plans, and during a lull in the fighting in 1974, they won agreement from moderate Protestants and Catholics to a power-sharing executive council for Northern Ireland. This was the Sunningdale Agreement. The council, which included representatives of the Catholic minority, was set up in January 1974; however, it amounted to only a temporary triumph of hope over reality. In the spring of 1974 a massive strike by militant Protestant trade unionists, supported by fanatics like Paisley, brought the council and the Sunningdale Agreement down. Direct rule was reestablished.

The horrors of the terrorist war continued. The IRA at some moments tried to extend the violence into England, hoping to force the British public to decide that keeping Northern Ireland was not worth the effort. In 1974, an IRA bomb blew up a pub in Guildford, killing five and wounding fifty-four, and then bombs killed twenty-one people in Birmingham pubs. In May 1979, the Conservative party spokesman on Northern Ireland, Airey Neave, was assassinated in the House of Commons parking lot; in that same year Earl Mountbatten, who had been Britain's last viceroy of India, was blown up on his yacht at Sligo. Shoppers as well as troopers of the Horse Guards were killed in London. In the summer of 1984, a terrorist bomb destroyed the Grand Hotel in Brighton, where the Conservative party was meeting, narrowly failing to kill the prime minister, Margaret Thatcher.

As we will see in Chapter 14, Thatcher has proved to be one of the most resolute and forceful prime ministers of the twentieth century. She was implacable in her opposition to Sinn Fein and the IRA. In 1981, for instance, she stubbornly refused to give in to a hunger strike staged by IRA and INLA prisoners in Belfast. These prisoners were demanding that they be treated as *political* prisoners rather than as criminals. They refused to eat until the British government changed their status. The first of the hunger strikers, Bobby Sands, died in May 1981, after going sixty-six days without food. By August of 1981, nine more hunger strikers had died. Despite immense pressure from British public opinion, Thatcher and her government stood firm and let the strikers die one by one. The IRA and INLA called off the strike. Yet it was Thatcher who went further than any previous postwar British prime minister toward reaching a settlement with Irish nationalism over Northern Ireland.

To understand the developments of the 1980s in Northern Ireland, one must realize that the Irish Republic itself became more hostile to the activities of the IRA. The government and people of the Republic were sympathetic to the Northern Ireland civil rights movement, and the traditional Irish desire for an end to the partition of Ireland resulted in support for the IRA in the early 1970s. Some Fianna Fáil leaders engaged in gunrunning to the IRA in 1970. But as the IRA violence spread into the Republic itself, with bomb blasts in Dublin and elsewhere, the Irish government turned against the IRA. It adopted strong antiterrorist legislation and imprisoned known IRA activists. In 1972 the Republic also tried to make itself less threatening to the Ulster Protestants by removing from the constitution Article 44, which gave special status to the Catholic church. By 1980 the Republic had admitted officially that Northern Ireland *is* after all a province of Britain and that although reunification remains the ultimate goal, it can occur only by *persuasion* of the Northern Ireland majority, not by force. Thus, the government of the Republic was increasingly willing to cooperate with the British in putting down IRA violence.

In that spirit, the Irish government reached an agreement with Thatcher over Northern Ireland. The first steps in this direction were taken by the Irish leader Charles Haughey, who ironically had been dismissed from the Irish cabinet in 1970 in the gunrunning scandal. Haughey met with Thatcher in a historic summit. It came to little in practical terms, but Haughey pledged that the goal of the Irish government was to obtain unification of Ireland "by agreement and in peace." He accepted that "any change of the constitutional status of Northern Ireland would only come about with the consent of a majority of the people of Northern Ireland." In 1983, a new Irish prime minister, Dr. Garrett Fitzgerald, who had long wished for peaceful reconciliation between Northern Ireland and the Republic, set up the New Ireland Forum. This was to be a conference of all constitutional parties, north and south, to consider ways of achieving that reconciliation. Neither the militant Irish nationalists nor the Unionists attended; however, the representatives of the other parties to the New Ireland Forum gave fresh and open consideration to various possible solutions to the Northern Ireland problem. The New Ireland Forum reported in favor of reunification, but one that recognized the rights of the Northern Ireland majority.

Although the British government received the recommendations of the New Ireland Forum coolly, the report nevertheless improved the atmosphere of Anglo-Irish relations. Out of this atmosphere came an agreement in 1985 that proved to be a most hopeful development for Northern Ireland. Prime Minister Thatcher wanted the Irish to agree to strengthened security arrangements in and for Northern Ireland. Fitzgerald in turn wanted British agreement to a plan for shared sovereignty in Northern Ireland, whereby Ulster Catholics would have a sense that their interests are recognized. Both sides got some of what they wanted in the Hillsborough Agreement of November 1985. This treaty between Britain and Ireland had five main points: (1) it acknowledged British sovereignty over Northern Ireland; (2) it declared that any change in Northern Ireland's status would come only when a majority in Northern Ireland so desired; (3) it acknowledged the existence of *two* cultures in Northern Ireland, the Catholic nationalist and the Protestant unionist; (4) it recognized the need to reconcile these two communities; and (5) it established a continuing "Intergovernmental Conference," with representatives from both Britain and Ireland, to advise both states as to matters of law enforcement, justice, culture exchanges, and the like.

The Hillsborough Agreement was not a solution to the Northern Ireland problem, but it was a step in that direction. Both the IRA and the militant Ulster Unionists, who wanted no reconciliation but victory over the other side, denounced the Agreement. Yet they were not able to force Britain and Ireland to abandon it, either by terrorism or by strikes. The best hope was that the Hillsborough Agreement would provide a framework in which trust between Ulster Protestants and Catholics would develop. If it did, the "sea" that supports the fanatical and violent "fish" would dry up. No student of Protestant-Catholic relations in Ireland had much reason to be confident, but it was conceivable, at least, that over time (and perhaps a very long time) the Agreement would lead to a peaceful reunification of the tragic province of Ulster with the rest of Ireland. As we shall see, the Hillsborough Agreement did lay the foundation for further steps towards peace in Northern Ireland.

Suggested Reading

Bowman, John, *De Valera and the Ulster Question, 1917–73* (Oxford: Clarendon Press, 1982).

Burk, Kathleen, *The British Isles since 1945* (New York: Oxford University Press, 2003).

Darby, John, *Conflict in Northern Ireland* (Dublin: Gill & Macmillan, 1976).

Devine, T. M., *The Scottish Nation: A History, 1700–2000* (New York: Viking, 1999).

Dickson, Anthony, and James H. Treble, eds., *People and Society in Scotland, vol. 3, 1914–1990* (Edinburgh: John Donald Publishers, 1992).

Donaldson, Gordon, *Scotland: The Shaping of a Nation* (Newton Abbot: David & Charles, 1974).

Elliott, Marianne, *The Catholics of Ulster* (London: Penguin Press, 2000).

English, Richard, *Armed Struggle: The History of the IRA* (New York: Oxford University Press, 2004).

Finley, Richard, J., *Independent and Free: Scottish Politics and the Origin of the Scottish National Party, 1931–1945* (Edinburgh: John Donald Publishers, 1994).

———, *Partnership for Good? Scottish Politics and the Union Since 1880* (Edinburgh: John Donald Publishers, 1997).

Hamill, Desmond, *Pig in the Middle: The Army in Northern Ireland, 1969–1985* (London: Methuen, 1985).

Hanham, H. J., *Scottish Nationalism* (Cambridge, Mass.: Harvard University Press, 1969).

Harvie, Christopher, *No Gods and Precious Few Heroes: Scotland, 1914–1980* (Toronto: University of Toronto Press, 1981).

———, *Scotland and Nationalism* (London: Allen & Unwin, 1977).

Kenny, Anthony, *The Road to Hillsborough* (Oxford: Pergamon Press, 1986).

Kinealy, Christine, *A Disunited Kingdom: England, Ireland, Scotland, and Wales, 1800–1949* (Cambridge: Cambridge University Press, 1999).

Lee, Joseph, *Ireland, 1912–1985: Politics and Society* (Cambridge: Cambridge University Press, 1989).

Lenman, Bruce, *An Economic History of Scotland, 1660–1976* (Hamden, Conn.: Archon Books, 1977).

Moloney, Ed, *A Secret History of the IRA* (New York: W. W. Norton, 2003).

Morgan, Kenneth O., *Rebirth of a Nation: Wales, 1880–1980* (New York: Oxford University Press, 1981).

Murphy, John A., *Ireland in the Twentieth Century* (Dublin: Gill & Macmillan, 1975).

O'Brien, Conor Cruise, *States of Ireland* (London: Hutchinson, 1972).

Osmond, John, ed., *The National Question Again: Welsh Political Identity in the 1980's* (Llandysul, Dyfed: Gomer Press, 1985).

Ruane, Joseph, and Jennifer Todd, *The Dynamics of Conflict in Northern Ireland: Power, Conflict, and Emancipation* (New York: Cambridge University Press, 1996).

Williams, Glyn, ed., *Crisis of Economy and Ideology: Essays on Welsh Society, 1840–1980* (Bangor: S.S.R.C.: B.S.A. Sociology of Wales Study Group, 1983).

Williams, Gwyn A., *When Was Wales?* (London: Black Raven Press, 1985).

Wilson, Andrew J., *Irish America and the Ulster Conflict, 1968–1995* (Belfast: Blackstaff, 1996).

Chapter 14

Thatcher's Britain, 1970–1990

The struggle over nationality and devolution in each of the Celtic countries has its own history, but together these histories make up part of another story: the breakup of the post–World War II consensus. As we have seen, the consensus consisted of public agreement on full employment, a welfare state, nationalization of some industries, and government direction of the mixed economy by Keynesian techniques. In the years after 1970, the consensus was destroyed by Britain's relatively poor economic performance, rising inflation, and growing conflict in industrial relations. Politics became polarized as Labour moved to the left, the Conservatives moved to the right, and the third parties emerged to fill the gap and to express popular frustration with the course of affairs. The chief political beneficiary of the ending of consensus was Margaret Thatcher, who was herself an adamant opponent of consensus. She became prime minister in 1979, the first woman premier in British history. By dint of her strong ideas and personality and her eleven consecutive years in office, she put her stamp on the nation more firmly than any peacetime prime minister in the twentieth century.

ECONOMIC TROUBLES AND INDUSTRIAL STRIFE IN THE 1970S

The long story of Britain's comparative economic decline continued through the 1970s. Indeed, the rate of comparative decline worsened as a number of troublesome problems deepened. For many decades the British had failed both to invest enough capital in industry and to increase productivity sufficiently from each unit of capital invested. Poor management, restrictive trade unions, and antagonistic labor relations were the prime culprits. In the 1970s, therefore, the British economy grew less rapidly than the other main industrial powers:

Table 14.1: Annual Growth Rates as Percentages, 1973–1977

Great Britain	1.9
West Germany	2.3
France	3.4
Japan	4.1
Italy	3.0

This relatively poor record of economic growth in the 1970s was the root cause of a number of unfavorable economic trends, each of which became a crucial political problem. Britain's share of world trade continued to fall. By 1975, for instance, Britain accounted for only 9.3 percent of the world's exports in manufactured goods. Britain's balance of payments was troublesome, for the British failed to export as much in visible goods as they imported in every year except 1971. Moreover, from 1973 on, the British had an *overall* payments deficit of visible and invisible goods and services, for their earnings on invisibles like international finance and insurance could not make up the gap between imports and exports of tangible goods. Inflation, which was driven in large part by the rising cost of imports, and above all by the skyrocketing price of oil imports after the Middle Eastern war of 1973, now became a serious problem. Retail prices had increased at a moderate rate in the 1960s, but between 1970 and 1974 they went up 9 percent annually, and between 1974 and 1979 the rate leapt upward to 15 percent a year.

The faltering of the British economy in the world's markets and the alarming inflation of prices caused severe unemployment for the first time since 1940 and an escalation of strikes. As the British lost out in global competition, many industrial firms either cut production or went out of business. The rate of unemployment, which had stood below 3 percent in the 1950s and 1960s, now climbed to 7 percent between 1974 and 1979. Rising prices plus rising unemployment made up a formula for rapidly worsening industrial relations. Workers sought to keep manning levels high and to raise wages in order to keep up with prices; managers resisted the workers' demands in order to keep manufacturing costs down. Strikes became more frequent and lasted longer than in the 1950s and 1960s. In the 1970s, the number of workdays lost because of strikes in industry tripled over the previous decade. Between 1973 and 1977, the British record in industrial work stoppages was worse than that of any other major industrial nation except the United States. The British rate of days lost per worker, for example, was twenty-five times as bad as the West German.

By the late 1970s, the British economy had reached a situation that most economists had regarded as impossible: "stagflation." This was a condition in which economic growth was stagnant and unemployment was high, yet inflation was rising. Stagflation created an atmosphere of crisis. It heated up the debate in Britain about the causes of the "British disease." As economists, politicians, businessmen, and trade unionists flung accusations at each other, the postwar consensus unraveled. British politics tended to become more ideological than usual. Scottish and Welsh nationalists, as we have seen, pushed their own claims, and Northern Ireland became locked in a bitter war of terror and counterterror. Britain appeared to many observers to be "ungovernable." These were the conditions in which successive British governments had to operate.

THE HEATH GOVERNMENT, 1970–1974

The general election of 1970, which revealed the first signs of the decline of consensus, brought to power the Conservatives under Edward Heath. A self-made man devoted to industriousness and efficiency, Heath was determined to reverse the unfavorable trends in Britain's economy and society. He hoped to make Britain into a more competitive, hustling nation like the United States. He proclaimed that his government had been "returned to office to change the course and the history of the nation." Heath spoke for a grass-roots turn inside Conservative circles against the Butskellite policies of the 1950s and 1960s; thus he wanted to reduce government intervention in the economy and to reemphasize capitalist enterprise. Yet Heath was not a full-fledged member of the Conservative party's right wing. He believed, as had Macmillan, that capitalism did indeed have an "unpleasant and unacceptable face" that had to be softened. Above all Heath wanted to lead Britain into the Common Market, which the Conservative right resisted. The question was whether Heath would be able to carry out all his goals simultaneously amid deteriorating economic conditions.

In his first two years in office, Heath pursued what has come to be called "neo-capitalist" policies. He sought to open up opportunities in the economy for talent and enterprise, not least by reducing taxes, and he tried to restore the competitive edge to British industry by withholding subsidies for failing companies. He denied that the state has a valid role in determining wages and prices. The Heath government, therefore, sold off some nationalized industries, such as the hotels owned by British Rail, and it abolished Wilson's price and incomes machinery, the National Board for Prices and Incomes.

Heath also sought to reform trade union law to make the unions responsible for their contractual agreements. In order to bring the unions under control, the Heath government attempted to redefine their legal standing. That standing had been established essentially in the years before the First World War, when the unions won immunity from suits brought by employers to recover damages caused by unionists' strikes or other industrial action. Likewise, the unions enjoyed the right to set their own rules of operation, including their procedures for calling strikes. Heath's legislation, the Industrial Relations Act of 1971, had a number of important and controversial features. First, it required all unions to register with the government if they wanted to keep their legal immunities. Second, registered unions had to change their rules to make elected officers responsible for strikes, and the act encouraged union-wide votes before a strike could be called. Third, it made sympathetic strikes illegal, as well as any strike that sought to alter a contracted work agreement. Fourth, it set up a National Industrial Relations Court to enforce the act. The new law was extremely unpopular with the trade unions, some of which went on strike or demonstrated against it. The act in the end was not on the books long enough to transform British industrial relations, but it soured the attitude of the workers against the Heath government and roused their antagonism to its efforts to hold down pay increases.

Heath's intention of moving away from these aspects of the prevailing consensus toward a revitalized free enterprise soon was stymied. As early as 1971, for example, the government found that the aeronautical division of Rolls Royce, which manufactured jet engines, had to be nationalized in order to keep it from collapsing. Then, in 1972, the coal miners went on strike for higher pay. Heath believed that the miners' wage claim was inflationary and therefore rejected it. A court of inquiry, which had been appointed by Heath because of the severe consequences of the strike, ruled in favor of the miners. Heath then began negotiations with the TUC in hopes of persuading the unions to moderate both their wage demands and their opposition to the National Industrial Relations Act. When these talks failed, Heath believed that he had no choice but to resort to legislation controlling prices and wages. This decision represented a "U-Turn," as it was called, in Heath's policy, for it showed that the neocapitalist approach was in shambles. Prices were going up, the unions were defying the government, and the government was intervening once again to keep companies afloat.

Following his new path, Heath enacted a bill that established a "Prices and Pay Code." It created a state council to rule on all claims for both wage and price increases. Although such a council might in theory seem rational, in fact it involved the government in the nightmarish task of distinguishing fair claims for wage increases from unfair ones, and it set Heath on the road to direct confrontation with the unions. This was to be his undoing.

Meanwhile, Heath had pressed on with his ideal of gaining British entry into the Common Market. As he had written some years earlier, he believed that only membership in the EC could make Britain efficient and competitive once again:

> We must pursue a policy which will enable Britain to become a member of an enlarged European Community. Technological advance is making nonsense of national boundaries. Britain's future lies in a larger grouping and that grouping should be the Europe of which the Common Market is already the nucleus.

The right wing of the Conservative party, led by Enoch Powell, opposed Heath on the Common Market, on a variety of practical and emotional grounds. The Labour left had always opposed entry, and now the party as a whole opposed Heath, even though Wilson's government had applied for membership in 1967. Labour attempted to keep a figleaf of integrity over this obvious inconsistency by focusing on the particular terms on which the Conservatives were seeking entry. Labour in addition demanded a referendum on the issue. Despite this opposition, Heath carried a Commons resolution favoring entry in 1971 and embarked on negotiations with the EC countries.

This time the British application was not to be denied. General de Gaulle had resigned the presidency of France in 1969, and his successor, Georges Pompidou, put up no major obstacles. The British, however, were forced to join on terms that, as we will soon see, favored the agricultural countries of the Continent. Britain officially signed the EC Treaty in January 1972 and became a member on January 1, 1973. Although membership in the Common Market did not immediately transform the British economy or convert the average provincial Briton into a worldly European, entry into the Common Market was one of the most significant events in modern British history. It symbolized the turn of Britain away from its traditional role as a world power, away from empire and Commonwealth, and away from the "special relationship" with the United States. It symbolized acceptance by the British of their new status—that of an ordinary European state.

Entry into the EC was Heath's one major victory. His moment of triumph did not last long, for the oil crisis resulting from the Arab-Israeli war began in October 1973. The OPEC countries began cutting oil production in order to raise world oil prices and so to force Britain and the other Western nations to abandon their support for Israel. Britain imported two-thirds of its oil from the Middle East and therefore suffered severely from the more than threefold increase in the cost of oil imports. A world wide recession swallowed the British economy, and inflation, already a serious problem, became acute.

British coal miners chose this moment of crisis to demand higher wages. As we saw in the cases of Wales and Scotland, British coal mining had been a declining industry for more than half a century. The industry had contracted after World War II, so that by the 1970s there were only 270,000 miners in Britain, compared to almost a million before World War I. Their wages were low relative to other skilled workers, and mining remained tough and dangerous work. As old mining communities withered and died, miners' morale sank and their militancy rose. For instance, the vice chairman of the National Union of Miners (NUM), Mick McGahey, was a communist. Indeed, while the Heath government was desperately fighting inflation, a number of unions were turning to militant leaders and to strikes for higher pay. For their part, the coal miners in 1973 realized that with oil prices going through the ceiling, Britain needed all the coal they could produce. They began to press for higher wages in October 1973 by banning overtime work. Heath responded by declaring a three-day work week in order to conserve electricity. In February 1974, the miners went on strike—the most serious industrial conflict since 1926.

Many Conservatives wanted to have a confrontation with the miners on the question of "Who rules Britain?" These Tories had decided with an increasing sense of urgency over the years that the unions were wrecking British industry and thwarting the government's efforts to stop inflation. On the other hand, the former prime minister, Macmillan, warned the Heath government that it was unwise "to take on the Vatican, the Brigade of Guards or the NUM." The bloody-minded Conservatives won this debate and persuaded Heath to call a general election for the end of February. The Conservatives thus sought from the electorate a mandate for strong government and an end of union power to influence political decisions. Labour shrewdly emphasized not who was to govern Britain but the cold facts of inflation, the balance of payments, and unemployment. The voters showed that they preferred to avoid confrontation. Labour won 301 seats to the Conservatives' 296. Perhaps most significant was the general unhappiness with both major parties: the Liberals, Plaid Cymru, the SNP, and the Ulster Unionist all took votes from the Conservatives and Labourites, who between them won only 75 percent of the total.

Heath was thus driven from office in a humiliating defeat. He had led Britain into Europe, but otherwise his government had not been a success. After his party in October lost a second general election in the same year of 1974, many Conservatives became restless with Heath's leadership. Early in 1975, he submitted to a vote of the parliamentary Conservative party. Those anxious for his departure cast about for a candidate to run against him, but none of the likely successors wanted to be seen as disloyal to the party leader. The person who stepped forward was Margaret Thatcher, who had served in Heath's cabinet as minister for education but was not regarded as ranking among the party's top leaders. She was expected to win enough votes to persuade Heath to step down and then stand aside for someone else. Thatcher, however, quickly impressed party backbenchers with her forthrightness and right-wing ideology, and she not only defeated Heath but also won the party leadership for herself. The Conservatives, the party of old-fashioned values, thus were the first major British party to have a woman as leader—a step made easier for them by the fact that she was not herself a feminist. Thatcher was to lead the Conservative party aggressively in the direction that Heath had taken initially but then turned away from.

THE LABOUR GOVERNMENTS, 1974–1979

Labour meanwhile made an inept attempt to restore the consensus. Following the general election of February 1974, Harold Wilson became prime minister for the second time. He led a minority government and won a small majority in the second election of 1974. Wilson remained in office until 1976, when he retired from office, apparently from weariness he felt in the face of Britain's seemingly intractable economic and social problems. His successor, James Callaghan, essentially continued Wilson's policies until 1979, when his government was defeated on a vote of confidence in the House of Commons. The Wilson and Callaghan governments alike tried to lead from the center of the Labour party; in failing they were a source of grave frustration to the party as a whole.

Perhaps Wilson's most important achievement in 1974–1975 was to avoid splitting his party over the issue of Britain's membership in the European Economic Community, as the Common Market was now called. Wilson had favored entry in 1967 but followed his party in opposing Heath's application in 1971. Wilson's strategy in 1971 was to focus on the *terms* of the British membership and to promise that in office he would renegotiate the terms. He also pledged to hold a referendum on British membership with the renegotiated terms. The areas for renegotiation were the EC's agricultural policy, Britain's relationships with Commonwealth countries, and Britain's contribution to the EC budget. During 1974, Wilson's foreign secretary won some modest concessions from the other EC states, enough to be able to claim that the terms were now favorable to Britain. After a spirited public debate, the promised referendum took place in June 1975. Although the voter turnout was light, the pro-EC position won by a two-to-one majority in the first referendum in British history.

Meanwhile, the Labour government was beset by the increasingly critical problems of low productivity, inflation, rising unemployment, and antagonistic industrial relations. Toward the end of his first administration, Wilson had adopted the idea of the "social contract" with the trade unions. By this vague notion, the unions pledged to moderate their wage claims in return for the government's promise to improve welfare programs and to promote "industrial democracy"—that is, workers' influence in running their industries. The social contract was an attempt to restore the postwar consensus and to formalize the process of consulting with the unions that had been a prominent part of it. Once Wilson was back in office after 1974, the social contract came to little. Wilson repealed Heath's Industrial Relations Act and gave up the Tories' income controls; further, Wilson settled the coal strike on the miners' terms and restored industrial peace. Soon, however, wages were going up faster even than prices, which themselves approached a 20 percent annual inflation rate. Naturally the trade deficit worsened, and pressure on sterling grew. Wilson's cabinet was forced to cut government spending, including social services.

To deal with industrial inefficiency and the shortage of investment, Wilson's government set up the National Enterprise Board (NEB). This was a state corporation to lend money to failing industries and acquire some companies outright. Instead of pursuing a long-range industrial investment program, however, the NEB spent its funds mainly in bailing out sick companies like British Leyland (the largest British-owned car manufacturer) and British Chrysler. British investment per employee remained one-third that of West Germany and one-fourth that of Japan. The best that can be said of the NEB is that it kept a number of companies afloat and prevented unemployment from becoming worse than it was. When he retired from office, Wilson was under savage attack from the British press, which saw him as a clever operator with no principles.

Wilson's successor, James Callaghan, represented the center and right of the Labour party. An able and experienced administrator, "Sunny Jim" Callaghan was above all a politician. He was more popular than Wilson with the rank and file of the party, whose loyalty he carefully cultivated. Callaghan reached an agreement with the Liberals in Parliament to shore up Labour's thin majority: the Labour government promised to consult with the Liberals in return for their support in the House of Commons. This "Lib-Lab" pact enabled Callaghan to sustain Labour's parliamentary edge while fighting the pressures of sterling crises, increases in unemployment, and union demands for higher wages. But the Lib-Lab arrangement confirmed the moderation of Callaghan's government. By 1979, militants in the unions and in the left wing of the Labour party were angry with the government's inability to reduce the gap between rich and poor in Britain, with its unwillingness to embark on a thoroughgoing campaign of nationalization of industry, and with its disinclination to abandon nuclear arms unilaterally. The left also remained unhappy over Britain's membership in the EC. By the end of 1978, union patience with the social contract had run out, and a series of unions struck for higher pay and won. Inflation surged upward again. Thus, when Callaghan lost a vote of confidence in March 1979 and resorted to a general election, the Labour left was disaffected, and the public was restless. The result was a decisive defeat for Labour, which won only 269 against the Tories' 339, the Liberals' 11, the SNP's 2, and the Welsh Nationalists' 2.

Prime Minister Margaret Thatcher. The first woman prime minister in Britain, Thatcher held office from 1979 to 1990—longer than any other prime minister of the twentieth century.

THATCHER IN POWER

The election of 1979 brought to power an outspoken opponent of the postwar consensus, Margaret Thatcher. "For me," she once announced, "consensus seems to be the process of abandoning all beliefs, principles, values and policies." To her mind, the Age of Consensus included permissiveness as well as compromise. In place of full employment, the mixed economy, the welfare state, and conciliation of the trade unions, Thatcher advocated, in the words of one historian, "markets, monetarism, and authoritative government."* To be sure, Thatcher could never have defeated the consensus by herself; the nation's revulsion from stagflation was necessary both to put her in office and to mobilize opinion in her favor. Nevertheless, her combative leadership had an immense impact, for better or for worse, in ending the consensus and altering the framework of politics and society.

Thatcher's policies derived from the combined influences of her family background and certain neo-right intellectuals. Born (1925) in the small market town of Grantham, the daughter of a grocer and ardent Methodist, Thatcher believed in ordinary middle-class values: the self-made person, individualism, and conventional morality. She won a scholarship to Oxford, graduated with a degree in chemistry, became a lawyer, and went into politics—showing remarkable determination and industriousness every step of the way. Despite her careers as a barrister and rising Conservative politician, she insisted on maintaining her role as wife and mother in a traditional family. Even as prime minister she rose early to fix breakfast for her

---

*Dennis Kavanagh, *Thatcherism and British Politics: The End of Consensus?* (Oxford: Oxford University Press, 1987), 2.

husband. She also brought to politics a belief in ideas. Not for her were the customary British ways of compromise and "muddling through." She was first attracted to the ideas of Enoch Powell, who had advocated control of immigration into Britain and a return to free-market, laissez-faire policies as early as the 1960s. Similarly, Thatcher, like many young Conservatives, became a disciple of two other free-market economists in the 1970s—the Austrian expatriate Friedrich A. Hayek and the American academic Milton Friedman, both of whom advocated monetarism as opposed to Keynesian policies. These two intellectuals inspired a bevy of Conservative think tanks that sprang up, and they influenced the British industrialist and politician Sir Keith Joseph, who was Thatcher's patron. Thatcher was, therefore, both a beneficiary of and participant in a swing to the right in Tory politics and ideas that began in the 1960s and gathered steam in the 1970s.

Thatcher believed in individual self-reliance, but she also advocated social order and strong government in the areas in which she thought that government has a proper role to play: national defense, law and order, and public morality. She was forced to cut defense spending on conventional forces, including the Royal Navy; nevertheless she insisted on maintaining Britain's independent nuclear deterrence by purchasing Trident submarines from the United States. Furthermore, she supported the American policy of installing medium-range and cruise missiles in Europe, even though she faced strenuous opposition from a revived CND, which demonstrated outside American missile bases in England. As for law and order, Thatcher was not able to persuade Parliament to restore the death penalty, nor did she roll back the increase in the crime rate. However, she supported a major buildup in the size of the national police force to 115,000 men and women. She encouraged the development of a nationwide police computer network, which some critics regarded as a threat to civil liberties. Along the same line, she forbade certain intelligence installations to be unionized and attempted to suppress publication of *Spycatcher*, the memoirs of one former intelligence officer. She sponsored the expansion of the scope of Britain's law controlling national security, the Official Secrets Act. Moreover, in what was to her a related matter, her government passed the British Nationality Act of 1981 to control immigration of former Commonwealth citizens into Britain. This act rejected the principle established in 1948 that all citizens of the Commonwealth enjoy British citizenship. In these ways, as well as her tendency to lecture people on their behavior, Thatcher sponsored the development of what her critics called a "nanny state."

Thatcher did not think that the government can play an effective part in directing the economy. To her way of thinking, the only valid economic tool of government is control of the money supply. As a *monetarist*, then, Thatcher believed that the nation's chief problem, inflation, could be defeated by restriction of the amount of money in circulation. As an advocate of free enterprise, she believed in *privatization* (selling off nationalized industries) and in cutting back the welfare state. She reduced income tax rates, especially for the well-to-do. She attempted to limit expenditures by local government authorities and replaced the traditional local rates (property taxes) with an extremely unpopular poll tax (head tax). Finally, she believed in curtailing the power of the trade unions, both because the unions have no right to legal privileges that allow them to behave irresponsibly and because their power to win high wage claims was destroying British industry. Taken together, these elements of "Thatcherism" represented the triumph of the middle-class business wing over the traditional, paternalist, landed gentlemen in the Conservative party.

Thatcher's political style was almost as important as her ideas. From her earliest days as prime minister, she adopted a very aggressive stance in the cabinet, the House of Commons, and the nation. She knew her own mind and did not hesitate to scold her colleagues or the public. She was quick to judge her fellow Conservatives as to whether they were *for* her neocapitalism (the "Drys") or *against* (the more paternalistic "Wets"). Though extremely articulate, she sometimes became overbearing and bullying in her speeches. She never enjoyed the great personal popularity of, say, a Churchill or a Macmillan. Opponents never tired of calling her names like "Attila the Hen," "the Iron Lady," and "the Abominable Hairdo." Nevertheless, she won respect and support from a large segment of the British public because of her resolution in trying to reverse what she regarded as Britain's disastrous march into socialism and into the second or third rank as an international power.

The record of Thatcher's government was mixed. In regard to welfare, she was not able to stop the overall growth of social expenditure. To be sure, her government made cuts in particular programs like old-age pension, public housing, and education. Her 20 percent cut in funding for the universities roused great opposition from the academics, a large number of whom denounced her for "anti-intellectualism" as they departed for higher-paying jobs in the United States. But Thatcher did not touch the core of pensions or the essentials of the National Health Service, which are highly popular programs, and spending on unemployment insurance went up as unemployment jumped up first to two million and then to three million. In general, most observers said that Thatcherism brought a certain shabbiness and stinginess to public services in Britain but not destruction of the welfare state.

In privatizing industry, Thatcher made more headway. The Thatcherites believed that state-run industries were inefficient and that the nation's economy ought to depend on free enterprise once more. As one Tory said of nationalized industries in 1982: "Look, we're bloody fed up with them. They make huge losses, they have bolshie unions, and they are feather-bedded." The Thatcher government, therefore, sold off many nationalized companies and even whole industries. These included British Petroleum, British Aerospace, Jaguar, and British Telecom. In a related move, the government encouraged renters of public council houses to buy their homes. More than a million did so. Privatization reduced the nationalized industries' share of the economy from 10 percent to 6 percent of the GDP. It also raised billions in cash, which the government used to balance the national budget. This windfall profit from the sale of public assets, plus earnings from North Sea oil, gave Britain a surplus in the national budget in the 1980s and temporarily ended the perennial balance of payments crises.

The Thatcher government also had a major impact on industrial relations. Pervious governments, as we have seen, came to the conclusion that the trade unions had to be brought under control, but they were not able to make their efforts stick. Once Labour's "social contract" had collapsed, many Conservatives were determined to limit closed shops, eliminate unofficial strikes, stop sympathetic strikes, and prevent picketing of companies not directly involved in a given dispute. In Employment Acts of 1980 and 1982, and the Trade Union Act of 1984, the Thatcher government passed a number of reforms: (1) restricting picketing to the strikers' place of work; (2) making unions liable for damages done in unlawful strikes; (3) providing that a closed shop must be approved by four-fifths of the workers in the company; and (4) requiring a prestrike vote before any industrial action. In addition, Thatcher refused to intervene to settle strikes, for she insisted that employers and employees take responsibility for, and the consequences of, their agreements. This way, she expected that employers would be tougher in resisting wage demands.

Thatcher's legislation helped break the power of the trade unions, but it was not the only factor involved. The TUC and a number of individual unions tried but failed to defy the new laws. Perhaps more important was the fact that, as the economy shifted from manufacturing to service industries, and as unemployment grew, trade union membership declined from 12.1 to 9 million. By 1990, only about 37 percent of the adult workers in Britain belonged to trade unions, as opposed to 51 percent in 1979. Whatever the causes of this decline, the erosion of union power was a key feature of the Thatcher years.

Finally, the economy. The Thatcherites wanted to reverse British economic trends in essentially two ways. First, they wanted to restore the spirit of enterprise, by withdrawing the government from the economy, by reducing income taxes, and by encouraging the attitude that profits and wealth were good. Second, they sought to defeat inflation by monetary policy. The Thatcherites succeeded in restoring the reputation of profits and wealth. They cut the top rate of the income tax from 75 percent to 50 percent though they also increased the Value Added Tax (VAT, a kind of sales tax) to 15 percent. These tax reforms helped the richest segment of the population while hurting most of the rest. In privatization of industry and sales of public housing, the Conservatives increased the number of property owners. In more general terms, the Thatcherites raised the reputation of money-making and self-interest, which had not stood as high in British public esteem since the early nineteenth century. It would be wrong to say that the British cultural bias in favor of landed life and against "trade" entirely disappeared, but a mood of "bourgeois triumphalism" and a public display of ostentatious consumerism certainly prevailed in the prosperous areas of the country.

The defeat of inflation was Thatcher's proudest claim. The rate of inflation continued its climb after Thatcher took office, reaching 21 percent in 1979 and remaining very high through the first half of 1980. Thereafter it began to fall. By 1984, the increase in prices was down to 5 percent a year, and it remained at that level until 1988, when it began to creep up again. However, it is not clear how much monetarism had to do with this record. The Thatcher government found that it had at best poor measures and controls over the money supply. To be sure, the government put up interest rates to 20 percent in 1979–1980 and kept them high through the mid-1980s. High interest rates do seem to have discouraged investment and therefore to have dampened demand. At the same time, the high interest rate caused massive unemployment, which reached 13 percent of the work force in 1984, and this certainly drove down demand and prices. Thatcher's strongest anti-inflationary weapon may well have been her willingness to see millions of people out of work for month after month. Perhaps most important of all was a collapse in oil prices, as OPEC output resumed and North Sea oil reached full production. In any case, it is not clear whether Thatcher's policies slew the dragon of stagflation or whether the monster will return under different world economic conditions.

High unemployment was the great disaster of the Thatcher years. The world-wide recession of the late-1970s and early 1980s hurt British employment, but so did high interest rates. Money was so expensive as to discourage investment in plant capacity, and British industry continued its decline. Whole industrial areas like the Clydeside of Scotland, the north and the west Midlands of England, and the coalfield of South Wales were idle. Industrial production dropped by 11 percent between 1979 and 1983. Thatcher came under great pressure to reflate the economy, but she stood firm, just as she did with the IRA hunger strikers. "This lady," she declared, "is not for turning." To her credit, while heavy industrial output languished, the economy as a whole, driven by financial services and some high-tech enterprises, grew at a rate of 2.5–3 percent a year between 1982 and 1989.

THE FALKLANDS WAR, APRIL–JUNE 1982

High interest rates, industrial disputes, and soaring unemployment all helped make Thatcher very unpopular in 1980–1981. The Conservative party in 1981 ran far behind the opposition in public opinion polls. But in April 1982 the course of British politics was shifted by events in the Falkland Islands, a small British-occupied archipelago in the wind-swept South Atlantic. On April 2, Argentine forces seized control of the Falklands, despite the fact that nearly all of the islands' inhabitants were of British descent and wished to remain British. Although the Falklands were of little value to Britain, and although the days of Britain's imperial glory were over, Thatcher decided to retake the islands by force.

Ownership of the Falklands (or "Malvinas," as the Argentines call them) had long been disputed by Britain and Argentina. Discovered by a British sea captain in the 1590s, the Falklands were not occupied until the eighteenth century, when the French, British, and Spanish successively put colonies there. The Falklands were claimed by the Argentines after they won independence from Spain in 1816, but the British reoccupied the islands in 1833. A small British community of sheep-farmers grew up during the nineteenth century. By the 1960s, the Falklands' residents consisted of 1,800 people, 650,000 sheep, and 10 million penguins. Britain and Argentina argued their cases before the United Nations from 1964 through 1981. The best British point was that the settlers wanted to remain British, and the best Argentine point was that the islands lie only 250 miles from Argentina but 8,000 miles from Britain. The Argentine military dictator, General Galtieri, decided

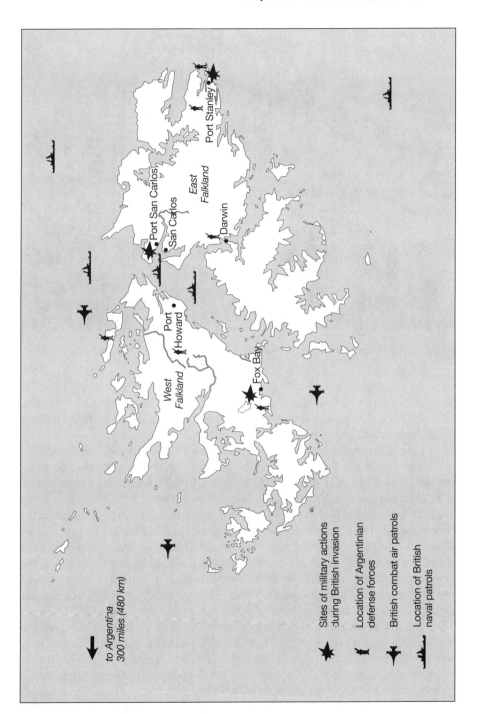

The Falklands War

British Royal Marine commandos raise the Union Jack over West Falkland Island, 1982.

to settle the dispute by occupying the islands, his motive being to divert public opinion in Argentina from the sorry record of his inept and oppressive regime. Little did he realize that he was saving Thatcher's political career or that Thatcher would be the ruination of his.

Prime Minister Thatcher handled the Falklands crisis in a way that pleased the great majority of the British public. She insisted that the use of force had to be stopped by force. Despite recent cutbacks in the Royal Navy, she assembled a task force to retake the islands. This was not easy, for the navy had been reshaped for an antisubmarine role in NATO; indeed, one of the two aircraft carriers that formed the core of the task force had already been sold to Australia, and the luxury liner *Queen Elizabeth II* had to be pressed into service to carry reinforcements. Meanwhile, after British forces set sail, Thatcher cooperated with the Americans and then with the United Nations in their attempts to mediate the dispute. Galtieri, however, would not compromise. These diplomatic efforts won essential American support for Britain. The British task force arrived at the Falklands early in May 1982.

The fighting in the Falklands lasted six weeks. During the month of May, the British ships fought a desperate battle with the Argentine air force. The British navy was not prepared for this kind of combat and lost six ships to Argentine bombs and air-launched missiles. British submarines, however, sank the Argentine cruiser *General Belgrano* and kept the Argentine navy bottled up in port. Thus British troops were able to land in the Falklands on May 21. These were highly professional forces, and they routed the Argentine occupying troops, who were vastly superior in number but only raw conscripts. On June 14, the Argentine commander surrendered his 12,500 men. Some 950 men had been killed, of whom 250 were British. The campaign cost the British about $1.3 billion, or about $750,000 per Falkland Islander.

At home Thatcher received much criticism from the opposition, the churches, and the liberal press, since it seemed so inappropriate for Britain to be fighting an expensive colonial war when the Empire no longer mattered. But the great majority of the British public felt real patriotic pride in the fact that the old British lion still had some teeth after all. Moreover, it was easy for the public to work up hostility to Galtieri, who was an especially loathsome dictator. (He fell from office not long after the war.) "Our Maggie" consequently enjoyed a powerful surge of popular approval, and the British for a time forgot about inflation, unemployment, and industrial decline.

REELECTION AND THE SECOND TERM, 1983–1989

Thatcher seized the rise in her popularity to call a general election in June 1983. Victory in the Falklands was a major element in the campaign, but perhaps an even greater factor was disarray among the opposition. Thatcher's electoral win in 1979 had caused a major split in the Labour party. Labour shifted to the left, and as a result a middle new party—the Social Democratic/Liberal Alliance—by 1983 was making a bid to become the principal opponent to the Conservatives. The curious effect of this situation was that Thatcher's Conservatives lost some popular support but gained a much bigger majority. This electoral victory in 1983 enabled her to push on with her program.

The failure of the Wilson-Callaghan governments between 1974 and 1979 led to Labour's swing to the left. The Labour governments' changes of policy on incomes, trade unions, and the EC had disgusted many party supporters. Moreover, many party activists, who tended to be left-wingers, were angry at the failure of the parliamentary leadership to follow the commands of the annual Party Conference. The party's defeat at the polls in 1979 eroded the strength of the moderates. Left-wing elements like Militant Tendency and the Institute for Workers' Control grew strong in the party and the trade unions. The leader of the left within the parliamentary Labour party was Tony Benn, who was the offspring of a prominent radical family and who had earlier renounced his title of Viscount Stansgate. Basing his radical socialism on Christianity rather than on Marxism, Benn argued for "democratic" control of industry—that is, workers' control—and for more power for Conference in the party as a whole. By 1980, the Labour party was ripe for a change in both its leadership and its constitution.

Benn was a shade too radical for the party; hence when Callaghan resigned the leadership in 1980, the M.P.s elected Michael Foot to replace him. Foot, however, clearly came from the party's left wing, for he was a disciple of Aneurin Bevan. Furthermore, the party in 1980–1981 accepted Bennite policies: unilateral nuclear disarmament, withdrawal from the EC, and a comprehensive program of nationalization of industry. In 1981, Conference altered the party constitution, providing that (1) the party leader be elected by an "electoral college" instead of the M.P.s; (2) in this electoral college the trade unions would have 40 percent of the votes, the constituency parties 30 percent, and the M.P.s 30 percent; and (3) Labour M.P.s would periodically have to submit themselves to "reselection" by their constituency party associations, which the left-wingers hoped to dominate. Activists now would play a dominant role in the party. These changes in the leadership policies, and constitution represented a sharp turn of Labour away from the consensus the party itself had done so much to construct.

The shift to the left was too much for some of the party's moderates. Led by the former cabinet ministers Roy Jenkins, David Owen, William Rodgers, and Shirley Williams, thirteen Labour M.P.s left the party and formed a new one, the Social Democratic Party (SDP) in 1981. The SDP stood for a mixed economy, the welfare state, full employment, and membership in the Common Market—that is, the post-1945 consensus. The SDP soon formed an alliance with the Liberals, who had elected eleven M.P.s in 1979. Within a few months the SDP/Liberal Alliance ranked higher in the polls than either Labour or the Conservatives. For once, it seemed that a third party in Britain had a great chance of success. But the Falklands war reversed the decline in Thatcher's popularity, and the deep animosity between Labour and the SDP/Liberal Alliance guaranteed a Tory electoral victory. In the election of 1983, the Conservatives increased their majority from 43 to 144 seats, even while their proportion of the popular vote decreased from 43.9 percent to 42.4 percent. The Alliance suffered a big disappointment, winning 25.4 percent of the votes but only 23 seats to Labour's 27.6 percent and 209 seats.

Emboldened by her triumph, Thatcher pressed on with her right-wing policies. She replaced a number of Wets in her cabinet with Drys, and she kept money tight to combat inflation. She pressured the National Coal Board to abandon inefficient pits in order to turn a profit, even at the expense of greater unemployment. This policy led to a strike by the coal miners that dominated her second term.

As the National Coal Board was scaling down the industry, the miners' union, the NUM, was turning to militant leadership. Its top official in 1984 was Arthur Scargill, a strong socialist who was devoted to keeping miners at work and mining communities intact. He and the NUM executive called a strike in the spring of 1984 to stop pit closures. Unfortunately for Scargill, not all the mining regions favored a strike, because the closures affected the older mining regions of Scotland, South Wales, and the North of England, but not the more efficient mines in the English Midlands. Thus the NUM executive dared not to have a general NUM ballot on the strike, and the Nottinghamshire miners refused to join the other miners in obeying the executive's call to lay down their tools. The NUM sent "flying pickets" to shut down the Nottinghamshire mines, but the government insisted on defending the right of the Nottinghamshire miners to work. Serious fights between picketers and police broke out in the summer and fall of 1984. This was the long-expected showdown between the union militants and the Thatcherites.

Thatcher refused to intervene to settle the strike or, mindful of Heath's mistake in 1974, to call a new general election. Her government had gathered ample stocks of coal to keep industry and power plants running. The NUM executive had committed the blunder of calling the strike during the spring and summer, when coal demand was lowest. By December 1984 miners were drifting back to work. In March 1985, the NUM admitted defeat. In subsequent months, Nottinghamshire miners broke away from the NUM to form a new union. Altogether, the strike of 1984 was the most serious defeat for the British trade unions since 1926; it did as much as Thatcher's legislation to curb union militancy.

The Labour party meanwhile made a surprising recovery from the electoral disaster of 1983. Michael Foot resigned the leadership, for it was clear that the voting public regarded him as an idealistic intellectual and not as prime ministerial material. He was succeeded by Neil Kinnock (b. 1942), an effective spokesman on television and an advocate of party unity . Kinnock came from a Welsh mining family and benefited directly from the welfare state; thus he was a passionate defender of the welfare state. He represented the center-left of the party's spectrum but moved somewhat to the right once he assumed the leadership. Kinnock stood aside from the miners' strike. He also worked to discipline or expel the militant socialists from the party, calling them "the dafties," who would rather be right than win. Alliance by-election victories over militant left-wing Labour candidates strengthened his hand. By 1986–1987, many leading British socialists were redefining their philosophy to reemphasize individual freedom. As one socialist wrote, "The true purpose of democratic socialism is the protection and extension of individual liberty." Likewise, Labour abandoned unilateral nuclear disarmament. This shift in Labour's outlook enabled the party to recover its position as the chief opposition to the Conservatives, but it also reflects the enormous impact of Thatcher in changing the terms of British political discourse.

The election of June 1987 gave Thatcher an unprecedented third consecutive victory. In her campaign for reelection, she called for a continuation of Thatcherism—free enterprise, monetarism, privatization, and reduction in government spending—so that it would become so well established as to be irrevocable. Kinnock and Labour ran a slick media campaign, focusing on the unemployment rate of 13 percent, the need for improved social security, recapitalization of industry by a capital levy and state-directed investment, and nuclear disarmament. The Alliance found the task of distinguishing itself from the other parties very difficult; it campaigned for full employment, welfare, devolution, and election of M.P.s by proportional representation. The voters gave Thatcher a majority of 101 seats over all other parties combined. Labour, however, made something of a comeback, winning twenty more seats than in 1983. The Alliance lost one seat and saw its bright hopes fading. (After 1987, the main body of the SDP formally merged with the Liberals.) The Conservatives, with Thatcher more than ever in control, stood triumphant.

THATCHER'S FALL, 1987–1990

Yet Thatcher fell from office less than four years after her victory. Her fall was as dramatic and unexpected as her rise, for she was deposed not by efforts of the Labour opposition but by the maneuvering of parliamentary leaders in her own

Conservative party. Thatcher had never been very popular in personal terms, and by November 1990 public opinion polls showed that the Conservatives under her leadership were running far behind the Labour party. A number of Conservative leaders feared that if Thatcher was not replaced, the party would suffer a defeat in the next general election, which by law had to be held by summer 1992. These Conservative M.P.s, many of whom were either present or former members of Thatcher's cabinet, succeeded in turning her out of office in November 1990.

Three factors combined to sow the fast-growing seeds of discontent with Thatcher. One was her customary high-handedness with her own cabinet. Not only had she expelled the "Wets" from office but she also ruled her cabinets with an iron hand. She always insisted on giving the last word in cabinet discussions, on interfering with decisions in the various executive departments, and on bullying her colleagues into silence. By autumn 1990, she had created a long list of bitterly resentful ex-ministers, among whom was Michael Heseltine, an aggressive and ambitious man who had resigned as defense secretary after a clash with Thatcher in 1986. Sensing that Thatcher had to go, such Conservative leaders began jostling with each other in hopes of replacing her at the top.

The second issue was the "poll tax," which she had insisted on passing in 1989 and which had provoked strong public protest, including a riot in London in the summer of 1990. The poll tax was a blow at progressive taxation. Traditionally, local taxes in Britain were based on property values, which meant that well-to-do families paid more than poorer ones. Thatcher preferred a flat tax, in which each member of a household—men, women, and children over eighteen years of age—would be taxed at the same rate. Thatcher hoped that dependence on this new method of taxation would cut the spending of local authorities, many of whom were under the control of Labour. After the poll tax went into effect, many families owning considerable property enjoyed a reduction in their local taxes, but the majority of families found that their taxes went up. Moreover, they thought that there had been no need for the change; the poll tax seemed to be the product of Thatcher's ideology alone. A number of Conservative leaders, not just Heseltine, believed that the poll tax had to be abolished, but Thatcher was determined to keep it.

Finally, the Conservative parliamentary leadership grew increasingly unhappy with Thatcher's stance on European unity. She seemed out of step with the progress of the EC toward unification and therefore likely to allow Britain to slip to the periphery of European affairs. This became especially noticeable when Germany reunited in 1989: if Britain did not become an enthusiastic participant in the EC, then major decisions would be made over which the British would have no influence. Thatcher did favor the completion of a European barrier-free market by 1992, but she resisted steps toward monetary union and expressed her dissent in abrasive terms. The EC was considering whether in the next decade to establish a single European currency and a central European bank. Thatcher's view was that she did not want to abandon the pound sterling, that old symbol of British power and influence, for a single European currency over which the British would have little control, and she loathed the idea of a central European bank making decisions that would profoundly affect the British economy. Her critics contended that since Britain was no longer a great power, the government had no choice but to go along with developments in European unity. A series of cabinet ministers had resigned over this issue, including the widely respected Sir Geoffrey Howe as deputy prime minister.

By November 1990, the movement to replace Thatcher as leader of the party had grown very strong among Conservative insiders. By party rules, Thatcher had to stand for reelection by Conservative M.P.s as leader of the parliamentary party. The simmering discontent with her leadership boiled over. Heseltine put himself forward as a rival for the post, arguing that the poll tax had to be replaced. Thatcher succeeded in keeping Heseltine from winning the leadership, but she failed to win enough votes for reconfirmaton herself. On November 23, 1990, she announced her withdrawal as a candidate for the leadership, which was effectively her resignation as prime minister. In the jockeying for position that followed, a relative unknown, John Major, emerged as the victor. He was sworn in as the new prime minister on November 28, 1990. Curiously, among the contenders for the leadership, Major was the one most clearly a Thatcherite, and he had been a Thatcher protégé from the time he entered Parliament in 1979.

THATCHER'S BRITAIN, THE 1980S

Whatever her unpopularity in 1990, Margaret Thatcher had an immense impact on Britain. Many observers think that Thatcher changed more than the terms of political debate in Britain. They say that she altered the very structure of the economy and society. Certainly the elections of 1983 and 1987 provided evidence that important economic and social changes were occurring, and Thatcher both contributed to and benefitted from them. Beyond returning the Conservatives to power, the elections showed a number of fundamental features of Britain in the 1980s. First, they demonstrated that there were in geographical terms *two* Britains. The Conservatives won in the South and Southeast, the Midlands, and East Anglia of England. Labour won in the North of England, in Scotland, and in Wales. The geographical pattern of the voting thus coincided with the dominant economic division of the country in the 1980s and early 1990s: roughly speaking, the prosperous South of England against the North of England and the Celtic "fringe." The southern part of England, including high-tech corridors near Oxford and Cambridge, had a thriving economy dominated by financial and service-oriented businesses. The old industrial areas of Northern England and the Celtic countries stood idle. In some of the formerly great industrial cities like Belfast, Glasgow, Merthyr, Liverpool, and Manchester, unemployment among young people reached 50 percent. There was a significant flow of population out of these areas into southern England, especially the London area. The Highland districts of Wales and Scotland long ago began to suffer depopulation and by 1980 were home to very few people. In the 1980s, only 9.3 percent of the British people lived in Scotland, 5 percent in Wales, and 2.7 percent in Northern Ireland.

Second, the elections of 1983 and 1987 revealed important changes in the social structure. The middle class, which had been solidly Conservative for more than half a century, was expanding but was less automatically loyal to the Conservative party. The middle class comprised about 40 percent of the population. Apparently the shift of Britain's economy from manufacturing to service industries increased the proportion of middle-class to working-class jobs. Moreover, Thatcher's policy of privatizing nationalized industries increased the number of stockholders (20 percent of the British people now owned shares in companies), and her policy of selling council houses increased the number of families who owned their homes (66 percent of all families owned rather than rented). Both of these changes can be seen as increasing the number of middle-class people. Privatization also shifted a large number of employees from the public to the private sector. This segment of the middle class voted Conservative, whereas public employees and professional people tended to vote Alliance or Labour.

The working class, meanwhile, seemed to be in a state of flux. We have seen that by 1990 only about 37 percent of the British workers belonged to trade unions, and of these less than half voted for the Labour party in 1987. Indeed, only about 42 percent of the working class as a whole voted Labour, the rest dividing themselves between the Conservatives and the Liberal-Democrat Alliance. The two key institutions of the British working class, therefore, the unions and the Labour party, seemed to be losing their hold on their constituency, which itself was declining as a portion of the population. Do these changes mean that the working class was dissolving or that the class system—that central creation of modern British history—was breaking up? Some observers thought so, but the hypothesis had to be very tentative. Certainly patterns of consumption and popular culture seemed to be producing a "homogenized" social structure, just as they tended to erode the significance of different national cultures within the British Isles. Inequalities of wealth and income still existed but had been reduced over the course of the twentieth century. On the other hand, a strong sense of social hierarchy, supported by a highly stratified educational system, the "public school tie," and the domination of key positions in government and industry by the Oxbridge elite, still pervaded Britain. Against this generalization is the fact that John Major himself appeared to be "classless": he attended neither a public school nor Oxford or Cambridge. Public opinion polls showed that class identity and class consciousness remained very strong; thus what was changing may simply have been the political allegiance of the middle and working classes, the issue being whether to return to the old postwar consensus or to stick with Thatcherism.

The elections of 1983 and 1987 pointed to yet another important social development: the growth of the immigrant population of peoples from Asia and the West Indies. An Asian and three blacks from inner-city constituencies won seats in the House of Commons in 1987. They hardly constituted evidence of a social revolution, but they were a reminder that about 2.2 million nonwhites by 1990 lived in Britain, about 4 percent of the total population of 55 million. They were concentrated in major English cities like London, Birmingham, Leicester, Wolverhampton, and Bradford. People of Asian and West Indian descent made up a large part of the shopkeeping and public transportation work force in such cities, with one result being that local shops stayed open longer because the Asians were willing to work long and hard. Asian doctors also became essential to the National Health Service, since many homegrown British doctors preferred private practice. In London, a large mosque was built near Regent's Park, and a number of old Christian churches in the cities where immigrants had settled were converted into mosques and temples. Muslims of Asian descent outnumbered Methodists in Britain by two to one. It is clear, therefore, that the British Nationality Act of 1981 and its predecessors of the 1960s and 1970s did not succeed in keeping Asians and West Indians from immigration into Britain and that England, which for many hundreds of years had absorbed Celtic people from Ireland, Scotland, and Wales, was no longer exclusively white.

Was Thatcher's Britain more European than Britain in the 1960s? Yes, but the Common Market did not have the decisive effects once predicted. Membership has remained controversial in Britain to the present day. The EC did not seriously limit British sovereignty, but neither did it pay off for Britain in the way that the EC's enthusiasts had expected. The EC's budget had been designed from the outset largely to assist the large (and relatively inefficient) agricultural sectors of the Continental nations, especially France. About 70 percent of the EC's annual budget was paid out in subsidies to farmers. The British, who had an efficient agricultural sector but also imported many foodstuffs from the Commonwealth and Scandinavia, benefited comparatively little from the EC's expenditures while giving up some of their advantages on imported food. At the same time, since the EC member nations paid into the EC treasury according to the value of imports, the British contributed more than their fair share as measured by GDP. Moreover, the British were not able to take advantage of the vast Continental market opened to them. In fact, from 1973 on, the British had a deficit on trade with the EC countries.

Yet if the EEC was not a bonanza for British manufacturers, and if it caused the British to pay higher food prices than they would have otherwise have done, it nevertheless seemed to most business people and financiers to represent Britain's best option. Thatcher in the 1980s succeeded in negotiating a somewhat more favorable arrangement of British contributions to the EC budget and payouts to the member states. The Commonwealth and the United States were simply no longer the best trading partners for the British, and it seemed possible that the British would be able to find a niche in the burgeoning European economy. By membership in Europe, the British had a voice in the evolution of a European political community and thus played a role through Europe in world affairs. In elections held in 1989 for the European Parliament, British voters showed themselves more favorable towards the EC than the Thatcherites.

Thatcher's Britain seemed in some ways a more aggressive, forward-looking country than the Britain admired by generations of American tourists—the Britain of quiet market towns, cozy villages, and well-mannered Londoners—but it was also a more harsh and divided society. For one thing, it was less peaceful and law-abiding than the Britain of the 1950s. Like most of the nations of the Western world, Britain experienced a rising crime rate between 1945 and 1990. Crime against both property and persons became more frequent. Football "hooligans," some of whom belonged to well-organized gangs, plagued the British stadiums and even terrorized Continental cities when British teams came to play. The police were still basically unarmed, but they now resorted to firearms much more often than at any time in the past. The division between the prosperous South of England and the impoverished old industrial districts of the North and the Celtic countries was startling. Parts of London were developing rapidly: Victorian districts that "gentrified" again; high-tech companies sprang up all over the greater London area; and splendid new "postmodern" shopping malls and condominium developments grew up along the Thames. Yet in London in the 1980s one also saw images of the other Britain: unemployed men sleeping on the steps of St. Martin's-in-the-Fields, Trafalgar Square; homeless people living in pasteboard boxes under Waterloo Bridge; and most ironic of all, impoverished children huddling under the theater marquee where *Les Misérables* was playing.

Suggested Reading

Abrams, Philip, and Richard Brown, eds., *U.K. Society: Work, Urbanism, and Equality* (London: Weidenfeld & Nicolson, 1984).

Black, Jeremy, *Britain since the Seventies: Politics and Society in the Consumer Age* (London: Reaktion Books, 2004).

Blake, Robert, *The Conservative Party from Peel to Thatcher* (London: Methuen, 1985).

Campbell, John, *Margaret Thatcher* (London: Pimlico, 2001, 2004).

Charmley, John, *A History of Conservative Politics, 1900–1996* (New York: St. Martin's Press, 1996).

Childs, David, *Britain Since 1945: A Political History*, 2nd ed. (London: Benn, 1986).

Coxall, Bill, and Lynton Robbins, *British Politics Since the War* (New York: St. Martin's Press, 1998).

Crewe, Ivor, and Anthony King, *SDP: The Birth, Life and Death of the Social Democratic Party* (Oxford: Oxford University Press, 1996).

Douglas-Home, Charles, and Saul Kelly, *Dignified and Efficient: The British Monarchy in the Twentieth Century* (London: Claridge, 2000).

Foote, Geoffrey, *The Labour Party's Political Thought: A History* (London: Croom Helm, 1985).

Freedman, Lawrence, *Britain and the Falklands War* (Oxford: Basil Blackwell, 1998).

Gamble, Andrew, *The Free Economy and the Strong State: The Politics of Thatcherism* (2nd. Ed.; London: Macmillian, 1994).

Hennessy, Peter, and Anthony Seldon, eds., *Ruling Performance: British Governments from Attlee to Thatcher* (Oxford: Basil Blackwell, 1987).

Hill, Michael, *The Welfare State in Britain: A Political History Since 1945* (Brookfield, Vt.: Edward Elgar Publishing, 1993).

Hopkins, Eric, *The Rise and Decline of the English Working Classes, 1918–1990: A Social History* (New York: St. Martin's Press, 1991).

Jacobs, Brian, *Racism in Britain* (London: Christopher Helm, 1988).

Kavanagh, Dennis, *Thatcherism and British Politics: The End of Consensus?* (Oxford: Oxford University Press, 1987).

Keegan, William, *Mrs. Thatcher's Economic Experiment* (London: Allen Lane, 1984).

Minkin, Lewis, *The Contentious Alliance: Trade Unions and the Labour Party* (Edinburgh: Edinburgh University Press, 1991).

Pelling, Henry, and Alastair J. Reid, *A Short History of the Labour Party* (11th ed.; New York: St. Martin's Press, 1996).

Perkin, Harold, *The Rise of Professional Society: England Since 1880* (London: Routledge, 1989).

Pugh, Martin, *State and Society: A Social and Political History of Britain, 1870–1977* (2nd ed.; London: Oxford University Press, 1999).

Raison, Timothy, *Tories and the Welfare State: A History of Conservative Social Policy Since the Second World War* (New York: St. Martin's Press, 1990).

Reitan, Earl A., *Tory Radicalism: Margaret Thatcher, John Major, and the Transformation of Modern Britain, 1979–1997* (Lanham, Md.: Rowman and Littlefield Publishers, 1997).

Riddell, Peter, *The Thatcher Government* (Oxford: Basil Blackwell, 1985).

Roth, Andrew, *Heath and the Heathmen* (London: Routledge & Kegan Paul, 1972).

Seldon, Anthony, and Daniel Collings, *Britain Under Thatcher* (London: Longman, 1999).

Seldon, Anthony, and Stuart Ball, eds., *Conservative Century: The Conservative Party Since 1900* (Oxford: Oxford University Press, 1994).

Skidelsky, Robert, ed., *The End of the Keynesian Era* (London: Macmillan, 1977).

Thatcher, Margaret, *The Downing Street Years* (New York: HarperCollins, 1993).

Williamson, Bill, *The Temper of the Times: British Society Since World War II* (Cambridge, Mass.: Basil Blackwell, 1990).

Young, Hugo, *The Iron Lady: A Biography of Margaret Thatcher* (New York: Farrar, Straus & Giroux, 1989).

Chapter 15

Post-Thatcher Britain, 1990– Present: New Labour, Prosperity, and Imperial Blowback

Thatcher's Britain, in all its complex mixture of decay and progress, was not the creation of Mrs. Thatcher alone. It was the consequence of the break-up of the post-World War II consensus, the relative decline of the industrial sector of the economy, the rapid growth of financial and technical services, and changes in the social structure that blurred the lines of class. Still, there is no question that Thatcher's electoral victories and the perceived successes of her policies of privatization, controlling the trades unions, and encouraging an "entrepreneurial culture" all shifted the center of the British political spectrum a couple of notches to the right. This conservative reorientation was reflected in the 1990s and after not only by the Tory government of John Major but also by the rise of New Labour and the government of Tony Blair. Thus it seems that between 1990 and 2007 a new consensus emerged in Britain—one that reflected the more service-oriented economy, a public mood that was more individualistic and less community spirited, and an eager embrace of "modernization" of institutions and attitudes. But the consensus paradoxically included the apparent division of Britain, as the Celtic countries won significant autonomy through the process of devolution. Moreover, while this new, modernizing Britain found an enormously popular spokesman and symbol in Tony Blair, leader of a radically reformed Labour Party, Blair's commitment of Britain to the support of an American invasion of Iraq caused fierce political dissent and contributed to "imperial blowback"—seething and sometimes violent anger among Britain's growing Muslim population.

THE TROUBLED TIMES OF JOHN MAJOR, 1990–1997

Shortly after John Major became prime minister in 1990, Mrs. Thatcher declared that she would remain active in politics and that she would be "a very good back-seat driver." Clearly, one of Major's tasks would be to mark out an independent position for himself. In a sense, he never did emerge from Thatcher's imposing shadow, and she and her anti-European disciples in parliament persistently split the Conservative party. But this was not the only difficulty that Major faced in his unusually turbulent and trouble-filled term of office. It must frequently have seemed to him that the gods were conspiring against him and Britain as the end of the millennium approached.

Only a person as resilient and resourceful as Major could have managed the discordant developments as long as he did. As a politician, he lacked vision and charisma; but he liked and understood people, and he was a clever and effective negotiator. His rise to the premiership was unusual—almost accidental. Born into the lower-middle class, Major left school at sixteen, without the benefit of either public school or a university education. He grew up in a tough inner-city section of London, which introduced him to a wide range of social types. He was a person of no clear class identity, and he genuinely believed in equality of opportunity and a classless society. For a time, these attitudes fit the mood of the nation. His only other fixed idea in political policy was concern about inflation, which he understood to have hurt his father in the 1960s. A tireless and conscientious party worker and a quick study on the job, he entered Parliament in 1979 and in the 1980s rose through a series of government offices in which he caught the eye of Mrs. Thatcher. He was colorless, but he was never in any office long enough to get the blame for bad mistakes. Hence he was a convenient and noncontroversial candidate to replace Thatcher when the more powerful Tory politicians had canceled each other out.

When Major took office in 1990, the Conservative party was in disarray and stood low in public opinion polls. Not even the Persian Gulf War, in which Britain followed the lead of the United States in a smashing victory over Iraq, gave Major much of a boost. The problem was that from 1990 through 1992 the British economy fared poorly: unemployment, inflation, and the balance of trade deficit all were up. British industry had contracted during the Thatcher years, and much of what was left could not compete with American, European, and Japanese industry. Britain thus suffered seriously from the worldwide recession of the early 1990s. Like his predecessor, Major focused on inflation as the main economic problem, and he tried to fight it by her methods—high interest rates, which drove exports and investments down and unemployment up. And as Major tried to hold down increases in public spending, the social services and public utilities, including the National Health Service and British Rail, were seriously underfunded. (Major's government sold off British Rail to private owners in 1996.)

These economic troubles provided the context for Major's difficult dealings with the European Community. During the 1980s, many of the states of the EC, led by Germany and France, sought to accelerate the pace of political and economic unification. They wanted to renegotiate the original Treaty of Rome, take the final steps in abolishing all internal European customs barriers, strengthen the EC's central political and administrative institutions, and move towards a common European currency. While many big businessmen and financiers in Britain supported British participation in these developments as the only way to stimulate and streamline the British economy, many Britons, especially Thatcher and her disciples, opposed them on grounds that they would infringe British sovereignty. Major himself believed that Britain's future lay with Europe, but he was constrained by the vigorous anti-European sentiment, most notably within his own party.

The European pot came to a boil at the EC conference in Maastricht (in the Netherlands) in December 1991. Major did not want to risk breaking up the European Union or to withdraw Britain from it; but he had to be mindful of Thatcherite opposition to any movement towards a "federal Europe." After a week of intense negotiations at Maastricht, Major scored a diplomatic victory. The Europeans got some of what they wanted, but Major avoided committing Britain to the most significant proposals. Specifically, Major won the right for Britain to opt out of the common currency, which was to come into effect by early 1999; he won the right for Britain to reject the "social chapter" of the Maastricht Treaty, whereby the European nations agreed to a level playing field in labor law and in certain social policies deemed too socialistic by the Conservatives; and he got the Europeans to drop the word "federal" from the Treaty.

Major's success at Maastricht helped him and his party pull off a minor miracle in the general election of April 1992. The Conservatives won their fourth straight victory since 1979, but their majority was reduced to only twenty-one seats in the House of Commons, which a series of by-elections was to shrink even further. However, considering that Britain was in a significant recession, the Conservative victory was a big surprise to every observer. Major's success was due not only to his success at Maastricht but also to the voters' inclination to regard the Tories as the natural party of government, to the division of the opposition between Labour and the Liberal Democrats, and to the widespread concern that Labour in office might adopt irresponsible tax-and-spend policies.

The electoral victory brought Major no respite. The Conservative party remained deeply divided over Europe. This wound was aggravated when the weakness of the pound sterling forced Major to withdraw Britain from the European Exchange Rate Mechanism (ERM) in September 1992. Britain had joined the ERM in 1989 because Thatcher had been persuaded by her advisers that belonging to the ERM, which pegged the exchange value of sterling to the deutsche mark, would be anti-inflationary. But it proved impossible for the government to support the pound at the required level, and an embarrassing withdrawal became necessary. Ironically, this defeat for Major worked to the benefit of the British economy because it devalued the pound and so encouraged British exports; employment consequently began a slow rise. But the small band of Thatcherite M.P.s frequently withheld their support from Major over the next few years over European issues. As by-elections reduced his already small majority, Major became frustrated to the point that he even insisted on reelection as leader by the parliamentary Conservative party—an extraordinary put-up-or-shut-up vote. He won, but by then his continuation as prime minister depended on the votes of a dozen Ulster Unionist M.P.s. As we shall see, this situation had serious consequences on his Northern Ireland policy.

With his majority dwindling and the polls running heavily against him, Major increasingly seemed indecisive and lacking a bold vision for Britain. Therefore, in 1993 he adopted a new strategy, which he called "back to basics"—the basics of supporting education, cracking down on crime, encouraging people to become more self-reliant in social insurance, and cutting the deficit. Unfortunately for him, the back-to-basics strategy was soon made to appear ludicrous by a series of revelations of "sleaze" among Tory M.P.s and even members of Major's administration. These included sexual scandals, mismanagement of personal and public funds, and acceptance by a few Conservative M.P.s of money from a foreign-born millionaire, Mohammed Al Fayed, for asking certain questions on his behalf in the House of Commons.

The troubles of the government over Europe, the high level of unemployment, the sleaze scandals, the rising crime rate, and the continued decay of social services all contributed by the mid-1990s to a widespread feeling among the British that something was seriously wrong with their nation. Accentuating that perception was the fact that an alarming number of the members of the royal family were seen as bringing the monarchy itself into disrepute. Of course, the British monarchy had lost its real political power long before the twentieth century; by the 1990s, its functions were essentially symbolic, philanthropic, and moral—that is, to serve as the prime exemplar of propriety. But in the early 1990s the monarchy's performance in this moral role was made to seem ridiculous, as escapades and messy divorces among Queen Elizabeth's offspring and their spouses were filling the pages of London's sensationalist tabloids. Plainly, too many "royals" had come to think of themselves as nothing more than celebrities and to behave accordingly. A considerable number of the British public became embarrassed and even disgusted by what some called the "royal layabouts," and many questioned whether the large sums spent from the public purse on the monarchy were worth it. The worst scandals of all stemmed from the unraveling marriage of Prince Charles and Princess Diana, whose squabbles went so far that each began to use leaks to the press against the other. (The two would be divorced in 1996.) Then, late in 1992, a year that the Queen called her *annus horribilis*, part of Windsor Castle was destroyed by fire; politicians as well as the public balked at paying for repairs. Prompted by all these malfunctioning institutions, many British newspapers, magazines, and television commentators by the mid-1990s were lamenting the decline of "British civilization."

TONY BLAIR AND THE RISE OF "NEW LABOUR"

The Labour party, and its new leader Tony Blair in particular, were the beneficiaries of the troubles plaguing John Major's government. For some years the Labour party had been struggling to adjust to the new political climate in Britain so effectively exemplified by Thatcherism. Neil Kinnock had begun the process of leading Labour to seek support from the middle instead of the left of the political spectrum after he won election as party leader in 1983. In the latter 1980s he succeeded in isolating the so-called "loony left" of the party and in dropping some of the party's more unpopular socialistic policies. In the general election of 1987, the Labour party had adopted as its symbol a red rose rather than the traditional red flag. Such efforts were moderately successful for Labour: even though in that year Thatcher's Conservatives won a third straight victory, the Labour party increased both its share of votes cast and its seats in the House of Commons.

By 1990, Labour's electoral prospects seemed very promising. Inflation, high unemployment, Thatcher's despised poll tax, and divisions over Europe sorely troubled the Conservative government. Under Kinnock, the Labour party continued to shift towards the right, abandoning the policy of unilateral nuclear disarmament and backing away from nationalization of industry—even in the case of nationwide monopolies. In 1990, the Labour Party Conference adopted several changes in the party constitution that were aimed at making the party more attractive to a middle-class electorate; these changes included selection of parliamentary candidates on the principle of one member, one vote, which reduced the long-standing power of the trade unions' block vote.

The Labour party thus faced with confidence the general election of 1992, against Major's Conservative party, which was in some disarray. The surprising Conservative victory, albeit with a reduced majority in the House of Commons, would eventually prove to be a poisoned cup for Major, but in the short run it was a bitter disappointment for Labour. Kinnock resigned the party leadership immediately, but the party did not swing back to the left. Kinnock was replaced by John Smith, another ideological moderate and party reformer. Smith worked hard to consolidate Kinnock's reforms and to unify Labour after the electoral defeat had unleashed divisive mutual recriminations within the party. His efforts were quietly successful, but Smith died in 1994, before he could lead Labour in a general election.

Smith's successor as leader of the party was one of his strongest supporters—Tony Blair, devout Anglican and a youthful public school- and Oxford-educated barrister who had long before rejected Marxism in favor of a more flexible commitment to the values of community and modernization that he had learned from reading Christian socialists like R. H. Tawney and John MacMurray. Blair had made a name for himself as shadow Home Secretary and an energetic party reformer. At the time of his succession to the party leadership, Blair was only forty-one years old, the youngest leader ever of the Labour party and a person of remarkable charisma, with a magnetic smile and a strong (some would say, ruthless) will. He meant to "modernize" the Labour party, appeal to the moderate center of the British electorate, and then revitalize the nation. How he meant to accomplish the latter remained fairly vague, for he enjoyed from the outset such a big lead in public opinion polls over Major that he could benefit from keeping a low policy profile. He simply made it clear that Labour was no longer a foe of business and no longer a tax-and-spend party. The main concerns he spoke of were decentralization of power within Britain, protection of civil rights, limitation of the power of the House of Lords, and removal from the Labour party's constitution of the famous "Clause 4," which from 1918 had committed the party to the public ownership of the means of production, distribution, and exchange. What Blair called "New Labour" abandoned Clause 4 in 1995. Blair therefore was the beneficiary of the process of moderating and modernizing the Labour party that had begun in 1983; but he soon put his own stamp on the process. New Labour clearly became Blair's party.

By the time of the general election of 1997, with Major's government troubled by the revelations of "sleaze" and by the divisions in the Conservative party over the European Union, the Labour party held a lead of more than thirty points in public opinion polls. Blair's campaign slogan of "New Labour—New Britain" was countered by the Conservatives' "New Labour—New Danger"; but the Tories' attempt to frighten the electorate with an image of a militantly socialist Labour now did not work. Meanwhile, the secession of moderates from the Labour party into the Social Democratic party had ceased, and the Social Democrats had been absorbed into the old Liberal party, now renamed the Liberal Democrats. In 1997 the Liberal Democrats drew more voters away from the Conservatives than from Labour. Blair proved to be a master of politics in the new-style public sphere, with its emphasis on television, sound bites, photo-ops, and slick public relations. Relying on Blair's youth, energy, and telegenic personality, Labour won a huge victory, the largest majority by a single party in the House of Commons in the twentieth century—177 seats over all other parties combined—and the Conservatives fell from 323 seats to only 165. Given that the Liberal Democrats would on most issues vote with Labour, Blair's new government would enjoy an even larger working majority. And two other electoral results were especially significant: first, the Tories were shut out of parliamentary seats altogether from Scotland and Wales and now stood as an exclusively "English" party; and second, 120 women won seats in 1997, most of them from the Labour Party, a development so significant that the House of Commons closed its rifle range and opened a child-care center!

Blair's government enjoyed remarkable success and popularity for the better part of three years, his approval ratings reaching the highest levels of any British prime minister since such polls began to be taken. Blair's success resembled that of his friend, President Bill Clinton of the United States, who had played a similar role in reshaping his own party into the "New Democrats." Given the relative vagueness of his campaign utterances, Blair in office felt the need to take command and act decisively in order to show that Labour had become the natural party of government. He immediately informed the European Union that Britain intended to be a constructive partner and accepted the social chapter of the Maastricht Treaty. Though he did not commit his government to joining the European common currency, and promised only a referendum on the issue, Blair appeared to favor acceptance of the euro at some future date. (Blair in fact never had to hold a referendum on the Euro, because in subsequent years, as the British economy surged ahead and the European economy sagged, the moment for Britain to accept the European common currency never seemed ripe.) He introduced a one-time-only tax on "windfall profits" earned by certain individuals on the sale of privatized industries, and directed the consequent revenue towards the National Health Service. He announced a massive welfare-to-work plan, radically increasing job-training and educational programs, while at the same time requiring most welfare recipients to enter training for work. And in 1998, Blair's Labour party passed the first national minimum-wage law in British history.

Blair benefitted greatly from the growing prosperity of the financial and service sectors of the British economy, which turned for the better in the late 1990s. Compared to France and Germany, the British did very well in the ten years of Blair's government. The GDP grew while inflation and unemployment remained low. Blair made sure that New Labour was friendly to business, accepted the basic structures of the market economy, and escaped from the old tax-and-spend image of the Labour left. He refused to abolish Mrs. Thatcher's regulations on the trade unions and rejected proposals from his party's left wing to raise taxes or to launch a serious attack on unequal income distribution. He restructured university financing, so that students would now pay a portion of their fees. After another big victory in the general election of 2001, Blair and his able Chancellor of the Exchequer, Gordon Brown, devoted much more money to recapitalizing the National Health Service, to eradicating pockets of poverty among old age pensioners and single-parent families, and to establishing a pre-school program for disadvantaged children. Still, while material standards of living in Britain generally remained high, inequality continued to grow under New Labour, if only slightly, for it was the rich who benefitted most from economic conditions: The share of the national income enjoyed the richest 1 percent of the population grew from 5.6% to 6.3% between 1995 and 2005.

Most important of all, Blair in September 1997 held referenda in Scotland and Wales on the issue of devolution. The Labour party had been committed to devolution since the 1970s, but, as we have seen, referenda in 1979 had failed to win approval by the required 40 percent of the electorate. After 1979, Labour retained its commitment to devolution, not least because Scottish and Welsh nationalism grew in popularity in the 1980s and competed effectively with Labour candidates for votes in both Scotland and Wales. The principal reason for the surge of support for Scottish and Welsh nationalism was that the recession of the early 1980s and the deindustrializing effects of Thatcher's deflationary polices hit the Celtic countries especially hard. Both the SNP and Plaid Cymru after 1979 had redefined themselves as left-of-center parties, devoted to asserting Scottish and Welsh independence in the face of Thatcher's British nationalism. Sensitive to the appeal of Scottish and Welsh nationalism, Blair in the campaign of 1997 had made devolution the key element in his policy of decentralizing power away from London. Many British (and especially English) nationalists argued that devolution of any significant power to a Scottish parliament and a Welsh assembly would lead to the break-up of Britain; and some Scottish and Welsh nationalists gave credibility to that point of view by envisioning devolution as the first step towards complete independence. Blair, however, contended that devolution would satisfy reasonable Scottish and Welsh national sentiment and thereby tie Scotland and Wales to the United Kingdom more firmly than ever.

The referenda of 1997 resulted in victories for devolution in both Scotland and Wales. In Scotland, 74 percent of the voters favored establishing a parliament and 64 percent favored tax-varying powers for the new parliament. In Wales, devolution won by a narrower majority. Elections for the Scottish parliament and Welsh assembly were held in May 1999, with Labour candidates given stiff competition by the SNP and Plaid Cymru. Both elections were conducted according to proportional representation, a constitutional innovation long advocated by the British Liberals and now adopted by Blair and Labour as part of their "modernizing" thrust.

Labour came out on top in both Scotland and Wales but failed to win an outright majority in either. Both the SNP and Plaid Cymru were encouraged by their second-place finishes, while the Conservative party did poorly. No doubt because of their weak showing in Scotland and Wales in both 1997 and 1999, some Tories by the year 2000 were speaking of making Conservatism the "English" nationalist party, a move that was in a sense consistent with the further turn of the party under its new leader, William Hague, against Britain's membership in Europe. Meanwhile, both of the new home rule legislatures convened in the summer of 1999, amidst much celebration by Scottish and Welsh nationalists—including in Edinburgh the actor Sean Connery resplendent in a kilt of green tartan. Plainly, both Scotland and Wales had embarked on a new era in their histories, and Britain had taken an important step towards becoming a federal state.

Devolution was not the only constitutional reform undertaken by Blair and New Labour. A second was acceptance in 1998 of the Human Rights Act, which was part of the process of bringing Britain into line with Europe. This for the first time gave Britain something of a bill of rights, for it guaranteed certain basic individual rights, though it was not clear how the British courts would interpret the Act. The third big step in constitutional change was reform of the House of Lords. As a self-proclaimed modernizer, Blair was determined to abolish or reform, he said, "all forms of conservatism that have so long held them [the British people] back." The House of Lords, long a bastion of conservatism, naturally was a prime target, even though the Lords' legislative authority had been reduced to delaying for only one year legislation passed by the House of Commons. Whatever formula should be adopted for reform of the Lords, Blair intended to end voting by the *hereditary* peers, of whom there were about 750 (there were 450 life peers). Various options for reform were hotly debated after 1997: outright abolition of the House of Lords; substitution for the current House of an entirely elected house; an all-appointed house of life peers (an option naturally attractive to any prime minister); or some combination of the latter two options. Blair appointed a commission to study the matter in 1999, and as an interim measure provided that 92 of the hereditary peers (elected by their fellows) would stay on, along with the life peers. There was some emotional opposition by traditional aristocrats, including one overwrought decla-mation by the Earl of Burford, who leapt upon the woolsack to accuse the Blair government of treason by abolishing eight hundred years of tradition: "Before us," he declared, "lies the wasteland: no queen, no sovereignty, no freedom." But the interim measure passed into law, and some 660 hereditary peers left their chamber at Westminster for the last time. The permanent composition of the House of Lords remained highly controversial, and the matter remained under consideration eight years later.

BRITAIN, IRELAND, NORTHERN IRELAND, AND THE GOOD FRIDAY AGREEMENT OF 1998

Important as these constitutional changes enacted by Blair's government were, perhaps the most important of all came in Northern Ireland. The events of the

1990s leading to the establishment of devolved government in Northern Ireland by the Good Friday Agreement of 1998—the most hopeful development in Anglo-Irish history since 1921—were tense, sometimes violent, and demanding of courage and determination by those in Northern Ireland intent on peace. But it is important to understand that the Northern Ireland peace settlement depended as well on longer-term developments not only in Northern Ireland itself but also in Britain and the Irish Republic.

The decisive point in those longer-term developments had been the normalization of relations between Britain and the Irish Republic epitomized by the Hillsborough Agreement of 1985. By then, Ireland had come to realize its own need for peace and security in Northern Ireland, and the British to recognize both the seriousness of Irish intentions and the reliability of the Republic as a negotiating partner. Crucial to the normalization of relations between Britain and Ireland were Irish entry into the European Community in 1973 and the consequent Irish economic development. In the 1970s and 1980s, Ireland took advantage of the EC's common agricultural policy as well as its industrial investment in the less developed European nations. By the 1990s, the opening of the huge European market to the agricultural and manufacturing products of Ireland had attracted much foreign investment to Ireland, freed Ireland from its long-standing dependence on the British economy, and enabled the Irish to achieve a much higher growth rate than Britain. Membership in the EC thus helped turn Ireland into the "Celtic Tiger." It also liberated Irish leaders from their traditional inferiority complex in dealing with the British and accustomed British leaders to dealing with the Irish on terms of equality.

Meanwhile, by the early 1990s, the military standoff in Northern Ireland had persuaded both the British government and a significant portion of the IRA that neither side could win. The British security forces realized that they could contain the IRA indefinitely but could not defeat them completely; and important elements in the IRA command recognized that the IRA could not drive the British army out of Northern Ireland. During 1993, John Hume, leader of the Northern Ireland Social Democratic and Labour Party, dared to open private discussions with Gerry Adams, former IRA soldier and now president of Sinn Fein. Hume hoped to persuade Adams and Sinn Fein that they stood a better chance of getting what they wanted by negotiations than by force. At the same time, the leaders of both major parties in the Irish Republic knew that Irish interests lay in peace and stability in Northern Ireland. These developments resulted in the "Downing Street Declaration" of December 1993, in which the Irish *taoiseach* (prime minister) Albert Reynolds and British prime minister John Major affirmed: (1) that Britain no longer had any selfish economic or strategic interests in Northern Ireland; (2) that reunification of Northern Ireland with the Republic was one acceptable solution to the Northern Ireland problem, provided that the majority in Northern Ireland agreed; (3) that the Northern Ireland Protestant Unionists should not be *forced* into reunification; and (4) that the Irish Republic would in the event of a peace settlement reconsider Articles II and III of the Irish constitution, whereby the Republic had long claimed sovereignty over Northern Ireland. Reynolds and Major also agreed that any organization in Northern Ireland, including Sinn Fein, could participate in peace negotiations, provided it renounced violence.

The Downing Street Declaration was a big step forward, yet peace talks among all parties proved enormously difficult to get started. Militants among neither the Catholic nationalists nor the Protestant unionists of Northern Ireland welcomed the Declaration. The IRA objected because the Declaration seemed to preserve the old "Protestant veto" over reunification and required the IRA to forswear violence, which they regarded as their only weapon. The Protestant paramilitaries for their part loathed the idea that under any circumstances Sinn Fein and the IRA, which they regarded as nothing more than criminal organizations, might be included in negotiating the fate of Northern Ireland. The unionists, as usual, feared that Britain was about to sell them out to Irish nationalism. But a majority in the IRA was persuaded by Adams to try the peace process, and in August 1994 the IRA declared a ceasefire, and the Protestant paramilitaries were coaxed into following suit in October. Even with the ceasefire, which led to the first peaceful Christmas season in Northern Ireland in twenty-five years, peace talks did not begin, largely because Prime Minister Major, whose parliamentary majority by then depended on the dozen Ulster Unionist M.P.s, now declared that for Sinn Fein to be allowed to participate, the IRA would have to disarm. Both Sinn Fein and the IRA strenuously objected to this demand, on grounds that IRA disarmament had not been part of the Downing Street Declaration. The IRA felt that to demand disarmament was to require them to surrender, and this they would not do.

The degree of mistrust between the paramilitaries associated with both the Protestant unionists and the Catholic nationalists were so high that the impasse over disarmament of the IRA soon led to a new spasm of violence. In February 1996, the IRA broke their ceasefire with a series of bombings in London, because the more militant faction for a time regained the upper hand in the IRA's bitter internal struggles over tactics. In June 1996, the IRA exploded a bomb in a Manchester shopping center, injuring more than 200 people. Former United States Senator George Mitchell, appointed by President Clinton to go to Northern Ireland as a neutral mediator, managed to get Major to drop the demand for disarmament in favor of restoration of the ceasefire by the IRA. But even this was not enough. Major now tried to force the issue in Northern Ireland by holding an election for representatives to the peace negotiations. Sinn Fein won seventeen of the seats, but the Sinn Fein delegates were turned away from the meeting place because the IRA had not yet disarmed. By the end of 1996, the IRA had begun bombing again in Northern Ireland itself, and the Protestant paramilitary organizations were responding in kind.

The logjam to beginning the peace talks was broken by the victory of Labour in the British election of May 1997. Unlike Major, Blair did not depend on the votes of Ulster Unionist M.P.s, and the British Labour Party for a long time had accepted that reunification of Northern Ireland with the Republic would be a "natural" solution to the problem. Blair thus acted quickly in Northern Ireland. He went to Belfast and made it clear that all parties should promptly join the negotiations. In

June 1997, he signaled the new British attitude towards Ireland by apologizing for the British role in the Great Famine of 1845–1848, and he directed British officials to meet with representatives of Sinn Fein. He reassured the Protestant unionists that no change would be made in the status of Northern Ireland without the consent of the majority in the province; but he told Sinn Fein that they could participate in peace negotiations if the IRA would simply renew their ceasefire for six weeks and agree to abide by democratic procedures. After public urging by Gerry Adams, the IRA agreed. The Ulster Democratic Unionist Party of Ian Paisley refused to participate if Sinn Fein was allowed in, but the larger Ulster Unionist Party, led by David Trimble, finally agreed to do so. The decisive factor in their thinking was a strong hint by Blair to all Northern Ireland parties that if *they* did not reach a settlement, then the British and Irish governments would do it *for* them.

The peace talks in Northern Ireland thus finally began in October 1997, under the chairmanship of George Mitchell. The negotiations proved to be exceptionally difficult, not least because the Protestant unionist and Catholic nationalists wanted very different things: the unionists wanted restoration of a provincial parliament dominated by themselves, disarmament of the IRA, and confirmation of the union of Northern Ireland with Great Britain; the nationalists wanted to see the first steps towards reunification of Northern Ireland with the Republic and general demilitarization of the province. Blair's plan, which he based substantially on a joint proposal issued in 1995 by John Major and the Irish prime minister, John Bruton, called for "devolution" in Northern Ireland, plus a "cross-border" council with advisory powers on Northern Ireland, made up of representatives from both Northern Ireland and the Republic. The new provincial assembly would be elected by proportional representation so as to ensure that the Catholic minority would have an adequate voice; and the provincial executive, which would be responsible to the assembly, would likewise be formed on a power-sharing basis. There would also be an advisory "Council of the Isles," with representatives from the British, Irish, Scottish, Welsh, and Northern Ireland parliaments. Finally, the Royal Ulster Constabulary would be reformed in order to reflect the whole population of Northern Ireland, and the province would be "demilitarized."

Almost every item in the agenda of the peace conference was extremely controversial because mistrust built over the decades, even centuries, still poisoned the atmosphere. At one point the Sinn Fein delegates were banished, only to be readmitted eighteen days later. Only the remarkable patience and transparent honesty of Senator Mitchell, as well as the ability of Trimble and Adams to drag their recalcitrant colleagues along, kept the talks together. Finally, on Good Friday (April 10) 1998, the various parties agreed to the main points of the settlement as proposed by Blair. The Good Friday Agreement was then ratified by referenda in Northern Ireland (71.1% to 28.9%) and in the Irish Republic (94% to 5.6%). It seemed to put an end to thirty years of "the troubles" in Northern Ireland. John Hume and David Trimble shared the Nobel Peace Prize in 1998.

Implementation of the Good Friday Agreement, however, proved to be far from easy. In the election for the new Northern Ireland parliament, Trimble's Ulster

Unionists won the largest number of seats, with the SDLP and Sinn Fein finishing in second and third place, respectively. Most important was the fact that parties opposing the Agreement did not win enough seats to stop implementation. But fringe groups of extremists on both sides tried to wreck the peace process by resorting to violence. For instance, a splinter nationalist faction called the Real IRA, exploded a bomb in Omagh (County Armagh), which killed twenty-three people. Public revulsion was so strongly expressed, however, that even the Real IRA called a ceasefire. On the other side, Ulster Unionists insisted that the demilitarization clauses of the Good Friday Agreement required the IRA to disarm before Sinn Fein representatives could take their places on the executive and before the cross-border body would be set up. Sinn Fein and the IRA strenuously disagreed, and the obstacle was overcome only when the IRA agreed to put most of its arms "beyond use"— that is in locked arms dumps verified by the disarmament commission. Moreover, the Ulster Protestants resisted the transformation of the Royal Ulster Constabulary into the Police Service of Northern Ireland. The Good Friday Agreement was finally put into operation in December 1999. The Irish government promptly abolished Articles II and III of the Republic's constitution.

As the twenty-first century opened, it still seemed that the Good Friday Agreement could unravel at any moment, so deep were the bitterness and mistrust in Northern Ireland. And unravel it did. The Ulster Unionist Party led by David Trimble continued to insist that the IRA disarm before Sinn Fein could be allowed to participate in any Northern Ireland assembly. The IRA's disinclination to go beyond putting its arms "beyond use" over time persuaded ever larger numbers of Protestant Unionists that Paisley and his Democratic Unionist Party had been right to oppose the Good Friday Agreement all along. By 2003 the DUP had become the largest Unionist party in Northern Ireland, and Trimble was pushed aside. With Unionist policy now controlled by Paisley, the Unionist demands on Sinn Fein and the IRA tended to escalate: The IRA must disarm and disband completely, and Sinn Fein must declare support for the police and judiciary of the Province. Given the IRA's belief that they constituted a legitimate army, the long history of oppression of the Catholic population by the Ulster police, and the now officially proven record of collusion among the British Army, the Ulster police, and the Protestant paramilitaries, this was an extremely bitter pill to swallow.

But Gerry Adams and Martin McGuinness, who had their eyes on the future of Sinn Fein in a united Irish Republic, continued to press the IRA for concessions. Finally, in July 2005 the IRA renounced violence altogether, and by September 2005 had decommissioned (destroyed) all of its arms. In 2007, Sinn Fein and the IRA agreed to cooperate with the judiciary and the Police Service of Northern Ireland. Paisley, who never expected this to happen, was taken aback; but when Blair and the Irish Prime Minster Bertie Ahern threatened to impose a settlement on Northern Ireland over the heads of the DUP, Paisley gave in. The Good Friday Agreement was finally implemented in the Spring of 2007, and Britons widely credited Tony Blair with his greatest achievement.

THE WAR IN IRAQ AND THE FALL OF TONY BLAIR

It was an achievement that Blair desperately wanted, not least because by 2007 he and his government had become extremely unpopular. Blair had been the longest-serving and arguably most effective of all Labour prime ministers, and by moving the Labour Party rightwards, towards the electoral center, he had succeeded in making the Party seem the natural party of government. Yet the huge Labour majorities of 1997 and 2001 had been cut to only sixty-six (on only 35.3% of the popular vote) by the general election of 2005, and Blair himself was being accused of playing fast and loose with the truth, subordinating British interests to those of the United States, and having misled Britain into a disastrous war in Iraq. Strangely enough, the opposition to Blair came principally from within his own party, and in effect he was forced out of office in June 2007, to be replaced by his long-time partner in the New Labour movement, Gordon Brown. How Tony Blair fell from grace is a complex and fascinating story that will long be debated by historians.

On the surface, the turning point seems to have been "9/11," the terrorist attack carried out by the Muslim extremist organization, al-Qaeda, on New York and Washington on September 11, 2001. There is no question that Blair was horrified by 9/11, not least because sixty-seven Britons were killed in the World Trade Center in New York. Blair immediately pledged support to the United States in its "war on terror." Later in 2001 he supported the invasion of Afghanistan, where al-Qaeda was rooted, and in 2003 he backed the American invasion and occupation of Iraq though al-Qaeda had no presence there. Blair in fact became a tireless international advocate of American policy, leading to the complaint from the anti-war opposition in Britain that he had subordinated British national interests to those of the United States. He had become, critics said, "President Bush's poodle."

The foundations of Blair's policy, however, pre-dated 9/11. Just as Blair had repudiated the stance of "Old Labour" on domestic issues, so he had long rejected traditional Labour tendencies towards pacifism and internationalism. He had, after all, opposed unilateral nuclear disarmament, and as a Christian he believed that there can be such a thing as a just war. He took a humanitarian and moralistic approach to foreign affairs and believed that Britain as a highly moral nation should play a key role in world affairs. In 1999, for example, Blair was a strong advocate of military action in Kosovo, even if ground forces were needed, to stop the oppression of ethnic Albanians by genocidal Serbian nationalists. In retrospect, it seems clear that Blair was an old-fashioned "liberal imperialist" who believed in British intervention overseas to bring the benefits of Western civilization to the former colonial world and to combat "barbarism" anywhere. Blair may have been a member of Labour's "soft left," but he was every bit as willing for Britain to follow interventionist policies as Mrs. Thatcher had been.

Though committed to a leadership role for Britain in the European community, Blair thought that Britain was well placed to serve as a bridge between Europe and the United States. This concept proved to be difficult to square with his pro-American views. Unlike many Labour politicians past and present, he regarded the United States as essentially a force for good in the world: he had learned from Margaret Thatcher that a British prime minister must make alliance with America, and friendship with the American president, a top priority in foreign policy. Blair was personally close to President Clinton, but he came to disapprove of Clinton's reluctance to use force to combat international terrorism. Blair was concerned well before 9/11 with terrorism among Islamic extremists, and he felt strongly the danger that such terrorists might somehow obtain weapons of mass destruction from rogue nations. Hence Blair agreed with people in the American administration after 9/11 who were eager to make war on al-Qaeda and Muslim extremist terrorism generally, and he was relieved to find that he had more in common with the new president, George W. Bush, than he or others had anticipated. He felt that he must stand shoulder to shoulder with Bush if Britain were to have any influence on American policy, even if that meant support for the American invasion of Iraq, and even if it meant breaking with Britain's allies in Europe. In all his discussions with the Bush Administration leading to war in Afghanistan and Iraq, Blair appears never to have raised directly the crucial issue of the likely effect of the war on Muslim attitudes at home and abroad.

Under Blair's aggressive leadership, therefore, Britain in March 2003 committed some 41,000 troops to the invasion of Iraq, about one-third of the total invasion force. The British forces performed very well, and soon had control of the Shiite Muslim area in southern Iraq. However, opposition of two different kinds swelled at home. The first was a conventional anti-war movement. Throughout 2002, many Britons doubted claims by Bush and Blair that Saddam Hussein's Iraq had weapons of mass destruction, and they believed that President Bush was dead set on invading Iraq, irrespective of the facts of Iraq's weapons programs. To such opponents of the war, Blair was trailing along uncritically after Bush, whom they regarded as ignorant in world affairs. Blair, they argued, was getting nothing in return for his support for Bush, and there was truth to that claim. During the run-up to the war, Blair argued strenuously to the Americans that America should join the world's struggle against global warming, that Britain and America should try to mollify the Muslim world by mediating the Arab-Israeli conflict in Palestine, and that they should seek the UN's support for disarming Saddam Hussein. Only on the latter point did he get American cooperation, and that was reluctant and half-hearted. Blair attempted to rouse British public support in September 2002 by publishing an intelligence dossier demonstrating that Saddam Hussein still had weapons of mass destruction, including some that supposedly could be deployed in forty-five minutes. But despite these claims by the Blair government, many Britons wanted Britain to support continued efforts by UN weapons inspectors in Iraq, not invasion. In February 2003 an anti-war demonstration in London gathered a million people—the largest demonstration ever in British history. Opposition came even from a few members of his own cabinet, two of whom (Robin Cook and Claire Short) resigned in the spring of 2003.

Blair, however, stood firm, for in this case he did not resort to opinion polls and focus groups. He was certain that he was right. However, once the invasion of Iraq began and no weapons of mass destruction were found, public opinion in Britain turned even more sharply against him. By the summer of 2003, his personal approval ratings had fallen very low, and the situation was made worse by controversy over the reliability of the intelligence dossier that Blair had published in the previous September. The most severe charges—that Blair had deliberately fabricated intelligence and lied to the House of Commons—were not borne out by subsequent investigations, but it seemed clear to most observers that he had in fact pressured the intelligence services to produce every possible scrap of information on Iraqi weapons of mass destruction, and at least indirectly caused them to rely on evidence from a few undependable agents and to exaggerate the readiness of Saddam's weapons programs. In short, by late 2003 a majority of Britons felt that Blair had rushed the country into an unnecessary war at the bidding of the United States. Blair was forced by dissent within his own party to declare that the general election of 2005 would be his last, and finally to resign as prime minister and leader of the Labour party in June 2007—earlier than he wanted to.

Yet the second form of opposition to Blair's Iraq policy at home was even more serious—and violent. This was a product of seething anger among British Muslims. By the early twenty-first century, there were between 1.5 and 2 million Muslims in Britain, most of them of South Asian descent—from Pakistan, Bangladesh, and India. The great majority of these Muslim families had originally settled in a few areas of London and the English Midlands, where their numbers became highly concentrated. South Asian men had emigrated to Britain to work in Midlands factories after World War II, but as British industry declined, they lost factory jobs and often were reduced to relatively low-paid shopkeeping and service work, or even unemployment. By the 1970s and 1980s, many Muslim neighborhoods in Britain were afflicted by unemployment, high crime rates, and drug addiction. In addition, many South Asians felt that the British public resented their presence, discriminated against them, and put obstacles in the way of their efforts to assimilate. British Muslims showed their discontent by their near unanimous condemnation of the British author, Salman Rushdie, whose novel *Satanic Verses* (1988) they took as an outrageous insult to Islam. British Muslim families themselves were often divided over the question of assimilating versus maintaining their traditional culture, but a growing number, especially in the younger generation, clearly identified themselves as Muslims rather than Britons.

These were conditions ripe for generating "imperial blowback"—in a sense the violent consequence of Britain's three centuries of empire. In some of the Muslim areas, a few young men reacted against the disfunction, drugs, and crime in their communities by resorting to extreme fundamentalist forms of Islam. They tended to break with the older, more moderate generation of British Muslims, to learn from new, radical, Imams who recently had come from South Asia, and to blame the secularism of British culture for their discontent. They increasingly argued that British culture was corrupt and degenerating. For them, a puritanical form of Islam would be the solution to their social and cultural problems. And some of these young radicals were driven to violent acts by the thought of British and American soldiers killing Muslims in Afghanistan and Iraq. In July 2005, home-grown British Muslim suicide bombers killed fifty-two people and injured seven hundred by bombing three tube stations and a bus in London. Moreover, British intelligence had foiled several other terrorist attempts as early as 2003, and other failed (so far) plots were to follow. Blair received credit for his coolness in handling the terrorist incidents, but the historical significance of these events was clear: Britain was paying a high price for their imperial past and for Blair's renewal, however idealistic, of Britain's imperial role in Iraq.

THE BRITISH ISLES IN THE NEW CENTURY: "COOL BRITANNIA" OR THE END OF BRITAIN?

By the end of Blair's time as prime minister, Britain seemed to many observers to be at a crossroads. Tony Blair's drive for modernization, as well as his own elegant personal style, typified at least the fashionable part of Britain's new appearance as prosperous and "cool." Blair had declared that "the new Britain is a meritocracy where we break down barriers of class, religion, race, and culture." Some of that claim seemed to be true, but other aspects had been exposed as merely a fantasy. True, Britain no longer seemed a quaint country of picturesque villages, reserved but polite people in sensible tweeds, and an ancient aristocracy deferred to by a working class that was conscious of its proper place. Class remained an important element in most people's identity, but the lines between classes had become blurred, and the middle and working classes now stood at about the same size. Class, in practical terms, no longer seemed to matter so much. London had become the home of more foreign business people than any other city in Europe, and it now boasted many fine foreign restaurants. London's ethnic diversity made it seem very cosmopolitan. All over Britain, curry shops now seemed positively British, and chicken tika had become a favorite dish in British pubs. Vast new developments along the Thames changed the very appearance of the metropolis, and urban renewal transformed the centers of many provincial cities. American popular culture continued its relentless infiltration of British life, with American television shows and movies, fast-food restaurants in all the main streets and malls, and American beer rather than traditional British ales in many pubs. "Cool Britannia" seemed an apt label for modernizing, entrepreneurial, increasingly Europeanized (and Americanized) Britain.

Yet there was underlying discontent among certain sectors of the British population. Many British blacks and Muslims, as we have noted, were unhappy with British culture and their place in British society. In addition, many country people—mainly but not exclusively of the old gentry set—felt that Blair's urbane New Labour movement was ignorant of rural life and agricultural problems. They rallied in surprising strength, on horseback and in tweeds, against efforts by the Labour and Liberal parties to end fox hunting. In early 2001, farmers joined truckers in bringing the nation to a halt in protest against high fuel prices, and in forcing a contrite Blair to promise that he would listen better in the future.

Moreover, there was increasing sense among old Labourites—trade unionists and moderate socialists who had long formed the core of the Party—that Blair and New Labour had betrayed the enduring principles and highest ideals of the social-democratic left. Many trade unionists were disappointed that Blair made no move to revise Mrs. Thatcher's legislation curbing the power of the unions. Others expressed opposition to New Labour's continuing of privatization and its determination to go forward with public-private partnerships in rail transport and the London Underground. And the British left generally disapproved of Blair's acceptance of Thatcher's idea of an "entrepreneurial culture," along with huge salaries for CEOs of private businesses and a widening gap between rich and poor. Blair believed strongly that only New Labour's policies enabled the Labour Party appeal to "middle England" and thus to be more than a party of protest, but many Britons thought that Blair was too devoted to politics by spin doctors, public relations experts, and focus groups, and not enough to genuine principles.

More generally, a number of social, economic, and constitutional changes by the first decade of the twenty-first century appeared to some observers to foreshadow the end of Britain—or at least of a distinctive British culture. Among these changes were (1) the growing "minority" population of nonwhites, which reached 6 percent overall and, concentrated as it was in certain urban centers of England, made Britain seem a multicultural society; (2) the contraction of industry to the point that Britain no longer seemed a major industrial nation; and (3) the blurring of class lines that had structured British society and social relations since the early nineteenth century. Mass culture—including a desire for consumer goods, youthful fashions, and pop music—and the mass media, both of which reflected a heavy American influence, shaped British attitudes to a degree that would have been unthinkable in the mid-nineteenth century. Perhaps the most remarkable change was the acceptance by the public of encroachment on privacy. The British had long prided themselves on the twin virtues of individualism and privacy, but as concern about crime and the uncertainties of a multicultural society grew, they embraced the rapid spread of surveillance cameras set up both by public authories and private businesses. By 2007, the ordinary Briton on average appeared on a closed circuit TV camera more than 300 times a day.

The extent to which British popular culture had changed amazed the world when millions of the British people engaged in a vast public outpouring of grief on the occasion of Princess Diana's death by auto accident in 1997. This outpouring apparently was not the expression of mourning and appreciation for a great public figure like Queen Victoria or Winston Churchill, but an emotional tribute to an international celebrity, a mistreated fairy-tale figure with whom participants in mass culture could identify, regardless of their class, religion, politics, or gender. Diana was, as Blair deftly described her, "the people's princess," and Elton John's vocal tribute at her funeral service in Westminster Abbey, his pop song "Candle in the Wind," seemed perfectly appropriate.

In constitutional terms, concerns about the possible end of Britain had to do with membership in the European Union on the one hand and devolution on the other. Participation by Britain in the European Union opened up possibilities of economic revitalization and political influence that Britain could no longer enjoy on its own or as the center of an empire, but it also entailed some loss of sovereignty to the European parliament and bureaucracy. Many in the British middle and upper classes in the early twenty-first century were clearly adjusting to thinking of themselves as "Europeans," and even large numbers of working-class Britons vacationed in Europe. But that Europeanization reduced to a degree the traditional British sense of differentness from Europe. At the same time, Blair's close support for the United States in Afghanistan and Iraq raised once again concern that in actuality Britain was becoming more like a dependency of America.

Devolution was contributing to certain problems in British national identity. This was particularly true of the English people. After the turn of the new millennium, devolution seemed not only to reduce English authority within Britain but also to suggest that the unity of Great Britain was fraying and might disintegrate altogether. The Liberal and Labour parties had hoped devolution would satisfy Scottish and Welsh nationalist desires and so quell the desire for independence, but in Scotland at least it was beginning to have the opposite effect. The Scottish National Party, in fact, became the largest party in the Scottish parliament as a result of elections in 2007. Many Scottish and Welsh nationalists could imagine that membership for Scotland and Wales in the European Union might be more advantageous than continued membership in the United Kingdom, just as it had proved to be for the Irish Republic. But some English nationalists in reaction were beginning to resent the fact that Scottish M.P.s could vote on purely English issues at Westminster, while English M.P.s could not vote on purely Scottish matters. There is now talk of one or more regional parliaments for England alone, with Westminster evolving into a parliament for pan-British issues and foreign affairs. Whether Britain would break up, remain united, or become a federal state was anyone's guess in the early twenty-first century. But even if Britain remains united, it will be a rapidly changing society—in some ways a "cool Britannia" but in others a "frazzled Britannia."

Suggested Reading

Adams, Gerry, *Before the Dawn: An Autobiography* (New York: William Morrow, 1996).

Anwar, Muhammed, *The Myth of Return: Pakistanis in Britain* (London: Heinemann, 1979).

Aughey, Arthur, *The Politics of Northern Ireland: Beyond the Belfast Agreement* (London: Routledge, 2005).

Bells, G. Gordon, *The Twilight of Britain: Cultural Nationalism, Multiculturalism, and the Politics of Toleration* (New Brunswick, NJ: Transaction Publishers, 2002).

Bogdanor, Vernon, *Devolution in the United Kingdom* (Oxford: Oxford University Press, 1999).

Cannadine, David, *The Rise and Fall of Class in Britain* (New York: Columbia University Press, 1999).

Davies, Norman, *The Isles* (New York: Oxford University Press, 2000).

Denver, David, *Scotland Decides: The Devolution Issue and the 1997 Referendum* (London: Frank Cass, 2000).

Devine, T. M., *The Scottish Nation: A History, 1700–2000* (New York: Viking, 2000).

Fitzgerald, Garrett, *All in a Life: An Autobiography* (Dublin: Gill and Macmillan, 1991).

Foley, Michael, *The British Presidency: Tony Blair and the Politics of Public Leadership* (New York: Manchester University Press, 2000).

Goulbourne, Harry, *Race Relations in Britain Since 1945* (New York: St. Martin's Press, 1998).

Harrison, Brian, *The Transformation of British Politics, 1860–1995* (New York: Oxford University Press, 1996).

Holland, Jack, *Hope Against History: The Course of the Conflict in Northern Ireland* (New York: Henry Holt and Company, 1999).

Hutchinson, I. G. C., *Scottish Politics in the Twentieth Century* (New York: Palgrave, 2001).

Major, John, *The Autobiography* (London: HarperCollins, 1999).

Mitchell, George J., *Making Peace* (London: William Heinemann, 1999).

Moloney, Ed, *A Secret History of the IRA* (New York: W. W. Norton, 2003).

Pilkington, Andrew, *Racial Disadvantage and Ethnic Diversity in Britain* (New York: Palgrave, 2003).

Seldon, Anthony, with Lewis Baston, *Major: A Political Life* (London: Weidenfeld and Nicolson, 1997).

Solomon, John, *Race and Racism in Britain* (New York: St. Martin's Press, 1993).

Appendix A

Kings and Queens of Great Britain, 1870–2007

Monarch	House	Reign
Victoria	Hanover	1837–1901
Edward VII	Windsor	1901–1910
George V	Windsor	1910–1936
Edward VIII	Windsor	1936
George VI	Windsor	1936–1952
Elizabeth II	Windsor	1952–

Appendix B

Chief Cabinet Ministers, 1868–2007

Minister	Post	Dates	Party
William E. Gladstone	Prime Minister	1868–1874	Liberal
Benjamin Disraeli	Prime Minister	1874–1880	Conservative
William E. Gladstone	Prime Minister	1880–1885	Liberal
Joseph Chamberlain	President of the Board of Trade		
Marquess of Salisbury	Prime Minister and Foreign Secretary	1885–1886	Conservative
William E. Gladstone	Prime Minister	1886	Liberal
Marquess of Salisbury	Prime Minister	1886–1892	Conservative (Unionist)
William E. Gladstone	Prime Minister	1892–1894	Liberal
Earl of Rosebery	Foreign Secretary		
Earl of Rosebery	Prime Minister	1894–1895	Liberal
Sir William V. Harcourt	Chancellor of the Exchequer		
Marquess of Salisbury	Prime Minister	1895–1902	Conservative (Unionist)
A. J. Balfour	First Lord of the Treasury		
Joseph Chamberlain	Colonial Secretary		
A. J. Balfour	Prime Minister	1902–1905	Conservative
Joseph Chamberlain	Colonial Secretary		
Sir Henry Campbell-Bannerman	Prime Minister	1905–1908	Liberal
H. H. Asquith	Chancellor of the Exchequer		
H. H. Asquith	Prime Minister	1908–1915	Liberal
David Lloyd George	Chancellor of the Exchequer		
Sir Edward Grey	Foreign Secretary		
Winston Churchill	President of the Board of Trade and later First Lord of the Admiralty		

Minister	Post	Dates	Party
H. H. Asquith	Prime Minister	1915–1916	Coalition
David Lloyd George	Minister of Munitions		
David Lloyd George	Prime Minister	1916–1922	Coalition
Andrew Bonar Law	Prime Minister	1922–1923	Conservative
Stanley Baldwin	Chancellor of the Exchequer		
Stanley Baldwin	Prime Minister and Chancellor of the Exchequer	1923–1924	Conservative
J. Ramsay MacDonald	Prime Minister and Foreign Secretary	1924	Labour
Stanley Baldwin	Prime Minister	1924–1929	Conservative
Winston Churchill	Chancellor of the Exchequer		
J. Ramsay MacDonald	Prime Minister	1929–1931	Labour
J. Ramsay MacDonald	Prime Minister	1931–1935	National
Stanley Baldwin	Lord President		
Neville Chamberlain	Chancellor of the Exchequer		
Stanley Baldwin	Prime Minister	1935–1937	National
Neville Chamberlain	Chancellor of the Exchequer		
Neville Chamberlain	Prime Minister	1937–1940	Conservative
Winston Churchill	Prime Minister	1940–1945	Coalition
Clement Attlee	Deputy Prime Minister		
Clement Attlee	Prime Minister	1945–1951	Labour
Ernest Bevin	Foreign Secretary		
Aneurin Bevan	Minister of Health		
Winston Churchill	Prime Minister	1951–1955	Conservative
Anthony Eden	Foreign Secretary		
R. A. Butler	Chancellor of the Exchequer		
Sir Anthony Eden	Prime Minister	1955–1957	Conservative
Harold Macmillan	Foreign Secretary		
R. A. Butler	Chancellor of the Exchequer		
Harold Macmillan	Prime Minister	1957–1963	Conservative
Sir Alec Douglas-Home	Prime Minister	1963–1964	Conservative
Harold Wilson	Prime Minister	1964–1970	Labour
James Callaghan	Chancellor of the Exchequer		
Edward Heath	Prime Minister	1970–1974	Conservative
Harold Wilson	Prime Minister	1974–1976	Labour
James Callaghan	Foreign Secretary		
James Callaghan	Prime Minister	1976–1979	Labour

Minister	Post	Dates	Party
Margaret Thatcher	Prime Minister	1979–1990	Conservative
John Major	Prime Minister	1990–1997	Conservative
Tony Blair	Prime Minister	1997–2007	Labour
Gordon Brown	Chancellor of the Exchequer	1997–2007	Labour
Gordon Brown	Prime Minister	2007–	Labour

Index

Credits

Page 11, 81 Banbury Road, Oxford: National Building Record. Page 13 New kinds of women's work: typists: Mary Evans Picture Library. Page 17, Late-Victorian urban poverty: City of Liverpool, Engineer's Department. Page 25, Herbert Spencer: Corbis/Bettmann. Page 32, William Morris's bed at Kelmscott Manor: A. F. Kersting. Page 33, Sidney and Beatrice Webb: Hulton Archive by Getty Images. Page 34, Missionaries at a dispensary in East Africa: United Society for the Propagation of the Gospel. Page 39 Bloomsbury: Bertrand Russell, John Maynard Keynes, and Lytton Strachey: Dr. Milo Keynes. Page 44, South Wales coal miners: National Museum of Wales. Page 51, Charles Stewart Parnell: Mansell/TimePix. Page 53, William E. Gladstone being kicked up in the air over Irish Home Rule (cartoon): Mansell/TimePix. Page 67, William E. Gladstone: Corbis/Bettmann. Page 69, Benjamin Disraeli: Corbis/Bettmann. Page 76, Joseph Chamberlain speaking in favor of tariff reform: Mansell/TimePix. Page 79, Emmeline Pankhurst: Museum of London Picture Library. Page 81, Ulster Unionist demonstration: Hulton Archive by Getty Images. Page 94, Imperial Rivalry (cartoon): *Puck*, February 19, 1896. Page 98, Boer riflemen at the siege of Mafeking: Hulton Archive by Getty Images. Page 103, *The Channel Squadron*, by E. de Martineau: National Maritime Museum. Page 112, Lord Kitchener's recruiting poster of 1914: Imperial War Museum. Page 115, A British trench at the Somme: Imperial War Museum. Page 124, Allied leaders: Lloyd George, Haig, Joffre, and Thomas: Imperial War Museum. Page 126, The Passchendaele battlefield, Flanders, 1917: Imperial War Museum. Page 139, Soldiers & civilians fighting, Easter Uprising, 1916: Hulton Archive by Getty Images. Page 144, Eamonn de Valera: Corbis/Bettmann. Page 158, Hunger marchers from Jarrow on the way to London: Hulton Archive by Getty Images. Page 161, Food convoy, General Strike, 1926: Hulton Archive by Getty Images. Page 168, The Hoover building, Perivale, London: Edgar Iones; B. T. Batsford. Page 179, Ramsay MacDonald and Margaret Bondfield: Corbis/Bettmann. Page 182, Stanley Baldwin: Corbis/Bettmann. Page 185, Mahatma Gandhi: Hulton Archive by Getty Images. Page 190, Neville Chamberlain departing for Munich: Hulton Archive by Getty Images. Page 197, British Spitfires taking off during the Battle of Britain, 1940: Royal Air Force Museum. Page 198, Winston Churchill inspecting air-raid damage to the House of Commons: Corbis/Bettmann. Page 199, St. Paul's Cathedral during the Blitz: Corbis/Bettmann. Page 210, Churchill, Roosevelt, and Stalin at Yalta, 1945: AP/Wide World. Page 218, Attlee and the Labour party celebrating electoral victory, 1945: Hulton Archive by Getty Images. Page 232, The Beatles: Corbis/Bettmann. Page 237, Henry Moore, *Recumbent Figure*: The Tate Gallery/Art Resource, NY. Page 252, Harold Macmillan, 1959: Corbis/Bettmann. Page 254, CND march, 1972: Hulton Archive by Getty Images. Page 256, Queen Elizabeth in Ghana, 1961: Corbis/Bettmann. Page 259, Harold Wilson: Corbis/Bettmann. Page 276, Anti-Catholic graffiti in Belfast: *Belfast Telegraph*. Page 292, Margaret Thatcher: Corbis/Bettmann. Page 298, British Royal Marines raise the Union Jack over West Falkland Island, 1982: Corbis/Bettmann.

POETRY